Translation as Innovation: Bridging the Sciences and Humanities

Traduction et innovation : une passerelle entre les sciences et les humanités

Translation as Innovation: Bridging the Sciences and Humanities

Traduction et innovation : une passerelle entre les sciences et les humanités

Edited by Patricia M. Phillips-Batoma
and Florence Xiangyun Zhang

DALKEY ARCHIVE PRESS

First edition, 2016

Library of Congress Cataloging-in-Publication Data

Names: Phillips-Batoma, Patricia M. | Zhang, Florence Xiangyun. |
Title: *Translation as innovation : bridging the sciences and the humanities* /
edited by Patricia M. Phillips-Batoma and Florence Xiangyun Zhang ;
Description: First Edition. | Victoria, TX : Dalkey Archive Press, [2016] |
Text in English and French. | Original title in French: Traduction et
innovation. | "Second biennial conference coordinated through a
partnership between the Center for Translation Studies at the University
of Illinois and the Centre d âEtudes sur la Traduction at the University
of Paris Denis-Diderot." | Includes bibliographical references and index.
Identifiers: LCCN 2015040720 | ISBN 9781564784094 (pbk. : alk. paper)
Subjects: LCSH: Translation studies--Congresses. | Translating and
interpreting--Congresses. | Interdisciplinary research--Congress. |
Interdisciplinary approach in education--Congresses.
Classification: LCC P306.94 .T7313 2016 | DDC 418/.02--dc23
LC record available at http://lccn.loc.gov/2015040720

Partially funded by a grant from the Illinois Arts Council, a state agency, and the Center for Translation Studies at the University of Illinois, Urbana-Champaign

Dalkey Archive publications are, in part, made possible through the support of the University of Houston-Victoria and its programs in creative writing, publishing, and translation.

Dalkey Archive Press
Victoria, TX / McLean, IL / London / Dublin

www.dalkeyarchive.com
Typesetting: Mikhail Iliatov
Cover by Katherine O'Shea

Printed on permanent/durable acid-free paper

Contents

Translation as Innovation:
Bridging the Sciences and Humanities

Traduction et innovation :
une passerelle entre les sciences et les humanités

Scientific Committee / Comité scientifique

Isée Bernateau

Rute Costa

Beatrice Daille

Fanny Dargent

Jean-Patrick Guillaume

Stephane Haffemeyer

Philippe Jaussaud

Laurie Laufer

Heba Lecocq

Marianne Lederer

Tony Lodge

Jean-Philippe Mathy

Victor Pan

Jordan Stump

Introduction (ENGLISH)

If translation is one of the world's "oldest professions," is there anything new to say about it? Jean-René Ladmiral asked this very question in the opening remarks of his keynote speech at the "Translation as Innovation" conference held in Paris in 2012, and whose proceedings constitute the present volume. The answer lies in Ladmiral's distinction between what we call in the United States the "hard sciences" (*les sciences exactes*) and the humanities (*les sciences humaines*). Whereas one of the major underpinnings of the former is the quest to discover and understand what is not yet known, research in the humanities consists of seeking to articulate new ways to see and understand what we already know. Translation studies today derives its research principles from the humanities, and yet is beckoned by rapid developments in science and technology to extend its reach to areas of inquiry that necessitate a blending of the hard sciences and the humanities. Such a shift is summarized in the subtitle to this conference, "Bridging the Sciences and the Humanities."

The interdisciplinarity that characterizes translation studies today is reflected in this collection of articles, organized into three categories, 1) Science and Terminology; 2) History and Literature; and 3) Psychoanalysis and Theory. Such categories are imperfect in this context, and some of the articles could have been placed in more than one of them, but we thought such an organization would provide the reader a useful framework for thinking about the many contributions that span such a large number of disciplines.

Scott Montgomery, one of the keynote speakers whose article opens this volume, provides us with the perspective of a scientist whose work as a geologist led him to explore scientific language and ultimately the relationship between translation and science. In his article entitled "English is the Global Language of Science: *Que faire*?" he explores the issue of English as the medium of global scientific knowledge exchange and challenges the often polemic assumptions that accompany this phenomenon. To the implicit question of what we should do about this, Montgomery replies that nothing should be done. He argues against the notion that English acts as a hegemonic device by reminding us that at any one time throughout its long history, science has always had a lingua franca whose existence enriches both source and target languages and cultures by establishing a flow of new knowledge in both directions. The status of English as a global language *tout court* presents a unique opportunity to researchers in translation studies, particularly terminologists. Large numbers of terms are created in English, and this volume provides terminology researchers with unprecedented amounts of data to query, which sometimes reveals unexpected phenomena.

John Humbley's article on *le déballage terminologique* illustrates this English-language research focus on two levels. Halliday's grammatical metaphor is the basis for many terms that emerge from the reformulation of clauses. Technical translators can benefit from understanding this "packaging process," which Humbley proposes to call in French "emballage." Further, term creation as well as translation in the target language might be improved through a process of "unpackaging," that is, going back to observe how the term was derived in the language of innovation. This "unpackaging" is what Humbley calls, "le déballage terminologique." Christopher Gledhill also uses Halliday's grammatical metaphor in his article on phraseological variation in French and English scientific discourse. The grammatical metaphors in this case take the form of light verb and anaphoric constructions, which are important non-technical components of both administrative and scientific discourses. Corpus analysis allows us to confirm the high density of these constructions within administrative and scientific discourse. Although these constructions exhibit predictable patterns, there is still a high degree of variation, an observation that provides a better understanding of the productive role played by these constructions as well as a deeper understanding of how translation works.

Danielle Candel makes the case for a more flexible approach to the creation of terms and neologisms, emphasizing the importance of identifying the cultural values that underpin the source language term—presently mostly US and UK terms—and ensuring that the new term in the target language reflects the values of the target culture. The one term / one concept rule is inflexible and does not account for the instability over time of the meanings of terms, even if these terms are fixed in official term bases. They will still take on lives of their own as usage and meaning constantly shift. Term success relies on a flexible approach to both term creation and to translation. Candel's argument is borne out by the findings of Pascaline Dury, who looks at the issue of equivalent terms in emerging medical fields. Using the example of the English term "translational research," Dury demonstrates through corpus analysis that the establishment of an equivalent term is not as straightforward as it appears. Indeed, the corpus revealed the existence of as many as four variant terms, each one endowed with subtle differences with respect to what aspect of the concept represented by the term is emphasized. Translators should thus be more aware of the subtle nuances of meaning and take pains to select the appropriate variant rather than yield to pressures of terminology standardization.

The complexity of managing large amounts of data for the creation of the bilingual (NL-FR) BabelIris medical corpus is described by Ward van de Welde. The methodology involves, on the one hand, theoretical decisions regarding what data to use and not to use, and whether to separate or combine texts written for experts or for the general public; and on the other hand, the practical steps to take to make sure that the texts to be used are converted from their different media into a single encodable format. The task itself revealed a surprising disparity between the data available in Dutch and in French, in spite of laws in place that require all medical information be available in both languages. The newly established corpus will provide opportunities for research on medical language, including the question of how to resolve the disparity between Dutch and French. Sandrine Peraldi exploits the existence of large amounts of data in chemical language corpora to ask specific questions and challenge some commonly held assumptions about the language of chemistry, specifically the nomenclature of organic chemistry. Whereas chemical nomenclature is viewed as one of the most highly standardized systems for term creation, Peraldi's findings indicate that there is much lexical creativity taking place as chemists attempt to express concepts and knowledge that are increasingly complex, and this in spite of the existence of not just one but several parallel systems of nomenclature rules. The creation of new terms that fully account for the increasingly complex set of skills required in the emerging profession of Language Mediation is the topic of the article by Elisabeth Navarro and Jean-Michel Benayoun. Increased migration has given rise to the need for individuals who mediate between the receiving country and the newly arrived immigrants from other cultures and other language communities. Too often the task at hand is conflated with what conference interpreters do, whereas the role of the Language Mediator involves interpreting, translating and mediating. Therefore, training programs in the university context should create curricula that accounts for this complexity.

It is the complexity inherent in the role of this new kind of translator that has given rise to vehement yet rich debate. Such debate is nothing new as can be seen in Doublas Kibbee's article on the *remarqueurs* of seventeenth-century France, the article which opens Part 2 of this volume entitled History and Literature. Kibbee's article takes us back to the era of the *Belles infidèles,* a time when the French language was considered to be so impoverished that translation was means to actively and intentionally enrich it. Through a close reading of the writings of Claude Favre de Vaugelas and Scipion Dupleix, Kibbee sheds light on the complex procedures brought into play as translators strove to both liberate the French language from its direct dependence on Latin, while at the same time investing it with the same level of prestige. Mairi Mclaughlin also looks at the role played by translation in both seventeenth and eighteenth-century France, with a specific focus on the periodical press that flourished at that time. It is a given, argues Mclaughlin, that the translation of journalistic texts has had a measurable influence on contemporary French, but can the same be said of this earlier period? Her data indicate that it is likely that translation within this genre was a major source of lexical borrowing as well as a locus for the conceptualization of translation itself.

An analysis of the French translations of the eighth-century *Kitāb al-Hayawān* (Book of Animals), written by the Arabic-speaking naturalist al Jāhiz, provides an opportunity to assess the importance of adequately trained translators to ensure the transmission of knowledge. In this article, authors Meyssa Ben Saâd, Mehrnaz Katouzian-Safadi and Philippe Provençal illustrate how a failure on the part of the French language translators to understand the full implications of the scientific terminology in Arabic gave rise to mistranslations of the text excerpts, which negatively affected the work's reception abroad, because the text was subsequently qualified as lacking in scientific rigor and therefore not worth exploring. For this reason an important work to the history of biology is still unavailable to most historians.

We move from zoology to fictional animal characters with an article by Sündüz Őztürk Kasar, who looks at five of the Turkish language translations of "The Wolf and the Lamb," a fable by La Fontaine. Following Jean-Claude Coquet's semiotic analysis of this fable, Kasar claims that semiotics can be extended to the translation process, viewed here as a speech act. Of the dozens of existing translations of this fable into Turkish, Kasar looks closely at five to explore how translations of polysemous words were rendered and to make the point that translation multiplies the points of view and "turns" our perspectives in different directions.

Aimée Lahaussois's work takes us to the remote regions of Nepal where linguists do field work that involves recording descriptive information about endangered oral languages in the translation tier of the Interlinear Glossed Text (IGT). This article not only sheds light on an area of translation that is unknown to most of us in the translation world, but also reveals a tendency within this profession to produce literal translations in this tier, whereas the standards indicate that such translations should be free. Absent a clear definition of what "free" means in this context, Lahaussois shows that the translation tier is increasingly taking on the role of providing semantic and morphosyntactic information on the source utterance. One solution lies in adding a fourth tier, with one tier designated for a free and one tier for a literal translation.

This section ends with a study of the Chinese translations of the novels of Jules Verne, an author who today is still a household name and whose writings blend rather than simply bridge the sciences and the humanities. Florence Zhang's study of the Chinese translations of Verne's novels reveals what motivated the different translators in the early 1900s, during the 1950s and more recently in preparation for the 2005 centenary commemoration of Verne's death. In each one of these periods we see the translators' motivations having profound effects on the final product. More importantly, as the gap between the sciences and the humanities deepened over the course of the twentieth century, Chinese literary translators with scientific backgrounds have proven difficult to find. The result is contemporary translations of Verne into Chinese that fail to reproduce the sequences of scientific reasoning that are so crucial to Verne's prose and to the science-fiction sub-genre.

Just as Verne's novels have undergone different translations at different periods, so too have the writings of Freud and Lacan undergone translation and retranslation. The third part of this volume covers psychoanalysis and theory, broadly conceived. In her keynote speech that opened the conference, Janine Altounian described herself as both a co-translator of the works of Freud into French and the child of parents who survived the 1915 Armenian Genocide, parents whose traumatic experiences were transmitted to her not through words, but rather, through unspoken channels reflected in the way her survivor parents lived in a country whose language and culture became their receiving language and culture. A translator herself of the writings of the father of psychoanalysis, Altounian reflects on the translational role played by children of the survivors of genocides, specifically describing how it falls to them to translate their parents' stories into the receiving language, without the parents ever verbalizing these stories to anyone. Translation for these heirs implies "consenting to the violent rupture of exile."

Rémy Potier and Olivier Putois construe translation as a means of rupture, in this sense a liberating one, as they describe the case of a psychotic patient, "Sybille," born in Morocco with a degenerative cochlear disease and who received cochlear implants in France against her family's wishes. From object within the Arabic-speaking family, the implants and the French-speaking therapeutic context provided her a pathway to subjectivity. Translation thus figures here as a means for a subject to free herself from the "body" of her mother tongue. The phenomenon of motherhood among immigrant women in Argentina is what interests Elise Pestre, who approaches this topic from the perspective of psychoanalysis. That pregnancy occurs among these women at higher rates and at younger ages than is customary in their home countries begs the obvious question of why women would literally burden themselves when already facing economic uncertainties. Pestre sees the situation of the subject in exile as one that places her in a translating position, a position which brings to the surface issues that have been suppressed, and the subject must reorganize her psychic space in order to create a new home space. For Pestre, pregnancy is a clinical manifestation of this translating position.

Elizabeth Kaluaritchige's article on the translations of Freud and Lacan into Sinhala describes the indirect path these writings took to get to India, going from German or French through English and into Sinhala, in which the equivalent terms coined were based on Hindu and Buddhist concepts. These terms derived from English do not adequately reflect the concepts that underly them in the original languages. She supports retranslations from the original German or French, but warns of resistance to this since the lexicon, although it is imprecise, is well established.

Nicolas Froeliger addresses the resistance among theorists of pragmatic translation to engage with the criticisms aimed at them by translation theorists whose work is associated with the "cultural turn," specifically gender and post-colonial studies. Froeliger presents the arguments behind these critics' view of pragmatic translation as a "lackey of imperialism," but also exposes the flaws in some of their reasoning. He argues that the cultural turn can enhance pragmatic translation provided there is a dialectical exchange between the field and its critics. Within the field of pragmatic translation, Patricia Minacori asks whether technical translation can be construed as a complex object as defined by Edgar Morin. The translation process can be aligned to Morin's four principles of complexity 1) dialogue; 2) feedback; 3) holism; and 4) the meta-point of view. Within this framework, the translation is conceived of as part of a much larger process of dialogue with and feedback from experts, conceiving of the translation as a whole, internally consistent piece of writing, and an outside reviser who works on the completed translation.

Jean-René Ladmiral's keynote address concludes this volume, and it is a fitting conclusion since he describes the extensive interdisciplinarity of the field and traces the different phases it has gone through, from the triangle of linguistics, philosophy and psychology to a square with the addition of comparative literature. Looking ahead to the future of translation studies, he makes the case for subjectivity and for placing the translating subject front and center to research in translation. Ironically, Ladmiral implores everyone, in the hard sciences and in the humanities, to refrain from writing too polemically within their disciplines and from writing too much, lest the researcher begin to confuse the "existential" self with the "scientific" or the "published" self. This is also the appropriate place to conclude my introduction to this volume, in which I expect the reader will find a vast array of approaches to translation studies as well as translation itself, a research topic whose boundaries appear to be expanding exponentially.

Patricia M. Phillips-Batoma
Urbana, Illinois

La traduction n'est pas un exercice neutre. Tout en étant l'outil de transmission des savoirs, elle influence leur constitution, et ses procédures ont une incidence sur les disciplines dans lesquelles elle intervient[1]. Dans le même temps, le champ de la traduction, structuré lui-même par ces disciplines, connaît d'importantes mutations. La traduction est facteur d'innovation, et elle-même est sans cesse innovée. L'histoire nous en apprend beaucoup lorsque nous observons le mouvement des frontières traditionnelles entre les champs disciplinaires et culturels.

Alors que la traduction remodèle certaines frontières des disciplines en sciences humaines, d'autres frontières, physiques, sont davantage franchies aujourd'hui par l'homme en quête de la liberté et de la prospérité. Devant les barrières linguistiques, et plus encore, celles qui sont ancrées dans la profondeur de notre psyché, la traduction est plus que jamais présente.

Les frontières physiques semblent pourtant ne plus exister pour la circulation de la science. Le monde actuel, avec sa technologie, mais aussi avec ses enjeux, économiques ou environnementaux, rend nécessaire la capacité de comprendre et d'apprécier les innovations de la science. Si l'anglais prend peu à peu la place de langue universelle de la science, où se situe la traduction ? Existe-t-elle comme une passerelle obligatoire, non seulement entre les hommes, entre les cultures, mais aussi entre les sciences et les humanités ?

Dans la perspective de revoir la traduction au carrefour de tous ces mouvements, le présent volume réunit vingt-et-un articles, correspondant au choix effectué parmi un large nombre de contributions présentées lors du deuxième colloque co-organisé par l'Université Paris Diderot et le Center for Translation Studies de l'université d'Illinois (University of Illinois at Urbana-Champaign), tenu à Paris du 13 au 15 décembre 2012, intitulé *Traduction et innovation - une passerelle entre les sciences et les humanités*. Des spécialistes de plusieurs domaines y ont apporté leurs points de vue très divers sur le rôle de la traduction non seulement dans la diffusion des innovations scientifiques dans le passé et à l'époque

1 Le présent volume fait suite aux travaux réunis par Antoine Cazé et Rainier Lanselle dans *Translation in an international perspective - Cultural Interaction and Disciplinary Transformation*, éd. Peter Lang, Bern, 2014

contemporaine, dans la transformation linguistique et le changement disciplinaire, mais également dans la prise en charge institutionnelle, médicale et psychique de l'homme en exil, phénomène nouveau de la société d'aujourd'hui. Les travaux sont donc regroupés dans trois champs thématiques qui sont : science et terminologie, histoire et littérature, psychanalyse et théorisation.

Dans la première partie, l'importance est accordée aux liens que tisse la traduction avec la science, en particulier par le biais de la terminologie. Dans l'article de Scott L. Montgomery qui ouvre le volume, « English is the Global Language of Science: *Que Faire?* », il expose un fait incontestable dans les journaux et revues scientifiques internationaux qui voient depuis 1990 la disparition des langues autres que l'anglais. Ce n'est pas pour autant synonyme de l'hégémonie linguistique car il rappelle qu'au cours de l'histoire, ont toujours existé des *lingua franca* de la science, telles que le grec, l'arabe et le latin, qui, au lieu de restreindre les autres langues, les ont grandement enrichies. Comme un réservoir, ces *lingua franca* de la science ont aussi servi à conserver les textes et données en provenance d'autres langues. Aujourd'hui l'anglais devenant cette langue universelle de la science, cela génère une demande considérable de la traduction à partir de l'anglais et vers celui-ci. Nombreux terminologues cherchent à comprendre comment les termes sont formés en anglais pour exprimer des concepts scientifiques nouveaux et surtout comment ces derniers peuvent être traduits dans les autres langues.

C'est ainsi que John Humbley emploie le mot « emballage » pour décrire le processus de création de termes car ceux-ci ne se stabilisent qu'après une série de reformulations qui leur permettent d'enfermer les concepts nouveaux avec nombreux éléments linguistiques ; dans son article « Le déballage terminologique pour traduire l'innovation », il montre la méthode de « déballer » et de « remballer » dans la langue d'arrivée afin de réapproprier les concepts scientifiques nouveau. De son côté, Christopher Gledhill observe la phraséologie du discours scientifique dans son article « Phraseological Variation and its Implications for Translation », et examine deux types de structures : 1) des constructions à verbe léger comportant un N prédicatif du type « effet », « impact » et « influence », 2) les reformulations basées sur les emplois anaphoriques de ces N. Il affirme que même s'il existe des schémas équivalents en anglais et en français, la traduction ne peut se faire que sur l'identification et l'analyse critique de ces constructions.

Danielle Candel étudie l'usage de la traduction en terminologie et en néologie dans le domaine médical. En confirmant que la création de termes en français passe toujours par une phase de traduction à partir de l'anglais pour remplacer les emprunts, elle démontre que la réussite du néologisme réside dans l'équilibre entre une plus ou moins grande fidélité formelle et sémantique aux termes d'origine, et une nécessaire liberté innovatrice. Pascaline Dury, quant à elle, se focalise sur la traduction en français du terme anglais *translational research* dans le cadre d'une discipline médicale émergente, et constate deux variantes : « recherche translationelle » et « recherche de transfert ». Dans son article intitulé « Quel(s) équivalent(s) pour traduire l'adjectif anglais translational ? Quelques remarques sur les difficultés à traduire la terminologie de domaines médicaux innovants », elle montre que les deux variantes sont utilisées par des experts médicaux et que le traducteur ne doit pas chercher à tout prix l'uniformisation terminologique.

Toujours dans le domaine médical, Ward Van de Velde relate un constat selon lequel dans les hôpitaux belges les patients d'origine étrangère ne peuvent pas bénéficier de la même prise en charge que les autres patients du fait de problèmes de communication. Participant au projet qui vise à produire des outils linguistiques d'accompagnement du personnel hospitalier bruxellois, il décrit les processus de compilation et d'encodage du corpus, composé de textes issus d'un réseau hospitalier public belge.

Sandrine Péraldi s'intéresse à la créativité lexicale dans « La chimie organique : une science en mouvement », et en analyse les procédés sur trois plans : au sein de la nomenclature, contredisant le caractère purement normatif du vocabulaire de la chimie ; à un niveau morphosyntaxique en apportant une validité permanente au terme ; enfin, au plan terminologique et combinatoire, témoignant du dynamisme des vocabulaires technoscientifiques.

Elisabeth Navarro et Jean-Michel Benayoun s'interrogent sur la nomination d'une profession nouvelle qui se situe entre l'interprétation, la médiation interculturelle et l'action sociale, dans un contexte où les phénomènes migratoires s'intensifient. En posant l'ethno sociolinguistique comme un socle interculturel indispensable à l'assise professionnelle de cette activité, l'article fait le point sur les enjeux politiques de cette nomination et précise les compétences exigées du métier. Ainsi ils proposent le terme d'« interprète-médiateur » pour mieux rendre compte de la spécificité de la profession.

La deuxième partie porte un regard historique sur le rôle innovateur de la traduction. Dans son article « La traduction et la création du bon usage », Douglas Kibbee remonte au XVIIe siècle où la langue française était considérée pauvre en lexique, instable en morphologie et désordonnée en syntaxe, et indique la façon dont le français utilise la traduction de textes anciens comme une source d'enrichissement. A cette époque de « Belles infidèles », c'est en effet la création du bon usage du français qui est en jeu. L'histoire de la langue française est à nouveau abordée dans l'article de Mairi McLaughlin, « La traduction et l'innovation linguistique dans la presse d'information sous l'Ancien Régime ». A travers des analyses linguistiques d'un corpus de textes journalistiques, elle démontre que la traduction faisait partie intégrante de la production et de la diffusion périodique des informations, et qu'elle était une source d'emprunts lexicaux du français aux XVIIe et XVIIIe siècles.

En passant à l'histoire de la zoologie dans laquelle la traduction a joué un rôle indispensable pour sa transmission, Meyssa Ben Saâd, Mehrnaz Katouzian-Safadi et Philippe Provençal examinent des extraits traduits en français du *Kitpasal-Ḥayawān* dtpasalḥiẓ (776–868) et relèvent de nombreux problèmes de traduction. Ils appellent ainsi à une nouvelle lecture de l'ouvrage, et de nouvelles traductions dans une langue scientifique « intelligible » afin d'en saisir toute la rigueur et toute la pertinence.

Loin de la science zoologique, « Le Loup et l'Agneau » de La Fontaine a connu en langue turque une dizaine de traductions. Sündüz Kasar propose ici une étude sémiotique de cinq traductions dans son article « Interaction entre la sémiotique et la traduction littéraire », et montre l'apport de la sémiotique à la traductologie et à la pratique de la traduction littéraire.

Plus à l'est de l'Asie, Aimée Lahaussois étudie la traduction utilisée dans les archives orales de langues en danger au Népal. Dans l'article intitulé « The Translation Tier in Interlinear Glossed Text: Changing Practices in the Description of Endangered Languages », elle met l'accent sur la tendance de plus en plus littérale de la traduction des données recueillies sur le terrain. A l'aide de nombreux exemples, elle avance l'hypothèse selon laquelle par cette traduction, il est important de rendre visibles les caractéristiques morphosyntaxiques de ces langues en danger.

Nous arrivons enfin en Chine avec l'article de Florence Xiangyun Zhang, « Relier la science à la littérature, la traduction de Jules Verne en Chine ». Selon elle, l'histoire de la traduction de Jules Verne depuis le seuil du XXe siècle reflète les rapports complexes entre les Chinois et la science. Le traducteur de 1900 adapte et simplifie le roman vernien car il y voit une source d'inspiration pour éduquer le peuple, en l'an 2000 l'œuvre de Verne retraduite satisfait plutôt des ambitions commerciales, mais entre 1950–1980 les traductions de Verne ont incité des écrivains chinois à innover l'espace littéraire en créant leur propre science-fiction.

La troisième partie sera consacrée à la vision de la traduction du point de vue psychanalytique et aux approches théorisantes de la traduction. Janine Altounian, dans « Traduire ce qui n'a pas pu se dire », nous fait partager son expérience et sa réflexion, en tant que traductrice de Freud, et en tant qu'héritière d'Arméniens survivants au génocide de 1915. Elle aborde la traduction au croisement de deux déplacements : la traduction entre deux langues et la traduction d'une transmission psychique en un langage partageable. En mettant en parallèle ces deux transferts, elle attire notre attention sur l'écriture d'une transmission psychique, cette traduction d' « un matériau originel ne disposant pas de mots pour se dire » et « transmis sans mots ».

Si le refoulement de la génération des survivants du génocide arménien a besoin d'être traduit par des descendants, dans « La traduction comme stratégie subjectivante en contexte de rééducation auditive post-implantatoire », Rémy Potier et Olivier Putois montrent que la traduction en langue étrangère par soi-même chez une patiente psychotique peut représenter une libération. Ici la traduction est utilisée dans un parcours thérapeutique pour une personne qui vit dans la psychose où sa langue maternelle est éprouvée comme *envahissement ou appropriation effective de son corps par l'Autre maternelle.*

Dans « Déplacement territorial, traduction et maternité. Quand la traversée des frontières favorise les phénomènes traductifs chez la femme » d'Elise Pestre, la traduction est envisagée comme un acte psychique et corporel, étudiant une population de femmes migrantes en Argentine. Même sans impliquer la langue étrangère, le déplacement territorial propulse le migrant à traduire, donc à s'approprier une nouvelle demeure par le biais d'importants réaménagements psychiques et pulsionnels. Ici c'est l'entrée précipitée dans la maternité des femmes migrantes peu après le déplacement qui révèle les actes de traduction. Ainsi Elise Pestre observe-t-elle l'avènement de la grossesse chez ces femmes en exil comme la traduction de nœuds refoulés jusqu'alors maintenus hors du conscient.

Elizabeth Kaluaratchige, quant à elle, traduit Freud et Lacan en cinghalais. Dans son article « La traduction de la psychanalyse en cinghalais : simple intérêt ou véritable défi », elle rend compte de l'insuffisance de la traduction existante faite à partir des traductions de langue anglaise, met l'accent sur la problématique de l'introduction de nouveaux concepts et termes, et insiste sur la nécessité de mener des recherches scientifiques afin de proposer une nouvelle traduction à la fois sourcière et accessible.

Nicolas Froeliger se propose d'être théoricien et avocat de la traduction pragmatique. Dans « Sommes-nous des laquais de l'impérialisme ? De l'apport du tournant culturel en traduction pragmatique », il rappelle que le « tournant culturel » dans les études traductologiques, résultat de deux principaux courants (études postcoloniales et études sur le genre), a en quelque sorte marginalisé la traduction pragmatique. Au lieu de faire l'impasse sur ce courant, il met en lumière les controverses dans l'argumentation de ses tenants théoriques et suggère une lecture dialectique des notions critiquées.

C'est sous l'aspect de la complexité que Patricia Minacori étudie la traduction pragmatique. Face à la complexité du texte pragmatique, le traducteur passe selon elle, par quatre phases (compréhension, expression, recherche et révision) et doit mettre en relation l'opération traduisante avec les principes de complexités définis par

E. Morin, permettant de penser à des stratégies qui mènent à l'innovation : « La complexité appelle la stratégie. Il n'y a que la stratégie pour avancer dans l'incertain et l'aléatoire » (Morin, 1990).

L'article de Jean-René Ladmiral « Sur la recherche en traduction », reprenant sa conférence hautement animée, constitue une conclusion parfaite de ce volume. En effet, comme l'illustre la variété du sujet des articles, la recherche en traduction s'est affranchie des limites traditionnelles de disciplines linguistiques, et s'ouvre vers une interdisciplinarité de plus en plus large. Il distingue alors deux interdisciplinarités. La linguistique, la philosophie, la psychologie et la littérature comparée forment l'interdisciplinarité interne qui assure les bases méthodologiques et conceptuelles de la traductologie ; tandis que l'interdisciplinarité externe désigne les liens qu'entretient la traduction avec tant d'autres disciplines, dans lesquels elle « sert de paradigme interdisciplinaire permettant de penser les conjonctures ethnosociologiques, les relations interculturelles, d'éventuels invariants anthropologiques, la communication, la sexualité elle-même ... ». Le champ d'étude de la traduction est alors illimité.

Florence Xiangyun Zhang
Paris, France

Part 1 / Première Partie

Science and Terminology / Science et Terminologie

English is the Global Language of Science: *Que Faire?*

Scott L. Montgomery

Abstract

This reflection on English as the global language of science starts with the premise that English is the global language *tout court,* and argues that we should see this not as a form of linguistic hegemony, but rather as a phenomenon that has reoccurred through-out history. Science has always had lingua francas, and these have worked to expand and enhance scientific knowledge. This growth in knowledge was driven partly by translation, as it was done both into and out of the scientific lingua francas. The widespread use of English today has led to an increased and unprecedented access to knowledge. Unlike lingua francas of the past, English as the global language of science is not dependent on the cultural and scientific dominance of the United States, and so the age of English as the global language of science has just begun.

Keywords: global language of science, lingua franca, English, access to knowledge

Résumé

Cette réflexion autour de la question de l'anglais comme la langue mondiale de la science part de l'idée selon laquelle l'anglais est la langue mondiale tout court. Nous voulons démontrer qu'il faut considérer cela non pas comme une forme de l'hégémonie linguistique, mais plutôt comme un phénomène qui est apparu régulièrement tout au long de l'histoire. La science a toujours eu des *lingua franca* qui lui ont permis de diffuser et renforcer le savoir scientifique. Le savoir s'est donc enrichi grâce en partie aux traductions, car elles ont été réalisées dans les *lingua franca* et à partir de celles-*ci*. L'usage très répandu de l'anglais aujourd'hui a conduit à une intensification sans précédent de l'accès au savoir. Contrairement aux *lingua franca* du passé, l'anglais comme la langue mondiale de la science n'est pas dépendant de la domination culturelle et scientifique des États-Unis, ainsi l'âge de l'anglais comme langue mondiale de la science ne fait que commencer.

Mots-clés : langue mondiale de la science, *lingua franca*, Anglais, accès au savoir

Introduction

This essay is intended as a series of informed thoughts on the role of English in science today, its possible future, and the impact on translation. Not a scholarly paper per se, it utilizes knowledge gained from research into past lingua franca in science and compares the trends and patterns observed there with the case of English today. As such, it puts to use much of the information gathered in my recent book, *Does Science Need a Global Language? English and the Future of Research* (Montgomery, 2013). Yet it extends beyond some of the conclusions presented there relevant to translation. A scientist who has worked as a translator, I should like to draw on my own experience and begin with a story that helps indicate the place of English at present.

In the mid-1980s, when a geoscientist in the energy industry, I was given the task to write a report on the geology of North Africa, specifically Libya, Tunisia, and Algeria. It was challenging work, but fascinating. The allure stemmed not merely from the geology involved, but the literature about it. Much of it included articles, monographs, and government documents written in French and German by intrepid explorationists who had spent months, even years living in isolated, extraordinary landscapes. From the pages of their work, one could find glimpses of the unblinking sun, moistureless air, and stinging dust they must have so often faced.

Nearly twenty years later, several geologists from Tunisia contacted me asking to collaborate on a paper dealing with the Ghadames Basin, a large oil and gas province extending from southern Tunisia into Algeria and Libya. I agreed and was sent a box of materials containing publications, raw data, and maps. Hoping to renew my acquaintance with those resolute geo-explorers of earlier times, I was disappointed to find none of their work included. All of the articles, published since the mid-1990s, were in English. Inquiring about material by the authors I had previously used, I was told it was either too old or not often read. It's nice, they said, that you can read French and German, but unnecessary. Indeed, I saw that the journal where I had found many helpful articles before, *Geologische Rundschau*, a prestigious international site of work in several languages, had changed its name. It was now the *International Journal of Earth Sciences* and carried papers only in English.

Many anglophone scientists over the age of fifty, who have worked in the places and languages of non-anglophone countries, have had similar experiences. The changeover to an all-English format in the world's prestigious international journals of science, has been swift, merciless, and nearly universal. Indeed, between 1990 and 2005, a mere fifteen-year period, practically all traces of what was once a linguistically diverse landscape has utterly abandoned the past and turned toward a monolingual future. Even the famous *Annalen der Physik*, dating from the eighteenth century, where Einstein published his epochal papers of 1905—known as the "annus mirabilis"—has eliminated all other languages but English. Only in its title, which remains unchanged, does it evince any linguistic loyalty to the past.

Status of English in Science

Such phenomena provide a keyhole to the broad reality defining English as the global language of science. One may ask whether this is a good thing or not, what burdens and benefits it may bring, what effects it may have on translation. There is little sense, however, in questioning whether it is true. That English has risen to such stature in science—which, in this article, is taken to include the natural sciences, mathematics, engineering, and medicine—the global scientific enterprise can not be called a result of centralized planning or policy. Though certain organizations—above all the bibliographic and bibliometric data company, Thomson Reuters—have had a distinct hand in advocating for English as a world scientific lingua franca—the actual reasons have been multiform, related as much to geopolitical events, such as collapse of the Soviet Union (and thus Russian as a competitor language) and, of course, the historical position of the United States and US science after World War II. History, in fact, defines an essential domain for understanding English as the global tongue of science, but not merely for the political dimension.

If we look carefully at the trends of Figure 1, we begin to understand why this is so. Curves on this graph show the number of articles published in the English language in scientific and engineering journals aimed at an international audience. Each curve represents a particular nation or group of nations, based on data collected annually (each curve actually shows an interpolation connecting these yearly totals). The top two curves reveal a significant fact: by 1995, Europe surpassed the United States in English language papers. In other words, by this year, European scientists had accepted English as the global language to the degree that they were out-publishing the primary anglophone nation. From the curves below the US and EU, it is apparent that the rest of the world, and above all Asia, has also increasingly turned to English, particularly since 2001. The most rapid increase exists for the so-called Asia-10, which includes China, India, Japan, South Korea, Malaysia, Taiwan, Thailand, Philippines, Singapore, and Indonesia. Curves for two nations, Japan and China, show opposite tendencies, with Japan decreasing its total English publications since the early 2000s and China more than doubling its own. Reasons for Japan's gradual drop are not entirely clear, but may be related to that nation's stagnant economy and declining population. Japan's pattern is clearly the exception. More striking even than China's rapid rise and that of the Asian-8 (same as Asian-10 minus Japan and South Korea), however, is the curve for "Rest of World."

Figure 1. Number, in thousands, of science and engineering articles published in journals with an international focus from the years 1995 to 2009. All articles are in English. Original graph from Science and Engineering Indicators 2012, National Science Board, USA.

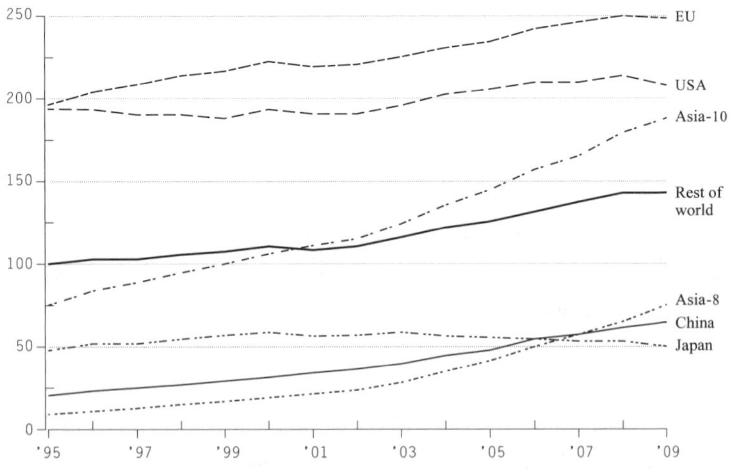

From one perspective, this defines the key trend. It represents data for most of the developing world—those nations, in other words, that until very recently have not been part of the modern scientific enterprise, yet that include most of the world's population. These are nations that can't afford to train a large number of scientists, that have limited scientific infrastructure, that tend to focus on a smaller range of fields, especially those of immediate relevance to their own domestic challenges (agriculture, for example). As the newest members of the scientific community of nations, they are a growing part of the future. Expanding the technical capability of these nations defines a key process in global modernization and a potential factor in long-term political liberalization. Their scientists now collaborate on a regular basis with researchers in advanced nations and also, to a somewhat lesser degree, with colleagues in other developing nations (Royal Society, 2012). Modern science, in short, no longer belongs to a few dozen wealthy states, as it has since the eighteenth century. The single curve on the graph of publications tells us that a new era has begun, an era of global science and a global language.

English in Perspective: Major Lingua Franca of Science Past

While much has been written on the history and growth of English as a world language (e.g., Seargeant, 2012; Crystal, 2005; Graddol, 2003; Baugh, 2002), very little has been said about its place with respect to former major lingua franca, particularly in science. As shown in Figure 2, English counts as the latest in a series of international tongues that have been crucial to the advance of knowledge in key societies. These tongues are plotted simply in chronological fashion but display complex relations.

Figure 2. Historical chronology of major international lingua franca of science. Figure indicates eras when each language served as medium of active advance and inscription (solid) and when it served more the purposes of preserving what had been written (dotted).

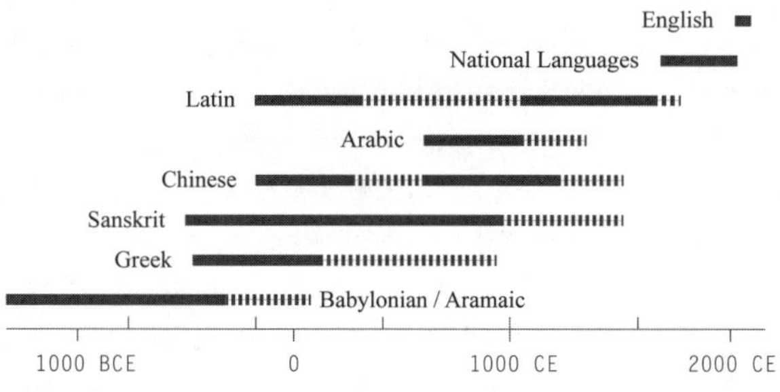

Figure 2 is far from complete, though it does include most of the languages important to the long-term growth and inter-cultural transfer of scientific knowledge. For each language, the chronological plot shows those periods when it served as an active medium for the advancement of knowledge (solid shaded portions)—meaning that significant texts were being written in this language, works were being translated into it, scholars from a variety of cultural-linguistic backgrounds learned it as a matter of course for their work. In short, the language provided a type of growing reservoir for the creation and gathering of new knowledge about the natural world. Also indicated are periods when this level of fertile increase was far less present (dotted portions), or not present at all, when existing knowledge was copied and perhaps taught in the particular tongue but not significantly increased (on the contrary, much was often lost). In addition, these periods of preservation were also times when considerable translation out of the relevant language took place and greatly helped further or inspire a period of advance in another tongue. Finally, Figure 2 shows a period labeled "National Languages." This refers to the time between the fall of Latin as a lingua franca of science in Europe (late seventeenth century) and the present. Starting about the 1680s (actual dates vary on a national and disciplinary basis), the great majority of new scientific work was being written in national languages. Such is distinctly a simplification, to be sure. French remained a powerful lingua franca in Europe for nearly the whole of the eighteenth century, while German became an international tongue in the physical sciences and medicine after about 1850, lasting till the 1920s.

It is only since the 1970s and, above all, the 1990s that English has come to be the new international lingua franca of science. The era of national-language science continues, without doubt, and Figure 2 reflects this. Yet, this era is now in the midst of transition. An overall sociolinguistic evolution is occurring within the sciences whereby English has been increasingly adopted within individual non-anglophone nations, initially for purposes of training (especially at the university level), and more recently for purposes of publication and international representation. This can be seen, for example, in the scientific data, reports, and other documents provided by websites of research institutions around the world, which now commonly provide such material in both the domestic language and in English. This is significant, since the internet has rapidly become the primary medium for scientific communication at many levels, as well as the global face of any specific group, project, university department, company, or organization. What this has meant linguistically, among other things, is that researchers using domestic languages—including other, less powerful lingua franca like Spanish and French—have increasingly adopted scientific terminology from English in order to keep their native tongues current, capable of expressing the latest knowledge.

Study of the evolving influences exhibited by the languages in Figure 2 reveals a number of recurrent phenomena that can be grouped into themes. These may well be of relevance to the present and future of English as a global lingua franca. In any case, they are the closest thing to "evidence" that we have on which to base such interpretations of the future. The following provides a summary of the more important themes:

Major lingua franca have brought many key benefits to science. These tongues created the possibility for researchers of many different scientific cultures to contribute their knowledge and skills through a single medium, advancing the prospects for cross-pollination.

Lingua franca have usually been installed by forms of hard power (military conquest, cultural dominance), yet greatly outlasted the force of these forms. This was as result of the language becoming integrated into the intellectual traditions of originally dominated states over time.

Over time (centuries), lingua franca were nativized to local settings and tended to develop into dialects and, eventually, new tongues. Their writing systems, however, could continue intact as international systems for inscribing and therefore teaching and sharing knowledge.

Major lingua franca have led to language death in many communities (Latin, Arabic, and European colonial languages, including Russian and English, are prominent examples), but have led to the creation of scientific cultures in others (e.g., the impact of Chinese in other East Asian areas).

There are few records that claim the learning of an international language was an insurmountable burden, though, in some cases (Arabic for European scholars) it was not easy. More often, multilingualism among scholars was routine in many settings, especially urban ones, and lingua franca were a major reason for this. Being capable in the principal tongue of knowledge was viewed as necessary, part of scholarly education.

International lingua franca of science became the source of new words, morphological structures, and entire terminologies in other languages. This allowed some tongues to develop and advance their own scientific discourse. More generally, it was a process repeated by successive lingua franca themselves, particularly as a result of episodes of translation. Examples include Greek and Sanskrit terms adopted into Arabic, then Arabic and Arabized Greek/Hindu terms brought into Latin, many of which have since become part of English.

A specific benefit: lingua franca that spread most widely, Arabic in particular, served as an unparalleled medium by which native knowledge could be preserved and used to fertilize science. The tradition of star worship in Harran (southernmost Anatolia) provides but a single excellent example.

Latin cannot be said to offer a useful analog for English today. After the late 6th c. A.D., Latin was a dead tongue outside of monasteries, available only to a tiny elite, limiting access to science for a thousand years. To note the obvious, English is a living language spoken to varying degrees by well over a billion people, with as many as two billion currently learning it, while it acts as a medium for science worldwide.

Major lingua franca of the past did not reduce but instead greatly expanded the role, importance, and volume of translation. For Greek, Arabic, and to a significant degree Latin and Sanskrit, there existed a strong motive by conquering leaders to collect the best, most advanced knowledge of every people—such was the distinct program behind the Library at Alexandria (as requested by Alexander the Great's lieutenants), the early Abbasid Caliphs, the translators of the twelfth-century Renaissance in Europe, and the Gupta Empire in northern India. Moreover, the very collection and advancement of scientific knowledge in a lingua franca like Sanskrit or Arabic meant that scholars who worked in later international languages of science would want such knowledge made available to them. Indeed, that brought from

Arabic into Latin over a period of several centuries proved an important basis for the Scientific Revolution itself (Montgomery, 2002).

Translation of scientific material from one lingua franca to another, moreover, was never a simple process of duplicating knowledge. Greek astronomical texts, for example, brought into Arabic were reorganized, sometimes rewritten, selectively edited, updated (e.g., star positions), provided with diagrams, and more. Translation was therefore a dynamic process of adaptation, and this adaptation often involved improving (or sometimes the opposite), adapting, the original texts for use in a new context. Such dynamism tended to make later versions of such texts more of an accumulation, an "edition" expanded by the varied changes, including additions and deletions, of previous scientific cultures. In this sense, it is essential to remember than no original manuscripts exist for all of Greek science, early Indian science, and much of Arabic science. It is often the case that the oldest near-complete (as far as can be discerned) versions are separated by over six hundred years from the author's lifetime and are in a different language as well.

Implications for English

How much of this can be applied to English as a global lingua franca? What, for example, are the implications for translation?

Taking these themes together, we see that lingua francas in science have brought both benefits and drawbacks. Yet, by almost any measure, the positives have greatly outweighed the negatives. Regional and even world-scale lingua franca have been a key factor in scientific progress, not least because of the increased mobilization of knowledge they create. Their benefits, in other words, have not in the least been restricted to their own original mother-tongue speakers, far from it. In the case of Arabic, for example, major contributions to Islamic science in Arabic came from all over the empire, from Asia Minor, Central Asia, the Iberian Peninsula, and particularly from Persia.

It is true that, as languages of power, these lingua francas have often been restricted to scholarly elites in their early stages. Yet over time, the borders of such elites have proven porous and non-exclusive. There are many individual examples of this: Adelard of Bath, born in late

11th century England in what appear to be modest circumstances, was sent to the local cathedral school, where he learned Latin, then, when a youth, traveled to France and taught there before deciding to journey east and acquire "what the Latins do not know" by studying Arabic. England's "first scientist" became, above all, a translator—from one great lingua franca into another, he brought Euclid's *Elements* and, still more significantly, al-Kwarizmi's *Compendium on Calculation by Completion and Balancing*, which introduced the basic concepts and methods of algebra, and also his *Astronomical Tables of Sind and Hind* that brought into Latin the Indian numerical system, including the zero, that we use today. Adelard's example reveals how possession of a lingua franca allowed, even forced, scholars to operate beyond the immediate limits of social class.

The themes above imply that it is in the early stages after a new language has been imposed on a people or established by some other means when challenges are greatest. Nations and communities have shown themselves far more willing to accept an international tongue with limited functions, including scholarly ones, rather than a total replacement of their own speech. A language of power, however, also creates a market, a trade in skills and status. Teachers of Greek to the sons of Roman patricians or the builders of Latin schools in twelfth-century France were responding to, and also helping further, a demand that was at once intellectual, professional, and economic. Anyone who had studied under the great polymath Posidonius on Rhodes or at the cathedral schools of Laon or Chartres acquired high value as a teacher themselves. Posidonius's fame, meanwhile, was due not merely to Greek-speaking scholars but to writers in Latin (Cicero, Seneca the Younger, Julius Caesar), who themselves knew Greek fairly well or fluently. Posidonius himself was in all likelihood (we have very little real information about his life) multilingual, have grown up in Apamea in northwestern Syria, a cross-roads between Mesopotamia and the eastern Mediterranean.

For science, in overview, one strong message from the past is that lingua franca have through history provided gateways and pathways. Shared, inter-cultural languages have proven to be a mode of access to intellectual material, opportunity, and fertilization. Far from acting in solely hegemonic fashion, such languages have helped to open scientific endeavor to new voices, ingredients, and possibilities. At the same time, as languages of power and opportunity, the status they were accorded often weakened local tongues in comparison. In some cases this aided language death significantly, in others not. Persian provides an instance where the lingua franca, Arabic, was itself resisted as a replacement and was eventually held to limited uses.

What of translation? Lingua franca, especially in science, have essentially forced—or perhaps better said, created the optimal conditions for—translation to occur, on a large and long-term scale. During the early stages of emplacement, the lingua franca of Figure 2 tended to act more as the target language. Again, this is one of the major functions of a scientific lingua franca: to gather like a great reservoir the knowledge from other linguistic communities into its embrace. With time, as it becomes the primary medium for scholarly knowledge and communication, it correspondingly shifts toward being the host language. Nearly always, the full history is much more complex and exhibits a series of translation phases. Greek, for example, began as a target language in the seventh and sixth centuries, into which material from Egypt, Mesopotamia, and possibly India as well, was brought. This continued, perhaps more sporadically but still significantly, down to the time of Hipparchus (second century BC) at least, even as Greek had become established as the premier scientific language and had been since Alexander's death in 323 BC the host *magnus* to Rome, to Asia Minor, Persia, and western India. After the Hellenistic era, it decayed as a lingua franca, entered a period of preservation, and then was resurrected as a host language first by Islamic thinkers in the eighth to eleventh centuries and then again by Latin-speaking scholars of science in the thirteenth through sixteenth centuries.

Major lingua franca of science past have therefore lasted for centuries and then been favored with multipart afterlives, all of which has served the cause of translation. A final point concerns the product of translation. The last theme listed above mentions the dynamism of scientific translation in the past, a dynamism that meant texts were sometimes adapted and paraphrased, thus recast. Texts in science, no less than in literature, were therefore unstable from a modern perspective. Such instability could be the source of invention and fertility as well as the opposite, incoherent literalism spiced with errors and omissions. A look at the translation of western scientific material into the languages of East Asia, Chinese and Japanese for example, would confirm that this continued as late as the final years of the nineteenth century (a famous example being Yan Fu and his rendition of Thomas Huxley in the classical Chinese of the 1880s). This might be compared with technical translation of today, where the dominant standard is fidelity—"don't spill a drop." Such, of course, is naïve since there is always matter lost and gained. Yet by the terms of such a standard, a global language, once it had become a basic skill for all scientists, would be much preferable to constant re-rendering of texts.

Future Possibilities

How applicable are these points to English in science? This is difficult to say, as the globalization of scientific English remains in its earliest stage and yet involves a wider array of nations and peoples than any lingua franca of the past. It is able to make use of—indeed, depends to a great degree on—electronic media that have altered human communication generally and obviously didn't exist until very recently. Moreover, the reasons for the rise of English, though attached in part to the economic, military, and cultural power of the United States, do not come from actual conquest and the centralized imposition of a ruling language. With these important caveats, we can't overlook the truth that major differences of this kind also distinguished past lingua franca from one another, yet important patterns still emerge for all of them. Here, then, are some ideas about the future based on the past.

First, the era of English has just begun. Many decades, perhaps a century or more—we may hesitate to say "centuries" at this point—lie ahead. Over this time period it might well penetrate further into domestic science communication, replacing national languages in many countries. This would accompany, and be supported by, the teaching of English as a basic skill, as David Graddol has suggested. Knowledge of English would then be similar to that of Latin in Renaissance or early modern Europe, i.e., part of every educated person's set of fundamental capabilities. On the other hand, a dynamic balance might well come to exist, whereby the functions of English settle into a limited set of domains—science for international uses, for the more basic types of research—while national languages continue to dominate where the public is the primary audience. These two particular possibilities have quite different implications for translation. The first would essentially make translation unnecessary in a majority of situations where technical material is communicated between scientists. The second scenario would render translation necessary in a larger number of cases, where non-scientists (e.g., policy makers) had need of scientific information.

At this point, it appears likely that the geopolitical standing of the United States will become ever more immaterial to all this. America may well decline over the coming decades in prestige and scientific preeminence (many feel this has already begun), but any such fall from the commanding heights will not, by itself, reduce the use of English as a medium of scientific exchange. This is because such use is already independent of any single nation: scientists who want to learn English do not necessarily want to become Americans, go to America, work in America, etc. The nature of a global language is extra-national. There are also practical challenges to switching from English to, say, Chinese or some other tongue. Rendering into another language the immeasurable corpus that has come to reside in English—which now exceeds by orders of magnitude the combined scientific writings of all previous eras, and whose volume is not merely increasing but accelerating in its growth on a daily basis—would present a major challenge, though perhaps, given future translation technology, not an impossible one for digital information.

In this vein, the idea that such technology, perhaps by mid-century, will reach a stage where it eliminates any need or motive for a lingua franca (Ostler, 2012) has to be considered. While the problems facing machine translation today, in the sense of achieving such a capability, are manifold and fundamental, this can't be said to rule out their solution (similar forms of challenge have existed for many successful technologies in the past, e.g., the automobile, or rather "steam wagon," in the 1770s and '80s). Indeed, recent advances by companies such as Microsoft are impressive, though still at a beginning level (Economist, 2013; Madsen, 2009). There is a basic question involved with MT, from the living translator's point of view: given the many different contexts in which human communication takes place—even when confined to professional interactions—and the varied contents that are transmitted, do the ambitions of replacing all needs for a lingua franca make sense? Is this not the age-old desire to replace the human dimension in communication with technology? What would scientists themselves prefer for the future (for their own children, for example), we might ask—knowledge of a language or use of a machine?

In truth, as the global language of science now, English has created a huge and growing market for human translation. International translation companies abound on the web, with many of them now specializing in technical subject areas—biomedicine, pharmaceuticals, engineering, energy, internet technology, legal material (including patents). Information from the company Common Sense Advisory (http://www.commonsenseadvisory.com), which tracts the global language services market, shows that the size of this market has grown from about $8 billion in 2005 to nearly $40 billion in 2012. The growing demand for translation is mainly due to companies and governments, which view English both as host and target language. Governments everywhere have had, or are having, online material for their various ministries and activities put into English for global access, and companies are doing the same. Yet the latter who seek to sell products and services worldwide are also spending the time and money to have their information translated into local languages. Thus, as English continues to expand as a global language of science, it generates further need for translation. This affects research scientists only to a peripheral degree and then dominantly in the private sector. As for the future, it seems more probable that English will remain a target language for scientific translation more than a host language. The main reason is that there are stronger motives for scientists and their employers to acquire a global presence than a local one. English is following the pattern of its predecessors.

These are but a few meditations on what past lingua franca suggest about the outlook for English in science. There is no blueprint or template for making such forecasts. The past can never be a precise model. Perhaps the main pattern we can derive from it at present is also the simplest, that of duration—there has never been a full-scale lingua franca of science, encompassing every area of scientific study and writing, that has not lasted several centuries or more. For some observers, this might be sobering. Yet for scientists everywhere, the reality of having a single, globally reliable tongue in which, like a vast reservoir, generations of the most important data and text will collect and remain accessible, will more likely be viewed as a gain, for themselves and those who come after them.

References

Brenzinger, Matthias, ed. *Language Death: Factual and Theoretical Explorations with Special Reference to East Africa*. Berlin: Mouton de Gruyter, 1992.

Crystal, David. *English as a Global Language*. Cambridge: Cambridge University Press, 2005.

Graddol, David. *English Next*. London: British Council, 2006.

Madsen, Mathias. "The Limits of Machine Translation". M.S. Thesis, University of Copenhagen, 2009. Online: https://docs.google.com/file/d/0B7-4xydn3MXJZjFkZTllZjItN2Q5Ny00YmUxLWEzODItNTYyMjhlNTY5NWIz/edit?pli=1

Montgomery, Scott L. *Science in Translation: Movements of Knowledge in Cultures and Time*. Chicago: University of Chicago Press, 2002.

---. *Does Science Need a Global Language? English and the Future of Research*. Chicago: University of Chicago Press, 2013.

Le déballage terminologique pour traduire l'innovation

JOHN HUMBLEY

Résumé

Il est admis que l'évolution de la terminologie représente la trace linguistique de l'innovation. La traduction de nouveaux termes reste toutefois un défi considérable. L'hypothèse développée ici part du principe que le processus de la création terminologique doit être identifié en vue de la recherche du meilleur équivalent dans la langue d'arrivée. Pour ce faire, on s'appuie sur une théorie de la terminologisation, adaptée de la métaphore grammaticale de M.A.K. Halliday qui fournit un cadre qui permet de rendre compte des transformations grammaticales qui reprennent les explications et les arguments concernant l'innovation sous la forme de condensés linguistiques—c'est-à-dire de futurs termes.

Mots-clés : traduction, terminologie, métaphore grammaticale.

Abstract

Changes in terminology represent the linguistic trace of innovation, and yet, the translation of these linguistic markers of change can present a number of challenges. The hypothesis developed here posits that it is advantageous to identify the manner in which the new term was created in the language of innovation because the strategy used originally can be exploited in order to find an effective equivalent. We rely here on a theory of terminology creation that is based on M.A.K. Halliday's grammatical metaphor. This provides an adequate framework, as it explains in mainly syntactic terms how explanations or arguments, concerning innovation in this case, are transformed into compact linguistic expressions which can serve as terms.

Key words: translation, terminology, grammatical metaphor.

Introduction

L'analyse systémique fonctionnelle telle qu'elle est formulée par M.A.K. Halliday est relativement peu sollicitée par les terminologues. Certes, Halliday lui-même en tant que syntacticien n'a jamais manifesté beaucoup d'intérêt pour le lexique et encore moins pour la terminologie elle-même, mais comme le font remarquer Antia et Kamal, ses écrits comportent des considérations qui se révèlent particulièrement pertinentes dans ce contexte.

> *It has been pointed out by Halliday (*1993*) that the difficulty of understanding science lies more with grammar than with the vocabulary. Even while admitting that, fundamentally, it is impossible to separate the vocabulary from grammar, Halliday claims that for us to really understand the challenges posed by science "we shall need to get rid of our obsession with words". He goes ahead to identify seven factors (which, in our reading, fall under lexical, syntactic and rhetorical considerations) which make science difficult. As an aside, Halliday's treatment of these seven points paradoxically makes terminology relevant in four.* (Antia & Kamal, 2006 136)

La technique que nous présentons ici dans le cadre de la traduction spécialisée, et que nous appelons le *déballage terminologique*, s'inspire de sa présentation de la formation de la langue scientifique à partir de la fin du Moyen-Âge. Halliday (2004 [1999]) explique comment, à partir de Chaucer en anglais, en passant par Newton, les scientifiques emploient des stratégies discursives fondées sur des transformations syntaxiques pour rendre la langue apte à exprimer les concepts scientifiques. Il fait également allusion à des stratégies comparables exploitées en italien par Galilé (Halliday, 2004 [1999] 114), ce qui laisse penser que le phénomène n'est pas propre à l'anglais mais qu'il concerne les langues en général. Halliday appelle le résultat de cette transformation une *métaphore grammaticale*, qu'il met en parallèle avec la métaphore lexicale bien connue, et le processus *packaging*, que nous proposons de rendre en français par *emballage :* "*… the grammatical metaphor "packages" the preceding assertion to function as the point of origin for the next.*" (Halliday, 2004 [1995] 20)

Nous affirmons que la métaphore grammaticale est à l'origine de très nombreux termes, qui commencent leur existence en tant que reformulation d'une proposition. Halliday lui-même prend l'exemple d'un terme de la mécanique de la rupture, *Griffith's energy balance,* qui est en fait une métaphore grammaticale fondée sur *Griffith's approach to energy balance*, dérivée à son tour de *Griffith approached the question of energy balance* .... (Halliday, 2004 [1998] 63).[1] Cet exemple montre que le terme qui finit par se stabiliser (bien que très partiellement dans ce cas précis) provient en réalité d'une série de reformulations que l'on peut dans de nombreux cas reconstituer. Le but de la proposition contenue dans cet article est de démontrer l'intérêt que peut avoir le traducteur spécialisé à *déballer* certains termes susceptibles de poser des difficultés de traduction. Le cas le plus fréquent est sans doute celui des termes nouveaux ou très spécialisés, soit des expressions de l'innovation, pour lesquels aucun équivalent consacré n'existe encore. Nous sommes convaincu par ailleurs que ce déballage terminologique doit faire partie des compétences du traducteur technique, qui aurait donc le choix, dans le meilleur des cas, entre un terme déjà consacré (et donc déjà bien emballé dans la langue d'arrivée) et une formulation discursive, résultat d'une opération de déballage. C'est selon la stratégie communicative de sa traduction, qui peut être différente de celle de l'auteur de l'original, que le traducteur choisira entre les différentes possibilités de formulation, gardant ses options ouvertes. L'ambition de cette contribution est d'explorer les options de terminologie et de traduction que le traducteur doit avoir à sa disposition, dont au premier plan le déballage.

La terminologie, expression de l'innovation

La réflexion prend comme point de départ la communication de l'innovation scientifique et technique, à la fois dans la langue des chercheurs ou des techniciens et sous forme de traduction. Il est généralement admis que les innovations réalisées dans les sciences et les technologies—ces dernières prises dans leur acception la plus large—sont exprimées par des formulations linguistiques ou extra linguistiques innovantes. Au niveau extra-linguistique, nous entendons par là les formules, les graphiques, bref le recours à toutes sortes de codes, généralement en lien direct les uns avec les autres aussi bien qu'avec la langue. Les textes spécialisés sont caractérisés par l'emploi de ces différents codes, de telle sorte que leur analyse doit se faire en convoquant les outils de la sémiotique aussi bien que ceux de la linguistique. Pour les besoins du présent article, toutefois, nous nous limitons aux expressions langagières de l'innovation.

La terminologie réserve à ces nouvelles expressions un traitement particulier. Généralement connus sous le nom de néologismes terminologiques (Rey 1979), ces formulations sont également appelées, à l'instar du pionnier québécois Guy Rondeau (1984), des néonymes. C'est à Rondeau que l'on doit par ailleurs la première modélisation de deux scénarios de création terminologique liés à la situation de l'innovation en question : le premier est celui du chercheur qui crée le nouveau terme dans sa propre langue.

Un terme nouveau apparaît dans une langue de spécialité (ou langage spécialisé) au moment où une notion nouvelle voit le jour, grâce à la découverte d'un savant, d'un technicien, d'un technologue, etc., bref, d'un spécialiste du domaine. La nouvelle notion est nommée par son concepteur dans sa langue de travail. Les termes nouveaux ainsi créés constituent des *néonymes d'origine* (NO). (Rondeau, 1984 123)

C'est toutefois le second cas qui nous concerne plus directement dans le cadre de la présente étude :

> Une nouvelle notion circule en général rapidement dans les milieux scientifiques et techniques. La dénomination qui lui a été rattachée par son premier concepteur peut, dans certains cas, passer d'une langue à l'autre, constituant ainsi un cas de néologie d'emprunt ; ou encore, elle peut faire l'objet d'une traduction littérale : c'est le cas du calque ; ou bien, enfin, une nouvelle dénomination (dans une langue autre que la langue d'origine) sera rattachée à cette notion, par un spécialiste du domaine, un traducteur ou un terminologue. Tous ces types de dénomination constituent des néonymes d'appoint (NA). (Rondeau, 1984 123)

Cette distinction est exprimée de manière analogue par Juan Carlos Sager (1987, 1990, 1997), qui parle lui de formation terminologique primaire et secondaire. Quelle que soit la dénomination, on comprend que le traducteur est susceptible de jouer un rôle important dans la transmission de la terminologie. Nous verrons toutefois qu'il s'agit d'un rôle secondaire par rapport à sa mission de traducteur. On voit également qu'il a le choix entre l'emprunt direct et la traduction, c'est-à-dire l'innovation langagière. Certaines études donnent d'ailleurs à penser que les traducteurs sont plus soucieux de trouver des équivalents dans la langue d'arrivée que les scientifiques et techniciens qui écrivent dans leur langue maternelle et qui eux préfèrent garder le terme établi dans l'autre langue—de nos jours inévitablement l'anglais. C'est le cas en particulier pour l'étude menée par Bernardini et Ferraresi (2011 241), qui attestent davantage d'emprunts directs à l'anglais dans les textes rédigés directement en italien par les informaticiens italophones que dans les textes traduits.

Nous savons par ailleurs que les termes nouveaux sont caractérisés par un fort taux de variation. Celle-ci est exploitée en traitement automatique du langage (Daille et al. 1996) ; certains terminologues s'en servent pour expliquer différents points de vue sociolinguistiques (Faulstich 2000). Freixa (2006) en donne un aperçu plus global, tandis que Pecman (2012) signale des fonctions rhétoriques et conceptuelles dans l'emploi des variations. Compte tenu de leur orientation méthodologique foncièrement onomasiologique, les terminologues ont privilégié l'aspect conceptuel de la variation, mais nous estimons que le traducteur est tout aussi concerné par les considérations expressives. Pour résumer ce qui est dit plus haut, on peut prétendre, sans schématiser grossièrement, que le traducteur a deux grandes options, le choix entre deux types de variation : ou bien il transmet l'innovation par un terme équivalent dans la langue d'arrivée (mais celui-ci existe-t-il ?) ou bien il rend le nouveau concept en employant une formulation discursive. A nos yeux, la formulation discursive inverse dans ses principes la démarche qui a présidé à la formation du nouveau terme (ou son emballage pour employer le terme de Halliday), aboutissant ainsi à un déballage terminologique.

On peut également supposer que le déballage qui permet d'exprimer par une construction verbale le concept nouveau peut servir de point de départ à un nouveau terme dans la langue d'arrivée, par une opération d'emballage. Il appartient encore une fois au traducteur de déterminer si cette opération est menée indépendamment de la manière dont le terme est motivé dans la langue d'origine, mais il semble raisonnable de vouloir reproduire le processus d'emballage de l'original afin de préserver autant que faire se peut la motivation conceptuelle du créateur.

Opérations d'emballages déballés

Les opérations d'emballage et de déballage terminologiques ont lieu dans différents contextes. Nous examinons ici d'abord la reformulation dans la langue de rédaction, ensuite dans une autre langue, sans que ce processus relève pour autant de la traduction en tant que telle.

Le déballage dans la même langue

Mojca Pecman (2012) montre comment le scripteur scientifique (généralement un scripteur pluriel dans la plupart des sciences naturelles et technologiques) emballe soigneusement son nouveau terme. Nous reprenons comme exemple le nouveau terme de *ice island calving*, le processus de création d'icebergs géants à partir de gros paquets de glace qui tombent d'un glacier (le processus est connu sous le nom de *vêlage*). Elle relève dans le même texte la forme discursive (que Halliday appelle *congruent form*) : *the ice shelf calved, creating an ice island*, qui représente soit un déballage terminologique, si la métaphore grammaticale est déjà employée, ce qui semble être le cas dans l'article cité, soit la forme à partir de laquelle l'emballage a été réalisé. Entre ces deux extrémités, l'auteur emploie plusieurs formes intermédiaires *calving of ice*, *calving of ice islands*, *iceberg calving*, qui constituent différents degrés d'emballage et donc de terminologisation de ce nouveau concept en glaciologie.

Le déballage dans une autre langue

Les stratégies d'emballage et de déballage font partie des techniques dont se servent abondamment—mais généralement inconsciemment — rédacteurs et traducteurs. Nous venons de voir comment un scientifique développe ou raccourcit les expressions désignant la même innovation dans la langue de la rédaction. Les scripteurs usent d'une stratégie comparable lorsqu'il s'agit d'exprimer dans une autre langue un terme déjà emballé dans une précédente. Il s'agit en fait de ce que Rondeau (1984 123) appelle la néonymie d'appoint et Sager

(1989 159) la formation terminologique secondaire, mais pratiqué dans un contexte expositif ou explicatif plutôt que dans un but dénominatif.

Examinons à titre d'exemple les reformulations que pratique un auteur suisse, travaillant en français dans le domaine de la criminalistique, pour rendre le terme néologique anglais *self-reported delinquancy survey*. Il en propose une formulation complètement déballée, qui présente tous les traits sémantiques du nouveau concept : *enquêtes qui mettent en relief la délinquance révélée, racontée ou confessée,* mais il ne se prive pas non plus de remballer cette expression sous différentes formes : *sondage de délinquance autoreportée, enquêtes d'autoconfession, enquête par autoportrait …*[2] Il s'avère donc que les spécialistes eux-mêmes se servent de cette stratégie de déballage et de remballage pour exprimer l'innovation pensée dans une autre langue, en graduant la forme précise aux besoins de la communication immédiate.

Traducteur et terminologue

Les fonctions de traducteur et de terminologue sont souvent combinées dans l'organisation matérielle du travail. De très nombreux terminologues sont en fait des traducteurs chevronnés, et dans de nombreuses organisations ce sont les traducteurs qui alimentent les bases de terminologie, sous le contrôle ou non d'un terminologue titulaire.[3] Malgré la proximité opérationnelle de ces deux métiers, il est important de souligner que les finalités sont en réalité très différentes. La mission du traducteur est de transmettre un message de la manière la plus efficace possible : les moyens qu'il choisit pour le faire sont multiples et variés et ne dépendent que de sa propre stratégie de communication, qui n'est pas nécessairement celle de l'auteur de l'original. Le terminologue, en revanche, doit proposer un équivalent. Pour schématiser, on peut dire que le traducteur travaille uniquement en discours tandis que le terminologue vise à combler une lacune lexicale en langue. Bien entendu, les frontières entre les deux sont perméables, comme le suggère la célèbre formulation de Marie-Françoise Mortureux (1997) : *le lexique entre langue et discours*. Et ce qui est vrai pour le lexique en général l'est encore davantage pour la terminologie.

C'est—entre autres—dans l'interaction entre traducteur et terminologue que le lexique spécialisé innove.

Il n'en reste pas moins que le traducteur n'a pas la même responsabilité que le terminologue. Celui-là l'assume à la fois envers l'auteur qu'il traduit et envers le public qui lira la traduction. Son action, ses choix, auront dans certains cas des répercussions sur l'évolution de la langue. Nous savons en effet que la néologie traductrice est une source importante d'enrichissement terminologique (Hermans & Vansteelandt 1999).

Le rôle du terminologue, en revanche, est de fournir un équivalent qui peut se substituer aussi directement que possible à l'expression d'un concept dans une autre langue. La forme retenue est donc relativement proche de celle du terme modèle, et renvoie généralement au mode de formation dans la langue d'origine. Certains termes sont formés consciemment de manière systématique, comme la nomenclature de la chimie, les dénominations de corps célestes récemment découverts etc. Ce sont des systèmes terminologiques qui peuvent avoir des équivalences systématiques, voire pas d'équivalent du tout, lorsqu'il s'agit d'une forme complètement internationale. Mais il s'agit là de systèmes quasi dérogatoires. On peut penser que la plupart des termes sont au contraire formés dans le discours, en variant les termes de l'expression. Le résultat en est des « condensés » linguistiques, qui suffisent aux experts pour échanger, y compris lorsqu'il s'agit d'innover, en variant le degré de concentration selon la situation—ils développent lorsqu'il convient d'expliquer, et ils raccourcissent lorsqu'ils font allusion à des phénomènes que le lecteur est censé connaître.

Le prototype de ces condensés linguistiques, qui vont plus loin que l'emballage—opération syntaxique—est bien entendu le sigle. C'est la forme la plus courte, qui fait appel à la loi du moindre effort ou, plus correctement, la loi de Zipf (Bully 1969). On constate que l'emploi des sigles constitue une des principales barrières linguistiques lorsqu'il s'agit de s'approprier un nouveau domaine, et que les spécialistes, lorsqu'ils changent de langue, répugnent à traduire le sigle. Celui-ci serait devenu une simple étiquette, tout aussi maniable lorsqu'il renvoie au développement dans la langue étrangère que dans la langue maternelle. Lorsqu'il s'agit de présenter un concept nouveau habituellement dénommé par un sigle dont le développement est étranger, on constate de la part des auteurs l'emploi d'un développement traduit. C'est ainsi en géologie que l'on constate parfois la formulation en français de *dépression quasi-circulaire* pour reprendre le sigle *QCD*, qui représente en fait l'anglais *quasi-circular depression*. Quelle que soit la décision du scripteur, il a à sa disposition une forme quasi codée, accessible aux seuls initiés, et une forme développée qui convient à un public moins initié au domaine concerné. Dans le cas des sigles donc, la marge de manœuvre du traducteur est relativement limitée, mais le développement (équivalent du déballage mais en plus mécanique) et sa traduction restent des stratégies privilégiées lorsqu'il s'agit d'une innovation encore peu connue dans la communauté linguistique et spécialisée concernée.

A l'autre bout de l'échelle conceptuelle, on constate que l'innovation est souvent exprimée au moyen d'une métaphore lexicale. Une bonne partie de la recherche de ces dernières années a été consacrée à l'exploration de ce que la linguistique cognitive peut apporter non seulement sur le plan de la néologie mais aussi et surtout sur celui des processus mentaux des scientifiques eux-mêmes lorsqu'ils abordent la nouveauté. L'étude marquante de Rita Temmerman (2000) montre comment les pionniers du génie génétique se sont appuyés sur le connu pour imaginer comment le génome peut fonctionner : en imaginant que l'ADN est un langage ils supposaient que celui-ci partage avec le langage un certain nombre de propriétés communes, d'où l'emploi du vocabulaire de l'information : *code*, *coder*, etc. Pour le scientifique non anglophone, tout comme pour le traducteur, la stratégie de transfert était simple : la métaphore faisant partie de la pensée des scientifiques est inhérente à la démarche et se transfère directement dans l'autre langue, par exemple en néerlandais ou en français. Ce n'est que lorsque la métaphore d'origine n'est pas bien comprise, par les spécialistes plutôt que par les traducteurs, comme ce fut le cas pour le *splicing*, que le transfert est bloqué et c'est l'emprunt direct — du coup démétaphorisé dans la langue d'accueil — qui est retenu. C'est ce qui s'est passé en néerlandais et en français, car les généticiens européens n'avaient pas compris l'analogie avec le montage de films ou répugnaient à employer une métaphore si peu scientifique. Temmerman fait une distinction avec les métaphores du domaine spécialisé qui sont transposées sans problème dans l'autre langue(Temmerman2010 : 555)etdonnedesexemplesd'expressionsen génie génétique qui proviennent de la métaphore mettant en parallèle la carte géographique et la carte génétique (*genetic map : carte génétique ; genetic linkage map : carte des liaisons génétiques ; landmark : point de repère*, etc.).

Plus généralement, il est permis de penser que les métaphores constitutives de théories (Boyd 1979, Van Besien, Pelsmaekers 1988, Knudsen 2003) peuvent être traduites littéralement, en invoquant une analogie commune, qui est inhérente à l'innovation scientifique en question. Nous l'avons observé dans le cas de la métaphore du virus informatique, innovation des années 1980 exprimée par l'analogie du comportement des fichiers contaminés et de l'action des virus informatiques, qui est rendu directement en français et en allemand (et probablement dans bien d'autres langues) en faisant appel au même ensemble de scénarios métaphoriques (Humbley 2001–3, 2006). Ce n'est que dans certains cas de métaphores de type plutôt catachrésique (Winter Froemel, 2011 308), qui remplit un vide lexical et qui est fondée sur une association linguistique plutôt que conceptuelle, que le transfert se trouve bloqué. C'est le cas de *bootstrap*, pour reprendre un autre exemple d'innovation informatique des années 1980, qui rappelle le dicton anglais *pull yourself up by your own bootstraps*,[4] mais dont l'analogie s'appuie sur la culture populaire et non scientifique, comme dans le cas de *splicing*. Dans le cas des métaphores de type catachrésique, le traducteur a l'option de renoncer à l'image et de traduire en faisant appel à la définition. C'est ce qui s'est produit pour l'équivalent français de *shotgun sequencing* (toujours en génie génétique) : il aurait été possible, du moins en théorie, de conserver la métaphore et de parler de *séquençage à la chevrotine**, mais les scientifiques français ont préféré conserver un vocabulaire scientifique, et emploient plutôt *séquençage aléatoire*,[5] et renoncent donc à une métaphore qui n'a pas de portée générale.

Tout porte de toute façon à croire que ce type de métaphore est avant tout local, tandis que celles qui sous-tendent une théorie se constituent en scénarios qui se prêtent à la transposition et donc à la traduction.

Déballer les métaphores grammaticales pour traduire l'innovation

Après ce tour d'horizon visant à baliser le paysage de la traduction des formes condensées de différentes sortes (sigles, métaphores lexicales de différents ordres ...), nous reprenons le cas précis qui nous préoccupe, celui des métaphores grammaticales, qui passent souvent inaperçues, malgré leur grande fréquence dans des textes scientifiques et techniques.

En réalité, la technique que nous préconisons figure déjà, sous une forme plus large, dans les manuels de traductologie, et est généralement connue sous la forme de transcatégorisation ou de recatégorisation (Delisle et al. 1999).

Prenons un exemple tiré de la traduction à réaliser vers l'anglais d'un texte qui présente la découverte de l'hominoïde *Homo floresienis :* l'auteur expose une théorie concernant l'isolement de cette espèce.

> On peut supposer que c'est une **éruption volcanique**, il y a 12000 ans, qui a éradiqué tous les représentants de cette **espèce insulaire**.[6]

Dans le cas de *éruption volcanique*, le traducteur a deux possibilités en anglais (contrairement au français) : soit de garder la forme emballée de *volcanic eruption*, soit de déballer et de remonter à la construction qui a donné le terme : *a volcano erupted* ... De même pour *espèce insulaire*, sachant que l'anglais dispose de moins d'adjectifs dénominaux que le français, le traducteur peut encore une fois déballer le syntagme pour prendre en considération une construction telle que : *species that lived on the island* ... Celle-ci se prête à une opération de réemballage, par modification du verbe, pour donner *island-dwelling species*. Suivant ces opérations, on aboutit à la proposition suivante:

> A volcano may have erupted 12,000 years ago, wiping out this island-dwelling species.

Bien entendu le déballage à partir des bases nominales nécessite la restitution de nombreux marqueurs, mais les opérations successives de déballage et d'emballage font partie de la pratique constante du traducteur. Elles peuvent donc être appliquées directement aux problèmes posés par les termes qui dénotent l'innovation. C'est fréquemment le cas dans les textes scientifiques où l'anglais sert de langue véhiculaire, mais la situation est la même quelle que soit la langue de la recherche. De même, les langues d'une entreprise sont celles où l'innovation est exprimée sous la forme de termes spécifiques soit à un secteur d'activités, soit à une entreprise, voire à des divisions internes d'une entreprise. Ces terminologies spécifiques font depuis de nombreuses années l'objet d'études sous le nom de *pragmaterminologie*, nouvelle branche de la terminologie développée par Dardo de Vecchi (2005, 2007) et dont le but est de rendre compte des expressions qui désignent la nouveauté au sein des institutions, commerciales ou non.

Examinons à ce titre ce bref extrait d'un bulletin d'information de l'association Artisans du Monde, organisation qui milite pour le commerce équitable, et qui mène des actions dans le monde entier, en particulier dans des pays hispanophones et anglophones. Les étudiants du master ILTS de l'Université Paris Diderot ont réalisé des traductions pour le compte de cet organisme, découvrant au passage les nombreuses innovations inhérentes à ses activités—souvent peu visibles à première vue, mais qui posent des problèmes d'équivalence du fait de leur nouveauté : aucun équivalent satisfaisant ne semble exister dans la langue cible. Prenons par exemple *évaluation mutuelle* dans l'extrait suivant :

> Ce nouveau système a deux piliers : d'un côté, l'***évaluation mutuelle***, menée par les acteurs du système ; de l'autre, la participation d'une instance nationale, pas en tant qu'auditeur, mais en tant qu'expert extérieur pouvant enrichir les discussions8.

Une des difficultés inhérentes du déballage des constructions nominales est de récupérer les informations perdues dans l'opération : les actants, les temps, les aspects, pour n'en nommer que les principaux. Celles-ci sont parfois fournies par le contexte, comme c'est le cas ici : pour déballer *évaluation mutuelle*, le traducteur dispose de l'identité des actants (*les acteurs!*), ce qui lui permet une formulation déballée du type : *the players in the system evaluate one another* ... Si le terme est repris par la suite dans le texte original, le traducteur peut commencer une série de remballages, par exemple en parlant de *eva-*

luation system, sans renoncer à employer ce qui peut être vu comme l'équivalent naturel : *mutual evaluation*. L'important, dans ce cas, est l'ensemble de la démarche : évaluation mutuelle n'est pas présentée tout de suite dans la traduction comme une pratique qui est censée être connue du lecteur, d'où la formulation discursive : s'il s'avère que le terme est indispensable, le traducteur peut commencer à introduire des formes emballées, reproduisant en fait en raccourci le chemin qui a dû être parcouru en anglais.

Le déballage terminologique est donc une méthode qui permet au traducteur de prendre du recul par rapport à l'innovation. Si dans une communauté linguistique donnée, celle-ci est déjà inscrite dans la langue — souvent une langue de spécialité qui n'est connue que des initiés, elle n'a pas encore atteint ce statut dans la langue d'arrivée. Ce recul ouvre la voie à une réappropriation du nouveau concept en suivant en raccourci le chemin discursif parcouru dans la langue où le concept a été élaboré, en reprenant les éléments linguistiques présents dans le terme emballé et en les réhydratant pour ainsi dire. Il est également possible, dans le même ordre d'idées, de prendre les éléments de la définition d'un nouveau concept et de les exploiter pour une reformulation du même type, mais sans pour autant exploiter directement le matériel linguistique. Ce faisant, on reprend en fait la technique du crochet terminologique cher à Robert Dubuc (1992 57–58). On se rappelle que celui-ci consiste à rechercher un équivalent d'un terme inconnu mais existant en prenant comme mot-clés les éléments de la définition. Ici nous suivons le même principe, mais en ayant à l'esprit que l'équivalent recherché n'existe pas encore ou n'est pas disponible.

Un exemple pour illustrer cette démarche, appliquée à l'expression de la nouveauté. Dans le programme de rénovation de la gare d'Annecy, les autorités entendent innover en ouvrant ce qu'ils appellent une *consigne à vélos*. Quel équivalent employer pour la traduction anglaise, sachant que la pratique n'est pas très répandue dans les pays anglophones ? Dans un premier temps, c'est-à-dire dans les présentations du projet avant réalisation, où cette consigne à vélos n'est mentionnée qu'en passant, parmi les autres innovations proposées, une formulation discursive peut suffire. Quelle en est donc la définition ?

somewhere to keep bikes in safety

L'équivalent discursif peut donc être identique :

somewhere to keep bikes in safety

L'emploi de termes qui ressemblent (trop?) à des définitions a déjà fait l'objet de critique de la part de terminologues. C'est un reproche que l'on peut faire à d'autres terminologues, mais pas nécessairement aux traducteurs, pour qui le recours à une expansion qui rappelle les éléments d'une définition peut constituer une stratégie locale de traduction tout à fait acceptable.

Cette technique consistant à partir d'éléments de la définition d'un néologisme pour retrouver un équivalent est exploitée par les organismes de politique linguistique comme l'Office québécois de la langue française, qui analyse la définition des nouveaux termes anglais et, à partir des éléments définitoires, conçoit une dénomination française qui est en réalité la forme remballée de la définition. Pour prendre deux ou trois exemples désormais connus et employés en Europe, on peut citer *drop-out*, défini comme un élève ou un étudiant qui décroche, en abandonnant ses études, qui est rendu en français par *décrocheur*, *commuter*, celui qui fait la navette entre son domicile et son lieu de travail (*navetteur*, plus connu en Belgique qu'en France), et *convenience store*, le magasin qui dépanne lorsque tout est fermé, qui devient *dépanneur*, appellation qui n'a guère traversé l'Atlantique.

Conclusion

Le déballage terminologique n'a donc rien de révolutionnaire : il s'agit tout simplement de l'approfondissement d'une technique bien connue des traducteurs. Il s'agit à nos yeux d'un apport de la linguistique à la traduction qui se révèle particulièrement pertinent lorsqu'il s'agit de traduire l'innovation. Le traducteur est invité à rechercher la stratégie de terminologisation dans la langue source, éventuellement à s'inspirer des tentatives de traduction de ses prédécesseurs (d'autres traducteurs ou très souvent des spécialistes de la discipline innovante qui écrivent dans la langue d'arrivée), et surtout à avoir à sa disposition des possibilités d'équivalents fonctionnels qui ne sont pas encore lexicalisés. C'est en travaillant ainsi qu'il respecte pleinement la déontologie du traducteur, son premier devoir, mais il préserve en même temps la formation terminologique dans sa langue en la laissant se former en douceur dans son discours et dans celui de ceux qui viendront après lui.

Le déballage terminologique illustre la pertinence de l'analyse linguistique dans le processus de la traduction. Au lieu de prétendre que la traduction n'a rien à voir avec la linguistique, il est important d'ouvrir les yeux et de profiter d'une démarche interdisciplinaire qui caractérise la linguistique appliquée. Celle-ci en effet cherche à proposer des solutions à des problèmes de la vie réelle—comme la traduction de l'innovation—en s'appuyant sur les recherches déjà menées en linguistique théorique, c'est en quelque sorte une démarche d'ingénieur appliquée aux sciences humaines.

Références bibliographiques :

Antia, Bassey & Richard Kamal. "African Issues in Terminology: An Educational Perspective." *Modern Approaches to Terminological Theories and Applications*. Ed. Heribert Picht. Bern: Peter Lang, 2006. 133–149.

Boyd, Richard. "Metaphor and theory change: What is "metaphor" a metaphor for?". *Metaphor and Thought*. Ed. A. Ortony. Cambridge: Cambridge UP, 1979. 356–408.

Bully, Philippe. « Zipf, créateur de la linguistique statistique ». *Communication et langage* 2/2 (1969) : 23–28.

Bernardini, Silvia & Adriano Ferraresi. "Practice, Description and Theory Come Together—Normalization or Interference in Italian Technical Translation?". *Meta* 56 (2011). 226–246.

Daille, Béatrice, Benoît Habert, Christian Jacquemin & Jean Royauté. "Empirical Observation of Term Variations and Principles for their Description." *Terminology* 3/2 (1996). 197–257.

Delisle, Jean, Hannelore Lee-Jahnke & Monique C. Cormier, eds. *Terminologie de la traduction / Translation Terminology / Terminología de la traducción / Terminologie der Übersetzung. Amsterdam : Benjamins publishing, coll. FIT Monograph,* 1999.

Dubuc, Robert. *Manuel pratique de terminologie.* Montréal, Linguatech (4° édition), 1992.

Faulstich, Enilde. « Principes formels et fonctionnels de la variation en terminologie ». *Terminology* 5/1 (2000) : 93–106.

Freixa, Judit. "Causes of Denominative Variation in Terminology: A Typology Proposal". *Terminology* 12/1 (2006). 51–77.

Halliday, M.A.K. "Language and the Reshaping of Human Experience". *Webster*, 2004 [1995]. 7–23.

Halliday, M.A.K. "The Grammatical Construction of Scientific Knowledge: the Framing of the English Clause". *Webster*, 2004 [1999]. 102–134.

Hermans, Adrien & Andrée Vansteelandt. "Néologie traductive". *Terminologies nouvelles* 20 (1999) : 37–43.

Humbley, John. "Metaphor and Secondary Term Formation". *Cahiers du CIEL* (2000–2003) : 199–212.

Humbley, John. "La traduction des métaphores dans les langues de spécialité : le cas des *virus informatiques*". *Lynx* 52 (2006) : 49–62.

Mortureux, Marie-Françoise. *La lexicologie entre langue et discours*. Paris : SEDES, 1997.

Pecman, Mojca. "Tentativeness in Term Formation: a Study of Neology as a Rhetorical Device in Scientific Papers". *Neology in Specialized Communication*. Eds. Cabré Castellví, M. Teresa, Rosa Estopá Bagot & Maria C. Vargas Sierra. Special issue of *Terminology* 18/1 (2012). 27–58.

Raad, B. L. "Modern Trends in Scientific Terminology: Morphology and Metaphor". *American Speech* 64/2 (1989). 128–136.

Rey, Alain. *La terminologie : noms et notions*. Collection " Que sais-je ? " N°1780. Paris : PUF. 1979 [1992].

Rondeau, Guy. *Introduction à la terminologie*. Chicoutimi : Gaëtan Morin éd., [1981] 1984.

Sager, Juan Carlos. "Term Formation". *Lebende Sprachen* 34, 1989. 159–61.

Sager, Juan Carlos. *A Practical Course in Terminology Processing*. Amsterdam: Benjamins Publishing, 1990.

Sager, Juan Carlos. « Term Formation ». *Handbook of Terminology Management*. Eds. S.E. Wright & G. Budin. Vol 1 (1997). 25–41.

Temmerman, Rita. *Towards New Ways of Terminology Description. The Sociocognitive Approach*, Amsterdam: Benjamins Publishing, 2000.

Temmerman, Rita. "Why *Special Language Translators Need Insight* into the Mechanisms of Metaphorical Models and Figurative Denominations".

The Meaning of Translation. Eds. Lewandowska-Tomaszczyk & Thelen. Frankfurt: Peter Lang, 2010. 351–369.

Van Besien, Fred & Katja Pelsemaekers. "The translation of metaphor", *Proceedings of XIth World Congress of FIT: Translation, our Future*. Ed. Nekeman). Maastricht: Euroterm, 1988. 140–146.

Vecchi, Dardo de. "La terminologie dans la communication de l'entreprise, approche pragmaterminologique ". *Cahiers du CIEL*, 2005, 71–83.

Vecchi, Dardo de. "La nomination et son suivi: entreprises et pragmaterminologie ». *Neologica* 1 (2007) : 49–63.

Webster, Jonathan. Ed. *The Language of Science*. London: Continuum. The Collected Works of M.A.K. Halliday, 2004.

Winter-Froemel, Esme. *Entlehnung in der Kommunikation und im Sprachwandel : Theorie und Analysen zum Französischen*, Beihefte zur Zeitschrift für romanische Philologie. Berlin: Niemeyer, 2011.

Notes

1 Un relevé aléatoire effectué dans des articles de langue anglaise publiés en ligne dans le domaine de la mécanique de la rupture donne les formes suivantes : *Griffith energy balance model, Griffith energy balance concept, Griffith's energy balance criterion, the Griffith energy balance postulate, the Griffith energy balance fracture criterion, Griffith energy balance model for crack-growth, the Griffith energy-balance concept of crack propagation, Griffith Crack theory, Griffith theory, Griffith cracks* ... et en français *théorie de la rupture fragile de Griffith, le critère de Griffith, théorie de Griffith pour la rupture fragile, calcul de type Griffith de l'équilibre d'énergie* ...

2 Aebi, M.F. (2000), « Les indications de la *criminalité», Revue internationale de Criminologie et de police* technique et scientifique LIII : 131–156.

3 Nous ne disposons pas de données statistiques sur l'évolution de ces métiers, mais les retours du master ILTS laissent penser que c'est la forme d'organisation la plus répandue à l'heure actuelle.

4 Le dictionnaire *Oxford* en ligne donne la definition suivante:"*pull (or drag) oneself up by one's (own) bootstraps* : improve one's position by one's own efforts." http://oxforddictionaries.com / definition / english / bootstrap.

5 [FAO] 2002 *Glossaire de la biotechnologie pour l'alimentation et l'agriculture* http://fr.scribd.com / doc / 32968277/Glossairede-La-Biotechnologie-Ang-Fr

6 http://www.hominides.com / html / ancetres / ancetres-homo-floresiensis.php

Phraseological Variation and Its Implications for Translation: The Role of "Effect" Nouns in Light Verb and Anaphoric Constructions in French and English Scientific Discourse

Christopher Gledhill

Abstract

In this paper, I explore two types of expression in scientific writing: 1) light verb constructions involving "process" nouns such as *effect, impact, influence;* and 2) the anaphoric use of these nouns to express reformulation. The hypothesis defended here is that these structures play a key role in the phraseology of scientific discourse, most notably in the expression of grammatical metaphor and "appraisal" (Halliday 1998). It is important for translators and terminologists to be able to identify patterns such as these, as well as to interpret critically the subtle differences which can be observed between analogous lexico-grammatical patterns in English and French.

Keywords: grammatical metaphor, lexico-grammatical pattern, phraseology, scientific discourse, systemic functional grammar

Résumé

Nous examinons ici deux types d'expression du discours scientifique : 1) des constructions à verbe léger comportant un N prédicatif du type *effet, impact, influence*, 2) les reformulations basées sur les emplois anaphoriques de ces N. Nous estimons que ces structures ont un rôle capital à jouer dans la phraséologie scientifique, notamment dans l'expression de la « métaphore grammaticale » et l'« évaluation » (Halliday 1998). Il est important que les traducteurs et les terminologues puissent non seulement identifier ces constructions mais aussi les examiner de façon critique, car il existe des subtilités entre les schémas équivalents en anglais et en français.

Mots-clés : discours scientifique, grammaire systémique fonctionnelle, métaphore grammaticale, phraséologie, schéma lexico-grammatical

Introduction

In this paper I attempt to demonstrate the relevance of "phraseology" to the study of specialised discourse and to specialised translation in particular. Whereas other members of this panel have emphasised the importance of variation in the process of terminological innovation (Pecman 2005, Humbley this volume), here I examine the role of variation in the creation of novel forms of wording and in the establishment of a "preferred way of saying things" in specialised discourse. I would suggest that translators need to be aware not only of the means by which innovative forms of phraseology are realised in source and target texts, but also the theoretical issues relating to the definition and identification of phraseology as a linguistic phenomenon (as distinct from related notions, such as "style" or "syntax').

A further point I wish to make here is that while the term "phraseology" has often been recognised as a key feature of language by translators and terminologists alike, the phenomenon, in my view, has still not been properly theorised. In the first part of this paper, I therefore provide a summary of the Systemic Functional approach to language proposed by Michael Halliday. I argue here that Halliday's theory, and in particular his notion of "lexicogrammar" allows for a systematic and productive way for terminologists and translators alike to talk about such difficult and sometimes poorly understood notions as "collocation', "style" and "phraseology'. In the second half of this paper, I attempt to demonstrate how this approach can be applied in practice. In particular, I examine two specific lexico-grammatical patterns in English and in French science writing: 1) light verb constructions built around the nouns *effect, impact* and *influence* and 2) the anaphoric use of these nouns in running texts.

The Systemic Functional Approach to Language

Systemic Functional Grammar (SFG) is an approach to language associated with the British linguist Michael Halliday. Broadly speaking, SFG has two interrelated aims: 1) to describe language as a set of lexical and grammatical resources for the creation of meaning, and 2) to explain how lexicogrammatical patterns function in discourse, that is to say in a cultural context and in a particular social situation. Humbley (this volume) has pointed out the relevance of Halliday's notion of "syntax" to our understanding of scientific discourse. However, there is clearly more to SFG than the study of syntax.

Broadly, SFG defines language as a "social semiotic system" and "a resource for making meaning'. Within this system, SFG posits three components of language: "signing" (graphology, phonology, sign-language, etc.), "wording" (also named "lexicogrammar" or "phraseology') and "meaning" (also known as "discourse-semantics'). Following the functionalists Martinet and Hjelmslev, Halliday sees these not as independent modules, but rather as increasingly higher-order semiotic systems which relate to each other in a process of "realisation": signing realises wording, wording realises meaning, (textual) meaning realises (social) value, and so on. It is important to note that the relationship of realisation always takes place in a particular context: in other words there is always a "text" without which meaning cannot be created, and in turn texts (whether visual or oral in form) are always engendered within a particular social context.

Clearly, the SFG approach has more in common with discourse analysis or anthropological linguistics than traditional accounts of syntax. Nevertheless, the observer might wonder what place notions such as syntax, morphology, lexis or terminology have in SFG. Rather than seeing these as independent phenomena, Halliday posits that grammar and lexis have essentially the same nature. Thus lexis is seen as "the most delicate zone within the lexicogrammar" where "terms [of meaning, of the system] are realized by lexical items rather than by grammatical items or grammatical structure" (Matthiessen, Teruya & Lam 2010: 131). It follows from this that each sign is seen as a particular instance or "lexicalisation" of a particular meaning, where the language user has a choice as to whether to express this meaning lexically or as a more complex grammatical structure. For example, POLARITY can be realised grammatically (*the glass didn't fracture*), semi-lexically (*the glass failed to fracture*) or lexically (*the glass resisted fracture, the glass showed resistance to fracture*). For Halliday, the latter example *(resisted vs. showed resistance)* involves a crucial feature of technocratic and scientific discourse: "grammatical metaphor", a structure in which a verbal process is reformulated as a nominal participant, and is thus made available as a potential discourse referent. For Halliday, grammatical metaphor is not a purely syntactic transformation or a handy piece of stylistic variation; it is a key resource for the creation of new meaning:

> Language—every human language—is a stratified system in which the content plane is split into a semantics, interfacing with the world of human experience (and of human social relationships), and a grammar, which is purely an abstract level of organisation; the two are coupled through a relation of congruence, but they can be decoupled and recoupled in other ways (which I am calling "grammatical metaphor'). This gives the system indefinitely large semogenic power, because new meaning is created at the intersection of the congruent and the metaphoric categories ('semantic junction'). (Halliday 1988: 222)

The "semogenic" analysis of grammatical metaphor leads Halliday to consider the different meanings (or more specifically, discourse functions) that are realised by structures such as pre- and post-modification within the noun group, structures which in scientific discourse lead to the gradual building up of multi-layered grammatical metaphors (compare: *the glass resisted fracture vs. the resistance of glass to fracture vs. glass fracture resistance vs. the limit of glass fracture resistance vs. the glass fracture resistance limit,* etc.) (for further discussion, see Simon-Vandenbergen et al. 2003, Halliday & Matthiessen 2004: 592–593, Schleppegrell 2004.)

I now turn to a second point raised by Humbley. Although Halliday and other proponents of SFG have made contributions to the study of lexis (Halliday 1966, Halliday, Teubert, Yallop & Čermáková 2004), it is true that lexis, and in particular the issue of terminology, is not central in SFG. I would suggest however that there are some justifiable theoretical reasons for this. As is well-known, Halliday's theory of language was heavily influenced by his mentor J. R. Firth (1957). Whereas Halliday developed an empirical, discourse-oriented theory of grammar, other followers of Firth (notably Sinclair 1991) developed a similar approach to the analysis of lexis, a perspective which ultimately led to the development of corpus linguistics (especially in English-speaking countries). This empirical approach to language (sometimes called "contextualism') holds that the meaning of a sign depends entirely on its habitual contexts of use or "collocations". This perspective directly contradicts structuralism, which defines the meaning of a sign in terms of its relative position within an abstract system "outside discourse". The contextualist approach also rejects realism, which posits that new referents (concepts or techniques) may exist without necessarily being associated with particular signs or a stable terminology. Rather, the contextualist approach holds that a new concept or technique has no stable social value unless it has a name (a "denomination"), and a denomination has no real meaning unless it is couched as a stretch of language in a particular situation (a "discourse")[2]. Here is how the semiotician Pierre Frath (2007) describes the process, using the terminology of C.S. Peirce:

> Lorsque l'enfant demande à son père ce que sont ces points qui brillent dans le ciel la nuit (une *désignation*, éphémère, construite, transparente), il apprend qu'il s'agit d'étoiles (une *dénomination* publique, stable, préconstruite, opaque). Désormais, il est prêt à recevoir d'autres signes développant tel ou tel aspect des étoiles : qu'elles sont très lointaines, qu'il y en a dans d'autres galaxies, que le soleil est une étoile, qu'il arrive qu'elles explosent, etc. Sans la dénomination, les signes interprétants ne seraient pas reliés entre eux par un lien stable et ne pourraient donc permettre l'accumulation du savoir. (Frath 2007: 88).[3]

Frath's notions of pre-construction and productivity are crucial to our understanding of phraseology. However, before returning to this idea, I would like to make a final point regarding terminology. It is notable that the field of terminology has itself become an increasingly central topic in the SFG approach. Matthiessen et al. (2010), for example, claim that terminology is a crucial resource in the process of theory-building, especially in areas which rely principally on a linguistic system of representation (as opposed to fields which exploit more varied semiotic resources, such as mathematics and chemistry). Matthiessen et al. (2010) also make the typically Hallidayan point that context, and in particular the notion of text-type (in their terms "register') is all-important in determining the different forms that terminology can take:

> [...] registers differ with respect to what meanings within the overall scientific model of a discipline are at risk—so they also differ with respect to how they deploy the resources of technical terminology. For example, procedures tend towards concrete and congruent terms because they are concerned with enabling people to manipulate real (as opposed to virtual) entities; but explanations are often abstract and incongruent because they are concerned with the construction of a theory [...]. (Matthiessen, Teruya & Lam 2010: 14).

Thus Matthiessen et al.'s point is that each register or text-type has evolved a particular configuration of lexicogrammatical forms in order to construe particular meanings. It is this emphasis on the particular functions of specialised discourse that leads me below to examine the phraseological patterns of scientific discourse in relation to those of other discourse types.

The Systemic Functional Approach to Phraseology

The systemic functional (or contextualist) approach to phraseology is rather different from the traditional definition given by lexicologists. In this paper I use the term "phraseology" to refer to "the preferred way of saying things in a particular discourse" and when I refer to the phraseology of a word, I am referring to "the lexicogrammatical patterns which make up a sign's typical contexts of use". Halliday himself does not develop the notion of phraseology in SFG and, as Humbley (this volume) has suggested, lexical items are not central considerations in his model. However, I would argue that there is a good theoretical justification for this difference in emphasis.

I mentioned above that an important principle of the contextualist approach is that the meaning of a word or sign can only be properly considered by observing its habitual contexts of use (its collocations).

A related principle is that each word has its own particular, even unique collocational environment, and such regularities of usage can be most efficiently observed within authentic, naturally-occurring discourse. Within the SFG framework, I and other corpus analysts (notably Hunston & Francis 2000, Tucker 2007) refer to these regular patterns of use as "phraseology'. This approach is however not compatible that of many other linguists. When lexicologists refer to phraseology, they are usually referring to something like "the study of idiomatic phrases, clichés and other idiosyncratic expressions'. The contextualist approach to phraseology is clearly much more inclusive than than this, and the definition I have given above is intentionally closer to that of the general language. I would claim that the general language use of the word may be more useful to linguistic analysis than competing terms such as "style'. This is because phraseology tends to refer to a type of language, whereas style has a much broader set of meanings (relating to non-linguistic semiotic systems). It is possible to show this by looking at the typical contexts of *phraseology* in English (these examples are from the British National Corpus: 100,000,000 words):

1a. In the time-honoured **phraseology** of football managers, there are no easy matches against the Scots any more.
1b. we must ask how far and in what circumstances he [Anselm] adopted the **phraseology** of the Gregorian reformers;...
1c. Porter's translation uses the well-known **phraseology** and verbosity of official pronouncements.
1d. an ignorant servant could not possibly be the writer of the elaborate legal **phraseology** of the threatening notes,

The equivalent word *phraséologie* is used in similar contexts in French (these examples are from a reference corpus of French administrative, journalistic and literary texts: 20,000,000 words):

1e. L'auteur démonte avec brio les rouages de la **phraséologie** d'entreprise, montrant sa froideur rationnelle et sa logique implacable aussi bien que ses formules ...
1f. Le jeu de mots sordide sur la "raie-publique" est typique de la **phra-**

séologie d'extrême droite et se place dans toute la tradition …

1g. Un débat largement influencé par les terminologies rabâchées par les journalistes. Eux-mêmes aiguillonnés par la **phraséologie** d'experts et de politiques.

1h. Ce qui est inacceptable c'est de voire *[sic]* un Conseil de Paris, institution démocratique, reprendre la **phraséologie** d'un tribunal militaire national.

Many speakers refer to *phraseology / phraséologie* ironically or ambiguously (as in 1g, for example, where it is used in the same context as "terminology'). Looking at general patterns of use, however, the corpus evidence shows fairly clearly that the word *phraseology* in English is typically pre-modified by epithets relating to typicality or appropriateness (*flamboyant, ingenious, right, time-honoured, well-known*) or by classifiers relating to specific types of text or languages (*German, legal, official, Norman, school-report,* etc.). In addition, in English and in French, the word is typically post-modified by *de / of* + the name of a person, a social group or a type of text or discourse (as in the French examples cited above: *entreprise, experts, extrême droite, tribunal miliaire*). The words *phraseology / phraséologie* thus have a very regular set of lexicogrammatical patterns in both English and French. It is notable that the core pattern is entirely predictable (epithet / classifier + *phraséologie / phraseology* + *de / of* + noun group), but there is of course a considerable amount of variation in the kinds of items that stand in pre- or post-modifier position. The fact that these modifiers have a relatively predictable set of meanings suggests that the words *phraseology* and *phraséologie* are both used in a very consistent lexicogrammatical pattern. This does not mean however that new items cannot be used in these positions; on the contrary, any novel lexical item can be used in this pattern, but it is likely that it will be interpreted in the light of the existing lexicogrammatical pattern (this is the principle of "semantic preference" and "semantic prosody" discussed by Kübler & Volanschi 2012 and Kübler, this volume.)

In this section, I have set out a brief analysis of *phraseology* and *phraséologie* in order to demonstrate some the basic principles of corpus linguistics and the contextualist approach. These can be summarised as follows:

- the meaning of a word depends on its typical context of use in discourse (its "phraseology"),
- the phraseology of a word is made up of the main lexical items with which the word is typically used (its "collocations"), as well as the main grammatical structures in which the word and its collocations typically occur (its "colligations"),
- the lexicogrammatical patterns of a word are highly predictable but also productive: any variation of form or function within the phraseological pattern can be interpreted in the light of its typical phraseology (or in other words, each pattern has "semantic preferences" and exerts a "semantic prosody").

In the following sections, I examine these principles in relation to specialised discourse. In particular, I suggest that the lexicogrammatical patterns of a specialised discourse are very highly consistent, but certainly not fixed in form: the key to understanding this balance between predictability and variability is to posit the notion of the "lexicogrammatical pattern'.

The Phraseology of Specialised Discourse

In the previous section, I examined the typical lexicogrammatical pattern of a noun in order to demonstrate that each lexical item in the general language has a predictable but also productive phraseology. In the second half of this paper I apply this principle to two related classes of expression which I believe to have an important role to play in technocratic, scientific and other specialised discourses: 1) light verb constructions (LVC) involving *effect, impact, incidence, influence,* and 2) the use of *effect, impact, incidence* and *influence* as "anaphoric nouns'.

The Role of Light Verb Constructions in Technical Language

A light verb construction is a compound verb which is made up of a semantically "light" verb (such as *have, make, take/avoir, faire, prendre,* etc.) and a "process" noun which specifies the semantic process of the entire predicate (e.g., *make a remark, take a decision / faire une remarque, prendre une décision,* etc). In some cases, LVCs involve a noun which is not related to an analogous verb (*make fun, take stock / faire le point, prendre conscience*) or other elements such as prepositional phrases and adverbials (*bear in mind, take seriously / mettre en cause, prendre en compte,* etc.). Generally speaking, French uses LVCs more productively than English, regularly deriving compound nouns from LVCs (*mettre en scène > mise en scène, prendre position > prise de position*) and compound verbs from bare nouns (*faire face, faire peur, prendre fin, prendre naissance,* etc.). I have suggested elsewhere (Gledhill 2008, Todiraşcu & Gledhill 2008) that LVCs play an important role in French and English administrative and legal discourse. This can be seen for example in the following extract from the multilingual parallel *Acquis Communautaire Corpus* (ACC, Steinberger et al. 2006: 20,000,000 words). In this translated extract the light verbs have been placed in bold, and the nouns which specify the semantic process for each of these verbs are underlined and in bold:

Example 2a)

Regulation (EC) No 138/2004 of the European Parliament and of the Council of 5 December 2003 on the economic accounts for agriculture in the Community

FOREWORD The revision of the European system of accounts (ESA 1995) in 1995(1) and the need to adapt to economic and structural developments in agriculture have led to a new basic methodology used for the EAA. The **<u>amendments</u>** **made** to the basic EAA methodology had to satisfy two, often conflicting, demands: on the one hand, methodological consistency was needed with the ESA to **allow** **<u>harmonisation</u>** of the EAA both between Member States and with the central framework of the national accounts; and on the other hand, the legislator had to ensure that the **<u>changes</u>** to be **made** were feasible. This manual has been drawn up with these considerations in mind as, in addition to the concepts, principles and basic rules for compiling the EAA, it also refers to any adaptations to specific characteristics in the field of agriculture.

Example 2b)

Règlement (CE) n° 138/2004 du Parlement européen et du Conseil du 5 décembre 2003 relatif aux comptes économiques de l'agriculture dans la Communauté

REMARQUES PRÉLIMINAIRES La révision du système européen des comptes (SEC 1995) en 1995(1) et la nécessité d'adapter les évolutions économiques et structurelles dans l'agriculture ont **donné lieu** à l'élaboration d'une nouvelle méthodologie de base utilisée pour les CEA. Les **modifications apportées** à la méthodologie de base des CEA ont dû satisfaire à deux exigences souvent contradictoires: d'une part, il fallait assurer une cohérence méthodologique avec le SEC pour **permettre l'harmonisation** des CEA entre États membres et avec le cadre central des comptes nationaux et, d'autre part, le législateur devait veiller à la nécessaire faisabilité des **changements** à **opérer**. La rédaction du présent manuel s'inscrit dans cette perspective puisqu'il est **fait mention**, au-delà des concepts, des principes et des règles de base de l'élaboration des CEA, des adaptations éventuelles aux spécificités dans le domaine de l'agriculture.

As can be seen in these extracts, the ACC contains a relatively a very high density of light verb constructions. Looking at the French text (2b), there is virtually one LVC per main clause. Four of the five LVCs in French have potential simple verb equivalents (*apporter des modifications > modifier, permettre l'harmonisation > harmoniser, opérer des changements > changer, faire mention > mentionner*). The English version (2a) uses three equivalent LVC expressions (*apporter des modifications / make amendments, permettre l'harmonisation / allow harmonisation, opérer des changements / make changes*). However, in two cases the French version uses a bare noun LVC (with no article) which is rendered by a full verb in English (*donner lieu / lead to, faire mention / refer to*).[4] This appears to be a general tendency in the ACC (for example elsewhere in the ACC *faire état* is regularly rendered by *to allege,* etc.).

Notwithstanding differences in the types and distribution of these constructions in English and French, LVCs appear to be an important feature of administrative discourse in both languages. The reason for this, I would claim, is that LVCs constitute a particularly productive form of grammatical metaphor. As mentioned above, the main function of grammatical metaphor is to reformulate a process as a noun in order to express a potential discourse referent. The purpose of this reformulation is to allow the process expressed as a noun to be specified or evaluated. This can be seen in the extracts above (2a-b): the process nouns in these LVCs are either heavily post-modified (this is the case of *modifications / amendments* and *harmonisation*) or explicitly evaluated (*la nécessaire faisabilité des changements / the changes . . . were feasible*). We shall see further evidence of this in the corpus analysis below.

Light Verb Constructions in Scientific Discourse

Generally speaking, it has been claimed (for example, in Banks 1994) that administrative and scientific discourse share a number of linguistic features:

- passive clauses (including thematicisation of inanimate nouns),
- complex pre-and post-modification of nouns,
- extraposed clauses (including indirect expression of evaluation),
- modal evaluation of verbs (including "hedging'),
- multiple subordination (including apposition and other types of post-modification).

These structures are associated with elaborate, impersonal, indirect forms of speech. In the remaining parts of this section, I set out some corpus evidence to suggest that LVCs also share these discourse functions and are perhaps just as prevalent in formal text types as these linguistic structures.

Corpus linguists use a standardised methodology for the analysis of specialised texts. In this type of analysis, it is necessary to a conduct a word-frequency count of the corpus under study and to compare these results with a reference corpus using statistical tools which calculate the statistical significance for each lexical item and thus provide a list of "keywords" (items which are statistically most likely to occur in the study corpus). In previous studies (Gledhill 2000a, b), I used this methodology to compare a corpus of scientific research articles ("Pharmaceutical Sciences Corpus" PSC, 150 research articles in cancer research and pharmaceutical sciences: 500,000 words) with general English (the Cobuild corpus: 20,000,000 words). Space precludes me from setting out the main results of that study here, but overall, I found it useful to divide the non-technical vocabulary of the PSC into three subtypes (the examples given here are the ten most statistically significant keywords of each category):

- grammatical items which occur more densely in this type of scientific discourse (*were, of, with, in, and, during, between, versus, these, due (to)*),
- generic lexical items which occur as keywords in this type of scientific reporting (*study, results, table, studies, significant, performed, significantly, using, data, age*),
- general terms which occur as keywords in this particular domain (*patients, cells, treatment, clinical, cases, tissue, disease, tumour, pregnancy, blood*).

For the purposes of this study, it is sufficient to point out that only a small fraction of the items in these lists are predicative nouns (de-verbal nouns such as *change*, *decision, harmonisation*) or process nouns (abstract nouns which can be used in light verb constructions, such as *effect, place, role* etc.). In addition, in the first 1000 keywords of the pharmaceutical sciences corpus, I find that only 12 nouns can be used in LVCs (involving the verb *have* as a light verb),[5] namely *(a/n) bearing, chance, effect, explanation, impact, incidence, influence, occurrence,*

Relational processes	X **has / have** a + greater / higher / high / low / lower / significant ... + **chance / occurrence / risk / tendency / role** ... + to (+ event) / + in (+ event / entity)

Mental processes	X **has / have** a + better / more sophisticated ... + **explanation, understanding** + of (+ phenomenon)
Material processes	X **has / have** a + beneficial / direct / key / important / negative / positive / preventative / protective / significant / substantial + **bearing / effect / impact / incidence / influence** + on (+ entity)

risk, role, tendency, understanding. These LVCs can be divided into three lexicogrammatical patterns, each expressing a different type of semantic process:

These examples suggest that LVCs have a more restricted range in scientific discourse than in other discourse types. Nevertheless, it can be seen that of the few LVCs which are used, they are exploited extensively in these types of texts, and that each of the major process types in English (relational, mental and material) are expressed by corresponding LVCs using the verb *to have*. It is also notable that each of these lexicogrammatical patterns involves a considerable degree of variation, not least in the key lexical items which make up the core of the expression, although the process nouns in each construction have roughly equivalent meanings (as mentioned above, this degree of lexical preference is a defining feature of phraseological patterns).

To what extent do these patterns have regular lexicogrammatical patterns or consistent functions in this particular text type? In order to answer this question, it is necessary to examine the typical contexts of these constructions in the form of concordances.

Light Verb Constructions Involving *Effect, Influence* and *Impact*

If we take the pattern *have a/n + effect, impact, incidence, influence (on),* we can see that this construction is regularly used in contexts in which the author summarises the results of previous studies in terms of the *effect, influence* etc. of a particular biochemical process (these examples are taken from the PSC):

3a. Previous studies have suggested that LPS-induced increase in prostaglandin synthesis **has** a negative **effect** on birth weight [20].
3b. Recent studies have demonstrated that SLS has a detrimental effect on epidermal lipid processing and, consequently, the formation of the lipid barrier domain [48]
3c. According to this publication, aloe vera extract **has** a significant **influence** on both erythema, infiltration and desquamation.

The same phraseology is at work in French. It is particularly interesting to compare these examples with a PhD thesis on cancer research published by Gyasi Johnson at the Université d'Angers (Johnson 2007). In each case, the author uses LVCs to summarise the conclusions of previous research:

3d. Il est communément observé une augmentation de la DER chez des patients cachectiques atteints de cancer du poumon (Staal-van den Brekel et al., 1997 ; Fredrix et al., 1991). En revanche, les cancers gastriques et colorectaux **auraient** moins d'**effet** sur la DER (Fredrix et al., 1991-b ; Dempsey et al., 1984).
3e. Au cours de ces travaux de thèse, nous nous sommes assurés que l'impact d'une restriction alimentaire sur le métabolisme énergétique mitochondrial (Article 1) ne serait pas un biais dans notre analyse chez l'homme. Nous avons observé que la restriction calorique **a** une **influence** sur la mitochondrie à court terme en fonction du degré de cette restriction.
3f. Ces résultats ont permis d'affirmer que la prise alimentaire **avait** peu ou pas d'**incidence** sur la perte de poids chez le patient cachectique, d'autant plus que certains présentent une perte de poids malgré des apports alimentaires inchangés (Bosaeus et al., 2001).

As we shall see in the following data analysis, there is a strong resemblance between the phraseology of Gyasi Johnson's thesis in French and the Pharmaceutical Sciences Corpus. It may be that these patterns have been in use for some time in both languages. But it may also be that there has been some accommodation between the phraseological patterns of Johnson and the PSC, especially since the subject domains are so close. In fact, Johnson (2007) cites many of the articles represented in the PSC (largely in relation to cancer cachexia, the subject of a breakthrough in the early 1990s and represented in the PSC in articles by Michael Tisdale and his research team).[6]

In this section, we have seen that the nouns *effect, impact, incidence, influence* are central lexical elements in one of the most productive LVCs in scientific research articles. In such texts, the particular function of these LVCs is to simultaneously express a particular process and to evaluate the extent of the process's effects (a biochemical entity or process *has + some / no / more* or *less + effect / impact / influence + on* a biochemical entity or process). I would suggest that these constructions have evolved within the particular context of scientific discourse, just as a range of different, but analogous, expressions have been developed in administrative discourse.

Anaphoric Constructions Involving *Effect, Influence* and *Impact*

Anaphoric nouns (Francis 1993, Hoey 2007) are non-technical words which are useful in expository discourse because they reformulate a preceding statement either in terms of a hyperonym (*this article, this mechanism, this study*) or an item which evaluates or implicitly changes the status of the referent (*this anomaly, this claim, this problem*). Anaphoric nouns are often (but not obligatorily) introduced by deictics such as *this, those, such, other,* etc., and despite their name they are not always anaphoric (they may also refer prospectively or forwards in the text, in which case they are "cataphoric"). In the previous section, the nouns *effect, impact, incidence, influence* were seen to have an important role in light verb constructions. In this section, we see that these items also have a key function as a specific form of anaphoric reference.

One of the reasons for the prevalence of *effect, impact, incidence, influence* and similar nouns in administrative, scientific and many other formal discourse types is their versatility: as we see in the following data, these items have variety of common semantic and structural properties. In particular, when one of these nouns is the head of a noun group, it can be (optionally) pre-modified by epithets and classifiers (expressing an evaluation or a particular type of metabolic process) and (optionally) post-modified by prepositional phrases such as *of* (expressing the "agent" or source of the process), prepositional phrases such as *on* (expressing the "medium" or participant affected by the process) as well as various other types of post-modifier (expressing various circumstantials). The following extracts (in English 4a-e and French 4f-k) give an idea of the different configurations of this pattern, as well as the ways in which the nouns *effect* / *effet* and *influence* are used as anaphoric nouns within the same running text:

4a. Fish Oil and Fighting Cancer[7]

4b. Researchers found that fish oil can significantly inhibit cholesterol production. The beneficial **effects** of fish oils come from their unique composition of high levels of the omega-3 polyunsaturated fatty acids eicosapentaenoic acid (EPA) and docosahexaenoic acid (DHA). Additionally, these omega-3 polyunsaturated fatty acids can increase the HDL (so-called good cholesterol) levels. Fish oil also provides anti-inflammatory and anti-aggregatory **effects** which play a crucial role in the formation of atherosclerosis and thrombosis. Due to these findings, it is believed that both healthy people and heart disease patients can benefit from fish oil supplementation.

4c. One exciting aspect of fish oil is its significant inhibitory **effects** against various human cancers in animal models, including breast cancer, colon cancer, skin cancer, pancreatic cancer, prostatic cancer, lung cancer, larynx cancer, etc. (3-8) Unlike fish oil which is high in omega-3 polyunsaturated fatty acids, fats that are high in omega-6 polyunsaturated fatty acids (like corn oil) can increase tumor growth. Using a chemical carcinogen-induced cancer model, researchers found that a high intake of fish oil significantly lowered the cancer incidence in animal studies as compared to animals fed either low fat diets or high corn oil diets. . . .

4d. Proposed Mechanisms For Fish Oil's Tumor Growth-Slowing **effects**

4e. Although there is no clear mechanism to explain fish oil's significant anti-cancer **effects**, researchers have uncovered several potential models of action. This indicates the significant beneficial **effects** of fish oil supplementation in cancer treatment. Additionally, fish oil showed a dramatic anti-cancer **effect** which was as effective as some chemotherapy drugs.

4f. Des acides gras oméga 3 contre la cachexie ?[1]

4g. Une étude néerlandaise attire de nouveau l'attention sur le **rôle** potentiel des acides gras oméga 3 en cas de cancer, en avançant que la prise de suppléments d'huile de poisson permettrait d'éviter la perte de poids.

4h. Cette étude de petite envergure impliquait 40 personnes atteintes d'un cancer du poumon « non à petites cellules », diagnostiqué peu de temps auparavant et soignées par chimiothérapie. Chez 69 % de ces personnes, la prise du supplément a eu un **effet** positif, avec une stabilisation du poids, mais aussi du volume et de la qualité de la masse musculaire. Dans le groupe qui ne prenait pas ce supplément, la stabilisation n'a été observée que chez 29 % des patients.

4i. Par ailleurs, l'huile de poisson exerce une **influence** positive dans le cadre de la prévention et du traitement des maladies cardiovasculaires, ainsi que sur la réduction du risque de cancer du sein chez la femme ménopausée. Ces suppléments pourraient être administrés à des patients atteints d'autres types de cancer et de diverses maladies chroniques s'accompagnant fréquemment d'une malnutrition et, par conséquent, d'une perte de poids et de masse musculaire.

4j. Ces dernières années, diverses études se sont focalisées sur l'**effet** des suppléments d'huile de poisson au cours d'un traitement anticancéreux. Il s'agit le plus souvent de suppléments d'EPA (un acide gras de poisson), administrés à raison de 2 g/jour et proposés sous forme de gélules ou de boisson lactée ...

4k. Mais les résultats d'études précédentes ne sont pas toujours concordants : certaines n'ont montré aucun **effet**, d'autres oui — y compris une survie plus longue. La seule **influence** positive manifeste des suppléments d'huile de poisson a été observée pour le cancer du pancréas. Par ailleurs, il semble que ces suppléments soient également intéressants dans le cadre d'un cancer du poumon « non à petites cellules ».

4l. Les travaux de recherche ont également permis de découvrir que l'EPA et le DHA (un autre acide gras de poisson)—qui constituent conjointement les « acides gras oméga 3 »—présentent d'autres **effets** : ils ralentissent la croissance de différents types de tumeurs et renforcent l'efficacité de la chimiothérapie. Toutefois, le nombre de ces études, réalisées encore seulement sur des animaux de laboratoires, est encore relativement restreint et il n'est pas encore possible de formuler des recommandations.

These extracts are not translation equivalents and they do not represent the same genres, but both deal with the same topic (cancer cachexia) and both are examples of "mediated" discourse, that is to say a reformulation of scientific research produced for a wider audience. There are many parallels in their wording, but here it is sufficient to point to ways in which the nouns *effect / effet* or *influence* play a role in the reformulation of the same basic referent. Thus, the first mention of *beneficial effects* in the English text (4a-e) is an evaluative reformulation of the preceding process: *fish oil can significantly inhibit* . . . Similarly, the compound noun *fish oil* is first used as a simple referent and then progressively integrated into a more complex noun group headed by *effects*: *fish oil* > *fish oil diet* > *fish oil's tumour growth-slowing effects* > *fish oil's significant anticancer effects* > *the significant beneficial effects of fish oil supplementation*. Another example of this can be found in the reformulation of the clause *high fish oil diet can slow tumor growth* as a noun group: *Fish Oil's Tumor Growth-Slowing effects*. As mentioned in the previous section, the function of *effect* in all of these examples is to express a biochemical process in the form of a noun which can be modified by evaluative epithets. This process forms a chain which runs throughout the text. A similar chain of reference can be seen in the French text (4f-l): *l'huile de poisson* > *l'effet des suppléments d'huile de poisson* > *La seule influence positive manifeste des suppléments d'huile de poisson* . . . The French text also involves an example of de-metaphorisation, in other words a move from a nominal to a verbal expression: *la prise de suppléments d'huile de poisson > Ces suppléments pourraient être administrés.* This process (*prise / administration de suppléments*) is then re-nominalised in a light verb construction, again expressing an explicit evaluation of the process: > *la prise du supplément a eu un effet positif > une influence positive.*

In all of these examples, it is notable that although the noun *effect / effet* is not involved in each phrase, the chain of reference eventually makes a link with a noun group headed by *effect / effet.* The net result of this is that in both the English and French texts, variations of the same complex noun group have been built up around the pivotal

determiner	**epithet**	**classifier**	**head**	**classifier**	**qualifier**
	beneficial		effects	of fish oils	
		anti-inflammatory and anti-aggregatory	effects		
	significant	inhibitory	effects		against various human cancers in animal models,
Fish Oil's		Tumor Growth-Slowing	effects		
fish oil's	significant	anticancer			
	Significant beneficial		effects	of fish oil supplementation	
	dramatic		effects		

items *effect / effet* or *influence.* This noun group essentially has the same structure and the same discourse referent, as can be seen in the following summary:
In French, a similar noun group is built up throughout the text (I have added *rôle* to the list: this phrase occurs under the title of the text; it

determiner	**head**	**epithet**	**classifier**	**qualifier**
Le	rôle	potentiel	des acides gras oméga 3	en cas de cancer
Un	effet	positif		avec une stabilisation du poids
Une	influence	positive		dans le cadre de la prévention et du traitement des maladies cardiovasculaires
l'	effet		des suppléments d'huile de poisson	au cours d'un traitement anticancéreux
La seule	influence	positive manifeste	des suppléments d'huile de poisson	

has a similar structure and expresses the same "macrotheme" as the other examples of *effet / influence*):

Although they are essentially similar, there are some minor but telling structural differences between the French and English noun groups: the determiners in English (the possessive *fish oil's*) are expressed by post-modifying classifiers in French (the first items introduced by *de* after the head), while the pre-modifying classifiers in English (treatment-related items) become post-modifying qualifiers (the second item introduced by *de* after the head).

I chose extracts (4a-l) because they contained a high density of the words *effect / effet* in close proximity. But these texts are also important because they involve most of the core phraseological patterns of *effect / effet* and their quasi-synonyms. In the final section of this paper, I sum up these patterns, using examples taken from the Pharmaceutical Sciences Corpus (PSC) and the French PhD thesis (Johnson 2007).

Phraseological Patterns Involving *Effect, Influence* and *Impact*

The nouns *effect, influence* and *impact* are used in three distinct lexicogrammatical patterns. It is perhaps no accident that these patterns correspond to the three major semantic categories of process in the SFG model: 1) mental, 2) relational and 3) material. In the first pattern, *effect* is the complement of a mental process verb (i.e., a verb expressing cognition, communication, perception, as seen in the previous section 4a-e: *explain, indicate, show* and in 4f-l: *montrer, observer, se sont focalisées sur*). In these contexts, *effect* is usually pre-modified (by a subjective epithet) and post-modified by an agent (*of* + formulations relating to "food restriction') or by the medium (*on* + formulations relating to body functions):

5a. Hypotheses proposed to **account for** the life-prolonging **effect** of CR include a decrease in ROS production and limited oxidative stress in macromolecules

5b. The aim of the present study is to **investigate** the early **effect** of FR on skeletal muscle mitochondrial proton leak kinetics and mitochondrial functions.

5c. Summary of studies **showing** the **effect** of calorie or food restriction on skeletal muscle mitochondrial respiration

The French corpus (Gyasi Johnson's thesis) also includes many examples of this type:

5d. l'objectif de cet article est de **déterminer** l'**effet** d'une restriction calorique à très court terme sur la fonction mitochondriale dans le muscle.

5e. Dejong et al. n'**observent** aucun **effet** de l'état inflammatoire sur l'expression d'UCP2 …

5f. Cette étude permet d'**observer** l'**effet** de la tumeur sur la DER indépendamment de la prise alimentaire tout en soulevant la question du choix des groupes contrôles

The discourse function of this pattern (5a-f) is to state the research goals or the essential findings of a study which is named in the neighbouring context. This function is different to the pattern *X has an effect on Y,* which expresses a material process in which the agent is thematicised as the grammatical subject, and the role of the researchers is not mentioned.

A second significant pattern (examples 6a-f) involves the attribution or description of *effect* using a relational process (*is* / *was*) or a circumstantial / existential process (*exist, exceed, come from* etc.). Both types are present in the English extract (4a-e): *One exciting aspect of fish oil is its significant inhibitory effects* and *The beneficial effects of fish oils come from their unique composition.* In the PSC, this pattern generally involves the expression of statistical findings, with some evaluation or hedging in the co-text (*no significant, should also be high*):

6a. Furthermore, there **was** no significant **effect** of FR on the oxygen consumed to drive ATP synthesis

6b. In addition to reducing the cachexia, both 3-hydroxybutyrate20 and EPA also inhibited tumour growth, although the **effect** on host body weight **exceeded** that of on tumour growth

6c. The high tumour-cell concentration of PIMO that can be obtained suggests that the radiosensitising **effect** of PIMO should also **be** high

This pattern is absent in the French text (4f-l) and does not quite have the same discourse function in Gyasi Johnson's thesis. In this text, relational processes are more likely to provide detailed biochemical explanations:

6d. Il s'agit d'une réduction de la consommation en oxygène en condition phosphorylante et découplée. Cet **effet** ne **concerne** que les mitochondries subsarcolemmales respirant avec du pyruvate comme substrat.
6e. l'**effet** de la restriction alimentaire sur l'adaptation énergétique musculaire **est fonction** aussi bien de la durée que de l'intensité de cette restriction et les mécanismes mis en œuvre semblent différents selon ces conditions.
6f. l'inflammation est une conséquence fréquente du cancer mais l'**effet** de cette inflammation sur l'hôte **est** probablement **lié** à la capacité de l'hôte à gérer cette inflammation.

The third and final pattern has a very similar form and function to light verb constructions, although here the verb is a lexical verb of causality rather than a light verb such as *have* (most usually *produce*, but also *cause, exercise, provide* … or in French: *exercer, induire, produire, provoquer*). One example can be found in the English example text (4a-e) *provide effects* and two in the French text (4f-l) *exerce une influence, présentent d'autres effets.* As mentioned above, these constructions express a material process in the form of a grammatical metaphor, a function which is similar to *have an effect on.* However, whereas the pattern *have an effect on* tends to express evaluation, these constructions express more specific biochemical explanations, with little explicit evaluation. The most frequent verbs used in this pattern in English are *exert* and *produce:*

7a. An association between PIMO and melanin could explain these results, especially if thenmelanin is remote from the DNA [34], thus spatially preventing PIMO from **exerting** its radiosensitising **effect**.

7b. This tumour is useful for the study of the mechanisms of cachexia, since in some cases growth of the tumour is not accompanied by weight loss [13], suggesting that the presence of the tumour alone is insufficient to **produce** the **effects** on host body tissues.

7c. The precise regulation **producing** such **effects** remains largely unknown, but it does imply a role of insulin …

It is notable that *have* cannot be used in place of *exert* and *produce* here: this suggests that these verbs are "full" lexical verbs, and that the noun groups they introduce as complements are more autonomous discourse referents (note the use of deictics and determiners such as *its, the, such*). It is possible to find several equivalent constructions in the French cancer research text, although these examples are closer to light verb constructions (the verbs in these examples can be replaced by *avoir*):

7d. Les résultats de ce premier article montrent que seule la restriction alimentaire de 50% **induit** un **effet** sur le métabolisme mitochondrial.

7e. Les études de cancérogénéité peuvent s'avérer inutiles si la substance active et ses métabolites:… - ne **produisent** aucun **effet** indiquant une (pré)néoplasie lors des essais de toxicité chronique.

7f. La leucine agit en antagoniste et **provoque** donc des **effets** inverses.

Finally, when nouns other than *effect* are used, there is preference for verbs such as *cause, make, exercise* and *exert.* Usually, these constructions are encountered in technical domains, but not in the pharmaceutical sciences (these examples are from the English version of the ACC). Whereas this pattern is used to express biochemical explanations in the PSC, in these contexts the emphasis is on the empirical evaluation of results:

7g. In accordance with FAA Order 1050.1D, Appendix 4 paragraph 4(j), regulations, standards and exemptions (excluding those, which if implemented may **cause** a significant **impact** on the human environment) qualify for a categorical exclusion.

7h. An investment company or a management company acting in connection with all of the unit trusts which it manages and which fall within the scope of this Directive may not acquire any shares carrying voting rights which would enable it to **exercise** significant **influence** over the management of an issuing body.

7i. [The authority …], particularly as regards traceability, has **exerted** a positive **influence** on consumption of beef.

Once again analogous constructions can be found in French, all belonging to domains other than medical research (these examples are from the ACC and a reference corpus of French literature and journalism):

7j. Le relief montagneux **exerce** un fort **impact** sur le comportement de l'atmosphère. Vents, précipitations, température et enneigement varient d'une vallée à l'autre selon l'altitude,

7k. Ces prévisions au long cours sont rendues possibles par la prise en compte d'un facteur jusqu'à présent ignoré : les océans. Plus exactement la température de surface des océans, qui **exerce** une **influence** déterminante sur le climat à moyen terme.

7l. Les critères sont fixés à des niveaux qui favorisent l'attribution du label à des amendements pour sols et à des milieux de culture **présentant** une plus faible **incidence** sur l'environnement pendant toute la durée de vie du produit.

Summary of Findings

The nouns *effect, impact, influence* (and a small set of similar items) are involved in the following lexicogrammatical patterns:

i) as "process nouns" in light verb constructions whose lexicogrammatical pattern is: *Biochemical participant / process + have /*

exert / produce + an + effect, impact, influence + on Biochemical participant / process),

ii) as "anaphoric nouns" in chains of reformulation whose lexicogrammatical pattern is: *Evaluative epithet / Biochemical classifier + effect, impact, influence + of (Agent) + on (Medium) + in (Circumstantial).*

The "anaphoric noun" pattern is itself be embedded in three more general lexicogrammatical patterns (each of which corresponds to one of the main categories of semantic process in systemic functional grammar):

1) complement of a Mental process verb *(observe + effect, impact, influence),* with the discourse function of "presenting the research goals',

2) subject / complement of a Relational process verb *(there was + (no) significant + effect, impact, influence +of/on etc.),* with the discourse function of "evaluating empirical findings',

3) process noun in a Material process *(exert / produce + an + effect, impact, influence),* with the discourse function of "explaining a biochemical process'.

Conclusion

In this study I have set out the case for seeing "effect nouns" (i.e., *effect, impact, influence* and a small set of similar items) as an important family of non-technical lexical items in administrative and scientific discourse. My analysis of the data, in particular the *Acquis Communautaire Corpus* and the *Pharmaceutical Sciences Corpus* suggests that these items share a very consistent set of phraseological patterns in these types of text. This finding that is entirely consistent with the "contextualist" approach to language, set out in the introduction to this paper, which contends that each lexical item has a unique and consistent set of phraseological patterns in the language, particularly in specialised genres. It is important to point out that these patterns are predictable but also by necessity productive. In fact, it is the relatively variability of these structures which allow us to string them together in order to create longer stretches of text and discourse. Many observers understand the concept of "collocation" to refer to fixed or entirely rigid sequences of signs. This opinion is often reinforced by computational tools (including translation memory) which can quickly identify sequences of "bundles" or "n-grams" (repeated sequences of signs, although often no longer than four or five words in length). But as I have shown above, it is extremely difficult to find the exact same phraseological pattern twice. Rather, what is significant about the lexicogrammatical patterns observed here is that even some of the core elements of these patterns are rather variable (hence the slight variation of the central noun in the light verb construction *have a(n) + [evaluative expression] + bearing, effect, impact, influence, incidence (etc.) + on.*

What are the implications of this kind of analysis for terminology and translation studies? In this paper I have set out a methodology that relies on detailed statistical and corpus-based study. There is no evidence that this kind of analysis will lead to better quality translations. But to my mind that is not the purpose of linguistic analysis: the purpose of a linguistic approach, especially from a "systemic functional" perspective, is to look at bilingual or translated texts in order to better understand how discourse is organised and how translation works. In this respect, it is important to realise that grammatical metaphors (in the form of light verb constructions) are a prevalent form of expression in some of the most frequently encountered text types in pragmatic (or "specialised') translation. Similarly, I would also claim that it is important to know that in many procedural and expository texts, there are many chains of reference which are often made up essentially of the same underlying phrase. It can be seen that the underlying phrases analysed above vary in form, but in very predictable ways, according to the discourse function that the phrase is being used to express at a particular point in the text. For a pivotal word such as *effect,* I would suggest that there are at most only three discourse functions, corresponding to each of the three main lexicogrammatical patterns observed above: "presenting the research goals', "evaluating empirical findings" and "explaining a biochemical process'.

References

Banks, David. *Writ in Water: Aspects of the Scientific Journal Article*. Brest: ERLA, Université de Bretagne Occidentale. 1994.

Bates, Ramona. "Fish Oil and Fighting Cancer". *eMaxHealth* 2011. http://intelegen.com/nutrients/fish_oil_and_fighting_cancer.htm

Chevalley J.-Y., & B. Chapuis. « Pichard Oncologie et anorexie : place des orexigènes », *Revue Médicale Suisse*, 2010. http://titan.medhyg.ch/mh/formation/print.php3?sid=20886

Fawcett, Robin. *A Theory of Syntax for Systemic Functional Linguistics*. Amsterdam: Benjamins. 2000.

Firth, John Rupert. *Papers in Linguistics* 1934–1951. Oxford: Oxford University Press, 1957.

Francis, Gill. *Anaphoric Nouns*. Discourse Analysis Monograph 11. Birmingham: Birmingham University English Language Research, 1985.

Frath, Pierre. *Signe, référence, usage.* Paris : Editions LeManuscrit, 2007.

Gledhill, Christopher. *Collocations in Science Writing*. Tübingen: Gunter Narr. 2000.

Gledhill, Christopher. "The Discourse Function of Collocation in Research Article Introductions", *English for Specific Purposes* 19(2000): 115–135.

Gledhill, Christopher. « Portée, Pivot, Paradigme : trois termes pour faire le point sur les expressions verbo-nominales ». *Zeitschrift für Französische Sprache und Literatur* 35(2008): 59–76.

Gledhill, Christopher & Frath, Pierre. « Collocation, phrasème, dénomination : vers une théorie de la créativité phraséologique ». *La Linguistique* 43-1(2007): 65–90.

Halliday, Michael. A. K. "Lexis as a Linguistic Level". *Journal of Linguistics.* 2.1(1966): 57–67.

---. "Things and Relations: Regrammaticising Experience as Technical Knowledge". *Reading Science: Critical and Functional Perspectives on Discourses of Science*. Eds. James Martin, Jim. R. & Robert Veel. London: Routledge, 1998. 185–237.

Halliday, Michael A.K. & Christian M.I.M Matthiessen. *An Introduction to Functional Grammar.* 3rd edition. London: Arnold, 2004.

Halliday, Michael A.K., Wolfgang Teubert, Colin Yallop & Anna Čermáková. *Lexicology and Corpus Linguistics*, London: Continuum,

2004.

Hoey, Mike. *Lexical Priming*. London: Routledge, 2005.

Hunston, Susan & Gill Francis. *Pattern Grammar—A Corpus-driven Approach to the Lexical Grammar of English*. Amsterdam: Benjamins, 2000.

Johnson, Gyasi. *Métabolisme énergétique au cours de la cachexie cancéreuse*. Thèse de doctorat, École doctorale d'Angers, 2007.

Kübler, Natalie & Alexandra Volanschi. "Semantic Prosody and Specialised Translation, or How a Lexico-Grammatical Theory of Language can Help with Specialised Translation." *Corpus-informed Research and Learning in ESP: Issues and Applications*. Eds. Alex Boulton, Shirley Carter-Thomas, and Elisabeth Rowley-Jolivet. Amsterdam: Benjamins, 2012. 105–135.

Matthiessen, Christian, Kazuhiro Teruya, Marvin Lam. *Key Terms in Systemic Functional Linguistics*. London: Continuum, 2010.

Mulligan Helen D. & Michael J. Tisdale 1991. "Metabolic Substrate Utilization by Tumour and Host Tissues in Cancer Cachexia". *Biochemistry Journal* 77(2): 321–326.

Pecman, Mojca. « De la phraséologie à la traductologie proactive : essai de synthèse des fondements théoriques sous-tendant la recherche en phraséologie ». *Meta* 50 n°4 (2005), 1492–1421.

Peirce, Charles S. *Collected Papers of Charles Sanders Peirce, vols.* 1–6. *Collected Papers of Charles Sanders Peirce, vols.* 7–8. Eds. Charles Hartshorne & Paul Weiss & Arthur W. Burks. Cambridge, MA: Harvard University Press, 1931–1935, 1958.

Schleppegrell, Mary. "Technical Writing in a Second Language: the Role of Grammatical Metaphor." *Analysing Academic Writing: Contextualized Frameworks*. Eds. Louise J. Ravelli & Robert A. Ellis. London: Continuum, 2004.

Simon-Vandenbergen, Anne-Marie, Myriam Taverniers & Louise J. Ravelli. *Grammatical Metaphor: Views from Systemic Functional Linguistics*. Amsterdam: Benjamins, 2003.

Sinclair, John. *Corpus, Concordance, Collocation*. Oxford: Oxford University Press, 1991.

Steinberger, Ralf, Bruno Pouliquen, Anna Widiger, Camelia Ignat, Tomaž Erjavec, Dan Tufiş & Dániel Varga. "The JRC-Acquis: A Multilingual

Aligned Parallel Corpus with 20+ Languages". *Proceedings of the 5th International Conference on Language Resources and Evaluation.* Genoa, Italy, 24–26 May 2006.2142–2147. PDF available at: http://langtech.jrc.it/JRC-Acquis.html

Todiraşcu, Amalia & Gledhill, Christopher. "Extracting Collocations in Context: the Case of Verb-Noun Constructions in English and Romanian". *Recherches anglaises et nord-américaines* 41(2008): 107–122.

Tucker, Gordon H. "Between Lexis and Grammar: Towards a Systemic Functional Approach to Phraseology". *Continuing Discourse on Language: A Functional Perspective.* Eds. C. Matthiessen, R. Hasan and J. Webster. Vol. 2. London: Equinox, 2007. 954–977.

Williams Geoffrey. « Les collocations et l'école contextualiste britannique ». *Les collocations : analyse et traitement. Travaux et Recherches en Linguistique Appliquée,* Eds. Grossmann, Francis. & Agnès Tutin, Amsterdam : DeWerelt. 33–44.

Notes

1 www.artisansdumonde.org/docs/.../BulletinAdMn2-Janvier2007.pdf

2 The distinction between *discourse* and *denomination* and their relation to phraseology is discussed further in Gledhill & Frath (2007).

3 "When a child asks his father what those points are shining in the night sky (an ephemeral, constructed, transparent *designation*), he learns that they are stars (a public, stable, pre-constructed, opaque *denomination*). Thereafter the child is ready to encounter other signs which develop various other features of stars: they are very far away, they are found in galaxies, the sun is a star, sometimes they explode, and so on. Without denomination, interpretant signs would have no stable relationship between each other, and thus would not enable us to accumulate knowledge." [My translation].

4 I say "rendered" rather than "translated" because the direction of translation cannot always be verified in the ACC.

5 Here I am only counting de-verbal and process nouns which occur in LVCs with *have*: other LVCs occur (with light verbs such as *give, make, take* and so on), but their distribution is very low in this corpus.

6 Mulligan Helen D. & Michael J. Tisdale 1991. Metabolic substrate utilization by tumour and host tissues in cancer cachexia. *Biochemistry Journal* 77(2): 321–326.

7 Extract from: Ramona Bates, 2011 Fish Oil and Fighting Cancer, eMaxHealth available at: http://intelegen.com/nutrients/fish_oil_and_fighting_cancer.htm

8 Extract from: Chevalley J.-Y., B. Chapuis C. Pichard Oncologie et anorexie : place des orexigènes, Revue Médicale Suisse, available at: http://titan.medhyg.ch/mh/formation/print.php3?sid=20886

Traduction et création terminologique en français médical (1997–2012)

Danielle Candel

Résumé

Nous proposons une étude portant sur l'usage de la traduction, en terminologie et néologie officielle en France actuellement. C'est le domaine du français médical qui sera étudié. L'analyse de quelques aspects du processus d'enrichissement de la langue permettra de souligner la variété voire l'ambiguïté contenue précisément dans les références à la « traduction ». Différentes attitudes et réactions sont observées ou exprimées par rapport à la traduction et à l'anglais. Leur analyse devrait permettre de proposer des clés du succès terminologique.
Mots-clés : terminologie, néologie, français médical

Abstract

We propose a study of the use of translation in the framework of the French official Terminology and Neology today, with a focus on medical French. The analysis of some aspects of the Language Enrichment Process will highlight the variety of viewpoints, sometimes even their ambiguity in what concerns "translation." Different attitudes and reactions are observed or expressed with respect to the translation process and to English. Their analysis allows us to propose a list of keys to terminological success.
Keywords: terminology, neology, medical, French

Introduction

L'innovation terminologique dans les domaines de spécialité est naturellement liée à l'évolution du monde contemporain. « Sciences dures » » et « sciences humaines » se rejoignent dans ce nécessaire mouvement d'enrichissement de la langue. C'est ce que l'on peut observer en sciences humaines, dans le secteur des sciences du langage que forment la lexicologie, la lexicographie ou la terminologie : des spécialistes linguistes y dénomment de nouveaux concepts et décrivent de nouveaux termes spécialisés de « sciences plus exactes » ou leurs nouveaux usages. Ils le font en s'inspirant de données textuelles ou en s'appuyant sur les avis de spécialistes de ces sciences. Un tel processus est mis en œuvre dans des dictionnaires de langue générale, par exemple les dictionnaires millésimés *Larousse*, *Robert*, et dans une moindre mesure, le dictionnaire d'Etat *Trésor de la langue française* voire, bien plus timidement, le *Dictionnaire de l'Académie* en cours. C'est aussi ce que l'on observe dans les dictionnaires de termes scientifiques visant le grand public, où l'on traite de termes du discours scientifique à l'adresse de non-spécialistes. C'est enfin ce qui caractérise tout répertoire de mots où l'on est amené à souligner et décrire des écarts entre des domaines de spécialisation. Il y a ainsi les dictionnaires dont les auteurs, spécialistes d'une discipline, s'adressent à des non-spécialistes ou bien à des spécialistes d'un domaine différent du leur. Et ces mêmes distinctions valent pour les échanges entre spécialistes du sous-domaine d'une discipline vers un autre sous-domaine de cette discipline, ou encore vers un niveau de spécialisation différent. L'étude qui suit porte sur le processus de terminologie et de néologie officielle en France actuellement, du point de vue de l'usage de la traduction. C'est le domaine du français médical qui sera étudié. Après un bref rappel du vocabulaire médical dans l'histoire, la présentation du processus officiel d'enrichissement de la langue française permettra de souligner la variété voire l'ambiguïté contenue précisément dans les références à la « traduction » et c'est finalement un nécessaire équilibre entre fidélité à la langue source et liberté en langue cible qui sera souligné.

Le vocabulaire médical dans l'histoire

Le vocabulaire médical « ne peut pas être aussi rigoureux que [celui] d'une science dite exacte » (Sournia : 10). Ce n'est qu'au cours du XVIe siècle que le français a pris chez les médecins le dessus sur le latin. « Une nouvelle terminologie devait désormais satisfaire la précision scientifique et convenir aussi bien aux savants qu'aux ignorants : cette exigence de deux intellections différentes (…) est maximale dans le monde de la santé et de la maladie, car le médecin ne peut s'isoler du public non spécialisé qu'il doit traiter » (Sournia 1997 : 33). Des termes du latin furent « déclassés » au cours de l'histoire et vulgarisés, et on emprunta au grec, avec « des hybrides gréco-latins qui devaient plus tard indigner les puristes » mais dont la médecine occidentale « ne saurait plus se passer » (*ibid.* : 34, 82). Sournia comprend que liberté doit être laissée à la création néologique. Les néologismes devraient certes selon lui ne pas être des hybrides mais comme ils sont « utiles, commodes, il serait vain de vouloir les supprimer par une sorte d'épuration, pour satisfaire un besoin artificiel d'esthétique linguistique » (*ibid.*, p. 83). Il opte pour un emprunt adapté ou traduit et critique l'emprunt direct à l'anglais mais tout en expliquant la valeur ajoutée qu'y voient les importateurs (*ibid.* : 148).

Le processus d'enrichissement de la langue française et le recours à la traduction dans le domaine de la Santé

L'enrichissement de la langue française émane en particulier de l'activité spécifique que représente le secteur de la néologie officielle. Cette activité, liée à la terminologie, est annoncée dans le cadre tracé par le *Décret* du 3 juillet 1996 (*Journal officiel*, n° 96-602) signé par le Premier ministre Alain Juppé. Telle qu'elle se développe en France depuis cette date, elle implique, en 2012, un grand nombre de participants, plus de six cents personnes en tout, spécialistes des domaines concernés, ou généralistes.[1] Dix huit grands secteurs scientifiques, techniques et économiques y sont identifiés, dont l'Ingénierie nucléaire, la Chimie ou les Sciences et techniques spatiales, ou encore l'Automobile, les Sports, l'Economie et les finances, les Affaires étrangères et européennes, la Santé et la Médecine. Ce cadre a été évoqué ailleurs, tout comme la raison d'être des commissions de terminologie et de néologie : celle de « proposer des termes (…) équivalant à des termes (…) nouveaux apparaissant dans les langues étrangères, accompagnés de leur définition » (voir notamment Candel 2010 et 2012, et Candel & Samain 2014 sous presse). C'est J.C. Sournia, professeur de médecine, qui a formé en juin 1997 la commission spécialisée de terminologie et de néologie de la Santé, de la Médecine et des Affaires sociales, et l'a présidée. Lui-même et plusieurs autres membres de la commission, comme ce fut ensuite le cas sous la présidence du professeur A. Laugier, participaient au dictionnaire de l'Académie de médecine, mais aussi au Comité d'études des termes médicaux français (CETMF). Avec ce Comité d'étude J.C. Sournia a publié en 1974 *Langage médical moderne*, et le professeur J. Chevallier, en 2010, *Pour un langage médical vivant et correct*. Les liens sont incontestables entre les deux instances, et nous évoquerons ci-dessous l'une et l'autre.

Le corpus du domaine de la santé et les sous-domaines

En se reportant aux données disponibles sur le site FranceTerme le 26 juin 2013, à côté du domaine « Biologie » (467 termes) — qui a aussi pour sous-domaines « Physiologie » ou « Immunologie » — et du domaine « Santé animale » (5 termes), on trouve le large ensemble « Santé et médecine ». Il est nuancé ou précisé par ses sous-domaines « Hématologie », « Neurologie », « Pharmacologie », « Chirurgie », « Imagerie », « Anesthésiologie », « Psychologie », « Toxicologie », « Biostatistiques », « Epidémiologie », « Orthopédie », « Endocrinologie », « Biochimie », « Génétique » et « Essais thérapeutiques ». On compte, en date du 3 décembre 2012, 90 termes pour l'ensemble « Santé et médecine », soit 1,65 % des 5493 fiches publiées au *J.O.* Les fiches comportent généralement, et au minimum, une entrée, une définition et un « équivalent étranger ». Ce qui influence largement la progression des travaux dans le secteur de la Santé — et qui peut tout aussi bien les retarder considérablement — si l'on considère le public à qui s'adressent les innovations terminologiques, c'est le va et vient entre les différentes cibles du traducteur-terminologue-néologue. Ces « cibles », ce sont d'abord la chambre d'hôpital, le couloir d'hôpital, le bureau des infirmiers/infirmières et le cabinet médical en ville. Ce sont aussi, outre les principaux interlocuteurs directs des médecins et des soignants, les sphères administrative, officielle, journalistique, et toujours plus ou moins académique et prescriptive qui interviennent dans les choix des traductions françaises des termes anglais, avec les variantes respectives qui les caractérisent. Sans parler des aspects relevant par exemple de situations dans lesquelles les patients parlent un idiome différent de celui des médecins (voir Léglise 2011). Ces éléments de variation font que le recours aux définitions des termes s'impose impérativement, notamment pour les traductions de ces termes innovants. Et les divers processus de transposition ou d'adaptation viennent enrichir, modifier et en tout cas moduler les processus de recherche d'équivalence ou de traduction.

Quelques commentaires instructifs exprimés dans les notes

Trente fiches officielles de terminologie et de néologie du domaine de la Santé sont accompagnées d'une note (une fiche en comporte deux). Près du tiers de ces notes sont de nature linguistique. Elles expriment des mises en garde contre l'emprunt : sous *guidance* (angl. *coaching*, *guidance*) (2008) on s'élève contre *coaching santé ;* sous *gymnastique de forme* (angl. *fitness training*) (2009), contre *fitness ;* sous *spondyloplastie expansive* (angl. *balloon kyphoplasty*) (2012), contre *cyphoplastie* et *kyphoplastie ;* sous *vierge de tout traitement* (angl. *naive*) (2008), contre *naïf ;* quant à la fiche *compliance* (angl. *compliance*) (2003), elle met en garde contre un fr. *compliance* qui serait un équivalent de l'angl. *compliance* avec le sens du terme *observance*. L'autre catégorie de notes veut préserver du calque, comme dans quatre fiches de 2008 : on y recommande *circulation générale* (angl. *systemic circulation*) et non *circulation systémique*, *effet de proximité* (angl. *bystander effect*) et non *effet bystander*, étude pivot (angl. *pivotal study*) et non *étude pivotale*, *renseignement médico-sanitaire* (angl. *medical intelligence*) et non *intelligence médicale*. Enfin, une note est consacrée au « Langage professionnel », marque que nous avons discutée ailleurs : le terme *parenthèse thérapeutique* (angl. *washout*), qui désigne « Suspension temporaire d'un traitement destinée à en évaluer les éventuels effets indésirables », est accompagné du synonyme *fenêtre thérapeutique* donné dans cette note. Il en est dit, comme par prudence, qu'il relève du « langage professionnel », or il est précisément, pour certains, l'équivalent effectif, dans les usages, de *washout*. On constate donc une tendance à corriger, à redresser les usages habituels, même lorsqu'ils sont ostensiblement des traductions, équivalents naturels, déjà en usage.

Diverses formes de recours à la traduction ; le métalangage des médecins

L'activité décrite fait émerger plusieurs formes de recours au processus de « traduction ». Il peut s'agir aussi bien du passage d'un niveau d'expression vers un autre, dans une même langue, que du passage d'une langue vers une autre. Les textes officiels ne mentionnent pas en particulier que les commissions de terminologie et de néologie ont pour tâches des activités de traduction. Il est simplement expliqué que l'on recherche des équivalents français pour les termes étrangers. Il est possible de distinguer (i) les reformulations « intralangues » dues en terminologie aux activités de dénomination aussi bien qu'aux activités de définition, (ii) les « traductions-équivalences » quelque peu artificielles que représentent les formulations d'« équivalents étrangers » — qui sont proposées à la fin des fiches de terminologie officielle publiées au *J.O.* —, et (iii) de rares formulations d'« équivalents étrangers admis ». Sur les quatre-vingt-dix fiches de FranceTerme relevant du domaine « Santé - Médecine », quelques-unes sont atypiques, car elles sont dépourvues d'un « équivalent étranger » : il s'agit de *corbeillage* (2000 [1975]), *pôle hospitalier* (2008), *remnographie* (2003), *sécurité alimentaire* (2007), *tépographe* (2003), *translocation* (deux entrées, 2000 [1975]) et *urgentiste* (2008) ; dans le cas de *pôle hospitalier* et d'*urgentiste*, ce sont des spécificités françaises qui sont à l'honneur, la première étant d'ordre quasi administratif, et le concept évoqué ne semblant pas avoir son équivalent ailleurs. Mais précisons aussi que nous disposons d'une seule fiche offrant un « équivalent admis » : *lissage* (2000 [1975]) est un terme français proposé mais l'usage de *lifting* reste officiellement admis. Ce dernier exemple est lié au peu de succès de *lissage* par rapport à *lifting*, donc d'une version française de l'anglicisme implanté.

Plusieurs valeurs de « traduire » et de « traduction »

Nous nous référons ici à Chevallier (2010), ouvrage non sans lien, on l'a vu plus haut, avec les travaux pour la commission de terminologie. Une chose y apparaît clairement : c'est une multiplicité de valeurs de « traduire » et de « traduction ». Par exemple, sous « addiction », on lit : « terme général pour traduire l'asservissement d'un individu à toutes sortes de comportements déviants, qu'il s'agisse de drogue, de jeu, d'alimentation, de sexe, etc. ». « Traduire » veut dire ici « désigner » ou bien « qui sert à définir », « par lequel on définit ». Mais juste après, sous *aidant*, on lit : « Ce terme est accepté pour traduire *care-giver :* membre, généralement bénévole, de l'entourage d'une personne dépendante, qui l'aide et contribue à répondre à ses besoins quotidiens : ici, « traduire » est utilisé à bon escient, avec sa juste valeur métalinguistique. Voici quelques exemples tirés de ce même ouvrage, dû à des auteurs divers, mais coordonné par un membre de la Commission de la Santé, avec pour collaborateur important un autre membre actif de cette commission. Ainsi, pour l'anglais *plug*, la traduction est *obturateur*, et suit une remarque, composée d'une définition (« bouchon conique en treillis pour obturer l'orifice herniaire ») puis de considérations sur la traduction elle-même : « la traduction de *plug* par bonde est réservée à l'évier ou au lavabo » (Chevallier 2010 : 67). Or le contexte comporte un raccourci métalinguistique : plutôt que de l' « évier » ou du « lavabo » eux-mêmes, il s'agit bien entendu des domaines d'application ou des contextes d'usage de ces objets. Mais il n'y a rien d'étonnant à ce que le métalangage de non-linguistes ne soit pas canonique.

Diverses attitudes exprimées quant à la traduction

Au fil des ans, on peut constater que certains membres des commissions officielles de terminologie et de néologie évitent de « traduire ». Ils émettent ainsi de manière récurrente des remarques contre ce qui se rapprocherait d'une activité de « traduction », qui risquerait de s'éloigner et de se distinguer de l'activité de terminologie. La notion de traduction peut alors être assimilée ou liée à celle de langue générale qui est riche en tournures phraséologiques. Mais en parallèle, dans d'autres cas, l'attrait de la traduction continue à se faire sentir. Peut-être est-ce davantage le cas chez les membres des commissions qui ne sont pas eux-mêmes linguistes, et qui se montrent particulièrement respectueux de traductions qui soient « exactes ». Des traducteurs professionnels présents dans les commissions, de leur côté, expliquent la nécessité qui est la leur de trouver des traductions de référence, agréées, voire officialisées, et en tout cas réutilisables dans le cadre de leurs travaux. C'est certainement dans un juste milieu qu'il fallait situer la remarque de Marc Fumaroli, président de la Commission générale de terminologie, lors d'une conférence de presse donnée le 19 janvier 2010. Il y insistait sur l'importance de traductions exactes et de correspondances précises entre l'anglais et le français. A ce stade de son exposé, il devait évoquer ces deux langues en général. En effet, dans le cadre précis des commissions de terminologie, les deux versions du terme ne se correspondent pas forcément avec exactitude, puisque, il faut le souligner, le milieu culturel intervient aussi. Quoi qu'il en soit, toute une gamme de « traductions » est donc à l'œuvre dans le processus de terminologie officielle, des plus littérales aux plus interprétatives.

Traduction et terminologie néologique, chez les non-spécialistes du langage : témoignages de spécialistes de la Santé

Le rôle joué par des acteurs non linguistes a sa place dans le présent ouvrage traitant de traduction. Il est intéressant d'analyser les positions des spécialistes des domaines scientifiques et techniques qui ne sont eux-mêmes ni linguistes ni traducteurs, mais qui participent activement au processus officiel d'enrichissement de la langue française par des propositions terminologiques et néologiques. En effet, les nouvelles propositions terminologiques et les « traductions » sont liées. Certains sont pour une correspondance exacte, mot à mot, entre l'anglais et le français. C'est précisément cette position que nous voudrions discuter.

Une partie de notre corpus, nous l'annoncions, comporte les travaux du Comité d'étude des termes médicaux français. Il se trouve que l'ouvrage *Pour un langage médical vivant et correct*, coordonné par le professeur Jacques Chevallier, a justement pour principaux acteurs des membres de la commission de terminologie et de néologie de la Santé. On y relève 280 fiches postérieures à 1997. Il y est expliqué en quatrième de couverture qu' « il ne faut pas laisser les journalistes et bien des médecins faire des traductions approximatives » et que « les anglicismes sont traduits ou francisés ». C'est dire la place qu'y tient la notion de traduction. L'introduction, par P. Lasserre, propose curieusement un recours au grec, qu'il donne comme une sorte de langue commune internationale pour la raison qu' « un mot formé sur le grec ancien n'a pas besoin d'être traduit : il suffit d'en modifier légèrement la graphie pour l'adapter aux exigences d'une autre langue » (p.6). Mais un problème majeur résiderait selon lui dans le fait que « le néologisme est intraduisible et n'a pas de correspondant en français » (*ibid.*). C'est ce qui lui avait fait proposer, au lieu de « aidant », dont voici la fiche officielle publiée :

Domaine : SANTÉ ET MÉDECINE
Définition : *Personne, le plus souvent bénévole, qui assiste une personne dépendante dans sa vie quotidienne.*
Équivalent étranger : *caregiver* (*en*) (*EU*), *carer* (*en*) (*GB*)
(06/09/2008, *Journal officiel de la République française*)

Une version issue du grec :

aidant : « Ce terme est accepté pour traduire *care-giver* : membre, généralement bénévole, de l'entourage d'une personne dépendante, qui l'aide et contribue à répondre à ses besoins quotidiens. Le mot équivalent, tiré du grec, serait *ophélète* (…) » (2004, dans Chevalier 2010).

Et l'auteur de souligner les difficultés de traduction de termes tels que *on-off*, *up regulation* ou *down regulation*, puisque les résultats en français ne peuvent présenter la même brièveté que celle de l'anglais. Le premier de ces termes, *on-off*, est commenté par : « qualifie un phénomène qui répond à la loi du tout ou rien. Par exemple, phénomène ou effet thérapeutique à début et fin brusques ». Il a droit au commentaire conclusif « pas d'équivalent en français ». Ce qui, en vérité, laisse les auteurs dépourvus, c'est que le terme peut renvoyer à plusieurs concepts, notamment ceux exprimés en français par « allumé-éteint » d'une part et « en service-hors service » d'autre part : comment, dans ces conditions, contourner ce *syndrome on-off* par lequel on évoque « cette perte brutale et très brève du tonus musculaire que l'on observe chez le parkinsonien avec chute et souvent blessures » ? Rappelons qu'à un terme anglais ne correspond pas une traduction française et une seule. Surtout lorsque le terme devient lui-même élément d'un autre terme, comme la forme *on-off* dans le terme *syndrome on-off*. Et les médecins désireux de proposer des termes français se voient ainsi acculés au renoncement. Mais finalement *up regulation* et *down regulation*, cas presque aussi désespérants, apparaissent, contre toute attente, accompagnés de leurs « traductions » : respectivement *augmentation compensatrice* et *diminution compensatrice* (Chevalier 2010).

Enfin, le signataire de l'introduction explique l'action selon lui la plus délicate : celle consistant à imaginer un correspondant à un terme anglo-américain « non traduisible directement en français à cause de son sens originel très différent de ce qu'il ou elle désigne » (p.7) ; il évoque à ce sujet les termes *buffy* et *burn out*. C'est en particulier à propos de ces derniers cas de figure que nous voudrions réagir. Avant de revenir à tout prix à l'étymologie du terme, il importe à notre avis de partir directement de ses valeurs actuelles, notamment dans la langue source et, le cas échéant, de les modifier pour les ajuster à leurs valeurs dans la langue d'arrivée. Les éléments culturels, dans la langue source—mais aussi dans la langue cible — sont primordiaux. Retourner à l'histoire est certes utile pour saisir le cheminement du terme dans sa langue d'origine, et si par hasard on peut arriver en français à imposer un terme en lien avec ce cheminement, on s'en félicitera. Mais en quoi la proposition officielle *syndrome d'épuisement professionnel*, certes un peu longue, devrait-elle nous faire regretter les valeurs et connotations de *brûler jusqu'au bout*, qui serait la traduction littérale de *to burn out ?* Les valeurs culturelles prises par ce terme anglo-saxon lorsqu'il est employé dans la langue cible sont les plus importantes à rendre dans l'équivalent français qui sera finalement à retenir.

Une nécessaire dualité fidélité/liberté : ce que l'on peut ou doit traduire en terminologie

A consulter des spécialistes de la traduction, on comprend qu'il faut garder à l'esprit, que ce soit dans les traductions de phrases, ou de mots, ce « débat liberté/fidélité (...) tranché par la dualité équivalences / correspondances de toute traduction réussie ». En effet, la liberté des équivalences et la fidélité des correspondances sont liées au cœur de la traduction. Et ce, même si « les correspondances sont nécessaires lorsqu'il s'agit (...) de termes techniques » (Lederer 2006 : 69). Jean-

René Ladmiral précise quant à lui que « la solution des problèmes théoriques ne passe ni ne commence par le dogmatisme subjectif de décrets terminologiques préalables » et « arbitraires » (Ladmiral 1994 : 24, 137). En effet, un « transcodage » parfait serait bien l'indice d'une « nomenclature quasi terminologique » mais il ne serait pas « en prise sémiotique sur la culture et l'histoire auxquelles il réfère », et ne tolèrerait pas cette nécessaire ouverture connotative qui entraîne un nécessaire « contresens minimal » (*ibid.*, 226, 244). Certes, chez les deux spécialistes traductologues cités, la terminologie représente le secteur qui permettrait des correspondances parfaites. Mais les deux auteurs concluent bien que de telles correspondances ne sont pas souhaitables.

Notre propos concerne surtout les usages de la traduction au sein des commissions de terminologie. Une coïncidence vient servir à point notre réflexion et nous aider à répondre à cette question : il se trouve que l'un des deux spécialistes traductologues cités, philosophe, et surtout connu comme traducteur et spécialiste de la traduction, est entré en 2010 dans la Commission de terminologie et de néologie de l'Education et de l'Enseignement supérieur. Il s'agit précisément de Jean-René Ladmiral. Un certain nombre de commentaires qui nous semblent liés à cette expérience, nouvelle pour lui comme membre d'une commission de terminologie et de néologie, sont disponibles dans Ladmiral 2012.

Deux de ces commentaires nous importent tout particulièrement. D'une part, l'auteur note que « le phénomène terminologique constitue l'une des tendances inhérentes au langage ». En effet, le besoin de disposer d'une définition pour un terme spécialisé est nécessairement présent dans le discours, qu'il s'agisse du domaine des sciences du langage ou de tout autre domaine de spécialité, comme les sciences de l'Education (intitulé de la commission dont l'auteur est membre), ou de sciences dures comme le Pétrole ou le Nucléaire. D'autre part, l'auteur rappelle que si l'on tend constamment à une correspondance entre terme et concept, une volonté outrée de rechercher et de vouloir décréter une « concordance biunivoque » entre « mot » et « concept » grâce à des « termes totalement désambiguïsés » relève dans de nombreux cas de l'utopie. Nous rappellerons à ce sujet les discussions sur le principe de biunivocité exprimé par Wüster, principe décrié par les tenants de la sociolinguistique et de la variation linguistique (Humbley 2004, Candel 2004). Ladmiral relève, même en terminologie, ce qu'il dénomme le « glissendo métonymique » : c'est ce qu'il observe entre ces acceptions proches qui posent problème aux non-spécialistes, à ceux qui ne sont pas les usagers habituels des éléments terminologiques étudiés. S'il souligne de « nombreux cas de polysémie bien marquée en terminologie », il ne manque pas de conclure qu'il s'agit en fait d'homonymie. Les « glissements métaphoriques », quant à eux, ne sont évoqués que dans la mesure où la métaphorisation d'un terme est à l'origine de sa détermination néologique, processus observable lors du passage d'une discipline à une autre, au cours d'échanges entre langue générale et discours spécialisés.

Ces caractéristiques observables dans les terminologies constituent pour Ladmiral « autant de fissures dans les murs de l'endiguement terminologique, par lesquelles la fluidité de la langue revient s'insinuer et tend à éroder la rigueur systématique imposée au vocabulaire pour en faire une terminologie ». Il conclut : « sans doute est-ce la traduction qui constitue l'opération qui met le plus directement en cause la clôture terminologique du lexique ». C'est là que Ladmiral fait intervenir son principe de la « quodité terminologique » (qui prend place dans celui de la « quodité traductive »), bref, ce qui détermine ce que l'on peut ou doit traduire en terminologie. On ne peut s'en tenir à la prise en compte du seul terme à rendre dans l'autre langue : il faut pouvoir analyser les contextes élargis dans lesquels il est employé, afin de retracer son sémantisme. Or Ladmiral suggère à juste titre la démarche consistant à se demander « si le terme considéré est employé dans son sens terminologiquement consacré, ou non », mais précisons que, dans la pratique de la terminologie officielle décrite dans ces pages, c'est ce dernier cas de figure qui prévaut, sinon le terme ne serait même pas mis à l'étude.

Il convient, pour contribuer à la description de la pratique en situation terminologique officielle, de souligner que le travail s'y déroule constamment avec des experts des domaines concernés. Positions, points de vue particuliers, pratiques de réflexion linguistique sont modulés par l'apport des autres membres des commissions, notamment les non-linguistes, qui sont spécialistes des domaines étudiés. L'ensemble des membres des commissions relèvent d'horizons diversifiés et se complètent. Aussi, si Ladmiral en vient à conclure, en parlant de la terminologie de la Santé, que « si le traducteur ne dispose que du compte rendu clinique (…) il ne pourra guère en fournir une traduction satisfaisante, s'il ne peut en appeler à une personne-ressource. », il convient de rappeler que, dans le cadre des commissions de terminologie, ces « personnes-ressource » sont effectivement présentes. Le linguiste (qui peut ici être aussi terminologue ou lexicographe) travaille en proche collaboration avec ces « personnes-ressource », ce qui fait justement le grand attrait des travaux de ces commissions de terminologie tels que nous les expérimentons nous-même depuis 1997.

Se pose enfin pour Ladmiral (2012) le problème de l'absence en langue cible d'un « équivalent immédiat » sinon littéral de l'item-source à traduire. Mais il relativise ce fait, soulignant l'importance des « langues-cultures ». Plutôt que des « traductions directes », ce sont en effet des « traductions obliques » qui interviennent, faites de décalages par rapport au texte-source, ou encore des « surtraductions » ou des « sous-traductions ». Deux cas de figure sont donc présentés à la fin de son raisonnement : soit une « terminologisation », soit une « idiomatisation », cette dernière revenant à trouver dans la langue cible un équivalent « sémantiquement adéquat et [qui] satisfasse à une exigence minimale d'aisance stylistique ». On retrouve ici ce nécessaire équilibre entre fidélité et liberté, où la culture de la langue d'accueil garde une importance primordiale.

Conclusion

L'usage de la traduction et l'idée que s'en font les spécialistes de la Santé et de la Médecine actifs dans le développement officiel de la langue française peuvent revêtir des formes variées. Nous avons étudié un ensemble d'attitudes et de réactions observées ou exprimées au sujet de la traduction et de l'anglais, qui ne sont d'ailleurs pas dépourvues d'ambiguïté, et qui entraînent souvent une confusion entre traduction et équivalence. La création terminologique passe couramment par une phase de traduction — à partir de l'anglais, au grand dam de médecins désireux de contribuer au développement officiel de la langue française contemporaine de la médecine tout en contournant l'angloaméricain ou en refusant ses influences. Souvent, pour reprendre finalement Chevallier 2010 (p. 118), c'est la « paresse de traduction » qui est stigmatisée. Comme il est souvent rappelé, de nouveaux termes français sont nécessaires pour remplacer les emprunts à l'anglo-américain. Il est selon nous indispensable, dans un tel but, de continuer à travailler à partir de contextes en anglais et en français, afin de rendre au mieux dans la culture française les usages des termes anglais qui pouvaient s'imposer en français ou qui commencent à le faire. Nous parlons là de contextes écrits, dans les deux langues, aussi bien que de l'inestimable discours produit séance tenante par les spécialistes médecins participant aux travaux. Le résultat auquel l'on parvient est acceptable même si, comparativement, dans la transposition en cours, les termes proposés et leurs usages diffèrent dans la culture d'accueil, celle du français, par rapport aux termes et à leurs usages dans la culture d'origine, celle de l'anglais. Car, et c'est souvent là le problème, dans le domaine de la Santé comme ailleurs, on cherche à s'éloigner de l'anglais, mais on ne veut pas non plus trop le trahir. La clé de la réussite d'un néologisme réside dans l'équilibre entre une plus ou moins grande fidélité formelle et sémantique aux termes d'origine, et une nécessaire liberté innovatrice.

Références bibliographiques

Candel, Danielle. « Wüster par lui-même ». *Des fondements théoriques de la terminologie*. Ed. Colette Cortès. *Cahiers du CIEL,* 2004: 15–32.

Candel, Danielle. « Pour une évaluation de la pratique néologique dans les commissions de terminologie et néologie en France ». *Actes del I Congrés Internacional de Neolofia de les Llengues Romaniques*. Ed. Maria Teresa Cabré i Castellví et al. Cineo Barcelona: Institut Universitari de Linguistica Aplicada, Universitat Pompeu Fabra, 2010 : 433–445.

Candel, Danielle. « Reformuler et définir les termes de spécialité ou tenter la traduction : études de cas en terminologie institutionnelle du français (1971–2010) ». *Dictionnaires et Traduction.* Ed. Michaela Heinz. Berlin : Frank & Timme, 2012 : 20–23.

Candel, Danielle & Didier Samain. "Translation as a Historically Situated Activity. Situational issues : the case of terminological transfer". *Paradigmes en mutation : du rôle transformateur de la traduction pour les sciences humaines*. Eds. Antoine Cazé & Rainier Lanselle. Berne : Peter Lang, 2014: 149-172.

Chevallier, Jacques. *Pour un langage médical vivant et correct*. Le Comité Clair-Dire - Comité d'étude des termes médicaux français. Paris : La maison du dictionnaire, 2010.

Comité Clair-dire, Comité d'étude des termes médicaux français. *Pour un langage médical vivant et correct. Etude critique des termes médicaux depuis* 1965 *jusqu'en* 2009. Paris : La maison du dictionnaire, 2010.

FranceTerme. *http://www.culture.fr/franceterme*

Humbley, John. « Wüster par lui-même». *Des fondements théoriques de la terminologie*, ed. Colette Cortès. *Cahiers du CIEL* 2004, Université Paris 7, 2004 : 15–32.

Ladmiral, Jean-René. *Traduire : théorèmes pour la traduction*. Paris : Gallimard, 1994 [1979].

Ladmiral, Jean-René. « La terminologie au risque de la traduction ». *Terminologie (II) : comparaisons, transferts, (in)traductions, Travaux interdisciplinaires et plurilingues* 17, 2012: 9–19.

Lederer, Marianne. *La traduction aujourd'hui - le modèle interprétatif*. Caen : Lettres modernes Minard, (nouvelle éd.), 2006.

Léglise, Isabelle. « Quel accès aux soins et aux services publics pour des citoyens non francophones ? ». *Culture et recherche* 125, 2011. 10–11.

Sournia, Jean-Charles. *Langage médical moderne*. Cilf - Comité d'étude des termes médicaux français. Paris : Hachette, 1974.

Sournia, Jean-Charles. *Langage médical français*. Toulouse : Privat, 1997.

Notes

* L'ensemble est géré par la Délégation générale à la langue française et aux langues de France. Nous bénéficions, au laboratoire HTL, d'une subvention annuelle de la part de la DGLFLF (ministère de la Culture) pour une expertise linguistique apportée aux commissions de terminologie.

Quel(s) équivalent(s) pour traduire l'adjectif anglais *translational* ? Quelques remarques sur les difficultés à traduire la terminologie de domaines médicaux innovants

Pascaline Dury

Résumé

L'article présente un travail mené sur les différentes traductions possibles, en français, du terme *translational research*, dans le cadre d'une discipline médicale émergente, la recherche dite « translationnelle ». A partir de données extraites d'un corpus bilingue, nous montrons qu'il existe plusieurs variantes terminologiques du terme « recherche translationnelle », parmi lesquelles le terme « recherche de transfert ». L'utilisation, par les experts médicaux, de l'une ou l'autre variante montre la volonté de mettre en avant telle information plutôt que telle autre. Il est donc important que le traducteur prenne en compte l'expression de ce sentiment linguistique d'expert et ne recherche pas à tout prix l'uniformisation terminologique dans son travail.

Mots-clés : Terminologie médicale, recherche translationnelle, recherche de transfert

Abstract

In this article I examine the different possible translations of the term "translational research" in French, and study one aspect of the new terminology of "translational research," which is an emerging discipline within medicine. A bilingual corpus was used to identify the different translations of this term such as "recherche translationnelle" and "recherche de transfert." When medical experts use "recherche de transfert" rather than "recherche translationnelle," they do so deliberately and appropriately in order to achieve a more nuanced meaning. Translators should thus take these linguistic choices more into account and avoid systematic terminological standardization.

Keywords: medical terminology, translational research

Introduction

L'adjectif anglais *translational* est d'une utilisation courante dans la langue médicale, mais sa traduction vers le français peut être source de difficultés, car il existe différents équivalents possibles (« traductionnel », « de traduction », « translationnel », « de la translation ») selon le domaine précis dans lequel il est utilisé (par exemple la biologie cellulaire, les essais cliniques, la chirurgie orthopédique, etc.), comme le montrent les courts exemples de traduction ci-dessous :

- Translational inhibition by cytomegalovirus transcript leaders → « inhibition de la traduction » / « inhibition traductionnelle »,
- Post-translational modifications, a key process in CD36 function: Lessons from the spontaneously hypertensive rat heart → « modifications post-traductionnelles »,
- Rotational and translational laxity after computer-navigated single- and double-bundle anterior cruciate ligament reconstruction → **« laxité de la translation ».**

Nous nous intéressons dans les parties qui suivent aux différentes traductions possibles de l'adjectif *translational* en français, lorsqu'il est utilisé en collocation avec le terme *research* dans un domaine émergent qu'est celui de la recherche dite « translationnelle ». Nous examinerons notamment l'utilisation des équivalents français « translationnelle » et « de transfert » dans le détail, à l'aide d'un corpus *ad hoc* bilingue anglais-français, contenant d'une part des articles médicaux écrits par des spécialistes pour d'autres spécialistes, et d'autre part, dans la partie française du corpus, des textes scientifiques destinés au grand public. A l'aide de données extraites du corpus visant à étudier les contextes précis dans lesquels ces deux termes apparaissent et en observant quelles sont leurs « préférences sémantiques » respectives, nous essaierons de montrer que l'emploi de « translationnnelle » et de « de transfert » par les spécialistes ne semble ni arbitraire, ni fortuit et indique au contraire la volonté de mettre en avant des informations différentes sur ce nouveau type de recherche. L'acte de traduction, lorsqu'il tient compte de la variation terminologique et ne recherche pas forcément l'uniformisation du vocabulaire, est donc envisagé ici comme un moyen de construire et de diffuser un savoir dans une autre langue, particulièrement un savoir innovant comme c'est le cas de la recherche « translationnelle ».

Remarques préliminaires sur l'émergence du concept aux Etats-Unis et en France

> *Translational research is defined precisely by the National Institutes of Health (NIH) as "the process of applying ideas, insights and discoveries generated through basic scientific inquiry to the treatment or prevention of human disease" (Fontana et al. 2).*

> *Cette nouvelle discipline décrite par la formule, maintenant consacrée, « de la paillasse au lit du patient » (from bench to bedside) vise à développer, au plus tôt, les interactions et les échanges entre recherche fondamentale et médecine clinique» (Institut de Cancérologie 2).*

Comme le laissent entendre ces deux définitions extraites du corpus, la recherche dite « translationnelle » est donc une nouvelle façon d'aborder la recherche médicale, dans le but d'accélérer le passage de la recherche fondamentale en laboratoire à des traitements réels pour des patients réels.

Le concept de *translational research* a émergé d'abord aux Etats-Unis il y a une vingtaine d'années, où il semble avoir très vite gagné en popularité dans les milieux médicaux : ainsi en 2001, le *Journal of American Medical Association* (JAMA) en fait le thème d'un numéro spécial, en 2003, les *National Institutes of Health* l'identifient comme un élément essentiel de leur programme d'actions et en 2005 un prix, le *Clinical and Translational Science Awards* (CTSAs), est mis en place pour récompenser les meilleurs travaux dans ce domaine. Enfin, en 2009, *L'American Association for the Advancement of Science* (AAA), lance la revue *Translational Medicine*, en partenariat avec la revue *Science* et en décembre 2012, cette même revue *Science* consacre un numéro tout entier, à destination du grand public, à ce nouveau concept.

Cet engouement extrême pour la médecine translationnelle se traduit également par la prolifération de revues scientifiques de langue anglaise qui y sont consacrées. Par exemple, depuis 2003, pas moins de 9 revues de disciplines médicales variées, mais traitant de médecine translationnelle ont vu le jour, parmi lesquelles le *Journal of Translational Medicine* (2003), *Translational Oncogenomics* (2006), *Experimental and Translational Stroke Medicine* (2009), *Clinical and Translational Gastroenterology* (2010), *Translational Biomedicine* (2010), *Translational Psychiatry* (2011), *Clinical and Translational Allergy* (2011), *Translational Neurodegeneration* (2012), *Stem Cells Translational Medicine* (2012).

Le concept gagne ensuite, et plus tardivement la France, mais semble y susciter le même intérêt parmi les scientifiques. Ainsi, sur le plan national, la médecine translationnelle est-elle inscrite au cœur des orientations stratégiques des deux Plans Cancer mis en place par l'Institut National du Cancer, celui de 2009–2013 et celui de 2014–2019[1] ; en 2010, l'Alliance pour les Sciences de la Vie et de la Santé (AVIESAN) et le ministère des Affaires sociales et de la Santé, en lien avec les centres hospitaliers universitaires (CHU) et les Centres de Lutte Contre le Cancer (CLCC), lancent un appel à candidatures pour l'établissement de contrats hospitaliers de recherche translationnelle, permettant de « renforcer la politique de soutien et de valorisation de la recherche translationnelle, composante majeure de la recherche biomédicale » (http://www.sante.gouv.fr/contrats-hospitaliers-de-recherche translationnelle.htm).

De nombreuses équipes de recherches hospitalières et universitaires se renomment ou se créent autour de ce nouveau concept scientifique, comme à l'Université de Strasbourg où l'on trouve une unité de recherche appelée « Physiopathologie et Médecine Translationnelle (PMT) »,[2] à l'Université de Nantes qui compte une unité de recherche mixte, « thérapie génique translationnelle des maladies neuromusculaires et de la rétine », à l'Institut de cancérologie Gustave Roussy de Villejuif qui possède un « Laboratoire de Recherche Translationnelle, LRT» ou à l'Institut Curie à Paris qui compte un département de recherche translationnelle.

La tâche du traducteur paraît donc ici facilitée, puisque le terme « recherche translationnelle » semble s'implanter avec autant de rapidité que le concept qu'il accompagne. En outre, la délégation générale à la langue française et aux langues de France (DGLGLF), par le biais de la Commission générale de terminologie et de néologie, fait publier au *Journal officiel* du 24/10/2012 le terme « recherche translationnelle » comme équivalent du terme étranger *translational research*, avec la définition suivante : « Phase de la recherche assurant le passage de la recherche fondamentale à la recherche appliquée » (http://www.franceterme.culture.gouv.fr/FranceTerme/).

Pourtant, nos lectures sur le sujet, tant de documents produits par des experts pour d'autres experts que de sites internet destinés à vulgariser le concept auprès du grand public, nous ont permis de constater que l'environnement dénominatif de ce nouveau concept est en réalité plus complexe qu'il n'y paraît au premier abord. On remarque en effet que même si le terme « recherche translationnelle » est utilisé dans de nombreux documents consultés comme l'équivalent de traduction « naturel » du terme *translational research*, il est pourtant encore souvent considéré, par les auteurs, comme un terme nouveau, pas encore adopté largement par la communauté scientifique et comme tel, il apparaît souvent entre guillemets et fait aussi souvent l'objet d'une explication, voire d'une définition.

> *La recherche « translationnelle » se réfère typiquement à la translation, c'est à- dire à la fois passage et traduction, de la recherche fondamentale au laboratoire en des traitements réels pour des patients réels.* (Corvol 49).

La recherche translationnelle doit :

> *transférer et interpréter le plus vite possible les connaissances et les technologies nouvelles vers des applications diagnostiques et thérapeutiques, au bénéfice des patients* (Dine 3).

Dans les documents étudiés, on rencontre également un certain nombre de variantes terminologiques du terme « recherche translationnelle », ce dernier n'étant pas systématiquement utilisé par tous les auteurs du corpus compilé pour cette étude. On trouve par exemple :

> *La recherche de transfert assure un continuum entre la recherche cognitive et la recherche clinique et inversement, fait poser des questions à la recherche fondamentale, déri-*

> *vées de l'observation des patients (ou de groupes et cohortes de patients)* (http://www.sante.gouv.fr/contrats-hospitaliers-de-recherche-translationnelle-chrt.html).

> *La recherche expérimentale est une recherche bidirectionnelle, du patient vers le laboratoire de recherche et vice versa. L'objectif de cette recherche translationnelle est d'améliorer la prise en charge des patients atteints de cancer : diagnostic, pronostic, choix thérapeutique, qualité de vie, effets à long terme* (Jobard et al. 24).

Exploitation des corpus et résultats

Ces deux constats nous conduisent donc à formuler la problématique suivante :

— De quelles autres variantes terminologiques du terme « recherche translationnelle » les experts font-il usage?
— Ces variantes sont-elles utilisées avec la même fréquence, et dans des contextes identiques ?
— Le traducteur doit-il tenir compte de l'existence de ces variantes, y compris si elles sont moins fréquentes que le terme « recherche translationnelle » ?

Afin de trouver des réponses à ces questionnements, nous avons décidé d'explorer de façon déductive un corpus bilingue (anglais-français) *ad hoc* contenant des articles spécialisés rédigés par des experts pour des experts, dans diverses disciplines médicales (mais plus particulièrement l'oncologie, la néphrologie, l'imagerie et la biologie cellulaire) et ayant trait à la médecine translationnelle. La partie française du corpus contient en outre des documents rédigés par des experts et destinés au grand public (sites internet, articles de vulgarisation, etc.). Ce corpus est également diachronique, puisqu'il contient des articles publiés entre 1998 et 2012 pour la partie anglaise et entre 2001 et 2012 pour la partie française. La partie anglaise du corpus compte 115 360 occurrences, la partie française 156 398 occurrences.

Le corpus a été analysé grâce à deux outils principaux, *Wordsmith*

Tools et *TermoStat Web TM* 3.0,[3] qui ont permis l'extraction de terminologie et de contextes.

Comme nous l'avons déjà mentionné, nos lectures préalables à cette recherche nous avaient permis de constater la présence d'un certain nombre de variantes terminologiques du terme « recherche translationnelle » : l'extraction effectuée en corpus a confirmé ceci et a mis en évidence l'existence de trois termes potentiellement synonymes présentés dans le tableau ci-dessous, avec leur nombre respectif d'occurrences dans le corpus.

Tableau 1 : variantes terminologiques du terme « recherche translationnelle » et leur nombre d'occurrences respectives.

Terme candidat	Nombres d'occurrences dans le corpus
recherche translationnelle	325
recherche de transfert	173
médecine translationnelle	95
médecine expérimentale	21

Il n'est pas tout à fait surprenant de constater que le terme « recherche translationnelle » compte un nombre d'occurrences plus élevé que les autres variantes possibles, car comme nous l'avons vu, il semble être considéré comme l'équivalent de traduction le plus « naturel » du terme *translational research*, et il a en outre été « officialisé » dans des documents de portée nationale comme le Plan Cancer 2014–2019.

Nous écarterons de notre analyse le terme « médecine expérimentale » pour des raisons numériques : le nombre d'occurrences de ce terme (21 occurrences) ramené à la taille du corpus en français (156 398 occurrences) le situe en dessous d'une ligne « de fiabilité numérique » en deçà de laquelle il nous semble peu prudent qu'un traducteur s'aventure. Nous nous intéresserons donc particulièrement aux variantes « médecine translationnelle » et « recherche de transfert » pour voir si elles apparaissent exactement dans les mêmes contextes que le terme « recherche translationnelle » et si elles peuvent être utilisées par le traducteur exactement dans les mêmes conditions.

« Médecine translationnelle »

L'extraction de contextes montre une assez grande confusion dans l'utilisation du terme dans la partie spécialisée du corpus, comme dans la partie vulgarisée ; certains auteurs le considèrent effectivement comme synonyme de « recherche translationnelle » et l'utilisent de façon interchangeable dans leurs propos (c'est le cas dans 31 contextes extraits sur 95) :

> *La recherche translationnelle, ou médecine translationnelle est une voie émergente naturelle issue de la pratique médicale, du développement des laboratoires de recherche médicale et de la meilleure connaissance épidémiologique et statistique* (Thervet 3).
>
> *La montée en puissance de la médecine ou recherche « translationnelle » s'appuyant notamment sur les techniques modernes d'imagerie devrait faciliter cette collaboration entre les acteurs impliqués dans chacune des étapes du développement* (Guilbaud et al. 55).

Alors que d'autres auteurs (dans 59 contextes extraits sur 95[4]), utilisent le terme « médecine translationnelle » non pas comme un synonyme, mais comme un hyperonyme de « recherche translationnelle » :

> *La recherche translationnelle est la base fondamentale de la médecine translationnelle. Il s'agit du processus qui conduit des résultats de la médecine fondée sur la preuve à des solutions viables à long terme pour résoudre des questions de santé publique* (De Azambuja et al. 352).
>
> *Nous avons voulu aussi dans ce dossier évoquer les autres aspects de la médecine translationnelle. En fait partie la recherche translationnelle de phase II et de phase III. La phase II explore la manière dont les découvertes vont trouver leur place en clinique, et la phase III permet de montrer que les solutions retenues sont viables et utiles à long terme sans occulter la dimension économique* (Ashton-Chess et al. 8).

Cette confusion dans l'utilisation du terme peut être due au caractère innovant de la discipline à l'étude : le sens de « médecine translationnelle » est encore instable parce que le terme est nouveau et il n'y a pas encore eu, en quelque sorte, de « consensus sémantique » à son sujet chez les experts qui l'emploient.

« Recherche de transfert »

Parmi les variantes terminologiques possibles de « recherche translationnelle » relevées dans le corpus, « recherche de transfert » est celle dont le nombre d'occurrences (173) est le plus élevé. Dans un premier temps, nous avons analysé les contextes d'apparition de ces 173 occurrences afin de tester l'hypothèse selon laquelle le terme « recherche de transfert », qui paraît moins « technique»[5] que « recherche translationnelle » est plutôt employé dans la partie du corpus composée de documents vulgarisés, et qu'il serait, en quelque sorte, plutôt destiné à un discours d'interface entre le monde médical et le grand public. Les données chiffrées extraites du corpus n'ont pas permis de confirmer cette hypothèse : le terme « recherche de transfert » apparaît aussi dans la partie spécialisée du corpus, et le terme « recherche translationnelle », bien que majoritairement présent dans la partie spécialisée, se trouve aussi assez fréquemment dans la partie contenant des documents destinés au grand public :

Tableau 2 : nombre d'occurrences pour les termes « recherche translationnelle » et « recherche de transfert » dans chaque partie du corpus.

Terme candidat	**Occurr./ corpus**	**Occurr./ textes spécialisés**	**Occurr./ textes destinés au grand public**
recherche translationnelle	325	209	116
recherche de transfert	173	78	95

Une seconde hypothèse reposait sur l'idée que ces deux termes, bien qu'apparemment utilisés dans le même type de documents, étaient peut-être employés, à l'intérieur de ces documents, dans des contextes différents et que les auteurs, en choisissant l'un plutôt que l'autre, mettaient en avant des informations différentes sur le concept, en quelque sorte s'exprimaient sur des traits conceptuels qui n'étaient pas les mêmes. Si elle s'avérait exacte, cette hypothèse tendrait à montrer en outre que les experts, loin d'utiliser leur terminologie professionnelle de façon passive, peuvent au contraire faire preuve d'un « sentiment linguistique»[6] averti et choisir les termes qu'ils emploient avec des intentions de communication bien précises. Comme le note Rogers (219) : « It is often assumed [...] that the author's use of synonyms rather than a single preferred term is arbitrary and by implication sloppy. But this is an assumption which requires investigation ».

L'idée selon laquelle les experts utilisent les variantes terminologiques à leur disposition de façon raisonnée n'est pas nouvelle, et a été décrite, notamment, par Temmerman (2000), qui montre que les biologistes utilisent telle ou telle variante terminologique pour décrire la technique du Southern blot en fonction de l'élément d'information qu'ils veulent accentuer :

> *[...] The naming of Southern's technique is motivated by—at least—three aspects of the (encyclopaedic) information concerning the technique. Depending on which of the three elements a language user wants to stress in a particular context the use of one or another of the synonyms can be appropriate for more nuanced communication* (151).

Enfin, selon Bowker et Hawkins (97), « different people prioritized different characteristics of a concept, which may result in different designations for that concept ».

Pour tester notre seconde hypothèse, nous avons recherché, dans notre corpus, les «préférences sémantiques » des deux termes à l'étude. Le principe des « préférences sémantiques » (*semantic preferences*) a été développé, pour la langue générale, par Sinclair (1987), puis a été repris par d'autres, notamment Louw (1993), Stubbs (2001), Partington (2004) et Blumentahl (2008). Il repose sur l'idée que certains termes peuvent montrer une « préférence » pour une famille de termes sémantiquement proches, avec lesquels ils sont associés, parfois en co-occurrence, selon une fréquence plus élevée que le simple hasard, et que cette préférence sémantique conduit à les utiliser dans des contextes plutôt que d'autres. Selon Partington (145) : « *semantic preference [is] the relation not between individual words, but between a lemma or word-form and a set of semantically related words* ». Pour Stubbs (65) : « *an item shows semantic preference when it co-occurs with a class of words which share some semantic feature* ». Nous avons donc examiné de très près, dans notre corpus, la rencontre non-fortuite de deux mots ou plutôt d'un mot et d'une famille de mots sémantiquement liés, et recherché ainsi les préférences sémantiques des termes à l'étude pour repérer les points communs et les différences éventuelles qui orienteraient l'utilisation de telle ou telle variante terminologique.

Des préférences sémantiques différentes

Les données extraites de notre corpus nous ont permis d'identifier trois familles principales de préférences sémantiques[7] pour le terme « recherche translationnelle ».

Une première préférence sémantique va aux termes et aux expressions rendant compte du caractère novateur du concept : dans ce cas, « recherche translationnelle » se trouve en compagnie des termes « nouvelle approche / voie émergente / approche innovante / nouveau paradigme / élaboration de nouvelles voies thérapeutiques / booster d'innovation / s'appuyant notamment sur les techniques modernes ».

On trouve par exemple le contexte suivant dans le corpus :

> *La recherche translationnelle est également une approche innovante dans la mise au point de nouveaux médicaments et des traitements qui centrent la recherche sur de nouveaux tests pour le diagnostic et la surveillance des maladies humaines* (Ashton-Chess et al. 10).

Une seconde préférence sémantique va aux termes et aux expressions véhiculant l'idée d'un transfert rapide et efficace des connaissances : - dans ce cas, on trouve le terme « recherche translationnelle » dans le voisinage immédiat des termes « facilite le transfert rapide entre / pour valider et transférer rapidement les techniques / transmission rapide de la connaissance entre / transfert rapide des connaissances vers / démarche efficace de transfert/ se réfère typiquement à la translation rapide et efficace », comme dans l'extrait suivant :

> *La recherche translationnelle porte sur le transfert rapide de connaissance ou de technologie, nécessairement innovant et, toujours en connexion avec un aspect de la biologie, vers les soins innovants* (Vassal 1107).

Enfin, une dernière préférence sémantique de « recherche translationnelle » va aux termes et aux expressions soulignant le caractère indispensable de cette recherche : on trouve ainsi « recherche translationnelle » en compagnie des termes « est la clef du succès / est un outil essentiel pour / est le chaînon manquant / son apport indispensable aux applications tangibles / aboutissement idéal du processus ». On trouve dans le corpus des contextes du type :

> *La Recherche Translationnelle est le chaînon manquant entre la Recherche Fondamentale et la Recherche Clinique* (Sigaux 196).

Qu'en est-il pour le terme « recherche de transfert » ? Partage-t-il les mêmes préférences sémantiques ? L'extraction de données issues du corpus montre que les préférences sémantiques de « recherche de transfert » sont radicalement différentes de celles de « recherche translationnelle ». Si le terme « recherche de transfert » tout comme « recherche translationnelle », apparait en compagnie de termes indiquant l'idée d'un transfert rapide des connaissances, il apparait peu ou pas en compagnie de termes indiquant le caractère novateur et indispensable de la recherche. En revanche, il est utilisé par les auteurs en association avec des termes indiquant très nettement l'idée d'intégration et de collaboration, comme par exemple « incorporation de technologies issues d'autres disciplines / interaction continue entre / programmes de recherches en collaboration / diverses équipes impliquées (dans la recherche de transfert)/études conjointes (de recherche de transfert)/s'enrichir d'une collaboration avec / une recherche intégrée au sein des hôpitaux / requiert l'implication forte et la collaboration des scientifiques et des médecins / étroite collaboration entre / assure un continuum entre ».

On trouve ainsi dans le corpus :

> *Une recherche de transfert efficace en cancérologie nécessite l'intégration d'un ensemble constitué de structures de recherche d'amont de qualité, d'un hôpital de notoriété incontestable dans la prise en charge des cancers et d'une structure de coordination* (Couderc et al. 344).

En guise de conclusion

Il nous apparaît donc que l'utilisation par les experts des termes « recherche translationnelle » et « recherche de transfert » n'est pas anodine ; elle semble montrer au contraire l'existence d'un « sentiment linguistique » chez les auteurs du corpus qui s'exprime, par exemple, par l'emploi raisonné d'une variante terminologique plutôt qu'une autre afin de nuancer leur communication et mettre en avant des informations différentes sur le concept.

Par conséquent, pour le traducteur, opter systématiquement pour la standardisation terminologique à l'intérieur d'un texte ou d'un groupe de textes, peut ne pas être un bon réflexe de traduction, comme le notent Bowker et Hawkins (84) : « *[translators] may be tempted to overrule the lexical choices made by a subject field expert in order to conform to standards, and this could have unfortunate results* ». Cette nécessité pour le traducteur de ne pas choisir la facilité en optant pour l'uniformisation terminologique est d'autant plus grande lorsqu'il s'agit d'un domaine émergent, dans lequel les besoins de communication et de transmission sont importants.

Sur le plan terminologique, on remarque que l'introduction d'un nouveau concept peut provoquer, par « effet rebond », l'apparition d'autres nouveaux concepts qui lui sont liés, complexifiant ainsi la tâche du traducteur : les contextes extraits de la partie anglaise du corpus montrent en effet qu'un concept nouveau lié à la « recherche translationnelle *», qui est celui de la médecine des « omiques » (omics*) est en train d'émerger dans les milieux médicaux, provoquant ainsi l'apparition d'une nouvelle famille de termes à traduire, comme *genomics*, *proteomics*, *transcriptomics*, etc.

> *Translational science is on the brink of generating a major revolution in medicine, thanks to advances in "omics", a term encompassing "genomics" (genetic complement),*

"transcriptomics" (gene expression), "proteomics" (protein synthesis and signalling), "metabolomics" (concentration andfluxes of cellular metabolites), "metabonomics" (systemic profiling through analysis of biological fluids) and "pharmacogenomics" (application of genomic information either to develop new drug therapies, tailor therapies for specific populations and/ordevelop new diagnostic tools) (Plebani 23) .

De la même façon, dans la partie française du corpus, des éléments contextuels indiquent que le concept de « médecine personnalisée » est en train d'émerger dans les milieux médicaux qui pratiquent la « recherche translationnelle » : *« Le développement d'une* nouvelle *« médecine personnalisée » pourrait donc dépendre, du moins en partie, de telles plateformes translationnelle »* (Hofman et al. 51).

Dans les années à venir, le traducteur devra, de toute évidence, participer à la diffusion de la terminologie propre à ces concepts émergents, en sélectionnant, utilisant, réutilisant, proposant parfois les équivalents de traduction qui semblent les plus pertinents et en cela, il se fait passeur de savoir et participe à la transmission des connaissances, dans notre cas médical.

Références bibliographiques

Ashton-Chess &al. « De nouveaux marqueurs biologiques de la tolérance chez l'homme ? ». *Le courrier de la transplantation* IX, 1 (2009) : 6–13.

Blumenthal, P. « Histoire de mots : affinités (s)électives ». *Actes du Congrès Mondial de Linguistique Française, CMLF'*08, (2008) : 31–46. http://www.linguistiquefrancaise.org/articles/cmlf/abs/2008/01/cmlf08338/cmlf08338.html

Bowker L. & S. Hawkins. "Variation in the organization of medical terms. Exploring some motivations for term choice". *Terminology* 12,1 (2006) : 79–110.

Corvol, P. « Le système rénine-angiotensine, un exemple de recherche translationnelle ». *Actualités Néphrologiques* (2006) : 49–50.

Couderc & al. « Cancer et vieillissement ». *M*édecine thérapeutique 16, 4 (2010) : 340–345.

De Azambuja & al. « La nouvelle génération des études cliniques sur le cancer du sein : la bonne drogue et la bonne cible ». *Bull Cancer* 95,1 (2008) : 352–357.

Dine, G. « Recherche translationnelle et biologie clinique ». *Biotribune magazine* 34 (2010) : 3–4.

Fontana & al. « Translational research in infectious disease: current paradigms and challenges ahead ». *Translational Research* (2012): 1–24.

Guilbaud & al. «Rôle de l'imagerie non invasive du petit animal dans le développement des medicaments anticancéreux ». *Bull Cancer* 92,1 (2005) : 45–57.

Hofman & al. « Les biobanques en France : enjeux et contraintes ». *Revue Francophone des Laboratoires* 418 (2010) : 49–53.

Hunston, S. et G. Thompson. Eds. *Evaluation in Text: Authorial Stance and the Construction ofDiscourse*. Oxford : Oxford University Press, 2000.

Institut de Cancérologie. « La recherche translationnelle, pour un transfert rapide des connaissances vers des applications diagnostiques et thérapeutiques », conférence de presse du jeudi 14 septembre 2006, Villejuif. Dossier de presse (2006) : 1–20.

Jobard & al. «La métabolomique : un nouvel outil pour la recherche translationnelle en cancérologie». *Biotribune magazine* 36 (2010) : 24–29.

Louw, B. «Irony in the text or insincerity in the writer? The diagnostic potential of semantic prosodies». *Text and Technology: In Honour of John Sinclair*. Eds. Baker, Mona, Francis Gill & Elena Tognini-Bonelli. Amsterdam: Benjamins, 1993. 157–176.

Moonen, G. « Sur des pensers nouveaux faisons des vers antiques (A. Chenier) », allocution du Professeur Gustave Moonen, Rev Med Liège 66, 9 (2011) : 461–463.

Partington, A. « Utterly content in each other's company: semantic prosody and semantic preference ». *International Journal of Corpus Linguistics* 9, 1 (2004): 131–156.

Picton A. et P. Dury « Les discours d'expertise en langues de spécialité : le point de vue du terminologue », Actes du colloque international *L'écriture experte : enjeux sociaux et scientifiques*. Sherbrooke, 13-14-15 juin 2013 (à paraître).

Plebani, M. «The changing scenario in laboratory medicine and the role of laboratory professionals in translational medicine», *Clinica Chimica Acta* 393 n.1 (2008) : 23–26.

Rogers, M. « Synonymy and Equivalence in Special-language Texts: A Case Study in German and English Texts on Genetic Engineering ». *Text Typology and Translation*. Trosborg A. Amsterdam: Benjamins Publishing, 1997.

Sinclair, J. «The lexical item». *Contrastive Lexical Semantics*. Ed. E. Weigand. Amsterdam: Benjamins Publishing 1998.

Sinclair, J. *Looking up: An Account of the COBUILD Project in Lexical Computing and the Development of the Collins COBUILD English Language Dictionary*, London, Collins, 1987.

Sigaux, F. « Les tumorothèques, ressources majeures pour la recherche sur le cancer et la prise en charge des patients ». *Bull Cancer* 93, numéro spécial (2006), 195–196.

Stubbs, M. *Words and Phrases*. Oxford: Blackwell, 2001.

Temmerman, R. *Towards New Ways of Terminology Description, the socio-cognitive approach*. Amsterdam: Benjamins Publishing, 2000.

Thaunat & al. « Un exemple de recherche translationnelle en transplantation : néogenèse lymphoïde au cours du rejet chronique ». *Le Courrier de la Transplantation*, IX, 1 : 14–17.

Thervert, E. « Recherche translationnelle : effet de mode ou réalité ? ». *Le Courrier de la transplantation* IX, 1 (2009) : 3–5.

Vassal & al. « Recherche translationnelle et plan Cancer ». *Bull Cancer* 94, vol. 12 (2007) : 1107–1111.

Sites internet cités

France Terme : http://www.franceterme.culture.gouv.fr/FranceTerme/. Dernière date de consultation : 17/06/2013.

Plan Cancer 2009–2013 : http://www.plan-cancer.gouv.fr/images/stories/fichiers/plancancer20092013_02112009.pdf. Dernière date de consultation : 17/06/2013.

Site santé du Ministère des Affaires sociales et de la Santé. http://www.sante.gouv.fr/contrats-hospitaliers-de-recherche-translationnelle-chrt.html. Dernière date de consultation : 17/06/2013.

TermoStat Web TM 3.0. http://olst.ling.umontreal.ca/~drouinp/termostat_web/. Dernière date de consultation : 18/06/2013.

Wordsmith Tools. http://www.lexically.net/wordsmith/. Dernière date de consultation : 18/06/2013.

Notes

1 On trouve ainsi, dans l'objectif 5 du nouveau Plan Cancer 2014–2019 :

il est impératif d'amplifier l'effort en faveur de la recherche clinique en continuité avec la recherche translationnelle, de faire évoluer les dispositifs encadrant l'évaluation et la valorisation des nouveaux médicaments, et d'accélérer les processus de reconnaissance des actes innovants.

2 Université de Strasbourg, Unité de Physiopathologie et Médecine Translationnelle, http://www-ulpmed.u-strasbg.fr/medecine/recherche/equipes_EA-4438.htm

Université de Nantes, « thérapie génique translationnelle des maladies neuromusculaires et de la rétine », http://www.medecine.univ-nantes.fr/90193/0/fiche___laboratoire/

Institut de cancérologie Gustave Roussy de Villejuif, « laboratoire de recherche translationnelle », http://www.gustaveroussy.fr/fr/page/recherche-translationnelle_4594,

Institut Curie, département de recherche translationnelle, http://curie.fr/fr/recherche/departement-recherche-translationnelle

3 Outil automatique d'acquisition de termes développé par Patrick Drouin de l'Université de Montréal et accessible gratuitement en ligne.

4 Dans les 5 cas restant, les auteurs mentionnent le terme pour relever qu'il leur semble impropre, comme le fait Moonen (461) : « *L'expression* **«médecine translationnelle»** *est dans l'air du temps, tout le monde en parle, mais en l'occurrence, le terme est impropre ».*

5 On peut penser que le succès du terme « recherche translationnelle », outre sa familiarité morphologique avec le terme anglais, repose aussi sur le fait qu'il dégage une « prosodie sémantique » (*semantic prosody*) positive, valorisante, plus technicienne que le terme « recherche de transfert ». L'idée de la « prosodie sémantique » a été développée pour la langue générale par Sinclair (notamment 1998), et repris par d'autres, comme par Partington (2004 : 132) et Hunston et Thompson (2000 : 5) qui décrivent la prosodie sémantique comme « the speaker or writer's attitude or stance towards, viewpoint or feelings about the entities and propositions that he or she is talking about ».

6 Voir aussi à ce sujet Picton, Aurélie et Dury, Pascaline (à paraître).

7 Nous ne conservons ici que les préférences sémantiques qui apparaissent plus de 4 fois dans le corpus.

La construction du corpus d'écrits médico-administratifs *BABELIRIS* : vers une méthodologie de compilation et d'encodage des textes

WARD VAN DE VELDE

Résumé

Cet article décrit les processus de compilation et d'encodage du corpus *Babeliris*, composé de textes issus d'un réseau hospitalier public. Concrètement, l'auteur traite des modalités de collecte documentaire dans le respect des contraintes déontologiques et juridiques, puis présente la manière dont les écrits ont été ventilés. Dans un second temps, il expose le processus « d'*XML*isation » du corpus selon la norme *TEI-P5* en portant un intérêt tout particulier à l'élaboration de l'en-tête.
Mots-clés : corpus, *Babeliris*, compilation, encodage

Abstract

This article describes the compilation and encoding processes used for *Babeliris*, a corpus of texts from a hospital network. In concrete terms, the author first describes how documents were gathered in compliance with ethical and legal restrictions, and how the texts were broken down into sub-corpora. In the second part, the process of *XML*ization of the corpus following the *TEI-P5* standard is presented and focuses on how the headers were produced.
Keywords: corpus, *Babeliris*, compilation, encoding

Le contexte

Le 6 octobre 2012, la Belgique célébrait le dixième anniversaire de l'entrée en vigueur de la *Loi relative aux droits du patient*. Celle-ci stipule que « *la communication avec le patient [doit] se déroule[r] dans une langue claire* » et que « *le patient peut demander que les informations soient confirmées par écrit* » (Ministère). Déjà dans son avis de 1977, l'Ordre des médecins belges énonçait que « *dans le cas où le médecin constate[rait] des troubles de communication lors de ses contacts avec ses patients, il devra[it] faire le nécessaire pour remé-*

dier à cette situation, en faisant appel, par exemple, à un interprète ou en renvoyant le patient chez un confrère parlant la langue de celuici » (14).

Parallèlement, à tous les échelons de la société, des efforts ont été entrepris pour réaménager les soins de santé avec l'idée d'atténuer d'éventuelles inégalités d'accès, d'une part, et de faciliter l'intercompréhension entre le médecin et le patient, d'autre part. L'*Evidence-Based Medecine* (Carretier 3–4), qui cherche à intégrer les préférences du patient dans le choix de sa thérapie, en avait jeté les bases dans les années '80. L'évolution du modèle de soins de santé « paternaliste » (*ibid.* 4) vers un modèle plus ouvert avait alors constitué la seconde grande ligne de fracture de la relation patient-professionnel de la santé.

Dès lors, le respect supposé des dispositions légales et l'expression de la parole citoyenne dans la thérapie laissent à penser qu'à Bruxelles — terrain de nos recherches —, le droit à un accès aisé à des soins de santé transparents serait acquis pour tous. Tant s'en faut. Malgré un bulletin de santé supposé honorable, la population bruxelloise n'est pas égale devant la démarche d'information médicale. Reflet parfois de fortes disparités sociales, économiques ou éducationnelles (Dcboosere et Fiszman) ou d'une méconnaissance de la langue (Maccioni *et al.*), cette inégalité peut aussi tirer son origine de coutumes héritées d'une culture éloignée de la nôtre, autrement dit d'une approche socioculturelle différente.

Résumés très analytiquement, tous ces points convergent vers le constat triste mais bien réel que la patientèle étrangère et/ou allophone semble souvent lésée sur le plan de la santé. L'un des hôpitaux *IRIS* a aussi abondé en ce sens : « *Lors d'un sondage réalisé en* 2009, *la moitié des soignants interrogés ont noté l'impression que les patients d'origine étrangère étaient moins bien pris en charge, notamment du fait de problèmes de communication.* »[1]

Afin de combattre ces inégalités, et affichant une « *volonté réelle d'accueillir au maximum les patients dans leur langue* » (Cliveti 7), ces hôpitaux ont lancé diverses initiatives adaptées à des populations ne maîtrisant pas les langues locales. À côté d'actions ponctuelles (Maccioni *et al.*), ils font ainsi régulièrement appel à des médiateurs interculturels avec pour objectif de « *résoudre, autant que possible, les problèmes liés à la barrière linguistique, aux différences culturelles et aux tensions interethniques* » (SPF), ou recourent à l'interprétation sociale et *ad hoc*, notamment par un référencement intranet des différentes langues parlées par le personnel soignant à solliciter en dernier ressort (Boiketé 10). Les autres actions concernent la formation linguistique continue des intervenants hospitaliers. Enfin, contexte belge oblige, ces hôpitaux ont mis en place des initiatives qui encouragent leur personnel, majoritairement francophone, à apprendre le néerlandais, comme le *Plan Langues* (*ibid.* 9). C'est dans la continuité de cet élan d'amélioration de l'offre hospitalière que s'inscrit le projet *Babeliris*.

La trame du corpus : le projet *Babeliris*[2]

La construction de notre corpus s'inscrit dans le cadre plus vaste de ce projet *Babeliris*. Celui-ci vise à améliorer la communication interculturelle au sein des hôpitaux publics bruxellois du réseau *IRIS*.[3] Ayant pour objectif de couvrir de multiples aspects communicationnels, il se ramifie en deux volets complémentaires : communications orale et écrite. Le premier pan est traité par le *Centrum voor Vaktaal en Communicatie*; le second, par nous-même, attaché au centre de recherche en linguistique appliquée TERMISTI.

S'agissant du volet écrit de la recherche, nous entendons produire des outils d'accompagnement du personnel hospitalier : un *Guide de bonnes pratiques rédactionnelles* en français et en néerlandais destiné aux rédacteurs et aux traducteurs *IRIS*, une banque de textes FR-NL alignés et une base de données terminologique multilingue « à vocation sociale » qui contiendra la langue médico-administrative sur laquelle est susceptible de butter la patientèle.

La nécessité de construire un corpus médico-administratif original

Afin d'appréhender la langue en usage dans les hôpitaux *IRIS*, nous avons décidé de créer un corpus textuel, en l'espèce de textes administratifs et médicaux. De fait, l'étude du langage *lato sensu* ou d'un phénomène linguistique isolé peut s'effectuer soit au départ de présupposés à attester par l'expérience des usagers versée en corpus, soit au départ d'observations empiriques de corpus d'énoncés, desquelles naîtront des théories (Crystal 117). C'est tout le paradoxe des approches « *corpus-driven* » et « *corpus-based* », décrites notamment par Tognini-Bonelli (65–100). Quelle que soit l'approche envisagée, un corpus demeure toujours un objet heuristique qui fait sens au regard des questions que l'on va lui poser (Mayaffre 55–59).

L'idée de constituer un corpus médical n'est pas novatrice en soi. En effet, de nombreux chercheurs ont étayé leurs travaux sur la langue médicale tantôt sur des corpus en diachronie (Vihla 74), tantôt sur des corpus de textes médicaux hybrides—vulgarisés et scientifiques—à l'instar de MEDICOR (*ibid.*), tantôt sur des corpus de textes très spécialisés tel MENELAS (Zweigenbaum). Pour le français, de nombreux corpus ont directement été construits au départ de thésaurus ou de textes spécialisés bilingues ou multilingues produits par des organismes internationaux.[4] Quant aux méthodologies d'élaboration de ces corpus médicaux, on peut citer les travaux de Jacquemart, de Dragos et Jaulent, de Zweigenbaum *et al.* ou encore, plus largement, de Habert *et al.* (143–159) et de Cabré.

Certes, notre enquête de terrain a le mérite d'exister, mais nous ne pouvons nous en inspirer que partiellement en raison de la nature composite de nos textes. En effet, l'élaboration d'un corpus suppose une définition bien établie de la population de textes à retenir et, partant, du dessein de ceux-ci (Cabré 61, Mayaffre 52 et Rastier 32) ainsi que de leur public cible (Biber 243–244). Dans ce cadre, nous avons décidé de ne réunir que les écrits médico-administratifs auxquels est susceptible d'être confronté le patient du réseau *IRIS* : brochures, dépliants, affiches, panneaux, page *Web*, etc. Ce faisant, nous avons écarté les communications internes au personnel et les rapports médicaux.

En raison du caractère original de notre corpus, nous avons opté pour une méthodologie adaptée à nos besoins et un encodage sur mesure de nos écrits. C'est de ces aspects que traitera cet article.

La constitution du corpus

La collecte des documents

La « *perspective sérielle difficilement contournable du corpus* » (Mayaffre 53–55) nous a très vite contraint à envisager la question de la collecte documentaire. Dans le contexte qui était le nôtre, il n'existait pas une infinité de manières de réunir des textes : la meilleure d'entre elles a consisté à se rendre sur le terrain afin de s'enquérir des documents existants puis de définir avec les acteurs hospitaliers[5] la meilleure approche de récolte.

Confronté à une masse de textes sans cesse croissante, nous avons rapidement opéré une sélection, décidant de ne prendre en compte que les écrits en usage, rédigés et publiés par le personnel du réseau *IRIS*. Cette stratégie nous a permis d'écarter les textes publicitaires ou obsolètes, ou encore ceux de l'Office de la naissance et de l'enfance (ONE) par exemple. Par ailleurs, avec la révolution technologique, l'Internet s'est peu à peu révélé une précieuse mine d'informations, si bien que de nombreuses brochures autrefois disponibles sous format papier classique sont désormais consultables en ligne exclusivement. Nous pensons d'emblée aux documents de l'Institut Jules Bordet. Fort de ce constat, il nous a semblé opportun d'inclure dans notre corpus les pages Internet du réseau *IRIS*.

Une élaboration de corpus dans le respect de contraintes déontologiques et juridiques

Habert *et al.* observent que «*peu de corpus sont dans le domaine public sans condition aucune*» (159). Il en est allé de même pour notre corpus *Babeliris*, bien qu'il soit à usage privé. De fait, certains textes requièrent un traitement particulier en termes de réappropriation, car ils sont soumis au régime du *copyright* ou *droits d'auteur*. Le caractère public des documents primaires colligés ne nous a toutefois pas contraint à prendre cette précaution. Ceci étant, nous avons veillé à préciser aux responsables hospitaliers que les écrits demeureraient la propriété du réseau *IRIS*, et que celui-ci disposerait d'un droit de regard sur les textes versés en corpus et d'un pouvoir de décision sur leur mode d'exploitation.

Par ailleurs, certains domaines d'activités traitent de matières sensibles, ce qui pose parfois des problèmes d'ordre juridique et/ou éthique. Au rang de ceux-ci figurent incontestablement la justice et la médecine. Citant le corpus MENELAS pour illustrer cette dernière spécialité, Habert *et al.* écrivent que, même anonymisée, « *la présence de données personnelles peut faire obstacle à la mise à disposition de la communauté* » (163). Attentif à ne pas avoir intégré des écrits confidentiels dans notre corpus et à circonscrire notre étude aux textes du domaine public, nous n'avons pas dû répondre aux préoccupations éthico-déontologiques de l'*IRIS*.

Néanmoins, les enjeux en présence[6] nous ont conduit à rédiger deux documents de nature juridico-descriptive, à caractère contraignant tant pour le réseau *IRIS* que pour nous-même, grâce auxquels nous avons aisément accédé aux écrits pour notre corpus : un accord de coopération, d'une part, et une méthodologie détaillée du projet *Babeliris*, d'autre part.

Un traitement primaire des textes

Très vite, la compilation d'écrits hétéroclites codés en divers formats[7] a soulevé la question de l'encodage textuel. De fait, soucieux de soumettre le corpus à des algorithmes de recherche, nous avons dû transformer les écrits *papier* en documents électroniques exploitables : nous les avons scannés puis numérisés à l'aide du logiciel de reconnaissance optique de caractères *Readiris*™. Ce travail de numérisation, long de sept mois, a été suivi d'une vaste tâche de révision aux fins de rendre lisibles les caractères mal interprétés par l'OCR et de calquer la mise en page des versions numérisées sur celle des écrits originaux. On sait que de mauvais transcodages et découpages textuels peuvent biaiser les résultats d'une analyse logicielle. Ce traitement liminaire des écrits est repris brièvement dans l'en-tête *TEI-P5*:

```
<p>Les textes imprimés ont été récupérés à l'aide du logiciel de reconnaissance optique de
   caractères Readiris™ puis minutieusement vérifiés et sauvegardés au format docx.</p>
<p>Les textes électroniques ont été également vérifiés puis sauvegardés dans ce même
   format.</p>
<p>Les documents ont ensuite été remis en forme selon les normes de la TEI-P5 (Text Encoding
   Initiative) à l'aide du modèle de conversion proposé par le logiciel tei-vesta (commande:
   docxtotei).</p>
```

Comme le suggèrent ces métadonnées, les textes sous format informatisé ont été enregistrés en **.docx** pour en permettre une « *XML*isation » automatisée. Nous les avons parallèlement renommés sur le modèle *Titre du document_Hôpital concerné_Langue_Public cible_Support* *textuel_Visée du document_Date de diffusion*, de manière à les assortir des informations qui les définissent au mieux. Ces métadonnées ont par la suite été insérées automatiquement entre les balises *ad hoc* de l'en-tête *TEI* lors de la phase « d'*XML*isation » des documents.

Le codage XML/TEI du corpus

Depuis les années '80, les chercheurs en TAL se sont intéressés à la question du marquage des corpus. S'il apparaît, à la lumière de leurs études, que les langages de balisage sont nombreux, il nous a fallu trancher pour un codage de textes reconnu et adopté par une large communauté de spécialistes. Le plus approprié à notre recherche est sans conteste le langage *XML*, et en particulier l'une de ses applications, plus adaptée aux exploitations linguistiques en contexte médical (Jacquemart 8) : la spécification *TEI*, dans sa version *P5* (Bauman et Burnard).

D'après celle-ci, tout document est formé d'un en-tête, reprenant les informations à propos de ce document, et d'un corps, contenant le document lui-même (Popescu-Belis 56). Sous un angle purement structurel, cette distinction s'opère au travers d'un jeu de balises hiérarchisées et structurées en arborescence : ainsi l'information descriptive sur le contexte de production et le contenu logique des textes sont respectivement encadrés par les balises `<teiHeader>` (Bauman et Burnard 17–54) et `<body>` (*ibid.* 800–802), à leur tour affinées par des sous-sections et leurs balises correspondantes.

Disposant à ce stade d'une banque de textes renommés et codés en **.docx**, nous avons transformé en masse ceux-ci en **.xml** conformes à la *TEI*, à l'aide de l'outil *Tei Vesta*. Dans le cadre de cette « *XML*isation », les sept métadonnées contenues dans le titre des documents ont été isolées puis injectées aux endroits *ad hoc* de l'en-tête.

La granularité du balisage retenue pour le corpus

Les métadonnées issues de la *TEI-P5* servant à coder le `<body>` peuvent se réduire à annoter un corpus ou un texte tout entier, à encadrer un paragraphe ou une phrase, ou encore à mettre en évidence un mot ou un morphème et, à chaque niveau, un phénomène linguistique ou discursif. En réalité, la granularité retenue pour marquer le corpus dépendra de l'exploitation que l'on envisage de celui-ci. Ce système d'annotation peut, bien entendu, être affiné en cours de recherche (Popescu-Belis 60). Dans le cadre de notre projet, nous nous sommes cantonné à un niveau de codage 1 `<p>`, correspondant au paragraphe (Zweigenbaum *et al.* 292 et Jacquemart 7).

Par ailleurs, à l'instar de Vihla (75), nous avons neutralisé les informations superfétatoires, à ignorer pour une quelconque analyse linguistique : adresses et courriels, contacts et numéros de téléphone, index et tables des matières, bibliographies et références bibliographiques et, enfin, mentions *réseau IRIS structuur* contenues dans le logo de l'*IRIS*. Certes, nous aurions pu adopter un balisage spécifique pour chacun de ces éléments, mais avons finalement choisi une balise générique, l'objectif consistant à masquer ceux-ci sans forme de spécification.

D'après Bauman et Burnard, trois balises *TEI* peuvent coder l'information superflue. En effet, les éléments à neutraliser peuvent être encadrés soit par une balise de commentaires du type `<!-- Passage à masquer -->` ou `<!-- Texte à neutraliser -->` (xxxvi-xxxvii), soit par la balise `<div type="ignore">` (900–902), soit par la balise `<del resp="Ward Van de Velde">` (884–886). À la différence des deux premières balises, la dernière d'entre elles indique que l'annotateur en revendique la paternité. C'est pourquoi nous l'avons retenue. Il convient par ailleurs de souligner que le marquage des données superflues dans le `<body>` a été réalisé de manière automatique.[8] Manquant parfois de précision, il mériterait une vérification manuelle, coûteuse en temps et en moyens.

La taille du corpus Babeliris

Le choix de la balise `<del resp="Ward Van de Velde">` posé, venons-en au volume de notre corpus. Le tableau *infra* mentionne, pour chaque langue officielle de la Région de Bruxelles-Capitale (FR et NL) puis pour les autres langues (EN, DE, ES, IT, SQ et TC), le nombre de documents, le nombre de mots et le nombre moyen de mots par document. La dernière colonne, elle, indique le nombre total de mots vierges d'informations superflues, masquées à l'aide de la balise `<del resp="Ward Van de Velde">`.

Tableau 1 - Taille du corpus *Babeliris*

Langue	**Nombre de documents**	**Nombre de mots**	**Nombre moyen de mots / document**	**Nombre de mots** `<del resp>`
Français	1126	531580	473	522491
Néerlandais	720	304348	423	300980
Autres langues	219	93808	428	92555
TOTAL	2065	929736	450	916026

À la lecture de ce tableau, on constate un déficit patent des textes disponibles en néerlandais par rapport au français. En outre, parmi les 1 846 écrits récoltés en français et en néerlandais, 665 écrits sont « alignables ». Cela signifie que 92,4 % des textes disponibles en néerlandais ont fait l'objet d'une traduction vers le français, contre 59,1 % dans l'autre sens.

Ces observations sont surprenantes du fait de la double tentative « *d'accord de courtoisie linguistique* » (Cliveti 6 et Boiketé 8) et de la règle du bilinguisme censément d'application dans les services hospitaliers. Sous réserve d'analyse plus approfondie, on pourrait y déceler une inégalité entre francophones et néerlandophones, qu'il conviendrait de résorber par un renforcement de la traduction vers le néerlandais.

Types et genres de textes : une distinction indispensable pour un compartimentage réussi

De tout temps, la question de la « classification des éléments » s'est posée aux scientifiques. Le domaine médical n'a pas non plus échappé à cette règle : comment hiérarchiser les disciplines médicales et les écrits qui y renvoient? Bien que discutées, les catégorisations textuelles les plus fréquentes sont celles du *type* et du *genre*. Biber opère leur distinction comme suit :

> *I use the terms genre or register to refer to situationally defined text categories (such as fiction, sports broadcasts, psychology articles), and text type to refer to linguistically defined text categories. Both of these text classification systems are valid, but they have different bases. Although registers or genres are not defined on linguistic grounds, there are statistically important linguistic differences among these categories, and linguistic feature counts are relatively stable across texts within a register. In contrast, text types are identified on the basis of shared linguistic co-occurrence patterns, so that the texts within each type are maximally similar in their linguistic characteristics, while the different types are maximally distinct from one another* (244–245).

Comme le précise aussi Lee (38–41), le *genre* exploite des critères externes au texte : contexte ou mode de production, situation d'énonciation, lecteur modèle, mode de publication, visée ou fonction et, surtout, thème ou domaine. Ce compartimentage répond ainsi aux intuitions communes, culturellement validées, de classification. S'appuyant sur les *types* textuels, la seconde catégorisation exploite les traits linguistiques du texte : lexique, syntaxe, recours à certains pronoms ou temps verbaux, etc. Cette catégorisation permet, en réalité, de distinguer à gros grain les livres des dépêches, ou encore les manuscrits des correspondances (Sharoff 3–4), quel qu'en soit le thème. Sa grande faiblesse réside toutefois dans l'élaboration de critères objectifs permettant de rattacher un texte à un type plutôt qu'à un autre.

Selon cette partition textuelle *a priori* et *a posteriori* (Habert), un même écrit peut ressortir à un seul genre, mais relever de deux ou plusieurs types, et inversement. Dans son article (37–39), Lee préfère la subdivision en genres, pragmatique et utile sur les plans théorique et pédagogique, et moins « fourre-tout » que la classification en types.

Par ailleurs, les genres, écrit-il, jouissent d'une légitimité *per se* auprès des spécialistes. De son côté, Biber (245) opte aussi pour un regroupement par genres, plus faciles à identifier au stade de l'élaboration du corpus en raison de critères externes. Jacquemart s'inscrit également dans cette lignée, mais concède que « *l'existence de types textuels distincts paraît intuitivement fondée, [quoique] délicate à étayer empiriquement* » (5). Enfin, si Atkins, Clear et Ostler (cités par Lee : 39) priorisent la relation qui unit le texte à son contexte de production, Sinclair précise que la dimension sociologique doit avoir préséance (7). La classification en genres paraît donc bien s'imposer.

Dans la sphère médicale, de nombreux travaux s'en sont inspirés. Zweigenbaum (291) liste ainsi 57 genres médicaux, fondés sur les situations de communication. Cabré, elle, recourt à une partition en 14 genres, basée sur le domaine, pour les textes médicaux de son corpus technique pentalingue. Tout écrit médical *stricto sensu* peut aussi intégrer l'une des rubriques de l'annuaire médical *CISMeF*. C'est de celui-ci que s'est inspiré Jacquemart (16) pour établir sa taxinomie des spécialités médicales dans le cadre de la constitution de son corpus.

Néanmoins, peu convaincu de l'applicabilité de ces classifications à notre étude, nous nous sommes tourné vers les catégorisations de la législation belge et la classification décimale universelle, sans toutefois nous en accommoder. Dès lors, nous avons composé notre propre taxinomie, souhaitant nous rapprocher du fonctionnement interne des hôpitaux *IRIS* (ou représenter au mieux tous les départements existants) et inclure des aspects (para)médicaux, administratifs, infirmiers et sociaux dans une seule liste. C'est ainsi que nous avons composé le ***Tableau 2***, qui rattache chaque écrit à un seul service et à une seule unité, alors même que nous sommes conscient qu'un texte peut relever de deux unités et, plus rarement, de deux services. Habert avait, lui aussi, dressé ce constat, argüant que « *les catégories ne s'excluent pas forcément [...] ou semblent être en intersection* ».

La *TEI-P5* ne prévoyant pas de balises spécifiques aux genres textuels, nous avons recouru à la balise générique pour termes techniques `<term>` (Bauman et Burnard 1377–1379), que nous avons insérée à l'endroit *ad hoc* de notre en-tête.

Tableau 2-Domaines retenus pour le corpus *Babeliris*, à insérer entre la balise <term>

Services	**Unités**
Administratif et logistique	Accueil—admission—consultation; archivage médical—bibliothèque; droits, devoirs et protection du patient (service juridique et contentieux); hygiène hospitalière; informatique—pages *Web*; médiation—communication—relations publiques; médiation interculturelle; service social; trésorerie—facturation; non catégorisé
Infirmier	Soins infirmiers
Médical	Anatomie pathologique et cytogénétique; anesthésiologie—réanimation; biologie clinique et prélèvements; cardiologie—chirurgie cardiaque; chirurgie cervico-faciale et thoracique; chirurgie mammaire et pelvienne; chirurgie plastique, réparatrice et esthétique; chirurgie vasculaire; dermatologie; endocrinologie; gériatrie; gynécologie—obstétrique—périnéologie—prénatale; hémato-oncologie—dépistage et prévention du cancer—cancérologie mammaire; hépato-gastro-entérologie—chirurgie digestive et abdominale; hôpital de jour; immuno-allergologie; infectiologie—maladies infectieuses; maladies tropicales; médecine interne; néonatalogie; néphrologie—dialyse; neurologie—neurochirurgie; ophtalmologie; ORL; orthopédie—traumatologie—chirurgie orthopédique; pédiatrie; pneumologie—tabacologie—médecine du sommeil; psychiatrie; radio-isotopes—médecine nucléaire; radiologie—imagerie médicale; recherche hospitalière—éthique; revalidation locomotrice, neurologique et cardio-pulmonaire; rhumatologie; sénologie; sexologie—urologie; soins supportatifs, continus et palliatifs; soins intensifs—urgences; stomatologie—dentisterie—orthodontie—chirurgie maxillo-faciale; non catégorisé
Paramédical	Diététique—nutrition; ergothérapie; kinésithérapie—ostéopathie; logopédie; pharmacie; psychologie

L'élaboration de l'en-tête TEI

Nous savons qu'un texte codé en *TEI* s'articule autour d'un `<body>` et d'un `<teiHeader>`, préférentiellement unique, fournissant des métadonnées sur le document en question. En réalité, l'en-tête « *donne des informations descriptives et déclaratives qui constituent une page de titre électronique au début de tout texte conforme à la TEI* » (*ibid.* 18). Son objectif est simple, et bien circonscrit dans la *TEI-P5 :*

> *The TEI header describes an encoded work so that the text itself, its source, its encoding, and its revisions are all thoroughly documented. Such documentation is equally necessary for scholars using the texts, for software processing them, and for cataloguers in libraries and archives. Together these descriptions and declarations provide an electronic analogue to the title page attached to a printed work. They also constitute an equivalent for the content of the code books or introductory manuals customarily accompanying electronic data sets* (*ibid.* 17).

Tout en-tête *TEI* se subdivise en quatre éléments : « *text itself* », « *source* », « *encoding* » et « *revision* ». Se succédant toujours dans le même ordre, ceux-ci se ramifient en sous-rubriques, en vertu de la structure arborescente du langage *XML*, et sont structurés à l'aide des balises (*ibid.* 18) :

`<fileDesc>` : contient une description bibliographique du fichier électronique ;

`<encodingDesc>` : documente la relation d'un texte électronique avec sa (ou ses) source(s) ;

`<profileDesc>` : décrit les aspects non bibliographiques du texte (langues utilisées et variantes, circonstances de production, collaborateurs et statut) ;

`<revisionDesc>` : fournit un résumé de l'historique des révisions d'un fichier.

Concrètement, le recours à ces éléments et surtout aux balises qui leur sont subordonnées doit permettre de travailler sur corpus de manière sélective suivant un (ou plusieurs) paramètre(s) de recherche et, partant, de générer des sous-corpus de travail. À côté des balises « fixes » utilisées pour tout document, il nous a ainsi fallu réfléchir aux autres balises à insérer dans notre en-tête *TEI*, spécifiques à chaque texte, lesquelles encadreront les variables à mettre en évidence—et que Biber comme Sinclair nomment «*dimensions*».[9] En réalité, il s'agit des sept méta-informations dégagées au moment de renommer les textes avant «*XML*isation». Le ***Tableau 3*** reprend ces «*dimensions*», les met en correspondance avec l'une de ces métadonnées, en précise la balise-mère parmi les quatre citées *supra* et en spécifie la référence dans la *TEI-P5 :*

Tableau 3[10] - « *Dimensions* » retenues pour le corpus *Babeliris*

Balise	**Métadonnée correspondante**	**Balise-mère**	**Référence *TEI***
<title>xxx</title>	Titre de l'écrit	<fileDesc>	pp. 1390–1392
<publisher>xxx</publisher>	Hôpital d'où émane l'écrit	<fileDesc>	pp. 1232–1233
<date when-iso="xxxx"/>	Année de diffusion de l'écrit (date à quatre chiffres)	<fileDesc>	pp. 875–877
<change who="iris hospitals" when-iso="xxxx"/>		<revisionDesc>	pp. 831–833
<language ident="xx"> xxx</language>	Langue de rédaction de l'écrit[10]	<profileDesc>	pp. 1071–1072
<channel>xxx</channel>	Support textuel (brochure, dépliant, affiche, page *Web*, formulaire, ordonnance, autre)	<profileDesc>	pp. 833–834
<interaction passive= "group">xxx </interaction>	Public cible (patient, responsable, non défini, autre)	<profileDesc>	pp. 1048–1050
<purpose type="xxx"/>	Visée de l'écrit (injonctif : "persuade", informatif : "inform")	<profileDesc>	pp. 1233–1234

Afin de disposer d'un balisage cohérent, nous avons décidé, comme le prévoient Bauman et Burnard (*ibid.* XLIII), de nommer en anglais les attributs et de rédiger en français le texte appelé à figurer entre balises. Voici un fragment de notre en-tête, centré autour de la balise <profileDesc> :

```
<teiHeader>
 <fileDesc> [...]
 </fileDesc>
 <encodingDesc> [...]
 </encodingDesc>
 <profileDesc> [...]
  <langUsage>
   <language ident="NL">néerlandais</language>
  </langUsage>
  <textClass>
   <keywords scheme="www.babeliris.org">
    <term>Service médical</term>
    <term>Ophtalmologie</term>
   </keywords>
  </textClass>
  <textDesc>
   <channel>dépliant</channel>
   <constitution type="single"/>
   <derivation type="original"/>
   <domain type="medicine"/>
   <factuality type="fact"/>
   <interaction passive="group">patient</interaction>
   <preparedness/>
   <purpose type="persuade"/>
  </textDesc>
 </profileDesc>
 <revisionDesc status="approved">
 </revisionDesc>
</teiHeader>
```

Enfin, nous avons veillé à ce que tous les documents aient été bien formés, et avons donc vérifié leur syntaxe—tant au niveau du <teiHeader> que du <body>—par l'éditeur *XML Oxygen*™. Une fois ce travail effectué, notre corpus était prêt pour l'analyse linguistique.

Conclusion et perspectives

De nos jours, l'étude empirique d'une langue repose souvent sur l'exploitation d'un corpus de textes aux contours bien définis. L'analyse de la langue en usage dans les hôpitaux du réseau *IRIS*, hermétique aux yeux de certains, n'a en rien échappé à ce *modus operandi*.

L'originalité de notre corpus, née du brassage de documents médicaux et administratifs, nous a toutefois contraint à mettre au point notre propre méthodologie. Dans ce cadre, le respect de contraintes déontologiques et juridiques s'est avéré crucial dans nos démarches de collecte documentaire. Nous avons ensuite dû concevoir une méthode de compartimentage textuel à la lumière des études existantes et avons aménagé celle fondée sur la partition en *genres*. Après informatisation des écrits, nous avons procédé à leur « *XML*isation » et les avons surmontés d'un en-tête *TEI-P5*, dans lequel sept *dimensions* ont été injectées automatiquement entre balises de manière à pouvoir travailler sur le corpus de manière sélective. Après quoi seulement notre collection de textes informatisée était prête pour l'analyse linguistique.

Les possibilités d'exploitation de notre corpus sont nombreuses : nous pourrions imaginer générer des sous-corpus en vue d'étudier, par exemple, les traits linguistiques propres à chaque hôpital *IRIS* ou à chaque support textuel, ou, après alignement des textes FR-NL, les procédés de traduction spécifiques au réseau *IRIS*. En réalité, ce sont toutes ces questions que nous approfondirons à l'avenir.

Références bibliographiques

Bauman, Syd et Burnard, Lou. *TEI-P5: Guidelines for Electronic Text Encoding*. Charlottesville, version 2.0.2., 2012.

Biber, Douglas. « Representativeness in Corpus Design ». *Literacy and Linguistic Computing* 8/4, OUP. 1993. 243–257.

Boiketé, Philippe. *État de la question. Emploi des langues à Bruxelles : mieux tenir compte de la réalité sociologique bruxelloise,* rapport commandité par la Fédération Wallonie-Bruxelles et réalisé par l'Institut Emile Vandervelde. Bruxelles, 2011.

Cabré, Maria Teresa. « Constituir un corpus de textos de especialidad: condiciones y posibilidades », *Les corpus en linguistique et en traductologie*). Arras : APU, 2007. 89–106.

Carretier, Julien *et al.* « Du langage expert au langage patient : vers une prise en compte des préférences des patients dans la démarche informationnelle entre les professionnels de santé et les patients ». *Sciences croisées* 6 2009.

Cliveti, Minodora. *L'accès aux soins et les problèmes linguistiques dans la région de Bruxelles-Capitale en Belgique*, rapport du Conseil de l'Europe, 2005.

Crystal, David. *A Dictionary of Linguistics and Phonetics*. Oxford: Blackwell Publishing, 2008.

Deboosere, Patrick et Fiszman, Pénélope. « Inégalités sociales et spatiales de santé en Région bruxelloise ». *Environnement et inégalités écologiques*. Bruxelles : PUB, 2007. 136–145

Dragos, Valetina et Jaulent, Marie-Christine. « Construction d'un corpus biomédical pour la recherche d'informations ». *Actes de la 8e conférence internationale « Terminologie et Intelligence Artificielle »*. Toulouse, 2009.

Habert, Benoît *et al. Les linguistiques de corpus*. U Linguistique, Paris : Masson et Armand Colin, 1997.

Habert, Benoît. « Des corpus représentatifs : de quoi, pour quoi, comment ? ». *Linguistique sur corpus. Études et réflexions*. Perpignan : PUP, 2000. 11–58.

ISO 639-1. *Codes pour la représentation des noms de langue. Partie* 1 *: Code alpha*-2. Genève : Organisation internationale de normalisation, 2002.

Jacquemart, Pierre. *Conception d'un corpus de textes médicaux*, rapport de stage effectué dans le laboratoire DIAM–SIM / DSI / AP-HP sous la direction de Zweigenbaum, Pierre, Paris, *s.d.*

Lee, David YW. « Genres, Registers, Text Types, Domains, and Styles: Clarifying the Concepts and Navigating a Path through the BNC Jungle ». *Language Learning & Technology* 5/3 2001. 37–72.

Maccioni, Johanna *et al.* « Accompagnement multiculturel de patients étrangers ». *Comprenne qui pourra* 289. Disponible sur http://www.cbai.be/revuearticle/566/.

Mayaffre, Damon. « Les corpus réflexifs : entre architextualité et hypertextualité », *Corpus* 1 2002. 51–70.

Ministère des Affaires sociales, de la Santé publique et de l'Environnement. *Loi relative aux droits du patient*, publiée au Moniteur belge le 26 septembre 2002 : 43719–43724.

Ordre belge des médecins. *Emploi des langues en pratique médicale*. 1977.

Popescu-Belis, Andrei. « Constitution de banques de textes multilingues : un mécanisme fondé sur le standard XML ». *Cahiers du Rifal* 23 2003. 56–60, Paris.

Rastier, François. « Enjeux épistémologiques de la linguistique de corpus ». *La linguistique de corpus*. Rennes : PUR, 2005. 31-45.

Sharoff, Serge. « Towards Basic Categories for Describing Properties of Texts in a Corpus ». Présenté à *Language Resources and Evaluation Conference* 2004, Lisbonne.

Sinclair, John. *Preliminary Recommendations on Corpus Typology*, rapport technique, EAGLES, Birmingham, 1996.

Service public fédéral — Santé publique, sécurité de la chaîne alimentaire et environnement. *Cellule Médiation interculturelle et Support de la politique*, dépliant remis aux patients du CHU Saint-Pierre, *s.d.*

Tognini-Bonelli, Elena. *Corpus Linguistics at Work*, Amsterdam: John Benjamin's Publishing, 2001.

Vihla, Minna. « MEDICOR: A Corpus of Contemporany American Medical Texts », *ICAME Journal* 22 1998: 73–80.

Zweigenbaum, Pierre. « MENELAS: An Access System for Medical Records Using Natural Language », *Computer Methods and Programs in Biomedicine* 45 1994: 117–120.

Zweigenbaum, Pierre *et al.* « Building a Text Corpus for Representing the Variety of Medical Language », *Medinfo* 2001. Lancaster : Proceedings Corpus Linguistics. 290–294.

Notes

1 Information tirée de la page http://www.chu-brugmann.be/fr/med/hematonco/multicultur.asp du CHU Brugmann.

2 Plus d'informations sur http://babeliris.be/.

3 Plus d'informations sur http://www.iris-hopitaux.be/fr/index.asp?ID=75.

4 Par exemple de l'*Agence européenne des médicaments* (*EMA*).

5 Par « acteurs hospitaliers », nous entendons le personnel *IRIS* avec lequel la patientèle étrangère ou allophone entre en contact dès son admission à l'hôpital : responsables de l'accueil, médiateurs interculturels et membres du service des urgences. Néanmoins, ce premier réseau de contacts s'est étoffé avec l'intégration d'infirmières, de responsables qualité, etc.

6 À savoir la crainte du personnel *IRIS* de savoir ses productions critiquées quand bien même nous n'avons guère l'intention d'en faire le procès, aspirant tout simplement à leur amélioration par la production de matériaux didactiques concrets.

7 Nous avons rassemblé des écrits sous différents formats « papier », .doc, .docx, .htm, .html, .pdf, .ppt et .pub.

8 Ces annotations ont été ajoutées par Cédric Libert, jeune linguiste de l'Université catholique de Louvain-la-Neuve (Belgique), qui se spécialise en informatique.

9 Pour une illustration de ces « *dimensions* », voir Zweigenbaum (293) ou Habert (152–153).

10 Eu égard aux spécifications de la norme ISO 639-1 : FR, NL, EN, DE, ES, IT, AL et TC.

La chimie organique : une science en mouvement

Sandrine Peraldi

Résumé

La présente communication aborde les phénomènes de créativité lexicale propres à la chimie organique. La présence d'une nomenclature chimique associée à de constantes activités normalisatrices a incité quelques rares auteurs à analyser les éléments nomenclaturaux à l'origine de la langue de la chimie, d'un point de vue diachronique ou synchronique. En revanche, aucune étude outillée sur corpus n'avait été proposée jusqu'à présent, s'agissant des processus de néologie et de construction de sens en discours. Nous proposons donc de passer en revue ces procédés selon trois angles spécifiques : en observant le fonctionnement de la nomenclature IUPAC en discours ; au travers de l'étude des formants morphosyntaxiques ; enfin, à l'aune des termes complexes de la chimie organique.

Mots-clés : chimie organique, terminologie textuelle, créativité lexicale, variation terminologique, indétermination, nomenclature, formants morphosyntaxiques

Abstract

The research presented in this paper explores the phenomena of lexical creativity in the field of organic chemistry. The existence of an international nomenclature and numerous standardizing activities in chemistry have prompted a small number of linguists to analyze the nomenclature principles that underlie chemical language, from a diachronic or synchronic point of view. However, no large-scale corpus-oriented analysis has ever investigated formal and semantic neology within chemical discourse. This article describes these lexical-creative processes from three perspectives: by observing the functioning of the IUPAC nomenclature in discourse; through the analysis of morpho-syntactic formants; and lastly, in light of complex terms.

Keywords: organic chemistry, textual terminology, lexical creativity, terminological variation, indeterminacy, nomenclature, morphosyntactic formants

Problématique et cadre théorique

Le présent article, qui relève de recherches doctorales menées en terminologie et en linguistique de corpus, propose de s'intéresser aux phénomènes de créativité lexicale propres à la chimie organique. Une créativité lexicale qui permet à cette discipline de s'adapter rapidement aux incessantes innovations qui la caractérisent et de remplir sa fonction de transmission des connaissances scientifiques. La présence d'une nomenclature chimique associée à de constantes activités normalisatrices au sein de la discipline a incité certains auteurs (Verkade 1985, Loening 1986, Sager 1990, Godly 1993, Cottez 1997, Deyne 1997, Gaudin 2007 - peu nombreux au demeurant - à analyser les éléments nomenclaturaux à l'origine de la langue de la chimie, à la fois d'un point de vue diachronique (en s'intéressant notamment à la nomenclature chimique de Lavoisier) et synchronique (via l'étude de la nomenclature IUPAC). En revanche, aucune étude de grande envergure, c'est-à-dire menée par le biais d'une exploration outillée sur corpus, n'avait été proposée jusqu'à présent, s'agissant des processus de néologie et de construction de sens dans le discours même de la chimie. En l'occurrence, c'est la volonté de mettre en évidence deux autres tendances méconnues en terminologie qui ont permis une analyse de ces phénomènes : à savoir l'indétermination terminologique et la multidimensionnalité en chimie organique.

En effet, pour resituer brièvement le cadre théorique et les objectifs de ces travaux de recherche, il s'agissait de remettre en question une certaine propension à la généralisation en terminologie, et plus spécifiquement la dichotomie existant communément entre sciences dures et sciences douces, d'une part, et entre domaines techniques et scientifiques, d'autre part. Étant donné que toute recherche scientifique vise *a priori* à établir un ensemble de certitudes en matière de connaissances et de catégorisation, on s'attend à ce que les langages appelés à désigner cette recherche soient tout aussi rigoureux et exacts, mésestimant souvent les difficultés d'ordre conceptuel et linguistique susceptibles d'apparaître dans ces domaines, notamment à l'aune des sciences humaines et sociales. Ainsi, nombre de linguistes (Gambier 1991, Weissenhofer 1995, Otman 1996) estiment souvent que les domaines scientifiques, au même titre que les disciplines techniques, se prêtent plus aisément à un traitement terminologique et notamment à une approche conceptuelle et logique des unités linguistiques. Ce postulat épistémologique et terminologique est d'autant plus vivace en chimie qu'il s'agit, comme évoqué précédemment, d'une discipline hautement normalisée.

Pourtant, diverses études préliminaires (comparaison des ressources terminographiques, interrogation des chimistes, etc.) semblent indiquer au contraire que, malgré l'existence d'une nomenclature et de pratiques normalisatrices, la communication entre experts, mais aussi entre spécialistes et non-initiés du domaine, est souvent floue, ambiguë, notamment en raison du caractère fluctuant ou extrêmement générique de certains concepts chimiques associé au caractère empratique du discours de la chimie (Peraldi 2012), portant préjudice à la structuration conceptuelle et à la transmission des connaissances spécialisées au sein de la discipline. Il semble d'ailleurs opportun de signaler que cette problématique de communication défaillante a été signalée de prime abord par un laboratoire de chimie organique (issu des Facultés universitaires Notre-Dame de la Paix à Namur), ce qui a permis d'ancrer ces travaux dans une véritable démarche de linguistique appliquée, avec pour objectif la construction d'une ressource onto-terminologique spécifique en chimie (Krief, Castillo-Colaux 2005, Krief, Castillo-Colaux, Henry, Juilliard, Peraldi 2008).

Aussi, pour éprouver le caractère indéterminé et multidimensionnel de la chimie organique, une exploration outillée d'un double corpus, pédagogique et spécialisé (Candel 2001), de plus de 1,5 million de mots a été menée,[1] associée à une analyse componentielle revisitée et corrigée des énoncés définitoires de certains termes clés.[2]

Or, bien que l'objectif premier de cette recherche ne fût pas d'ordre néologique, l'analyse discursive qui en a découlé a permis de mettre en lumière de manière assez frappante un certain nombre de spécificités en matière de créativité lexicale. Nous avons donc analysé, en parallèle, la façon dont les chimistes exploitent le stock lexical qui est à leur disposition pour créer de nouveaux termes ou leur assigner un nouveau sémantisme.

Ces phénomènes de créativité lexicale et sémantique se sont manifestés selon trois angles d'approche spécifiques : en premier lieu, lors de l'observation du fonctionnement de la nomenclature IUPAC qui, nous le verrons, correspond à la dimension et au cadre de communication le plus formel de la chimie. Dans un deuxième temps, au travers de l'étude des processus créatifs dans un cadre semi-formel, processus qui portent indubitablement les traces du passé, notamment sous la forme d'unités ou de formants issus de la première nomenclature chimique élaborée au XVIIe siècle. Enfin, à l'aune des termes complexes de la chimie organique, aspect que nous aborderons néanmoins de manière plus concise dans la mesure où il a déjà été traité (Peraldi 2012).

Analyse de la nomenclature IUPAC

Règles dénominatives

Comme nous le savons, la chimie en général (et la chimie organique en particulier) constitue une des rares disciplines technico-scientifiques à être dotées d'une nomenclature standard et mondialement reconnue et elle bénéficie, à ce titre, de l'activité et des avancées d'un organisme de normalisation. Le domaine dans son ensemble est en effet régi ou du moins encadré depuis de nombreuses années par l'Union Internationale de Chimie Pure et Appliquée (que nous appellerons IUPAC, acronyme anglais de *International Union of Pure and Applied Chemistry*). Il s'agit d'un organisme international cherchant à promouvoir la compréhension des sciences chimiques auprès du public et à nourrir une culture scientifique. IUPAC publie des recommandations systématiques, notamment pour désigner les composants organiques ; il codifie les pratiques langagières acceptables, classifie et évite les usages ambigus et propose, au demeurant, un certain nombre de glossaires terminologiques dans les domaines clés de la chimie.

La chimie est donc fondée sur un système de termes faisant autorité, établi et développé selon un ensemble de règles dénominatives et de pratiques extrêmement précises (presque canoniques), rendant le processus néologique extrêmement rigide et codifié. Plus spécifiquement encore, les règles dénominatives qui fondent la nomenclature IUPAC ont pour rôle d'associer à chaque formule développée un nom ne pouvant appartenir qu'à cette dernière et permettant, à l'inverse, de déterminer sans aucune ambiguïté, à partir d'un nom unique, la structure du composé désigné. L'accélération du nombre de substances chimiques et notamment organiques, qui a été particulièrement tangible à partir du 20e siècle, a en effet mené à l'absolue nécessité d'instituer une nomenclature encore plus systématique (afin de prévenir la prolifération arbitraire de noms de substance) et d'assurer, de façon générale, un langage commun entre les chimistes :

> *It is recognized that exactness in communication is essential to effective progress in science; and a good system of nomenclature is a fundamental necessity for exact communication. Chemical nomenclature is defined here as the total language of chemistry and relates to everything that people talk or write about when conveying chemical information. It covers a much wider field than simply assigning names to chemical compounds; it embraces quantities and units, symbols, acronyms, abbreviations and even pronunciation. Even though chemists frequently communicate by means of structural formulas, the role of nomenclature and terminology is as important to chemistry as in any other discipline.* (Loening 1986 : 92)

On considère que 10 % des règles de la nomenclature IUPAC permettent de couvrir à peu près 90 % des cas de figure. En revanche, les 10 % restants demeurent les plus problématiques et requièrent de fait le plus grand nombre de règles. Bien que ce pourcentage puisse paraître anodin, il concerne en réalité un très grand nombre de composés notamment d'origine naturelle, couramment utilisés, présentant une structure complexe, et par conséquent difficile à décrire et à nommer. Malgré l'utilisation, en chimie organique, d'un petit nombre d'éléments, près de 50 000 nouveaux produits sont découverts en moyenne chaque année, soit par synthèse, soit par extraction de plantes ou d'animaux (des produits naturels). En 1880, 12 000 composés organiques étaient connus des chimistes, 150 000 en 1910, 500 000 en 1940, 1 000 000 en 1968, 7 000 000 en 2001 et, enfin, plus de 14 000 000 en 2012.

Sur un plan syntaxique, cette construction dénominative se fait systématiquement en deux étapes : en premier lieu, on établit le nom de la chaîne carbonée, c'est-à-dire le nom de l'hydrocarbure ayant le même squelette carboné et constituant la base du nom du composé. Puis, on ajoute à ce nom les préfixes et / ou suffixes, les indices numériques indiquant la nature et la position sur la chaîne des atomes ou groupes particuliers contenant la molécule. Par conséquent, les différentes parties composant une désignation ont une signification structurale précise et permanente. À titre d'exemple, nous décomposons le terme *pentane* : *penta-* signifie cinq (atomes de carbone) tandis que le formant *-ane* indique qu'il s'agit d'un alcane. La désignation 4,5,6,7-*tetrabromocyclo-hept*-2-*ene*-1,3-*dicarbonitrile*, plus complexe, est aussi composée exclusivement de fragments, de symboles et de chiffres pouvant être considérés comme systématiques. Les éléments *-cyclo*, *-ene*, *-bromo* et *-carbonitrile* auront toujours la même signification. C'est également le cas des préfixes multiplicateurs *-di* et *-tetra* qui signifient 2 et 4. Ce système dénominatif permet ainsi de créer des familles entières de molécules, à l'image des hydrocarbures acycliques saturés illustrés au Tableau 1 et dont le nom générique est *alkane*. À chaque modification du nombre d'atomes ou de la nature de la liaison, il y a un changement de terminaison et/ou éventuellement de préfixe :

Tableau 1 : Les hydrocarbures acycliques saturés

Terme anglais	Terme français	Définition
alkane	alcane	Hydrocarbure **acyclique saturé**
alkyl	alkyle	Hydrocarbure **acyclique saturé** dont on a enlevé un atome d'hydrogène
alken	alcène	Hydrocarbure **acyclique non saturé** comportant une double liaison
alkyne	alcyne	Hydrocarbure **acyclique non saturé** comportant une triple liaison
cycloalkane	cycloalcane	Hydrocarbure **monocyclique**

Nous sommes donc en présence d'un système dont les désignations visent clairement "à l'économie d'un discours descriptif sous la forme d'un encodage univoque".[3] Gaudin (2003 : 69) va jusqu'à affirmer que le passage de concepts construits dans le discours vers l'établissement de nomenclatures s'apparente à l'emploi de représentations figuratives. Les règles dénominatives de la chimie seraient donc fondées sur un rapport de paraphrase entre le code limité que représente la nomenclature et ses équivalents en langue d'usage :

> Un exemple : en écrivant “norbornène = 5 CH_2 + 2 CH”, j’écris l’équivalent de “Le norbornène est constitué de cinq groupements méthylènes CH_2 et de deux groupements méthane CH, connectés d’une certaine manière” (Laszlo, 1993 b : 33). Le terme méthylène et la formule CH_2 sont ici en position de synonymie, l’équivalence étant faite entre deux systèmes sémiotiques. (Gaudin 2003 : 69)

En d’autres termes, il s’agit d’un système dénominatif qui laisse extrêmement peu de place à la liberté néologique tout en participant bien évidemment à l’idée que le vocabulaire de la chimie est parfaitement structuré et biunivoque.

Variation terminologique

Or, une observation de la nomenclature dans le discours notamment nous montre qu’il existe en réalité un nombre important de variantes terminologiques au sein de ce système. Le premier indice de variation est l’existence au sein de la nomenclature IUPAC de trois catégories distinctes de désignations : les noms systématiques évoqués précédemment, les noms triviaux (à savoir des termes consacrés par l’usage, mais ne conférant aucune information sur la structure chimique de la substance désignée) et les noms semi-systématiques qui constituent une combinaison des deux premières catégories. Le tableau suivant illustre l’existence de deux dénominations concurrentes pour un même concept / substance :

Tableau 2 : Hydrocarbures benzyliques

Nom systématique	**Nom d’usage**
Methyl benzene	Toluene
Vinyl benzene	Styrene
Isopropyl benzene 2-Phenylpropane (1-Methylethyl)benzene 2-Phenylpropane Benzene, (1-methylethyl)-i-Propylbenzene Isopropylbenzene	Cumene / Cumol / Cumeno

Pour illustrer plus avant nos propos, le terme *quinoline-4-carbaldehyde* témoigne, quant à lui, est né de la combinaison d'éléments triviaux (*quinoline*) et officiels (*carbaldehyde*), faisant de cette désignation un nom semi-systématique.

Il est à noter qu'une grande partie des noms d'usage concerne essentiellement des composés simples extrêmement courants (*acetone, chloroform, toluene*, etc.) ou, à l'inverse, des composés particulièrement complexes (*chlorophyll, penicillin, cholesterol, saccharose*, etc.). En effet, cette multiplicité dénominative répond le plus souvent à des besoins de communication divergents, dans la mesure où la variation permet de compenser partiellement la complexité des dénominations engendrées par IUPAC. L'appropriation et l'utilisation des appellations systématiques sont effectivement extrêmement difficiles dès lors qu'il s'agit de satisfaire des besoins classiques de communication, notamment orale ou informelle :

> *These names, however, may not meet objectives in textual and oral presentation of brevity, pronounceability, creativity (coinal names), proprietary availability (trade or generic name), or even of obscurity (code designations, alchemical names, trade secrets). For general communication, a name that is either unique or unambiguous may be sufficient.* (Merritt, Bossenbroek 1997 : 222)

En revanche, l'élément sans doute le plus surprenant issu de notre analyse est la substitution de termes systématiques au profit de dénominations d'usage au sein même de la nomenclature officielle, ainsi qu'illustré ci-après :

Tableau 3 : Alcanes linéaires

CH_4	Methane	C_8H_{18}	Octane
C_2H_6	Ethane	C_9H_{20}	Nonane
C_3H_8	Propane	$C_{10}H_{22}$	Decane
C_4H_{10}	Butane	$C_{20}H_{42}$	Eicosane
C_5H_{12}	Pentane	$C_{30}H_{62}$	Triacontane
C_6H_{14}	Hexane	$C_{40}H_{82}$	Tetracontane
C_7H_{16}	Heptane	$C_{50}H_{102}$, etc.	Pentacontane

Enfin, il semble important de signaler que la présence de variantes terminologiques en chimie tient pour une grande part à l'existence de systèmes dénominatifs concurrents, existant en-dehors de l'Europe (à l'image du système CAS américain), mais également au sein même de la nomenclature IUPAC puisqu'il n'existe pas moins de sept systèmes dénominatifs différents au sein de cette dernière,[4] tous constitués de règles divergentes, menant de fait à des dénominations multiples et donc conflictuelles. L'ensemble de ces nomenclatures sont, qui plus est, non exclusives. En d'autres termes, le chimiste est libre de sélectionner la nomenclature qui lui convient. Cette concurrence nomenclaturale témoigne une nouvelle fois du manque d'harmonisation du système IUPAC, bien que ce dernier soit toutefois essentiel pour prévenir la prolifération arbitraire de noms de substances.

Héritage de Lavoisier

Une révolution morphosyntaxique

L'exploitation du corpus a permis de mettre à jour une seconde spécificité d'ordre néologique en chimie : celle de l'héritage direct du système de dénomination établi par les pères fondateurs de la première nomenclature chimique, à savoir Lavoisier, Guyton de Morveau, Berthollet et Fourcroy (Guyton *et al.,* 1787*)*. Nous faisons référence ici au recours à des morphèmes sémantiquement pleins et notamment à ce que Corbin et Paul (2000 : 58) appellent des fracto-constituants,[5] à savoir des représentants tronqués, dans des mots composés, d'unités lexicales dont ils conservent une partie de la forme et le sens référentiel. À titre d'exemple, le formant *-ol dans le terme glycerol désigne le groupe hydroxyle -OH des alcools et des phénols.*

Nous rappelons en effet que les deux principaux apports des quatre chimistes à l'égard de la discipline furent non seulement l'instauration du principe de motivation interne au sein du système de dénomination qu'ils créèrent, mais surtout l'introduction d'une suffixation de nature grammaticale et sémantique autorisant une identification et une classification beaucoup plus fines des substances chimiques. En effet, face à la multiplication des appellations ésotériques héritées des alchimistes, la présence considérable d'appellations concurrentes associée à une forte polysémie des termes de la chimie, Lavoisier et ses compères sont convaincus de la nécessité de réformer la langue afin que cette dernière permette à la fois de clarifier les concepts et de stimuler les découvertes :

> Un peu de vrai était tellement dissout dans une grande quantité de faux, qu'il en était devenu invisible et tous deux presque inséparables [...] Les métaux sympathisaient avec les planètes et avec les principales parties du corps humain. [...] Les opérations de la chimie étaient décrites dans les livres d'une manière énigmatique, et souvent chargées à dessein de tant de circonstances impossibles ou inutiles, qu'on croyait que les auteurs n'avaient voulu que s'assurer la gloire et le savoir et jeter les autres dans le désespoir d'y réussir. (Fontenelle) cité par Bensaude-Vincent (1993 : 43)

S'inspirant de la philosophie de Condillac, Lavoisier instaure une véritable *« méthode de nommer » (Cottez* 1994 *:* 676*)* fondée, en premier lieu, sur une sorte de parallélisme chimico-morphologique. Les désignations attribuées aux substances chimiques doivent systématiquement laisser transparaître la nature ainsi que la composition des corps chimiques qu'ils désignent, notamment en s'appuyant sur le trait sémantique le plus saillant pour dénommer l'objet : « Nous avons fait en sorte d'exprimer par ces nouveaux noms la propriété la plus générale, la plus caractéristique du corps qu'ils désignaient. » (Lavoisier, III, 19)

Ce système permet ainsi d'assurer une validité permanente au terme, et ce, malgré les découvertes qui sont susceptibles d'être faites par la suite. Par ailleurs, comme évoqué précédemment, l'introduction d'un système d'affixation (à titre d'exemple, la série de suffixés *-ine*, *-éne*, *-ane*, *-one*, *-yne*, *-ide*, *-ile*, *-ime*, *-ite*, *-yle*, *-ol*, *-ose*, *-ure*, *-al*, *-ate*, etc.) qui sera appliqué tout aussi bien aux substantifs qu'aux adjectifs va également permettre de faire coïncider le sens régulier (qui peut être déduit par analogie avec d'autres formes) et le sens avéré des unités concernées. Ces morphèmes ont un véritable rôle de classifieurs dans les domaines technico-scientifiques, tout en veillant à la cohérence du stock morphologique. Les chimistes attribuent, en effet, aux morphèmes des valeurs sémantiques régulières qui en font « *d'authentiques produits d'une grammaire lexicale particulière.* » (Gaudin 2003 : 67). Autrement dit, ils ouvrent la voie à un système dénominatif extrêmement productif, l'originalité cette méthode tenant également au recours à des morphèmes au sémantisme plein d'origine grecque :

> Le plus remarquable, dans ces appellations, c'est que si quelqu'unes étaient empruntées (forme et sens) ou adaptées (forme seulement) du grec, la plupart étaient de véritables productions, associant de manière inédite des morphèmes d'origine grecque auxquels effectivement, comme le disent les auteurs du Rapport, on "fait signifier" en liaison ce qu'ils ne signifiaient pas en liberté. (Cottez 1994 : 682)

Le recours massif au grec constitue d'ailleurs une spécificité supplémentaire s'agissant du système imaginé par les quatre chimistes. Et, bien que Cottez (1994 : 68) s'étonne du manque de justification de ces derniers à ce sujet, ce choix linguistique reflète clairement une volonté de s'affranchir du latin. Dagognet (1969 : 53–54) y voit notamment une conséquence des positions anti-jésuites que Guyton de Morveau affiche dans son Mémoire sur l'éducation publique (1764), le grec étant souvent considéré comme la langue de la science, tandis que son concurrent direct, le latin, est pensé généralement comme étant la langue de la religion. Il est à noter également que la langue hellénique est usitée à foison dans de nombreuses autres disciplines scientifiques (mathématiques, physique, médecine, anatomie, grammaire, rhétorique) dont la botanique de Linné. Or, Lavoisier, Guyton de Morveau, Fourcroy et Berthollet cherchent également à œuvrer à l'internationalisation de la discipline, et ce, par le biais de son support linguistique. Comme certains de leurs contemporains, ils sont persuadés de la nécessité de convaincre l'ensemble des chimistes, et ce, quelle que soit leur nationalité :

> Quand un mot nouveau devient nécessaire, il faut l'admettre. Il est convenu dans l'Europe savante que, pour être entendu dans toutes les langues, un mot doit tirer son origine du grec qui, pour toutes les nations civilisées, est la langue génératrice de mots, la langue mère ; souscrivons à cette loi. Ce mot

> sera plus aisé à admettre que nombre de mots insignifiants que le monde introduit journellement. (Citation historique de l'Empire napoléonien) cité par Brunot (1967 : 1221).

Enfin, dans une adjonction d'une traduction latine à la nomenclature de 1787, on constate également que l'originalité du grec sert d'argument aux chimistes :

> Les racines des noms nouveaux créés pour exprimer des corps également nouveaux ou inconnus des anciens chimistes sont constamment prises dans la langue grecque. À l'avantage de n'avoir aucun rapport avec des mots déjà connus et de ne pouvoir par conséquent être confondus avec les noms appartenant à des substances différentes. (Fourcroy 1801) cité par Dagognet (1969 : 55).

Quant à Gaudin (2003 : 72), il voit dans cette préférence du grec, la confirmation que les nomenclatures ne sont pas uniquement désignationnelles. Elles sont le lieu des conflits d'ordre intellectuel, politique et économique qui entourent leur création. Les nomenclatures nc peu vent être exclues du fonctionnement social et éventuellement conflictuel des langues. C'est, en effet, le débat (scientifique, théorique, etc.) existant entre locuteurs qui nourrit et enrichit la langue de sens nouveaux et d'unités nouvelles. La langue doit être perçue comme un outil d'échange, de combat, de déchiffrement mutuel et de construction perpétuelle.

Composition savante

Toujours est-il qu'une grande partie des termes relevés dans notre corpus est effectivement constituée de formants directement empruntés à la langue savante et dont voici une brève illustration :

Tableau 4 : Formants liés à la situation

intra	intramolecular / intramolecularity / intramolecularly, etc.
inter	interatomic, interesterification, interionic, intermolecular, internuclear, interstellar, etc.
exo	exocyclic, exohedral, exothermic / exothermicity, etc.

Tableau 5 : Formants liés à l'action mise en œuvre

scopy	microspectroscopy, spectroscopy, etc.
metry	spectrometry, spectrophotometry, stoichiometry, thermogravimetry, diffractometry, stoichiometry, polarimetry, etc.
phoresis	electrophoresis
lysis	alcoholysis, aminocatalysis, autoprotolysis, biocatalysis, bioelectrocatalysis, biohydrolysis, brominolysis, catalysis, deuterolysis, deuteronolysis, electrocatalysis, electrolysis, glycerolysis, glycolysis, hemodialysis, heterolysis, homolysis, hydrazinolysis, hydrogenolysis, hydrolysis, iodinolysis, methanolysis, organocatalysis, ozonolysis, photolysis, protolysis, pyrolysis, radiolysis, retronitrolysis, thermolysis, thiolysis, solvolysis, etc. N.B. La plupart de ces unités correspondent à des termes entiers issus du latin ou du grec.

D'après Soubrier (2005 : 281), l'utilisation de formants d'origine savante permettrait de « *renouer avec le vieux rêve d'une langue scientifique universelle* », favorisant largement l'intercompréhension interlinguistique, notamment par le biais d'une réduction des différences de graphies et de prononciation entre les langues.

Éponymes

Nous avons également noté le recours très important aux dénominations éponymiques, ces dernières désignant le plus souvent des notions fondamentales, en plus d'être d'une grande transparence interlinguistique. Elles se caractérisent, qui plus est, par une grande stabilité notionnelle et terminologique. Les quelques exemples proposés ci-après portent sur les mécanismes réactionnels :

> Arndt Eistert synthesis, (intramolecular) BaeyerVilliger reaction, (intramolecular/samarium) Barbier reaction, Barton reaction, Beckmann rearrangement, Birch reduction, Brook rearrangement, (intramolecular) Cannizzaro (rearrangement) reaction, Chichibabin reaction, Chugaev reaction, Claisen (rearrangement) reaction, Claisen & Dieckmann condensation, Claisen Schmidt reaction, Clemmenson reduction, Cope elimination, Cope rearrangement, CoreyWinter reaction, Curtius rearrangement, De Mayo reaction, Dieckmann

> condensation, (intramolecular) DielsAlder reaction, Edman degradation, Favorskii rearrangement, Fischer esterification, Fischer indole synthesis, Friedel Crafts alkylation & acylation, Gabriel synthesis, (samarium) Grignard reaction, Grob fragmentation, Heck reaction, Hofmann (elimination/rearrangement) reaction, Horner-Wadsworth-Emmons reaction, Hunsdiecker reaction, Leuckart reaction, Leuckart-Wallach reaction, etc.

En outre, contrairement aux éponymes de la médecine qui se caractérisent par des variations syntaxiques et sémantiques significatives,[6] notamment dans le cadre d'une traduction interlinguistique (Van Hoof 1986 : 59–84), les désignations de la chimie n'entraînent aucune difficulté d'ordre traductologique dans la mesure où elles se maintiennent d'une langue à l'autre. En revanche, elles témoignent de l'extrême liberté combinatoire et lexicale des chimistes organiciens, spécificité que nous exposons plus avant dans la section suivante, puisque les spécialistes n'hésitent pas à accoler à ces désignations éponymiques des unités de nature grammaticale diverse ou à juxtaposer au sein d'un même syntagme des réactions parfaitement opposées, ainsi qu'illustré ci-après :

- anti-Markovnikov reaction
- Beckmann-like rearrangement
- bromodifluoro-Reformatsky reaction
- Crafts type Michael reaction
- oxy-Cope rearrangement
- retro-Diels-Alder rearrangement
- Williamson ether synthesis
- Wittig-Emmons reaction, etc.

Termes complexes

Comme évoqué précédemment, l'un des objectifs de la thèse fut d'éprouver le caractère indéterminé de certains concepts de la chimie. Qu'il s'agisse des termes génériques de la chimie ou des unités dénotant des réactions organiques spécifiques, l'analyse componentielle revisitée et corrigée de certains termes clés, a effectivement permis d'établir de manière satisfaisante que le domaine se caractérisait soit par une indétermination conceptuelle, c'est-à-dire un manque de consensus au niveau des notions de la chimie, soit par une indétermination définitoire, autrement des définitions ne répondant pas aux critères d'exhaustivité et de technicité requis par la terminologie traditionnelle.

Or, une analyse approfondie des variantes syntaxiques, menée selon la méthodologie de Daille, Habert, Jacquemin et Royauté (2000) sur un ensemble de syntagmes de longueur 2 à 5, a permis de constater que cette indétermination était non seulement compensée par une liberté combinatoire, syntaxique et néologique extrêmement forte de la part des spécialistes organiciens (menant à la création de nouvelles unités sémantiques), mais également par un mode de créativité par incrémentation (Portelance 1987 : 359) extrêmement productif, grâce à l'utilisation notamment d'éléments sémantiques forts tels que les adjectifs, contredisant une nouvelle fois le « tout » substantif et dénominatif qui caractérise *a priori* les terminologies des disciplines technoscientifiques (Peraldi 2012).

Ce système est, à notre sens, extrêmement révélateur de la dynamique du vocabulaire technoscientifique, une dynamique qui repose à la fois sur le potentiel combinatoire des unités composant les nomenclatures et sur le potentiel taxinomique de ces dernières. Il permet de générer des séries de syntagmes à noyau commun parfois extrêmement développées et potentiellement de longueur infinie. Ces nominalisations permettent d'organiser les objets dans plusieurs sous-classifications. Cela montre également que les scientifiques communiquent souvent leurs savoirs communs dans un langage qui montre la complexité croissante de leurs connaissances. Et, contrairement aux propos d'Ormrod (2001 : 10) et ceux de Soubrier (2005 : 291) qui estiment que ce mode de dénomination peut engendrer des problèmes de lisibilité et de compréhension conceptuelle, Portelance (1987 : 359) affirme, quant à elle, que la longueur et la technicité de ces syntagmes seraient compensées par la « *capacité de la mémoire de compréhension* » qui agit dans toute nomenclature. Autrement dit, le terme de base, à condition d'être suffisamment explicite, permet de créer des combinaisons également explicites par le biais d'unités lexicales elles-mêmes identifiables grâce à la mise en contexte des termes et grâce à l'ensemble des liens logiques et indirects existants entre ces unités :

> Avec une telle capacité générative, toute notion élaborée dans une discipline pourra être nommée et distinguée des autres notions par le jeu des références et des oppositions selon le même principe qui permet à un système linguistique d'engendrer un nombre infini de phrases. (Portelance 1987 : 359)

Conclusion

La recherche menée a non seulement permis d'établir que les notions de la chimie ne se prêtaient pas à un traitement classique des termes, mais surtout que paradoxalement les chimistes organiciens cultivaient sciemment une forme d'imprécision autour de certains concepts notamment génériques, et ce, par le biais de termes amalgamés, afin de gérer l'extrême complexité des processus réactionnels à décrire, tout en ayant recours en parallèle à des syntagmes d'une densité et d'une longueur exponentielle. Néanmoins, bien que ces phénomènes d'indétermination (et à terme de multidimensionnalité) constituent une difficulté évidente, ils font aussi partie intégrante du processus de construction et de transmission des connaissances spécialisées en chimie, en ayant recours à des procédés de créativité lexicale originaux et performants. Ces procédés sont activés sur trois plans : au sein même de la nomenclature, contredisant le caractère purement normatif du vocabulaire de la chimie ; à un niveau morphosyntaxique en apportant une validité permanente au terme ; enfin, sur un plan terminologique et combinatoire, témoignant du dynamisme des vocabulaires technoscientifiques.

Références bibliographiques

Bensaude-Vincent, Bernadette. *Lavoisier. Mémoires d'une révolution.* Paris : Flammarion, collection Figures de la science, 1993.

Brunot, Ferdinand. *Histoire de la langue française des origines à* 1900. *Tome IX : La Révolution et l'Empire.* Paris : Armand Colin, 1967.

Candel, Danielle. « La définition chez les scientifiques ». *Terminologies Nouvelles* 21 (2000). 52–57.

Candel, Danielle et al. « Aspects du Groupe nominal dans l'activité définitoire des scientifiques ». *Revue française de linguistique appliquée VI* (2001). 17–28.

Condamines, Anne et Josette Rebeyrolle. « Construction d'une base de connaissances terminologiques à partir de textes : expérimentation et définition d'une méthode ». *Ingénierie des Connaissances, évolutions récentes et nouveaux défis*. Eds. J. Charlet, M. Zacklad, G. Kassel, D. Bourigault. Paris : Eyrolles, 2000. 225–242.

Corbin Danielle et Jérôme Pau. « Aperçus sur la créativité morphologique dans la terminologie de la chimie ». *La banque des mots* 60 (2000). 51–68

Cottez, Henri. « Les bases épistémologiques et linguistiques de la nomenclature chimique de 1787 ». *Meta* 39 (1994), numéro 4. 676–691.

Daille, Béatrice, Benoît Habert, Christian Jacquemin, Jean Royauté. « Empirical Observation of Term Variations and Principles for their Description ». *Terminology* 3-2 (2000). 197–257.

Fradin, Bernard. « Combining Forms, Blends and Related Phenomena ». *Extragrammatical and Marginal Morphology*. Eds. U. Doleschal and A. Thornton. München: Lincolm Europa, 2000. 11–59.

Freixa Aymerich, Judit, Sabela Fernandez Silva, Maria Teresa Cabre Castellvi. « La multiplicité des chemins dénominatifs ». *Meta* 53(2008), numéro 4. 731–747.

Gambier, Yves. « Présupposés de la terminologie : vers une remise en cause ». *Cahiers de linguistique sociale* 18 (1991). 31–58.

Gaudin, François. *Socioterminologie : une approche sociolinguistique de la terminologie*. Bruxelles : De Boeck & Larcier et Duculot, 2003.

--- « La révolution dénominative en chimie : un coup de force ? ». *Neologica* 1 (2007). 65–74.

Godly, Ted. « Terminological Principles and Methods in the Subject Field of Chemistry ». *Terminology: Applications in interdisciplinary communication*. Amsterdam: Hrsg. v. H. Sonneveld, K. Loening, 1993. 141–164.

Guyton de Morveau, L. Guyton de Morveau, A. Lavoiser, C. Berthollet et A.

Fourcroy. *Méthode de nomenclature chimique proposée par MM. Morveau, Lavoisier, Bertholet et Fourcroy*, 1787. Paris : Le Seuil, 1994.

Krief, Alain, Catherine Castillo-Collaux, Julie Henry, Claudie Juilliard, Sandrine Peraldi. "Building the EnCOrE Dictionary Collaboratively: Strategy and Practice ». *International Journal of Knowledge and Learning* 4 (2008), numéro 2–3. 203–216.

Lavoisier, Antoine. *Traité élémentaire de Chimie, Mémoires, tableaux et Synonymie de* 1787, réunis dans le 3e tome, Nouvelle édition, Cuchet.

L'Homme, Marie-Claude. *Terminologie : principes et techniques*. Montréal : Presses de l'Université de Montréal, 2004.

Loening, Kurt L. « Terminological Guidelines and Their Application in the International Union of Pure and Applied Chemistry (IUPAC) ». *International Co-operation in Terminology Work*. Ed. M. Krommer-Benz. Munich: K. G. Saur, 1986. 92–116.

Ormrod, Janet. « Construction discursive de noms composés dans des textes scientifiques anglais ». *Le groupe nominal dans le texte spécialisé*. Ed. D. Banks. Paris : l'Harmattan, 2001.

Otman, Gabriel. *Les représentations sémantiques en terminologie*. Paris : Masson, 1996.

Pearson, Jennifer. *Terms in Context*. Amsterdam: John Benjamins Publishing. 1998.

Peraldi, Sandrine. « L'anglais de spécialité en chimie organique : entre indétermination terminologique et multidimensionnalité », *ASp* 62 (2012). 5–24.

Portelance, Christine. « Fertilisation terminologique ou insémination terminologique artificielle ». *Meta* 32 (1987) n° 3.

Sager, Juan C. *A Practical Course in Terminology Processing*. Amsterdam: John Benjamins Publishing, 1990.

Soubrier, Jean. « Transparence et opacité de l'anglais scientifique ». *De la mesure dans les termes, Travaux du CRTT*. Eds. Béjoint H. et Maniez F. Lyon : Presses Universitaires de Lyon, 2005. 280–295.

Temmerman, Rita. *Towards New Ways of Terminology Description. The sociocognitive approach*. Amsterdam: John Benjamins, 2000.

Thoiron, Philippe, Pierre Arnaud, Henri Bejoint, Claude-Pierre Boisson. « Notion d''archi-concept » et dénomination ». *Meta* XLI (1996), n°4. 512–524.

Tournier, Jean. *Introduction descriptive à la lexicogénétique de l'anglais contemporain*. Paris : Champion-Slatkine, 1985.

Verkade, Pieter. *A History of the nomenclature of organic chemistry*. Dordrecht / Boston: Reidel, 1985.

Van Hoof, Henri. « Les éponymes médicaux : essai de classification ». *Meta* 31 (1986) n° 1, pp. 59–84.

Weissenhofer, Peter. *Conceptology in terminology theory, semantics and word-formation: a morpho-conceptually based approach to classification as exemplified by the English baseball terminology*. Wien : TermNet, 1995.

Notes

1 L'exploration du corpus a impliqué notamment le recours à des critères sémantiques de conservation / filtrage terminologique (Condamines, Rebeyrolle 2000) et des marqueurs linguistiques spécifiques (Pearson 1998, Candel 2000, L'Homme 2004) afin de cibler les contextes « riches en connaissances ».

2 Dans la lignée des travaux de Thoiron, Arnaud, Béjoint et Boisson (1996 : 512–524), de Temmerman (2000) et de Freixa, Silva et Cabré (2008 : 731–744)

3 Nous avons volontairement choisi un exemple simple avec les alcanes. Mais, les composés organiques de structures cycliques complexes - comportant des cycles accolés ou des « hétérocycles », par exemple - ont longtemps suscité des problèmes de nomenclature. Ce n'est que tardivement que IUPAC a pu les résoudre et proposer des règles univoques. Des produits bien connus ou d'usage courant, évoqués ci-après, sont également concernés.

4 On dénombre en effet la nomenclature substitutive, radico-fonctionnelle, additive, soustractive, conjonctive, celle de remplacement et celle par assemblage d'unités identiques.

5 Les fractoconstituants peuvent être considérés comme une variante des fractomorphèmes de Tournier (« un fragment de lexie qui la représente dans un mot construit » (1985 : 86) ou encore des fractoformants de Fradin (2000).

6 En anatomie, par exemple, les règles établies dans le cadre de la nomenclature internationale ont exclu les anciennes dénominations éponymiques (*Ganglion spinal* se substituant à *Ganglion de Corti*, etc.), entraînant des phénomènes de variation intralinguistique.

Interprétation-médiation : Une étude pragmatique de la désignation d'un nouveau métier

ELISABETH NAVARRO, JEAN-MICHEL BENAYOUN

Résumé

Dans un marché linguistique en plein essor, les langues migrantes font l'objet d'une attention nouvelle. Un nouveau cadre est apparu ces dernières années, celui de la médiation linguistique et avec lui, de nouvelles compétences langagières. Entre médiation interculturelle, action sociale et pratique linguistique, cette activité cherche sa place dans le monde de la traduction. Cet article fait le point sur les enjeux politiques de la nomination de cette profession novatrice et approche la complexité des compétences exigées en posant l'ethnosociolinguistique comme un socle interculturel indispensable à l'assise professionnelle de cette activité.

Mots-clés : interprétation, médiation, ethnosociolinguistique, migration, interculturalité

Abstract

In a booming language market, the languages of migration have generated much interest and renewed debate. Over the past few years, a new framework has emerged, Language Mediation, a practice which carries with it a new set of language-related skills. This article considers the broader, political issues invoked by the names used to describe this novel profession. We also attempt to describe the complexity involved in defining the competencies it requires. Specifically, we argue that an ethno-sociolinguistic approach can provide the intercultural theoretical scaffolding around which Language Mediation can be built as a professional activity.

Keywords: community interpreting, languages, interculturality, socio-ethno-linguistics

Introduction

L'intensification des phénomènes migratoires, et la présence sur le territoire national de populations étrangères d'origines très diverses s'établissant durablement dans le pays d'accueil, imposent la mise en place de structures appropriées. C'est dans ce contexte démographique et politique spécifique, que de nombreuses associations, des organisations non gouvernementales, et des institutions privées se sont attribué les services de « médiateurs linguistiques », dont la mission principale est de proposer un lien linguistique et culturel entre le migrant et les institutions.

Parce qu'elle se situe au croisement de l'interprétation, de la reformulation et de la médiation, cette activité de « médiateur linguistique » constitue une nouvelle branche au sein des métiers de la traduction. En cela, elle exige une dénomination qui lui soit propre, d'autant que la modalité de cette interprétation très spécifique adaptée aux milieux dans lesquels elle intervient, requiert une attention toute particulière car elle pose des problèmes éthiques et déontologiques qui exigent qu'apparaissent nettement, dans la désignation de la profession, ce à quoi peuvent s'attendre les personnes qui sollicitent une *interprétation.*

Il appartient, dès lors, aux instances en charge des opérations de nomination de délimiter les contours de ces termes descripteurs, qui s'inscrivent dans un ensemble conceptuel complexe. La médiation ne peut être éludée car elle est au cœur des consultations médicales, ethnopsychiatriques, ou sociales, et devient *de facto* constitutive du métier d'interprète en milieu social.

Une activité traditionnelle mais novatrice

A priori, décrire un métier qui s'inscrit dans une pratique ancestrale peut faire penser que nous nous éloignons des descripteurs de l'innovation. Pour autant, si l'interprète-médiateur a joué un rôle fondamental dans l'histoire des peuples, l'activité professionnelle qu'il exerce n'a pas fait jusqu'à présent l'objet d'un investissement scientifique de l'Université française.

Or, c'est la forme que peut revêtir la reconnaissance institutionnelle de cette profession, qui est au cœur de la nouveauté, dans la mesure où il ne s'agit pas simplement de l'appropriation par l'université d'un métier que certains voient comme adjacent à l'activité d'interprète de conférence[1], mais plutôt de l'intégration dans un cursus universitaire spécifique et adapté d'une profession déliée encore des enjeux qu'offrent la diplomation.

En quoi l'acte de traduction de l'interprète-médiateur est-il spécifique et engage-t-il des processus particuliers de traduction ?

De quelle manière la désignation de cette profession peut-elle être l'acte fondateur et politique, qui lui permettra d'établir et d'assurer, à long terme, la pérennité et la spécificité de ce métier ?

L'enjeu de la nomination

Il s'agit de nommer, de définir et de normaliser, en 2013, une activité qui s'est construite empiriquement. Il est clair que l'acte de nommer, au-delà de la fonction symbolique qu'il revêt, engage une inscription dans un contexte socio-politique.

Or, ce n'est qu'une partie de la difficulté liée à l'acte de nommer. Il est clair que nommer consiste à poser des limites, des termes et des fins ; ce qui revient, en réalité, à donner un sens[2] au signe-référent, à le délimiter, à le déterminer et donc à le définir, dans la mesure où l'opération de nomination appartient aux opérations de définition. Afin de ne pas diluer notre propos, nous évoquerons simplement ici, les trois opérations fondamentales de la nomination, que nous décrirons brièvement.

L'une, tout d'abord, est orientée vers l'avenir. Il s'agit de poser la désignation d'un objet qui vient d'être créé. Cette désignation sera le reflet « du rôle, de l'usage et du but » (Mounin, 1969) prévu pour cet objet. La deuxième catégorie d'opérations de nomination, elle, est une écriture / réécriture d'éléments appartenant au passé, sous une forme ou sous une autre. C'est l'acte conjugué des archéologues, préhistoriens et lexicologues, que décrit Georges Mounin[3], qui doivent, entre autres, nommer des objets qui ont existé à partir de fonctions que l'on reconstruit. La dernière catégorie, enfin, s'inscrit doublement dans l'histoire des termes et des concepts, dans la mesure où la désignation de l'objet s'appuie tout d'abord, sur un capital sémique construit au fil du temps (donc capitalisant le passé), puis sur une projection de la fonction socio-économique (orientée donc vers le futur). En résumé, la nomination se répartit schématiquement en trois types d'opérations, selon les orientations définitoires : un type visant l'avenir et l'usage qui sera fait de l'objet, un autre capitalisant le passé, le dernier type, enfin, qui fait le lien entre le descriptif fonctionnel d'une activité pré-existante et qui, simultanément, lui donne le moyen de s'adapter aux applications futures de l'objet ainsi désigné.

Pour revenir précisément à notre propos, il faut nous appuyer sur un descripteur qui rende compte à la fois de l'activité telle qu'elle s'est inscrite dans l'histoire sociale, mais qui en décrive également la réalité présente, sans pour autant freiner une évolution possible de la définition du métier. Or, si l'Histoire a permis d'apporter des limites définitoires au terme d'*interprète*, il n'en va pas ainsi du terme *médiateur*. Le premier est référencé depuis le 14ème siècle[4] ; l'autre, médiateur, n'apparaît, dans sa valeur moderne[5], qu'au 20ème siècle pour décrire une activité qui « doit beaucoup au modèle d'*ombudsman* suédois»[6].

En nous recommandant ici d'une approche fondamentalement sociolinguistique, nous décrirons, dans un premier temps, les pratiques-métiers ; nous en organiserons ensuite la description, pour enfin répondre à la problématique de la désignation. Comme nous le voyons à travers les travaux en cours concernant la future norme ISO[7], la désignation, acte fondamental en terminologie, permet la reconnaissance sociale et inscrit le statut socio-professionnel tout en référençant le métier.

Les traductologues et les scientifiques dont l'une des activités est de décrire les métiers de la traduction dans leur ensemble, ont également un rôle à jouer, s'ils souhaitent s'approprier véritablement cet objet, pour en définir les contours et en délimiter les approches.

Des pratiques professionnelles des plus variées

Les pratiques professionnelles s'organisent principalement selon les lieux d'intervention, selon les demandeurs et bien sûr, en fonction des besoins d'interprétation-médiation. Ce sont ces mêmes lieux d'intervention qui vont, tout d'abord, définir les modalités de l'action de ces interprètes-médiateurs ; chaque lieu, et parfois chaque représentant de l'institution, ont recours à des méthodes et à des exigences qui lui sont propres.

Les domaines d'intervention, sans prétendre ici à l'exhaustivité, vont du secteur médical[8] au secteur social[9] ; ces deux domaines s'entendent dans leur acception la plus large. Sont également concernés tous les lieux et domaines liés à la demande d'asile,[10] et aux actions diverses mises en œuvre par les Cours de justice ou les tribunaux.

Les interprètes-médiateurs accompagnent parfois le migrant à l'hôpital,[11] dans les aéroports ou les tribunaux. Ils apportent leur aide dans les actes du quotidien : à la pharmacie, au bureau de poste ou dans les gares, par exemple. Ils se rendent dans les institutions scolaires, ou dans les structures d'accueil dédiées à la petite enfance, y rencontrent des assistants sociaux, des assistants maternels. En outre, leur présence est souvent requise, voire indispensable, dans les services de la protection maternelle et infantile (PMI).

On attend, également, de ces professionnels qu'ils soient en mesure de résoudre des problèmes d'incompréhension, des conflits dont certains prennent source dans des espaces où la médiation transculturelle est à l'œuvre. Ici, la traduction à proprement parler n'est plus l'objet principal de leur activité. Dans ces cas précis, ils ne traduisent pas simplement, ils sont en fait, amenés à régler ou à apaiser les conflits générés par les origines culturelles différentes.

Dans d'autres lieux, ils sont écrivains publics. A ce titre, ils peuvent assurer des permanences. La Poste et les principaux services publics, n'en sont que quelques exemples. Les écrivains publics expliquent, traduisent les actes administratifs, vont même jusqu'à rédiger des récits de vies. Ils collaborent à la rédaction de courriers à vocation administrative, ou les rédigent entièrement. Le plus souvent, ils travaillent au sein d'unités du secteur associatif, qui organisent ces permanences.

En raison de la grande diversité des lieux d'intervention, la sphère de compétences requises pour exercer le métier d'interprète-médiateur va bien au-delà de la simple compétence linguistique. En effet, ce qui est déterminant est lié à la réception de ce qui est dit et à ses modalités, d'une part et à ce qui est interprété d'autre part[12].

On pourrait tout simplement considérer que les compétences requises pour exercer une activité duelle s'additionnent, ce qui reviendrait à combiner les compétences attendues pour un interprète de conférence à celles que l'on attendrait d'un médiateur.

Mais cela n'est pas possible, tant la réalité de cette activité professionnelle est complexe. Or, lister les compétences techniques de l'une ou l'autre de ces deux activités est réalisable, et nous en proposerons plus loin une perspective synthétique. Mais, et cela est vrai de toute profession, les compétences techniques ne sont qu'une partie de la réalité du métier, puisqu'il ne suffit pas de les maîtriser pour être interprète. Et il ne suffit pas non plus d'être conscient de l'écart culturel pour être médiateur. Il faut maîtriser un certain nombre de savoir-faire et posséder des qualités personnelles et interpersonnelles pour être en mesure d'intervenir dans toutes les situations que nous venons d'évoquer. Ces derniers éléments constituent les prérequis pour devenir interprète-médiateur.

De la nécessité de définir savoir-faire et compétences pour nommer

Bien évidemment les compétences linguistiques sont fondatrices. Et de ce point de vue, la détermination de connaissances et de compétences dans les deux langues de travail est un préalable indispensable. Les interprètes-médiateurs doivent, en effet, être en mesure de traduire, à vue ou non, des documents écrits. En outre, leur niveau de maîtrise des deux langues doit leur permettre d'interpréter en mode consécutif entre autres, et sur le mode bidirectionnel, tout échange verbal entre un migrant et un représentant d'associations ou d'institutions.

C'est à partir de ce point précis que s'évalue toute la difficulté d'une activité plurielle. Les réalités de la compétence linguistique dépassent même ce qui vient d'être dit. Nous avons évoqué deux langues de travail ; or, ce sont souvent plus de deux langues qui sont requises lors de la prestation. En effet, les migrants pour lesquels ils interprètent, ne possèdent parfois pas la langue nationale de leur pays d'origine. Leur expression se fait par l'intermédiaire d'un dialecte local, tribal ou même d'un type de jargon. Le linguiste sait bien toute la difficulté qui réside dans la maîtrise de l'ensemble de ces registres, et variantes d'une langue, qui se répartissent entre le langage écrit et le langage parlé, en passant par l'argot. Et pourtant, quel que soit le lieu d'intervention, l'interprète se doit d'être à même de réagir immédiatement, (Seleskovitch, 1985)[13]. Il s'adapte aux conditions linguistiques qu'il rencontre, qu'il s'agisse de langues de travail, ou de langues de communications simplement, ce qui est le cas d'un dialecte local par exemple. Il apprécie immédiatement les registres du « parler » de chaque migrant, et en restitue le « dire ». L'immédiateté de la réaction face aux situations linguistiques les plus diverses constitue l'une des compétences, dites personnelles, les plus souvent sollicitées.

Par ailleurs, l'interprète-médiateur est également au fait de l'existence de variantes du dire qui, en France, se sont créées au fur et à mesure de l'arrivée de groupes de populations migrantes. Construites essentiellement autour d'un lexique propre aux immigrants, ces variantes métaphorisent des lieux de convocation, de rencontres. Ce sont par exemple, les structures administratives dont la mission est de prendre en charge l'accueil des étrangers. En surface, ces variantes sont les traces complexes de formes d'appropriation d'objets de l'extralinguistique les plus divers : sigles, requêtes, documents, aides administratives[14]. C'est au sein de ces lieux de fusion[15] et de rencontres tant linguistiques que culturelles que l'on trouvera, entre autres, les outils mis en œuvre pour exprimer des unités terminologiques non transférables.

Interpréter et rendre compte

Mais au-delà de la simple traduction, au-delà de l'interprétation elle-même, ces professionnels doivent restituer, et commenter à l'aide d'outils linguistiques ce qui est à l'œuvre au sein de l'échange communicationnel.

C'est ce que Juan M. Ortega Herraez et Ana I. Foulquié Rubio soulignent à travers la description qu'ils proposent de situations d'interprétation en contexte policier : « Communication implies much more than words; it also implies gestures and non-verbal elements. Interpreters have to be aware of this kind of non-verbal information and have different ways of dealing with it»[16].

En d'autres termes, ils doivent rendre compte : du verbal mais également du non verbal, du paratexte dans le respect de ses limites ; rendre compte enfin, de l'ensemble des signaux non linguistiques, mais pourtant signifiants.

Toutefois, certains institutionnels (les tribunaux, les services de police, les Cours de justice ou parfois les psychothérapeutes, les médecins) attendent un rendu plus littéral des mots. D'autres psychothérapeutes demandent souvent que la prestation de l'interprète aille au-delà de la simple traduction[17]. Pour aider leur patient, ils ont besoin de savoir quelle relation celui-ci entretient avec sa propre langue : son niveau de maîtrise, bien sûr, mais pas seulement. Il leur faut également repérer les images qui construisent son discours ; être à même de décoder les hésitations fortuites ou non ; déterminer les troncatures implicites. Les segmentations lexicales, en effet, sont souvent signifiantes, et disent plus, ou autre chose que les mots eux-mêmes[18]. En d'autres termes, il leur appartient de mettre en mots, l'écart entre l'intention de dire, et la réalité de ce qui est dit. Pour donner le sens, ils n'hésitent pas à interrompre, à intervenir afin d'expliquer ce qui est à l'œuvre dans la structure profonde des énoncés. Ils signalent les modalisateurs, les outils d'euphémisation, ou indiquent les répétitions. Ils commentent les métaphores et les images signifiantes, et mettent en relief les outils, verbaux ou non, dont la fonction en discours relève de la dénotation. Cela explique, en partie, la raison pour laquelle de nombreux interprètes intervenant en consultations ethno-psychiatriques, sont qualifiés de *co-thérapeutes*. Il ne nous appartient pas d'émettre ici un jugement sur cette désignation. Il est clair, toutefois, que leur rôle dépasse le cadre de l'interprétation pure ; ils prennent une part différente en apportant leurs connaissances culturelles, essentiellement, mais aussi en participant activement à la phase de conceptualisation linguistique, sous-jacente de la thérapie.

La construction de la relation de confiance

En réalité, ce qui transparaît derrière cette désignation de *co-thérapeute*, relève de la relation qui s'établit entre le thérapeute et l'interprète-médiateur. Cette relation passe par la confiance que l'un et l'autre s'accordent, confiance qui se construit essentiellement sur la conscience partagée de ce qui est à l'œuvre dans l'échange communicationnel.

C'est là une autre facette de l'exercice de cette profession, qui passe à la fois par la conscience des liens entre les faits, les mots, et les outils langagiers de leurs représentations, mais également par la maîtrise d'éléments qui relèvent du non-verbal.

Là se situe la base de la confiance nécessaire à l'exercice de ce métier. L'installation de cette relation passe principalement par la mise en œuvre de trois données : la conscience de l'interaction d'unités linguistiques et non verbales, la maîtrise d'éléments implicites, sous-entendus, dont certains relèvent de l'éthos, et enfin, de la description « transparente » de ce qui est en cours.

En effet, la construction de la confiance au sein de ces échanges communicationnels passe nécessairement par le contrôle d'éléments qui sous-tendent la communication non verbale, et qui tiennent à l'individu, à la personne, à ce qu'elle dégage, à ce qu'elle véhicule, à son genre aussi, mais également, et peut-être surtout, à son origine ethnique[19]. Un travail sur l'être, l'existence et l'identité est indispensable. De par sa formation, le thérapeute a conscience et maîtrise ces éléments qui relèvent, pour partie de *l'ethos ;* l'interprète-médiateur, lui, doit apprendre seul, à maîtriser un certain nombre d'éléments sous-jacents à la mise en œuvre de son activité.

Gérer préjugés et codes culturels

Si l'on requiert du professionnel d'être familier des deux cultures qui interagissent au cours de l'intervention, il lui est également demandé d'avoir conscience de ses préjugés personnels, pour mieux les maîtriser afin qu'ils ne prennent jamais le pas sur le message interprété. Or, si les connaissances culturelles peuvent s'acquérir, la gestion des préjugés, elle, relève d'un travail plus difficile à mettre en œuvre.

Sa qualité de migrant, le plus souvent, place l'interprète dans une situation objectivement « non neutre ». Et afin de ne pas « orienter » sa prestation, il lui faut prendre conscience, entre autres, de ses propres préjugés, et de ce que son origine personnelle peut générer de barrières ou de freins. Cette prise de conscience est indispensable pour en maîtriser lui-même les effets sur la qualité de sa prestation, mais également pour en anticiper les implicites chez le migrant en attente d'interprétation.

Il s'agit de connaître le sens et la signification de tels ou tels signes extérieurs, qu'ils soient vestimentaires, ou simplement liés au genre. Les interprètes doivent en maîtriser les représentations et les analogies possibles en dépit des évidentes multiplicités liées aux différents codes culturels qui fondent l'identité des migrants, même s'il nous faut reconnaître que dans de nombreux pays, ces codes diffèrent d'une région à l'autre, d'une ethnie à l'autre, et parfois même d'une tribu à l'autre.

Nous n'en citerons ici que quelques exemples signifiants : le costume, la coiffure, la barbe, la jupe, le pantalon pour les femmes, le voile,... Ce ne sont pas de simples signes, symboliques d'une culture, ce sont également les manifestations physiques de ce que chacun véhicule, de ce que chacun représente. Ces manifestations, signifiantes par analogies[20], relèvent également de *l'ethos*.

Gérer son émotion

L'implication émotionnelle de l'interprète-médiateur doit faire l'objet d'une prise en compte spécifique en amont et en aval de la séance elle-même, et ce, afin de le libérer de la charge émotionnelle de ce qui vient d'être entendu. Dans le cas de consultations psychiatriques, pour ne choisir que cet exemple, il s'agit d'aider et de prendre en charge les migrants victimes de tortures ou de violences. L'interprète peut parfois se retrouver lui-même en situation personnellement délicate : migrant lui-même, il connait parfois certaines de ces situations. De plus, son interprétation se faisant souvent à la première personne[21], il lui est difficile de lutter contre toutes les formes d'implication. Or, l'objet de l'interprétation est tel que le professionnel accède souvent à des parts privées, voire intimes, de la vie du migrant. Il est facile de comprendre que les phénomènes d'assimilation de l'interprète-médiateur sont à l'œuvre dans certains cas. Dans cette mesure, la gestion de l'implication émotionnelle est une nécessité, mais elle relève des compétences éminemment difficiles à mettre en œuvre sans l'aide de séances adaptées et construites à cet effet.

Nous le voyons, il est difficile de délimiter les champs des savoir-faire qui relèvent de la sphère non-linguistique, dans la mesure où elle-même ne s'inscrit pas dans un périmètre figé. En effet, selon l'origine des migrants que l'on interprète, les compétences linguistiques relèvent déjà des compétences interculturelles et transculturelles.

« Verbe » et transculturalité : des unités non transférables

Et ce n'est qu'en apparence que *culturel* et *transculturel* ne relèvent pas du domaine linguistique. En effet, la mise en œuvre de l'interculturalité sous-entend de complexes va-et-vient. Nous ne développerons ici que deux exemples pour mettre en relief la difficulté de tracer une frontière nette entre les grands domaines de compétences que nous venons de citer.

Tout d'abord, l'ensemble des partenaires sociaux représentés en France par les organismes dont nous avons parlé, n'ont souvent pas d'équivalent local ; les règles sociales et la hiérarchie sociale n'ont parfois pas de rapport avec celle du pays d'accueil ; et l'interprète-médiateur n'a pas d'autre choix que celui d'adapter le mot à traduire, puisque la transposition terme à terme est impossible. Ainsi, en malinké, la fonction de *psychothérapeute* sera-t-elle rendue par le recours au terme *marabout*[22]. La fonction d'*assistant social*, pour choisir cet autre exemple, est difficilement traduisible ou explicable. Ambigu dans certaines cultures, ce rôle est souvent assimilé à celui de *chef de village*, ou même à celui de *parent*, et sa fonction fait souvent l'objet d'un questionnement auquel il est malaisé de répondre. Savoir rendre compte d'unités non transférables, être en mesure de combler l'écart entre des unités linguistiques propres à des langues de communication et de travail et des unités propres à des langues exclusivement de communication sont des compétences qui se situent aux frontières des savoir-faire explicites.

L'interprète-médiateur : un interprète social, médical, judiciaire, de proximité ?

Nous avons jusqu'ici délimité les contours des compétences attendues et requises pour exercer cette profession. Il ressort de cette première analyse que cette activité, telle qu'elle se définit dans le contexte français, se distingue d'autres activités à l'œuvre en Europe. Tout du moins, l'analyse des nombreuses désignations de cette profession dans les principaux pays qui accueillent des populations étrangères met-elle en évidence des différences épistémologiques et conceptuelles. En effet, ce ne sont pas les mêmes champs qui sont couverts par les différentes façons de nommer cette activité.

En Belgique, on désigne ces professionnels par le terme *d'interprète-social*. En Italie, ils sont nommés *mediatori linguistico culturale*. En Grande-Bretagne[23], ce seront des *community interpreters*.

La désignation italienne de médiateurs linguistiques et culturels[24] pose le problème de la hiérarchisation des domaines et des compétences. En effet, proposer comme compétence première, la médiation, ne saurait résoudre la pluralité des termes de l'équation. Certes, il est à la fois clair et évident que cette forme d'interprétation s'inscrit dans une logique de transculturalité, car cette activité permet de combler les manques de compréhension que génèrent les écarts culturels et les différentes origines ethnosociales. La désignation anglo-saxonne d'interprète communautaire[25], quant à elle, soulève un problème d'un autre type. En mettant en évidence la réalité du groupe auquel est destinée la prestation, cette désignation pose un implicite social non négligeable, celui de la différence communautaire. En France, l'État s'installe d'emblée dans une conception politique d'un autre ordre[26], en refusant la possible confusion culturelle et contextuelle qui consiste à qualifier de *communautaire* un groupe professionnel, échappant ainsi à la virtualité d'un contresens constant.

Or la problématique de la désignation est celle de la synthèse et celle de la réconciliation d'unités terminologiques, dont il arrive que certains critères divergent. Cette réconciliation est impossible si l'on recourt à l'étiquette d'*interprète social,* car elle semble réduire l'activité au domaine uniquement social, et en ce sens, elle est exclusive de tous les autres champs d'activité que nous avons exposés. Qui plus est, parler d'*interprète social*[27] et l'opposer à *interprète-médical* ou *interprète-judiciaire* revient à définir un métier, en ne considérant qu'un seul lieu d'intervention. Et il est évident que procéder de la sorte ne permet pas de réunir et de solidariser des acteurs, qui, par essence et parce qu'ils proviennent de pays différents, ont doublement besoin d'une reconnaissance de la société et de ses réponses en matière de professionnalisation. Il n'est donc pas souhaitable de limiter la désignation en l'enfermant dans une définition par restriction, alors qu'il semble plus constructif de procéder par addition. C'est pour cette même raison que nous ne pourrions choisir ici l'étiquette d'interprète de proximité, qui, décrit une activité non professionnelle que pourrait exercer un voisin, un ami, un parent[28].

Parler d'*interprète de conférence*, enfin, revient à installer la conférence elle-même comme le fondement de la désignation professionnelle. Or ces professionnels doivent pouvoir faire état de la médiation culturelle et interculturelle comme d'un autre aspect de leur activité. Il convient donc de mettre l'accent sur la notion de lien, de médiation, et sur les qualités interpersonnelles[29] qui, à la fois, se déduisent et vont au-delà de leurs acquis linguistiques. La désignation doit se faire le reflet de l'ensemble de ces unités définitoires.

Désigner pour synthétiser la réalité d'une activité plurielle

Normaliser sur une absence de fondement social est problématique. Or, fonder c'est nommer car la nomination engage en ce qu'elle contient d'implicites, la structure, les modalités d'une pratique, et donc son avenir. Elle engage, comme nous l'avons vu, la problématique de l'identité professionnelle et de l'identité linguistique.

Ce qui est attendu de cette profession appartient à un code déontologique implicite. A l'heure actuelle, rien n'est véritablement mis en place pour permettre à l'interprète de se former et d'embrasser la complexité de ce qu'il doit accomplir.

Certes, il doit traduire, interpréter. Mais il doit également mettre en œuvre des compétences qui définissent une autre profession à part entière : celle de médiateur. A l'intersection de ces deux métiers se trouvent les principes, admis et reconnus, des liens entre les langues et la culture.

Or l'activité de l'interprète-médiateur est à la croisée de l'interculturalité et du plurilinguisme. Il montre au quotidien que la langue est le véritable outil de la médiation[30] et que l'interprète-médiateur en est l'acteur. Cette médiation, nous l'avons vu, se construit sur la triade "conscience-maîtrise-transparence": conscience de soi, de l'autre, du migrant comme de l'institutionnel ; maîtrise de soi, de l'autre en gérant les aspects non verbaux ; en n'étant jamais complice ; mais en comprenant simplement, en étant présent pour l'un et pour l'autre, voire proche, au cours de l'intervention, mais ni avant[31], ni après[32].

Il doit être présent, mais ne jamais prendre le pas sur l'institutionnel. Il doit savoir quand interrompre la prestation pour expliquer ou commenter ce qui se dit. Il se doit apprécier les sources de conflit potentiel pour permettre l'échange communicationnel. C'est parfois à lui qu'il revient de mettre en œuvre des stratégies efficaces d'intervention pour résoudre les problèmes.

Il doit rester neutre, mais doit pouvoir tenir la main du malade en situation d'isolement ; rester parfois seul avec lui, une fois le médecin sorti, afin de commenter un diagnostic douloureux. Être neutre en toutes circonstances. Or, le plus souvent et dans les faits, c'est bien le contraire que l'on attend de lui[33]. La posture de neutralité et d'effacement est véritablement remise en cause par les prérequis mêmes, que l'on exige de ces professionnels au travers des normes référentielles.

Nous le voyons bien, certaines désignations par adjectivation sont problématiques, puisqu'elles nous conduisent sur des représentations figées de l'autre : l'autre social en ce qu'il est représenté par l'immigrant, mais l'autre individuel également. L'ambiguïté symbolique prend ici une place fondamentale. Cet espace n'est pas le simple creuset métaphorique d'une juxtaposition de trois individus, chacun étant l'autre de l'autre. L'échange communicationnel, en devenir d'interprétation-médiation, est au contraire, l'espace au sein duquel trois identités vont de l'une à l'autre, pour mieux communiquer, et pour mieux s'aider.

Ici, l'interprète-médiateur n'est pas un Autre « communautaire ». Il rend compte de la parole des uns ; il est là pour eux, mais pour les autres aussi. En aucune façon, on ne peut le définir par l'altérité. S'il la symbolise comme une sorte d'allégorie éphémère, il n'en est pas le dépositaire professionnel.

C'est pourquoi la médiation qui s'effectue dans les actes d'interprétation est une variable qui annonce la spécificité d'un métier qui souffre encore de ses indéfinitions et de la conception que le grand public a de cette activité. Relier *interprétation* à *médiation*, donnerait un sens à cette profession qui, parce qu'elle est installée dans les approches interculturelles elles- mêmes en proie à une crise définitionnelle, manque toujours de repères.

Références bibliographiques

Amselle J.-L. *Vers un multiculturalisme français, l'empire de la coutume.* Paris : Flammarion, 2001. 125–126.

Backes S. « L'interprétariat et la traduction en milieu social. Un instrument garantissant les droits fondamentaux ». Écarts d'identité 113 (2008). En ligne : http://www.revues-plurielles.org/_uploads/pdf/6/113/ei_113_backes.pdf

Gile D. « Rôles d'interprètes ». *Les pratiques de l'interprétation et l'oralité dans la communication interculturelle.* Lausanne : l'Age d'Homme, 2010. 52.

Goguickian Ratcliff B., Suardi F. « L'interprète dans une consultation thérapeutique. Conceptions de son rôle et difficultés éprouvées ». *Psychothérapies*. Paris : Éditions Médecine et hygiène, 2006. 37–49.

Hofstadter D., Sander E. *L'analogie, cœur de la pensée*. Paris : Odile Jacob, 2013.

Ladmiral J.-R. « Le concept d'interprétation et l'oralité dans la communication interculturelle » *Les pratiques de l'interprétation et l'oralité dans la communication interne culturelle*, Lausanne : L'Age d'Homme, 2010. 18.

Mounin G. *Introduction à la sémiologie*, Paris : Les éditions de minuit, 1970. 129–133.

Ortega Herraez J. M., Foulquié Rubio A. I. « Interpreting in Police Settings in Spain, Service Providers' and Interpreters' Perspectives ». *Crossing Borders in Community Interpreting, Definitions and Dilemmas*. Amsterdam: John Benjamins Publishing 2008. 124–146.

Pöchhacker, F. « Interpreting as Mediation ». *Crossing Borders in Community Interpreting, definitions and dilemmas*. Amsterdam: John Benjamins Publishing, 2008. 9–26.

Rey, A., dir. *Dictionnaire historique de la langue française,* Paris, 2010.

Seleskovitch, D., M. Lederer. *Interpréter pour traduire*. Paris : Didier Érudition, 1984.

Notes

1 Après plus de 60 ans de pratique, l'activité de l'interprète de conférence, elle, est clairement définie et normée. Elle prend ses racines profondes dans l'histoire des deux derniers millénaires et ses racines récentes dans le procès de Nuremberg. C'est depuis ce procès que l'interprète de conférence se définit dans l'histoire sociale, économique et politique des États.

2 A comprendre également comme *direction*.

3 Mounin G. (1970) *Introduction à la sémiologie*, Les éditions de minuit, Paris. p. 129–133.

4 « Interprète (...), attesté isolément au début du XIXe siècle (1321, *interpreite*), apparaît sous la forme moderne à la fin du XIVe siècle. C'est un emprunt au latin classique *interpres-etis,* « intermédiaire, courtier, chargé d'affaires » puis « commentateur » et « traducteur », en particulier par oral. Le mot est probablement un ancien terme juridique composé de *inter-(inter-)* et d'un élément *–pres,* qui représente peut-être une forme nominale d'un verbe disparu, signifiant « acheter » ou « vendre » et qui serait apparenté à *pretium* (prix)." DHLF, p.1108

5 Il est intéressant de noter qu'un des champs d'application communs de l'usage de ces deux termes relève de la théologie et de l'intermission entre Dieu et l'Homme. Cette fonction précise prend toute sa valeur dans la relation symbolique qui s'établit entre le Haut et le Bas.

6 « Médiateur, trice (…) est emprunté (v. 1265) au bas latin *mediator*. Il est apparu en français dans un emploi spécialisé en théologie chrétienne, Jésus étant dit *médiateur* entre Dieu et l'Homme. Puis, il a pris le sens plus général de « personne qui s'entremet pour effectuer un accord » (v. 1355), spécialement en droit international (1437) ou l'acception doit beaucoup (1973) au modèle de l'*ombudsman* suédois. » *DHLF*, p. 1298

7 Norme ISO/10 DIS 3611

8 Nous citerons ici les services hospitaliers de l'Assistance Publique qui maillent le territoire national. Ces interprètes interviennent en accompagnement, lors de consultations publiques ou privées. Certaines sont organisées dans le cadre de rencontres ou de consultations psychiatriques. Des consultations à vocation transculturelle accueillent ces professionnels au sein de centres spécialisés. Ce seront, à Paris, le Centre Minkowska, La Maison de Solenn, à l'Hôpital Cochin). D'autres consultations sont plus généralistes et regroupent les activités purement médicales, psychiatriques, juridiques ou même transculturelles. Nous trouverons là les COMEDE (Comité Médical pour les Exilés), la CIMADE qui se définit comme un « service œcuménique d'entraide » : « La Cimade a pour but de manifester une solidarité active avec ceux qui souffrent, qui sont opprimés et exploités et d'assurer leur défense, quelles que soient leur nationalité, leur position politique ou religieuse. » (http://www.lacimade.org/)

9 Les centres de rétention pour étrangers, « Sangatte » (aujourd'hui fermé), les zones d'attente dans les aéroports (La Croix Rouge à Roissy Charles de Gaulle), les prisons, les commissariats, l'ASE (Aide Sociale à l'enfance) et le travail avec les travailleurs sociaux ; Inter Service Migrants, Migration Santé Alsace, (les associations, prestataires de service d'interprétation), L'association Mana de Bordeaux (Association de médecine transculturelle)

10 L'OFPRA (Office Français de la Protection des Réfugiés et des Apatrides), la CNDA (Cour Nationale du Droit d'Asile), l'OFII (Office français de l'immigration et de l'intégration)

11 Il lui faudra être un véritable « accompagnateur social », assister également le brancardier, ou tout simplement soutenir l'immigrant dans des situations personnellement douloureuses (lui tenir la main, lui parler à l'oreille, annoncer la mort d'un proche ou la maladie …).

12 Pour une introduction de la médiation dans les actes d'interprétation, voir le film documentaire *Les Arrivants* (Bories Claudine, Chagnard Patrice, 2009).

13 « Traduction immédiate, elle ne subit de corrections que linéaires, aucune retouche n'efface la version première, aucun remords ne gomme ce qui a été dit. », Seleskovitch, D. (1985), « Interprétation ou interprétariat », Meta: Translators' Journal, vol. 30, n°1, 1985, p. 20

14 Il est rapporté par plusieurs interprètes qu'un jargon se crée autour des principaux documents ou lieux auxquels sont confrontés les migrants : « Il y a (…) l'APS (Autorisation Provisoire de séjour) qui est le premier document de la préfecture donné pour un mois. Les demandeurs d'asile l'appellent « le jaune » car le document est de couleur jaune. De plus, après l'APS, la préfecture donne aux demandeurs d'asile un récépissé de trois mois, qui est un document de couleur verte. Les migrants appellent le document : « le vert ». Il faut donc comprendre de quoi ils parlent quand ils disent *j'ai eu mon vert »*, Arakelian, Monica, *Mémoire de fin de diplôme universitaire (*DUIM, session 2013)

15 *Fusion* fait allusion, ici, au creuset, récipient propice à la fusion, que nous rapprocherons du *melting pot*, terme tiré du titre de la pièce d'Israël Zangwill, dont l'usage métaphorique s'est répandu au XXe siècle, aux États-Unis, pour décrire l'assimilation des migrants, qui pouvaient accéder à la citoyenneté américaine, dès lors qu'ils acceptaient l'ensemble des valeurs qui composaient « le creuset fédérateur », tout en y contribuant eux-mêmes.

16 Herraez, Juan M. Ortega et Foulquié Rubio, Ana I., « Interpreting in police settings in Spain, service providers and interpreters' perspectives », *in* Crossing Boarders in Community Interpreting, definitions and dilemmas, John Benjamins Publishing Company, Amsterdam/Philadelphia, 2008. p. 139.

17 « Chez les interprètes de service public, on ne trouve pas les mêmes exigences formalisées de « fidélité » que dans le domaine judiciaire … En revanche, les besoins personnels des particuliers que sert l'interprète sont au moins aussi présents, de même que l'importance de certaines interventions allant au-delà de la transformation translinguistique des paroles des interlocuteurs—avec les épineux problèmes que cela pose. », GILE Daniel (2010), « Rôles d'interprètes » in *Les pratiques de l'interprétation et l'oralité dans la communication interculturelle*, p. 52.

18 Omar Guerrero, psychothérapeute, cite cet exemple d'un patient qui commente le rêve qu'il vient de faire d'un oiseau enfermé dans sa cage ; oiseau qui n'est autre qu'un corbeau. La décomposition en deux syllabes du terme corbeau détache *cor* de *beau* et permet la lecture d'un autre signifiant : un corps beau. *Séminaire DUIM*, juin 2013.

19 Il ne suffit pas à l'interprète-médiateur d'être capable d'analyser l'origine ethnique, sociale, géographique, religieuse des personnes pour lesquelles la prestation est mise en place. Il lui faut également posséder une juste appréciation des relations géopolitiques et donc connaître les situations de conflits géographiques que ce soit entre tribus, groupes religieux, ou même entre groupes sociaux d'origine diverse. Cette connaissance lui permettra d'anticiper et donc de déjouer un éventuel conflit sous-jacent. L'interprète-médiateur et la personne pour laquelle il va interpréter, peuvent parfois appartenir à des communautés qui vivent dans leur pays des situations de conflit. Ce simple fait peut constituer une véritable barrière à l'échange communicationnel, et entraver la prestation elle-même.

20 Voir sur ce point, Douglas Hofstadter et Emmanuel Sander (2013), *L'analogie, cœur de la pensée*, Odile Jacob, Paris (chapitre 1)."L'analogie est le mécanisme qui, sans que nous en ayons conscience, dicte le choix de nos mots et notre compréhension des situations les plus délicates."

21 Le passage par le JE ôte le seul filtre que la langue puisse mettre entre les mots douloureux entendus et celui qui les rapporte. Portée ainsi à son comble, l'assimilation de l'interprète à la victime est source de danger psychologique. Ici, le psychothérapeute a un rôle fondamental à jouer. C'est lui qui doit permettre de mettre en mots certaines des images les plus fortes, et ainsi laisser se libérer la charge émotionnelle de ce qui a été entendu et rapporté. A cet égard, les professionnels dont l'activité se fait essentiellement par téléphone, souvent la nuit, sont parmi les plus exposés. Exposés, ils le sont doublement, dans la mesure où ils ne voient pas leurs interlocuteurs, d'une part, mais aussi, parce qu'ils restent seuls, une fois l'intervention terminée, et le téléphone raccroché.

22 En fait, la traduction du terme *thérapeute* par celui de *marabout* semble véhiculer

une réelle confusion, dans la mesure où le marabout s'inscrit essentiellement dans un rapport hiérarchique, tant social que religieux : « Les marabouts (…) sont à la fois des religieux musulmans et des locuteurs berbères. » Ils sont donc les représentants d'une « catégorie sociale hybride ». Voir Amselle J.-L., *Vers un multiculturalisme français, l'empire de la coutume*, pp. 125-126.

23 En Grande-Bretagne, et dans le contexte anglo-saxon, plus généralement.

24 Désignation parfois reprise en France, également.

25 C'est cette même étiquette qu'a choisi la Confédération Helvétique.

26 En Suisse, c'est l'étiquette d'interprète communautaire qui est adoptée. Ici, il ne s'agit que d'une traduction de « *community interpreter* ». La nomination de cette activité professionnelle en référence à *interprète communautaire* pose un ensemble de problèmes sous-tendus par la polysémie de l'adjectif *communautaire* elle-même.

27 Cette étiquette a été choisie par la Belgique.

28 Rôle que joue, par exemple, le jeune enfant qui accompagne ses parents non francophones.

29 La conceptualisation de cette notion passe souvent par la mise en relation des termes *médiation* et *interpersonnelle*. C'est, par exemple, ce que nous propose Franz Pöchhacker, dans l'extrait suivant : "*In contrast to the simple image of a " from-to', or " back-and-forth" movement between language systems and culture (however defined), interpersonal mediation cannot be discussed without reference to such features of human interaction as intentions, objectives, expectations, attitudes, status, power or conflicts.* », Pöchhacker, Franz, « Interpreting as mediation », *Crossing Boarders in Community Interpreting, definitions and dilemmas*,. p. 13.

30 À propos des liens qui se nouent entre l'oralité et la médiation, Jean-René Ladmiral considère que « la médiation de la communication (orale) s'opère alors « sur le tas » et devient un enjeu relationnel, où interfèrent des rapports de pouvoir de séduction, les clivages idéologiques, ou nationaux, les enjeux d'argent, etc. entre individus et entre sous-groupes plus ou moins « communautarisés » L'ensemble des rapports décrits ici relèvent de l'ethos, comme nous le verrons plus tard, LADMIRAL, Jean-René (2010), « Le concept d'interprétation et l'oralité dans la communication interculturelle » in *Les pratiques de l'interprétation et l'oralité dans la communication interne culturelle*, p. 18.

31 Dans les salles d'attente par exemple, l'interprète attend souvent assis à côté de la personne pour laquelle il va effectuer une prestation d'intervention. Lorsque le dialogue s'engage entre eux, toute neutralité est d'ores et déjà perdue.

32 Il arrive souvent que l'interprète-médiateur retrouve le migrant pour lequel il est intervenu, à l'arrêt du bus, ou sur le quai du métro, par exemple.

33 Dans les PMI, il leur est demandé de commencer le dialogue avec les patients, dès la rencontre dans la salle d'attente, afin de préparer et d'optimiser la consultation.

Part 2 / Deuxième Partie

History and Literature / Histoire et Littérature

La traduction et la création du bon usage

DOUGLAS KIBBEE

Résumé

Dans la première moitié du XVIIe la traduction était d'abord une source d'enrichissement de la langue française, celle-ci toujours considérée pauvre en lexique, instable en morphologie et désordonnée en syntaxe. La traduction sert à exemplifier les notions de clarté dans les *Remarques sur la langue françoise* de Claude Favre de Vaugelas (1647) et dans la réponse de Scipion Dupleix, *La liberté de la langue françoise dans sa pureté* (1651). Les termes disputés dans leurs remarques sont souvent trouvés dans les difficultés de la traduction, et les solutions reflètent la nouvelle esthétique de la clarté, parfois en conflit avec la « tyrannie de l'usage » tant prisée par Vaugelas.
Mots-clé: génie de la langue, synonymie, périphrase, ordre des mots, clarté, netteté, Vaugelas, Dupleix

Abstract

In the first half of the seventeenth century, translation was first a means to enrich the French language, still considered lexically impoverished, morphologically uncertain, and syntactically confused and confusing. Translation serves both to exemplify the notions of clarity in the *Remarks on the French Language* by Vaugelas (1647) and in the response to this work, *The Freedom of the French Language in its Purity* (1651) by Scipion Dupleix. The words and structures to be debated by these two *remarqueurs* are often found in thorny problems for translation. The solutions proposed reflect the new esthetic of clarity, which sometimes clashes with Vaugelas' cherished "tyranny of usage."
Keywords: Genius of the language, synonymy, paraphrase, clarity, exactitude, word order, Vaugelas, Dupleix

Dans la première moitié du XVIIe siècle, la traduction des langues anciennes vers le français passe d'un modèle à imiter à un outil de perfectionnement d'une langue devenue partenaire égal dans le monde des lettres, selon la perspective des auteurs de l'époque. Nous examinerons dans cette contribution le rôle de la traduction dans l'élaboration des notions du bon usage. Claude Favre de Vaugelas (1585–1650) et Scipion Dupleix (1569–1661) sont en accord pour affirmer que les traductions sont égales ou même supérieures aux textes originaux. Pourtant la traduction a un rôle différent dans leurs remarques et observations, ce qui reflète leurs conceptions de la source du bon français.

La traduction est omniprésente dans la pensée grammaticale de la première moitié du XVIIe siècle. Malherbe croyait que si l'on lisait attentivement sa traduction de *Tite-Live*, elle pourrait servir de grammaire du français (Sorel 1664: 234, cité dans Lebègue 1941: 179).[1] D'autres produisaient des grammaires et des collections de remarques plus traditionnelles, dans la confection desquelles les traductions servaient d'exemples. Après avoir passé en revue la traduction dans les années 1640, nous regarderons de près les renvois à la traduction insérés dans les remarques de Vaugelas et dans les observations sur ces remarques produites par Dupleix.

Quelles sont les règles du bon usage et comment se relient-elles aux règles de la bonne traduction? Au milieu du XVIIe siècle plusieurs théoriciens de la traduction veulent imposer des règles, à l'instar des règles du théâtre et de la versification. Cette manie pour les règles se voit également chez les premiers remarqueurs. Eux aussi recherchent les moyens de limiter la variation et la créativité linguistique, invoquant, selon les cas, l'usage social, la raison, le génie de la langue, et l'histoire pour justifier leurs choix.

Presque tous les participants aux débats linguistiques du XVIIe siècle étaient en même temps traducteurs, Malherbe de *Tite-Live*, Vaugelas de *Quinte Curce*, Chapelain du *Gueux* de Guzman parmi d'autres. Dupleix est exceptionnel à cet égard, parce qu'il a écrit plutôt des synthèses que des traductions, d'abord en philosophie, ensuite en sciences et en histoire.[2] Mais même ceux qui n'ont jamais publié de traduction ont appris leur sens du style et de la rectitude grammaticale et lexicale dans les exercices de traduction. La traduction sert à « former [le] stile & acquerir la facilité d'écrire », rappelle Godeau, dans sa préface à Giry (1630). Justement, la décennie qui suit l'officialisation de l'Académie Française voit une petite explosion de traductions non-érudites dont le but est de polir le style des auteurs, et d'instruire un public de courtisans qui rejettent les lourds tomes de traductions commentées et annotées dans le style pédantesque (Martin 1999 [1969], I, 197, II 607 sqq et Zuber 1968, 52–63).[3] Il y a même une petite réaction humoristique à l'emploi des traductions comme exercices de style, dans les « traductions travesties » ou « bouffons » des années 1650 (voir Leclerc 2008).

La traduction est non seulement un exercice de style, mais en même temps une façon de faire du français l'égal des langues anciennes (selon la perspective de l'époque). Nicolas Perrot, sieur d'Ablancourt (1606–1664), un auteur estimé par Vaugelas comme « un de nos meilleurs Escrivains » (1647 : 64), voit dans la traduction un moyen de réaliser son dessein « d'enrichir ma langue de ce que l'Antiquité a de plus beau » (Préface aux *Guerres d'Alexandre*, d'Arrian, 1646). En effet, le TLF note plusieurs mots pour lesquels la première attestation est dans une de ses traductions (*obligeamment, lesbien*). Vaugelas, en reconnaissant que la cour est la source du bon usage, admet que :

> nous avons encore un grand nombre d'autres phrases, qui ne viennent pas de la Cour, mais qui sont prises de tous les meilleurs Autheurs Grecs et Latins, dont les despoüilles font une partie des richesses de nostre langue, et peut-estre ce qu'elle a de plus magnifique et de plus pompeux. (1647, Préface II, 3)

Le modèle offert par les langues anciennes a toutefois ses limites, dans les constructions et dans le vocabulaire.

L'équivalence des langues dépend d'une conception où un sens indépendant des langues se réalise différemment dans chaque langue particulière, selon le génie de cette langue. Les structures qui rendent clairement le sens selon le génie d'une langue manqueront de clarté dans la langue cible. Isaac Lemaistre de Sacy note que la « brièveté » du latin, « plus courte & plus serrée » que le français, peut être une source d'obscurité : « ... la brefueté, qui est vn peu obscure, ayant quelque grace & quelque dignité dans la langue Latine, passe d'ordinaire pour vn vice, & ne se souffre presque iamais en nostre langue » (Préface au *Poeme de S. Prosper contre les ingrats*, 1650). L'obscurité chez Thucydide vient, selon Perrot d'Ablancourt, de « tant de l'affectation des termes et des frases qui sont hors d'vsage, que de l'embarras de la construction où aucune parole n'est en son lieu, ce qui donne de la force, mais derobe la clarté ; ioint qu'il entasse pensées sur pensées au lieu de les demesler ... » (Préface à *L'histoire de Thucydide*, 1662).

Ces contrastes des langues anciennes et du français mènent à une discussion des mérites d'une traduction littérale ou d'une traduction plus libre. Les libertés prises par Perrot d'Ablancourt pour résoudre ces problèmes lui ont valu l'approbation de Ménage, qui a inventé l'expression « belle infidèle » pour décrire ses traductions. A quoi Perrot d'Ablancourt a répondu qu' « il vaut mieux estre infidelle dans les petites choses, pour estre plus fidelle dans les grandes » [*ibid*].

Lemaistre de Sacy veut chercher le bon équilibre entre la liberté et la littéralité :

> je me suis efforcé d'éuiter égallement les deux extremitez où tombent aisément ceux qui traduisent; dont l'vne est vne liberté qui degenere en licence, & qui rend le Traducteur semblable à vn Peintre, qui voulant représenter le visage d'vn homme, en fait vn tout different selon son imagination & sa fantaisie : & l'autre est vn assujettissement qui degenere en servitude, & qui rend vne traduction semblable au modele qu'elle a voulu exprimer, comme vn homme mort est semblable à vn homme viuant. (Préface au *Poeme de S. Prosper contre les ingrats*, 1650)

Cette formulation reprend les termes de liberté et de tyrannie dans les débats politiques et linguistiques de l'époque dont nous avons parlé ailleurs (Kibbee 2011). La liberté de l'expression est nécessaire pour revendiquer la gloire de la France qui veut monter sur le trône de l'éloquence, mais l'innovation trop hardie met en risque cette ascendance.

En même temps qu'on proclame la libération du français du joug des langues classiques, les rapports entre ces langues, établis par la traduction, continuent de générer la discussion. Vaugelas craint l'influence exercée par la traduction et cherche la pureté de la langue française, le vrai génie de la langue, dans l'usage des femmes. Elles seraient moins corrompues par les connaissances d'autres langues, et en particulier du latin et du grec. Dupleix n'y croit pas du tout :

> L'absurdité de ces paradoxes est si evidente, que sous le respect de l'Auteur, ils sont ridicules. Les ayant desia impugnés en mon observation sur le Principe I. ie diray seulement icy

> qu'il ne nous doit plus proposer l'autorité des plus doctes & plus celebres Escrivains touchant la pureté de nostre langue, puis qu'il leur prefere les personnes qui n'ont point estudié: & que luy mesme est moins croiable que les ignorans & les femmes: parce que (suivant ses propres maximes) estant bien versé en la langue Greque & en la Latine, il peut corrompre la Françoise, qui luy est naturelle, par le commerce de celles là comme estrangeres. (1651 : 89)

La source du bon usage est ainsi en jeu : pour Vaugelas, la « plus saine partie » de la Cour et particulièrement ceux qui ne sont pas contaminés par les connaissances de langues anciennes ; pour Dupleix, les meilleurs écrivains, y compris les traducteurs, en somme, les doctes. Dupleix raconte sa propre formation, qui comprend une forte dose de traductions :

> je n'ay pas esté si incurieux que je n'aye aussi espuré & poly mon style par les conferences que j'ay euës avec ceux qui sont en la plus haute reputation d'elegance, de politesse, & de pureté de langage à la Cour, & en l'Academie: par la lecture des escrits, tant de ceux qui ont produit des ouvrages de leur invention, que de ceux qui ont traduit en nostre langue des pieces les plus belles & les plus riches des Latins, avec vn si heureux succez, que l'elegance de la traduction egale, & bien souvent surpasse celle de la piece traduite. (1651 : 7)

Cette différence entre les sources du bon usage s'exprime dans les jugements de syntaxe et de lexique, et dans la façon dont les traductions sont utilisées comme exemples.

Les ornements de l'éloquence des auteurs antiques ne correspondent plus aux goûts du public français du milieu du XVIIe siècle. Un premier exemple concerne la confection de longues périodes. Godeau préface ainsi la traduction de Cicéron offerte par Giry :

> Ceux qui entendent les secrets de la langue Latine, sçauent qu'elle n'a point, ou fort peu de rapport auec la nostre ; que la phrase, les figures, le tour des periodes, & les liaisons qui les doiuent attacher les vnes aux autres, sont toutes differentes ; & qu'il arriue souuent qu'vne pensée, dont la force est renfermée

> dans la hardiesse ou la brieveté d'vne maniere de parler, deuient languissante, & ne se recognoît quasi plus, à cause des circonlocutions dont il faut user pour l'expliquer à nostre mode. (1630, préface)

Vaugelas lui-même déplore ces périodes, dont la longueur est « fort ennemie à la netteté du stile » (1647 : 592). Pour Vaugelas la période est un exemple des raisons pour lesquelles il faut délaisser les modèles de l'antiquité, et la traduction exemplifie cette différence entre le génie des deux langues. Une règle qu'il fournit dans ce sens condamne l'emploi du pronom relatif *qui* au début de la phrase :

> [*qui*] est incapable de commencer une periode, ny d'avoir jamais *un point* devant luy, mais tousjours *une virgule*, tellement qu'il faut joindre à la periode precedente, et alors elle se trouve d'une longueur demesurée et monstrueuse (1647 : 86)

Pour soutenir cette règle il cite un exemple de sa traduction de *Quinte Curce*, notant que « les Latins se donnent ordinairement cette licence … mais nous sommes plus exacts en nostre langue, et en notre stile ».[4] Vaugelas ne fait ici que de répéter un lieu commun parmi les traducteurs de l'époque : dans les traités de règles pour la traduction qui foisonnent dans les années 1640 et 1650, on recommande souvent le découpage des périodes.[5] Le français est supérieur au latin et la traduction en est la preuve. Dupleix ne conteste pas la règle grammaticale, mais reproche à son adversaire son arrogance et son inconsistance, ainsi que la prétention que le français est plus régulier et plus exact que le latin (1651 : 112–113).

Dans la syntaxe de l'accord, *toute sorte* ou *toutes sortes*, Dupleix a recours aux exemples de traductions pour appuyer sa règle contre l'indécision de Vaugelas. Vaugelas propose que « d'ordinaire » *toute sorte* se met avec le singulier et *toutes sortes* avec le pluriel : *toute sorte de bon-heur ; toutes sortes de maux* (1647 : 130). Mais il ne se prononce pas fermement, citant Coeffeteau. Dupleix juge cette règle « erronée & trompeuse » (1651 : 591), basant sa propre règle sur la logique, la grammaire, et des exemples tirés de Cicéron et de Virgile, pour lesquels il fournit une traduction en français.

Quand Vaugelas cite les traductions, comme généralement dans ses citations littéraires, c'est pour critiquer un usage dont il ne trouve pas d'écho dans le parler des courtisans. Par exemple, Vaugelas s'étonne des fautes contre le bon usage qu'il trouve dans les traductions de Perrot d'Ablancourt, comme l'emploi de *tandis* sans *que :*

> Il [*tandis*] ne se doit jamais dire ny escrire, qu'il ne soit suivy de que ... Cette faute néantmoins se trouve dans un ouvrage de l'un de nos meilleurs Escrivains, qui soutenoit alors qu'on en pouvait user ainsi; Mais depuis il s'est rendu à l'opinion generale, et ne s'est plus servy de cette façon de parler dans ses Ouvrages suivans, que toute la France estime comme un des plus grands ornemens de nostre langue (1647 : 64)

Toutefois, Vaugelas estime que la recherche de l'élégance peut permettre au traducteur de transgresser certaines règles qui contraignent les autres. Dans sa remarque « *Certaines constructions et façons de parler irregulieres* », Vaugelas accepte les « fautes qui passent pour une vertu », d'abord une faute contre la logique (*s'empescher* pour *empescher*), et ensuite une faute contre la grammaire et contre la netteté (*laissant sa mere avec sa femme et ses enfans prisonniers*) (1647 : 397–398). Dans le premier cas, Vaugelas conclut que « l'expression non seulement en est bonne, mais elegante selon le sentiment de la pluspart de nos meilleurs Escrivains, que j'ay consulté là dessus », et dans le deuxième, « tant s'en faut donc que ceux qui en sont juges capables, la condamnent, qu'au contraire ils la loüent, et la preferent de beaucoup à la reguliere ». En citant ces autres juges, peut-être que Vaugelas exprime ses propres hésitations devant de telles constructions. Cette soumission à l'usage des courtisans est souvent critiquée par Dupleix, dans les traductions comme ailleurs. L'abus ne peut constituer l'usage approuvé.

Le recours à la traduction se voit surtout dans les commentaires sur les mots, soit l'emprunt direct aux langues anciennes, soit le maintien d'une distinction exprimée en latin mais plus parmi les courtisans, soit la création d'un néologisme pour éviter l'équivoque. Le plus souvent, Vaugelas veut supprimer un mot et critique son emploi par des traducteurs. Par exemple, selon Vaugelas, ceux qui sont influencés par la traduction emploieraient *onguent* pour *parfum*, mais l'usage veut limiter *onguent* au sens de « médicament » (1647 : *458). Mais

Dupleix estime que cette distinction est toujours utile (1651 : 378–379). Pour Dupleix, cette utilisation dans la traduction peut justifier l'emploi d'une forme directement empruntée au latin, comme *héroïdes* pour *héroïnes*, « puis qu'Ovide en use ainsi dans une elegie qu'il escrit à sa femme » (1651 : 292).

Quant aux archaïsmes, Vaugelas juge vieilli l'emploi de la préposition *ès* (1647 : 167), « bannie du beau langage », mais Dupleix cite la traduction du rite catholique pour la garder (1651 : 252). Pareillement les traductions de l'écriture sainte justifie pour Dupleix la distinction entre *je croy* (du verbe *croire*) et *je crois* (du verbe *croistre*).

Les deux remarqueurs disputent également la néologie dans la concurrence entre *conjurateur* et *conjuré*. Comme un de ses principes, Vaugelas déclare que la formation de nouveaux mots « est bon en la langue Latine, & plus encore en la Greque : mais non pas en la nostre : où jamais cette hardiesse n'a reussi à qui que ce soit » (1647 : Préface, XI), une condamnation qu'il reprend dans sa remarque sur le barbarisme (1647 : 569), notant que les néologismes de Ronsard et du Vair ont eu « un mauvais succes ». Dupleix répond que la fabrication de nouveaux mots est nécessaire (1651 : 93) et encore qu' « il y a beaucoup plus de raison que la langue Françoise fasse des mots nouveaux extraits de la Latine, que la Latine n'en tire de la Greque », et confère le privilège d'en faire aux « hommes de rare doctrine & suffisance » (1651 : 99). D'ailleurs

> Ronsard, le Cardinal du Perron, M. du Vair, Vigenaire & autres grands personnages du siècle dernier, & du present, ont travaillé en cela si heureusement, qu'ils se sont acquis autant de loüange en enrichissant de nouveaux mots la langue Françoise, que ces nouveaux Reformateurs de langage se sont chargés de blasme par l'abolition & retrenchement de plusieurs termes energiques & utiles (1651 : 100).

Un exemple de mot inventé serait *conjurateur*. Vaugelas (1647 : 518–519) déclare que *conjurateur* n'est pas français, expliquant que ceux qui ont inventé ce mot se sont trompés dans leur notion de voix : *conjurateur* est actif, et désigne une personne qui agit, tandis que *conjuré* a l'air d'être passif.

Dupleix (1651 : 212) objecte que nombreux sont les mots à forme passive et au sens actif; la bonne question est de savoir si *conjuré* et *conjurateur* sont vraiment synonymes. Ce n'est pas la voix, mais l'aspect qui est en jeu. *Conjuré* peut être actif ou passif, selon Dupleix, et pour soutenir son argument il cite Cicéron, lui-même citant Euripide[6]:

> Juravi lingua mentem iuratam[7] gero
> I'ay iuré de la langue & mon ame est iurée
> C'est à dire, mon ame est astreinte & obligée par serment.

De cette manière, *conjuré* est équivoque, parce que actif ou passif, et la preuve est dans la traduction du latin. La traduction dépasse, en effet, la simple étymologie, en fournissant un contexte d'usage. La distinction entre *conjurateur* et *conjuré* est plutôt aspectuelle—*conjurateur* signifierait « l'habitude à se porter aux conjurations & conspirations », tandis que *conjuré* désignerait une participation ponctuelle. En évitant ces équivoques, selon Dupleix, le français peut espérer accéder au premier rang des langues.

Ce but s'atteindra par la recherche de la clarté, un principe que les deux remarqueurs soutiennent, mais qui doit se soumettre, selon Vaugelas, à l'usage des courtisans, même si cet usage est ambigu. Dupleix cite une traduction des *Annales* de Tacite[8] qu'il profère pour garder le terme *accoustumance*, que Vaugelas croit vieilli. Vaugelas veut le bannir au nom de l'usage, tout en reconnaissant son utilité. *Coustume* est équivoque, admet-il (1647 : 383), et « *accoustumance* exprime bien mieux & uniquement ce qu'il signifie. Mais il n'y a point de raison contre l'Usage. »[9]

Que faire si le recours à l'usage comme l'arbitre de la langue entraîne l'appauvrissement de la langue, lui enlève sa capacité pour des distinctions toujours utiles ? Pour Dupleix, l'utilité de termes latins dans la traduction est une raison suffisante pour les maintenir. C'est la traduction de Tacite (II, 62) qui justifie la distinction voulue :

> Degenerabat a labore *[ac virtute]* miles assuetudine voluptatum & contemptu Ducis La soldatesque quittoit ses exercices ordinaires par l'accoustumance aux voluptés & par le mespris qu'elle faisoit de son General (1651 : 123[10])

Il poursuit : « C'est pourquoy *[nous soulignons] accoustumance* ne signifiant qu'un acheminement à la Coustume, ce mot, *Coustume*, qui marque une habitude entierement formée, ne luy peut pas estre proprement subrogé » *ibid.*) La traduction dépasse son rôle d'exemple pour assumer celui d'explication, une explication basée sur l'aspect. Bien traduire est la raison pour laquelle il faut maintenir l'emploi du terme *accoustumance*.

Dupleix utilise sa traduction de cet exemple pour soutenir sa conception de la clarté. *Coustume*, le mot préféré par Vaugelas, est selon Dupleix un terme équivoque, avec une interprétation juridique et une autre morale. *Accoustumance* ne mène qu'à la *coustume*, sens moral.[11] La recherche de la clarté s'exprime également par l'ajout de l'adjectif *ordinaire* pour opposer le comportement attendu et le comportement dégénéré, par l'emploi de la préposition *par* pour spécifier le rapport logique exprimé par l'ablatif, par la répétition de cette préposition pour expliciter l'équilibre entre les deux parties, et par l'insertion du deuxième verbe (*faisoit*) pour montrer qui est contempteur de qui.

Un deuxième exemple—l'emploi de *superbe* comme nom. Vaugelas note qu' « une infinité de gens & particulierement les Prédicateurs » emploient *la superbe* comme équivalent de *l'orgueil*, mais prononce tout de même que « ce mot est tousiours adjectif, & iamais substantif » (1647 : 31). Cette infinité de gens ne se trouve évidemment pas à la Cour. Ce qui gêne davantage Dupleix c'est que les deux mots ne sont pas synonymes, ou, au moins, qu'il y a une nuance qui les distinguent pour qu'ils peuvent être complémentaires—lorsque *orgueil* est fastueux, ils sont équivalents, mais *superbe* combine toujours faste et orgueil. Son raisonnement se base sur la traduction de *Tite-Live*, où, selon Dupleix, le mot *orgueil* aurait moins de force,[12] et représenterait moins bien la hauteur stéréotypique des Rhodiens :

> Superbiam verborum iracundi oderunt, prudentes irrident, vtique si inferioris adversus superiorem, capitali pœna nemo vnquam dignam judicavit:
>
> Les hommes coleres s'offensent de la superbe des paroles: mais les prudens s'en moquent, mesmement quand elles sont dites de l'inferieur au superieur: & iamais perſonne ne l'a iugée digne du dernier supplice.

Dans sa traduction Dupleix adhère aux principes de la clarté que lui, comme Vaugelas, a tant prisée. D'abord l'ordre des mots : dans la première partie, Dupleix met l'objet direct après le verbe, pour transformer une phrase OSV en SVO ; dans la dernière partie l'original latin sépare l'adjectif *dignam* de son complément (*poena capitali*) insérant le sujet et l'adverbe entre les deux, et l'adjectif se trouve devant plutôt qu'après le verbe. Voilà un bel exemple de la façon dont le français suit l'ordre dit « naturel ». Dans la deuxième partie, Dupleix insère un pronom (*elles*) pour renvoyer à *paroles* et un verbe (*sont dites*) pour expliciter les rapports sous-entendus dans la version latine. Notons aussi comment il emploie *colere* comme adjectif, comme pour renforcer l'opinion de Vaugelas, transformant l'adjectif *iracundi* en nom substantif qualifié par un adjectif (*hommes coleres*) ; en utilisant ce mot générique pour l'être humain, et ensuite en mettant l'article défini devant les adjectifs *prudens, inférieur* et *supérieur*, Dupleix marque comment l'ambassadeur rhodien veut établir, dans l'abstraction, la réponse raisonnable à leur comportement imprudent.

La traduction opère donc à plusieurs niveaux dans le travail de ces remarqueurs. Ils ont tous été formés par la traduction, sont tous critiques de traductions de leur époque et des précédentes (Amyot, Vigenere, etc.), et la plupart d'entre eux sont des traducteurs actifs. La confrontation de différentes langues et les exigences d'un nouveau public les obligent à embrasser la clarté. La traduction sert à résoudre des questions linguistiques, et sert de modèle pour la nouvelle esthétique. Elle vise l'innovation tout en essayant de la brider, et la bride tout en embrassant une expressivité toujours en train de se perfectionner.

Références bibliographiques

Arnauld d'Andilly, Robert. *Histoire des Juifs, ecrite par Flavius Joseph, Sous le Titre de Antiquitez Judaïques, traduite sur l'Original Grec reveu sur divers Manuscrits*. Bruxelles: Eug. Henry Frick, 1676.

Ballard, Michel. « Gaspard de Tende: théoricien de la traduction ». *La traduction à l'âge classique*. Eds. Michel Ballard et Lieven d'Hulst. Lille : Les presses universitaires de Lille, 1995. 43–61.

Blampain, Daniel.. « Aux origines du français de référence, la traduction ». *Cahiers de l'Institut de Linguistique de Louvain* 26, 2000. 43–54.

Camus, Jean-Pierre. « Issue aux Censeurs ». Postface à *Alcime, relation fvneste ou se descovvre la main de Dieu sur les Impies.* Paris : Martin Lasnier, 1625.

De Nardis, Luigi, éd. *Regole della traduzione. Testi inediti di Port-Royal e del « Cercle » de Miramion (metà del XVII secolo)*. Naples : Bibliopolis, 1991.

Dotoli, Giovanni. *Littérature et société en France au XVIIe siècle. Vol.* 4. Paris : Presses de l'Université de Paris Sorbonne, 2004.

Dupleix, Scipion. *La liberté de la langue françoise dans sa pureté*. Paris: Denis Bechet, 1651.

Estienne, Henri. *Deux dialogues du nouueau langage françois italianizé & autrement desguizé : principalement entre les courtisans de ce temps : De plusieurs nouueautez que ont accompagné ceste nouueauté de langage : De quelques courtisanismes modernes, & de quelques singularitez courtisanesques*. Genève : H. Estienne, 1578.

Giry, Louis. *Dialogue des causes de la corruption de l'eloquence*. Paris : Iean Camusat, 1636. (Première édition, 1630)

Harlay de Champvallon, Achilles de, Marquis de Bréval. *Les oeuvres de C. Corneille Tacite, traduites de latin en François*. Paris: veuve Jean Camusat & Pierre Le Petit, 1644.

Kibbee, Douglas A. 2011. « 'Liberté' et 'tyrannie' dans le discours normatif ». *Langue commune et changements de norme*. Ed., Sonia Branca-Rosoff. Paris: Champion, 2011. 45–60.

Labègue, Raymond 1941. « La traduction de Tite-Live par Malherbe ». *Bibliothèque d'Humanisme et Renaissance* 1, 1941. 173–185.

Lebègue, Raymond. « La syntaxe de Malherbe, traducteur de Sénèque ». *Cahiers de l'Association Internationale des Études Françaises* 8, 1956. 139–146.

Leclerc, Jean. *L'antiquité travestie et la vogue du burlesque en France,* 1643–1661. Ste-Foy (QC) : Presses de l'Université Laval, 2008.

Lemaistre de Sacy, Louis-Isaac. *Poeme de S. Prosper contre les ingrats. Traduit en Vers & Prose. Seconde edition. En laqvelle on a adiovsté l'excellente Lettre du mesme S. à Ruffin. Avec vn abregé de tovte sa Doctrine touchant la Grace & le libre Arbitre, tiré de ses autres Ouurages. Le tout en Latin & en François*. Paris : Martin Dvrand, 1650.

Martin, Henri-Jean & Roger Chartier. *Livre, pouvoirs et société à Paris au XVIIe siècle*. 1598–1701. Genève : Droz, 1999. (Première édition, 1969)

Monet, Phililbert. *Ligatvres des langves, françoise, et latine, reciproqvemant appariees, & propremant randues, les vnes par les autres. Ov*

Explication des menus mots, François, & Latins, qui font la liaison de la structure, au langage. Lyon : Abraham Cloqvemin, 1629.

Muntéano, Basil. « Port-Royal et la stylistique de la traduction ». *Cahiers de l'Association Internationale des Études Françaises* 8, 1956. 151–172.

Perrot d'Ablancourt, Nicolas. *Les guerres d'Alexandre par Arrian.* Paris : veufue Jean Camvsat et Pierre le Petit, 1646.

Perrot d'Ablancourt, Nicolas. *L'histoire de Tacite, ov la svite des Annales.* Paris : Avgvstin Covrbé, 1651.

Perrot d'Ablancourt, Nicolas. *L'Histoire de Thucydide, de la guerre du Peloponese, continuée par Xenophon. De la traduction de N. Perrot, sieur d'Ablancourt.* Paris : A. Courbé, 1662.

Soll, Jacob. « Amelot de la Houssaye and the Tacitean Tradition in France. » *Translation and Literature* 6, 1997. 186–202.

Tende, Gaspard de, sieur de l'Estang. *Regles de la traduction, ov moyens povr apprendre a tradvire de latin en françois. Tirez de quelques-vnes des meilleures Traductions du Temps.* Paris : Damien Fovcavlt, 1660.

Vaugelas, Claude Favre de. *Remarques sur la langue françoise, vtiles à ceux qui veulent bien parler et bien escrire.* Paris: Augustin Courbé, 1647.

Zuber, Roger. *Les* « B*elles infidèles* » *et la formation du goût classique : Perrot d'Ablancourt et Guez de Balzac.* Paris : A. Colin, 1968.

Notes

1 Mlle de Gournay ne partageait pas cette opinion. Voir la note 1 de l'article de Labègue.

2 Il note pourtant avoir traduit un texte mathématique de Clavius, qui n'a jamais été publié.

3 Notons en passant que la traduction de Tite-Live de Malherbe n'a pas été publiée que pendant cette période (1639), un autre signe du goût pour la traduction non-pédante. Voir Lebegue 1941 : 173.

4 Pareillement Vaugelas estime que « Les Latins ne sont pas si scrupuleux en plusieurs façons parler » (1647 : 489 et *487).

5 Par exemple, Arnauld d'Andilly conseille que « lors qu'une periode est trop longue et trop embarassée dans le latin ou dans le grec, on peut en la traduisant la couper en plusieurs petits membres: ce qui fait d'une part qu'au lieu qu'elle auroit esté languissante on la fortifie et on la fait mieux soustenir, et de l'autre on rend clair et intelligible ce qui auroit esté remply d'une obscurité vicieuse » (*Remarques sur la Traduction*, 33 recto, dans de Nardis 1991 : 63).

6 Ennius ou Euripide? Cicéron ou Horace? Dupleix dit Ennius, mais il s'agit vraiment d'Euripide. Comenius attribue la citation à Horace (*Lexicon atriale latino-latinum*, 1657: 540). En effet, la citation semble provenir d'Euripide (*Hippolyte*, 612; édition Loeb), cité dans Cicéron *De Officiis*, III, 29.

7 En fait, *iniuratam*, non pas *iuratam.*

8 Tacite est l'objet de multiples traductions dans les années 1640, en partie pour exemplifier les différentes approches à la traduction, et en partie parce que la matière décrite, Rome sous les empéreurs, offrait des leçons dans la bonne conduite du roi et de ses sujets sous l'absolutisme. Voir Zuber 1968.

9 Pourtant, selon les recherches de Marzys, le mot *accoustumance* reste en pleine vigueur jusqu'à la fin du XVIIe siècle.

10 Cf la traduction contemporaine de Harlay de Champvallon (1644 : 450) : « les soldats se relaschoient du trauail & de la vertu, pour l'accoustumance des voluptez, & par le mespris qu'ils faisoient de leur General ». Également la traduction de Jean Baudoin : « les soldats se forlignoient de la fatigue & de la vertu militaire, tant par vne accoustumance aux voluptez, que par le mespris qu'ils faisoient de leur Chef» (1619 : 608). Rodolphe Le Maistre : « Le soldat par l'accoustumance des voluptez, & par le mépris de ceux qui commandoient, s'alienoit de ses exercices, & de la vertu » (1627 : 588). D'Ablancourt (1651 : 165) ne traduit pas *assuetudine*, « la valeur des soldats abastardie par les voluptez, & par le mépris qu'ils faisoient du Prince ». Soll (1997 : 187) a identifié la publication 11 traductions différentes de Tacite (33 éditions) entre 1582–1663.

11 Le maintien d'*accoustumance*, quoique vieilli, permet à Dupleix d'éviter non seulement l'équivoque, mais également l'anachronisme tellement typique des traductions des « belles infidèles ». Zuber note l'emploi dans les traductions d'Ablancourt de plusieurs termes modernisés pour accommoder le lecteur du XVIIe, comme *ministres* et *sergent* (1968 : 290–292). Toutefois, on pourrait, pour les mêmes raisons, critiquer chez Dupleix la traduction de *ducis* par « général ».

12 La force est un élément clé de l'équivalence dans les théories de la traduction au XVIIe siècle, ce qui nous aide à comprendre la fréquence de l'évocation de l' « énergie » des mots chez Dupleix, surtout dans son maintien de mots que Vaugelas trouve inadmissibles — par exemple *longuement/longtemps* (1651 : 317–318) et *notamment* (1651 : 362–363).

La traduction et l'innovation linguistique dans la presse d'information sous l'Ancien Régime

Mairi McLaughlin

Résumé

Cet article vise à attirer l'attention sur la traduction comme facteur de diffusion de l'innovation linguistique et scientifique dans la presse d'information aux XVIIe et XVIIIe siècles. Nous utilisons des analyses linguistiques d'un corpus de textes journalistiques pour étudier l'apport linguistique de la traduction. Il sera démontré que la traduction des articles était une source d'emprunts lexicaux aux XVIIe et XVIIIe siècles tout comme elle l'est de nos jours. Nous montrerons également que le statut et la conceptualisation de la traduction auraient pu être influencés aussi.

Mots-clés : traduction journalistique, histoire de la presse, emprunt lexical, *Journal des savans, Gazette de France*

Abstract

The aim of this article is to draw attention to the role of translation in the diffusion of both scientific and linguistic innovation in the seventeenth and eighteenth centuries. We use linguistic analysis of a corpus of journalistic texts to explore the effect that translation had on the French language. We show that the translation of articles was a source of lexical borrowing in this period just as it is today. It will also be seen that the status and conceptualization of translation in this period could also have been affected.

Keywords: News translation, history of the press, lexical borrowing, *Journal des savans, Gazette de France*

Introduction

Les linguistes ont depuis longtemps souligné l'importance de la traduction pour l'évolution de la langue française au XVIIe siècle. Tout récemment, Ayres-Bennett et Seijido (2011) ont montré que les traductions — surtout de textes classiques — représentaient des modèles de style pour ceux qui s'intéressaient au bon usage au siècle classique. Elles ont noté que les auteurs de livres de remarques sur la langue française tels que Vaugelas « citent fréquemment les traductions contemporaines mais beaucoup moins les textes que nous considérons aujourd'hui comme les grands représentants du classicisme » (*ibid.* : 241). Le but de cet article est d'attirer l'attention sur un type de traduction qui n'est que rarement examiné en linguistique, à savoir la traduction journalistique.[1] Il n'est pas nouveau de suggérer que la traduction qui s'effectue dans le domaine de la presse peut avoir des conséquences pour l'évolution de la langue. C'est une hypothèse qui est avancée depuis au moins la fin du XIXe siècle et nous avons nous-même exploré le rôle joué par la traduction journalistique dans le changement linguistique en français contemporain (McLaughlin 2011).[2] La contribution innovatrice de ce travail est l'adoption d'une perspective historique : nous examinerons si la présence et la représentation de la traduction dans la presse d'information ont pu influer sur l'évolution de la langue française aux XVIIe et XVIIIe siècles. Cette période a été choisie parce que la première moitié du XVIIe siècle coïncide avec l'avènement de la presse périodique de langue française, et parce que la Révolution française s'est accompagnée de grandes perturbations dans l'évolution de la presse.[3]

La recherche présentée ici fait partie d'un projet plus large en linguistique historique sur les origines et l'évolution du français journalistique. L'objectif principal du projet est de fournir la première description systématique de la langue de la presse francophone dans les deux premiers siècles de son existence. Le projet répond à un désir fréquemment exprimé de diversifier les types de textes utilisés comme sources de données pour la recherche sur l'histoire de la langue française ; l'histoire de la langue traditionnelle se base pour l'essentiel sur l'histoire de textes littéraires.[4] Si la description des différents niveaux linguistiques (orthographe et ponctuation, morphologie, syntaxe, et lexique) constitue le noyau du projet, nous avons été frappée par l'importance du rôle joué par la traduction dans la presse périodique historique. Nous nous sommes donc intéressée à la problématique de la présence de la traduction dans la production et la circulation des informations pour savoir si elle a pu être la source de changements linguistiques aux siècles XVIIe et XVIIIe tout comme elle peut l'être aujourd'hui. L'article commence par un bref survol du rôle joué par la traduction dans le domaine de la presse aux XVIIe et XVIIIe siècles. Ce survol se base sur la recherche effectuée par les historiens travaillant sur l'histoire de la presse en général ou dans le domaine de la circulation transculturelle et translinguistique des informations dans la période pré-moderne.[5] La deuxième partie de l'article présente trois études de cas qui permettent d'explorer le lien éventuel entre la traduction des informations et l'innovation linguistique. Les études de cas se basent sur le corpus que nous avons construit pour notre projet linguistique sur l'histoire du français journalistique et nous utilisons la même méthodologie qui combine des analyses quantitatives et des analyses qualitatives. Notons dès le début que l'objectif de cet article n'est pas d'offrir une étude systématique des effets linguistiques de la traduction, mais de déterminer si l'hypothèse avancée ici mérite d'être retenue et si l'on devrait consacrer un projet plus large à cette question.

La présence de la traduction dans la presse

Pour explorer la possibilité d'un lien entre la traduction journalistique et le changement linguistique aux XVIIe et XVIIIe siècles, nous commençons par un bref examen du rôle qu'a joué la traduction dans la production et la circulation des informations. La première publication périodique de langue française de longue durée est la *Gazette*, fondée à Paris par Théophraste Renaudot au mois de mai 1631.[6] Elle sera suivie bientôt par de nouveaux titres tels que le *Journal des savans* (1665) et le *Mercure galant* (1672).[7] Il est à noter qu'il s'est également développé une importante presse de langue française publiée hors de France avec des titres tels que la *Gazette d'Amsterdam* (1688), la *Gazette de Leyde* (1677) et la *Gazette d'Utrecht* (1689?).[8] Dès le début, la traduction a joué un rôle central dans la production des informations qui circulaient en Europe car les publications périodiques constituaient l'une des sources d'informations majeures pour les journalistes. Ceci est très-bien illustré par une citation de la part du rédacteur de la *Quintessence des lettres historiques, critiques, politiques, morales et galantes*. En 1719 il a critiqué les journaux concurrents en disant que pour fonder une nouvelle publication tout ce qu'il faut faire c'est de : « piller adroitement ses confrères gazetiers, et, à la faveur d'une traduction, revendre en français ce que d'autres ont déjà débité en flamand, ou, faisant venir les mêmes nouvelles de trois ou quatre endroits différents, remplir son papier à peu de frais » (cité par Trenard 1969 : 149). Cette citation témoigne de l'importance de la traduction dans la pratique journalistique européenne aux XVIIe et XVIIIe siècles.

Pour mieux cerner la fonction de la traduction à cette époque, nous allons nous concentrer sur deux périodiques principaux : la *Gazette* et le *Journal des savans*. Ces deux titres serviront de représentants de deux sous-genres distincts. Les gazettes traitent des informations sérieuses en publiant des dépêches envoyées par des correspondants de différentes villes telles que Londres, Constantinople, Amsterdam, et Vienne. Dans un certain sens les informations diffusées par les gazettes ressemblent à celles publiées par les agences de presse contemporaines telles que *Agence France Presse* et *Thompson Reuters*. Par contre, le *Journal des savans,* le premier journal scientifique, se compose principalement de comptes rendus d'ouvrages savants.

Considérons d'abord les gazettes. L'histoire de l'édition de la *Gazette* montre que la traduction figure dans la production de ce type de périodique dans trois circonstances principales : a. la publication entière peut provenir de la traduction d'autres périodiques;[9] b. la gazette peut publier un certain nombre de traductions d'articles publiés dans d'autres périodiques ; c. les articles peuvent comprendre des extraits traduits. A son tout début, la *Gazette* dépendait de la traduction. Dans son étude approfondie de la presse d'information en France sous l'Ancien Régime, Feyel (2000 : 172–190) offre une description détaillée des sources des dépêches d'information publiées par la *Gazette* entre 1631 et 1723. Outre les sources internes comme le roi, Richelieu et ceux qu'il appelle « les Parisiens bien informés » (*ibid.* : 172), il cite les correspondants qui travaillaient à l'étranger. Son analyse nous intéresse tout particulièrement parce qu'il a également trouvé que « Renaudot disposait, aussi et surtout, des gazettes étrangères que lui traduisait Jean Epstein » (*ibid.* : 187). En fait, dès son premier numéro publié en 1631, la *Gazette* se compose de deux parties : la *Gazette* et les *Nouvelles ordinaires de divers endroicts*. Cette deuxième partie traitait surtout des pays du Nord et elle se composait de dépêches qui avaient été traduites par Jean Epstein des gazettes néerlandaises et allemandes.[10] Les *Nouvelles ordinaires* aurait été publiées entre janvier et mai 1631 comme un périodique autonome. Même s'il nous manque la comparaison textuelle qui fournirait des preuves linguistiques du rapport entre la *Gazette* et ses équivalents allemands, nous avons accès au contrat signé par Epstein et Renaudot qui témoigne de l'importance de la traduction. En voici un extrait cité par Feyel (2000 : 140) :

> C'est assçavoir que ledict sieur Epestein a promis et promect faire venir et apporter toutes les septmaines d'Allemagne les nouvelles courantes communément appellées Gazettes, les rendre traduictes et translatées en françois en telle sorte qu'elles puissent estre receues et avoir cours.

Pourtant ce n'est pas que dans les *Nouvelles ordinaires de divers endroicts* que l'on trouve des traductions : on peut également trouver des articles particuliers qui sont des traductions d'articles étrangers, et même les dépêches non-traduites peuvent présenter des extraits de textes traduits d'une autre langue comme par exemple des décrets officiels ou des accords diplomatiques.[11]

Passons maintenant à la presse scientifique où la traduction figure dans de nombreuses circonstances : a. certains journaux se composent entièrement de traductions d'articles publiés dans d'autres périodiques[12] ; b. un journal peut inclure un certain nombre d'articles qui sont des traductions d'articles publiés ailleurs[13] ; c. un journal comme le *Journal des savans* publie des comptes rendus de traductions, d'ouvrages publiés dans d'autres langues et d'ouvrages qui traitent de la traduction comme thème et ces comptes rendus peuvent contenir des phrases individuelles qui sont traduites à d'aurtres langues.[14]

Le Tableau 1 présente un résumé de tous les comptes rendus publiés dans un échantillon qui représente tous les numéros du *Journal des savans* publiés dans un mois tous les 25 ans à partir de 1682.[15]

Tableau 1 Langue des ouvrages dont rend compte le *Journal des savans*[16]

Mois	**Français (original)**	**Français (traduction)**[17]	**Langue étrangère**	**Total**
Mai 1682	4	0	3	7
Juillet 1707	6	1	4	11
Septembre 1732	5	2	3	10
Novembre 1757	7	3	1	11
Janvier 1782	4	2	0	6
Total	**26**	**8**	**11**	**45**

La distribution des comptes rendus dans le Tableau 1 témoigne de l'importance des livres publiés dans d'autres langues et de l'importance des traductions. Au mois de septembre 1732, par exemple, les comptes rendus d'ouvrages traduits et d'ouvrages en langues étrangères représentent la moitié de l'ensemble des comptes rendus. Le journaliste rend compte de deux traductions : la traduction des *Métamorphoses* d'Ovide par l'abbé Banier et les *Lettres pastorales de Monseigneur l'Evêque de Londres aux fidéles de son diocése, contre les libertins & les incrédules* traduites de l'anglais (*Journal des savans*, septembre 1732). Les comptes rendus qui traitent d'ouvrages publiés dans d'autres langues sont plus fréquents que ceux traitant de traductions. Au mois de mai 1682, par exemple, trois comptes rendus sur sept concernent des ouvrages écrits en d'autres langues, à savoir deux textes historiques rédigés en latin et un ouvrage espagnol, qui est lui-même une traduction d'un livre flamand, intitulé *Pyratas de la America y luz a la defensa de las costas de Indias Occidentales* (*Journal des savans*, 11 mai 1682). Si dans le cas des ouvrages écrits en langues étrangères il ne s'agit ni de comptes rendus traduits ni de comptes rendus de la traductions, la traduction y joue toujours un rôle. Nous voyons dans les exemples suivants une vulgarisation du savoir qui comprend un effet de traduction parce que l'on passe d'un livre en langue étrangère à un compte rendu en français; le changement de genre s'accompagne d'un changement de langue. Il est évident que nous parlons intentionnellement de plusieurs types de traduction distincts dans cet article : il y a la traduction plus ou moins directe du matériel publié dans d'autres périodiques, mais nous prenons également en considération les processus traductifs impliqués dans la rédaction de comptes rendus d'ouvrages traduits ou en langues étrangères. Même si nous nous éloignons de la conceptualisation étroite de la traduction comme reproduction *fidèle* d'un texte de la langue source dans la langue cible, nous verrons dans ce qui suit quels peuvent être les effets linguistiques de tels types de traduction non-canoniques.[18]

La traduction dans la presse et l'innovation linguistique

La Gazette

Ayant exploré les contextes dans lesquels figure la traduction dans la presse périodique des XVIIe et XVIIIe siècles, il convient alors de s'interroger sur ses éventuels effets linguistiques. De nouveau, nous nous concentrons sur la *Gazette* et le *Journal des savans* comme représentants de deux sous-genres journalistiques historiques. Nous analyserons tous les numéros de la *Gazette* publiés au début de la période qui nous intéresse : il s'agit de cinq numéros publiés en janvier 1632 et qui comprennent chacun deux parties, la *Gazette* et les *Nouvelles ordinaires de divers endroicts*.[19] Étant donné l'opinion reçue selon laquelle les dépêches publiées dans les *Nouvelles ordinaires* sont des traductions, nous avons comparé les traits textuels de la *Gazette* et des *Nouvelles ordinaires* pour déterminer si la présence de la traduction aurait pu avoir un effet sur l'évolution de la langue. L'hypothèse qui nous intéresse est inspirée par Haffemayer (2002 : 212) qui lie la relative concision des informations présentées dans les *Nouvelles ordinaires* à la présence de la traduction dans le processus de la rédaction :

> Il n'est pas impossible que la concision de l'information dans les Nouvelles Ordinaires soit due à un travail préalable de traduction et puis d'élimination, effectué sur la base d'informations qui parvenaient à la Gazette par la voie allemande.

Haffemayer a observé une relative concision dans les *Nouvelles ordinaires* grâce à ses lectures de ce périodique. A l'aide de notre propre transcription intégrale de tous les numéros de la *Gazette* et des *Nouvelles ordinaires* publiés au mois de janvier 1632, nous avons pu vérifier cette relative concision quantitativement. Bien que les deux titres soient de la même longueur, à savoir de quatre pages, le Tableau 2 montre que la *Gazette* utilise un nombre de mots plus important que les *Nouvelles ordinaires*.[20]

Tableau 2 Longueur de tous les numéros de la *Gazette* et des *Nouvelles Ordinaires* du mois de janvier 1632

	Gazette	***Nouvelles ordinaires***
Mots	10 303	9 923
Pages	20	20
Mots par page	515.15	496.15

De plus, comme le montre le Tableau 3, les *Nouvelles ordinaires* comprennent toujours un nombre plus élevé de dépêches.

Tableau 3 Nombre de dépêches publiées par la *Gazette* et par les *Nouvelles ordinaires* (janvier 1632)

Date	***Gazette***	***Nouvelles ordinaires***
2 janvier 1632	8	10
9 janvier 1632	10	11
16 janvier 1632	11	16
23 janvier 1632	13	17
30 janvier 1632	10	15
Total	52	69

Ces deux observations confirment chiffres à l'appui le constat fait par Haffemayer que le texte des *Nouvelles ordinaires* est plus concis que celui de la *Gazette*. Il semble probable que ces différences entre la partie traduite et la partie non-traduite proviennent surtout du processus de la traduction. On peut faire appel ici à ce que l'on sait du processus de la traduction journalistique contemporaine qui est reconnue pour la présence de la révision du contenu informationnel. Les chercheurs qui s'intéressent à la traduction journalistique se servent du terme *trans-editing* pour indiquer que dans le domaine de la presse, la traduction s'accompagne de révision du contenu.[21] Bien que l'on puisse être plus ou moins certain que les différences entre la *Gazette* et les *Nouvelles ordinaires* sont l'effet du processus de la traduction, cette « lecture à distance » du périodique ne permet pas de déterminer si ces différences auraient provoqué des changements notables au niveau de la langue. Il reste à déterminer dans une étude future si le processus de la traduction ici mis en évidence a laissé ses traces linguistiques en contribuant à l'introduction d'emprunts, par exemple au niveau lexical. C'est un des objectifs d'une étude de la présence de mots d'emprunts dans la presse historique qui fait partie de notre projet linguistique plus large. Il sera important aussi d'explorer la possibilité que la présence généralisée de la langue de la traduction aux tous débuts de la presse périodique aurait pu participer à l'établissement de conventions stylistiques du genre journalistique des dépêches (emprunt stylistique/générique).[22]

Le Journal des savans

Au lieu de faire le même type d'analyse quantitative du matériel publié par le *Journal des savans*, nous avons effectué cette fois-ci une analyse qualitative qui se base sur les comptes rendus d'ouvrages publiés dans d'autres langues pour déterminer s'ils représentent une source potentielle de mots d'emprunt.[23] Considérons d'abord un compte rendu de l'ouvrage espagnol *Pyratas de la America y luz a la defensa de las costas de Indias Occidentales* publié dans le *Journal des savans* le 11 mai 1682. Ce livre concerne la piraterie dans le nouveau monde mais « pour ne nous pas trop étendre là-dessus », l'auteur du compte rendu a décidé de ne parler que de la description offerte par l'auteur de l'Isle Espagnole. Dans l'introduction, le journaliste discute brièvement de l'histoire de l'île, mais se penche sur la faune et flore dans le reste de l'article. L'introduction est suivie par quatre paragraphes, dont deux traitent des plantes de l'île ; un autre traite des animaux, à savoir les crocodiles ; et le dernier traite des insectes, à savoir les lucioles. Etant donné le sujet de cet ouvrage, il n'est pas surprenant que l'auteur se soit servi de termes propres à l'histoire naturelle. Ces quatre courts paragraphes contiennent des termes qui avaient été en usage depuis l'ancien français (*palmier, crocodile*) mais l'auteur emploie également des mots empruntés à l'espagnol ainsi que des calques. Le mot *cayman* avait déjà été attesté dans une traduction française d'un ouvrage espagnol en 1584,[24] mais ce compte rendu contient les premiers exemples des termes *Genipe* et *Mançanilla* qui sont empruntés à l'espagnol et les premières attestations de calques comme *palmier vineux* (< *palmera de vino*) et *mouches de feu* (< *mosca de fuego*) pour *luciole*. Aucun de ces quatre termes n'est resté dans la langue donc ils ne peuvent pas être considérés comme des emprunts établis ; il s'agit plutôt d'emprunts spontanés. Néanmoins, leur présence soutient l'hypothèse que la production de comptes rendus d'ouvrages étrangers a pu servir de réseau de transmission d'emprunts et de calques parce que ce sont précisément de tels emprunts spontanés qui sont à l'origine des emprunts qui se diffusent et s'intègrent dans le vocabulaire d'une langue.

En effet, nous avons trouvé un exemple révélateur concernant le mot *inoculation* utilisé dans son acception médicale.[25] Cet emprunt sémantique en français est attribuable à l'influence de l'anglais car c'est Lady Mary Wortley Montagu qui est responsable de la diffusion de cette technique qui a ses origines en Turquie.[26] La première attestation du mot anglais de *inoculation* utilisé avec cette nouvelle acception se trouve dans les *Philosophical Transactions* de la *Royal Society* en 1714.[27] Selon le *Trésor de la langue français informatisée*, le mot a été utilisé pour la première fois avec ce nouveau sens en français dans une lettre publiée sous forme de livre au mois d'octobre 1723 mais nous avons trouvé une occurrence de ce mot neuf mois plus tôt dans le *Journal des savans*. Le mot a été utilisé dans un compte rendu d'une lettre écrite en anglais par un docteur britannique contre l'usage de l'inoculation contre la petite vérole (*Journal des savans*,

18 janvier 1723).[28] La proximité de ces deux dates reflète le grand intérêt que présente la méthode de l'inoculation qui était fortement débattue à l'époque.

Ces deux exemples montrent que la presse savante a pu jouer un rôle dans le processus de l'emprunt linguistique aux XVIIe et XVIIIe siècles que ce soit de mots neufs, de calques ou d'emprunts sémantiques. Il y a plusieurs facteurs qui expliquent pourquoi il y a un lien entre la presse savante et l'emprunt à cette époque. Citons par exemple la nature des sujets traités. Les journalistes s'intéressent surtout à la sphère intellectuelle et aux développements scientifiques où il y a un besoin de néologismes constant, comme le remarquent Duris et Ducos (2008 : 7). De plus, le fait que l'activité intellectuelle que couvre le *Journal des savans* s'étende au-delà des frontières nationales implique naturellement le recours aux emprunts. L'exemple du mot *inoculation* sert à souligner le fait que la presse est capable de répondre dans un délai plus court à l'urgence de la communication que ne le permet le monde des livres. Comme le signale Banks (2010 : §1), la diffusion de l'information par le canal des livres est un « processus lent et couteux[29] » par contraste avec le système des périodiques. Vittu (2005 : 545) a également souligné les avantages du support périodique pour l'échange savant parce que « les périodiques savants s'ouvrent à des contributions d'origines très diverses qu'ils publient rapidement ». Il les compare au monde relativement clos des sociétés académiques parce qu'ils « s'adressent à un public élargi et non institutionnel ». Même si nous n'avons pas encore eu l'occasion d'analyser le lexique des gazettes, il est très probable que les gazettes aient également participé à la création et à la diffusion des emprunts linguistiques. Il se peut que les sujets dont elles traitent suscitent moins souvent l'usage des emprunts mais elles restent importantes parce qu'elles ont été diffusées à une échelle plus large et elles ont donc touché un lectorat plus important.

La représentation de la traduction

Avant de conclure, il convient d'examiner un dernier effet possible de la présence de la traduction dans la presse savante. Cet effet ne concerne pas l'évolution de la langue mais plutôt celle des attitudes. La question est de savoir si la conceptualisation et le statut de la traduction ont pu être touchés par la présence de comptes rendus discutant soit des ouvrages traduits, soit des ouvrages qui traitent de la traduction comme thème.

Il est d'abord évident que l'importante présence de comptes rendus de traductions dans le *Journal des savans* a dû suggérer que la traduction occupe une place centrale dans l'entreprise scientifique. Qui plus est, les auteurs du périodique n'ont fait aucune différence entre les ouvrages originaux et les traductions. Le journaliste n'a certes pas caché le fait que l'ouvrage espagnol *Pyratas de la America y luz a la defensa de las costas de Indias Occidentales* est une traduction parce qu'il a fait imprimer le titre entier qui contient l'indication suivante : « *traducido de la lengua Flamenca en Española, por el D. Alonso de Buena* » (*Journal des savans*, 11 mai 1682). Pourtant il n'a pas traduit cette indication et il n'y a rien dans le corps du compte rendu qui mette en évidence le statut traduit de l'ouvrage. En effet, le journaliste ne s'intéresse qu'au contenu du livre, tout comme s'il s'agissait d'un livre français non-traduit. La présence de comptes rendus d'ouvrages qui traitent de la traduction comme thème a dû également renforcer le prestige de la pratique de la traduction car elle suggère que la traduction est un sujet qui mérite d'être discuté et une pratique qui mérite une histoire. Les premiers exemples de tels comptes rendus paraissent vers la fin du XVIIe siècle et ils concernent tous la traduction de textes sacrés. Les auteurs du périodique ont eux-mêmes expliqué l'intérêt de cette question de manière explicite. En 1693, le journaliste note que l'histoire des traductions de la Bible avant la Réforme protestante « fait voir qu'il n'est pas vrai que les Pasteurs de l'Eglise Romaine défendent au peuple la lecture de l'Ecriture en langue vulgaire, ni que les Protestans ayent les premiers travaillé à la traduire, comme ils le publient » (*Journal des savans,* 1 juin 1693). Tout comme les histoires de la traduction, les comptes rendus de ces histoires sont à comprendre dans le contexte du débat central à cette période concernant la publication de la Bible en langue vernaculaire.[30]

Le traitement de la traduction par le *Journal des savans* a aussi pu influencer la conceptualisation de la traduction comme pratique. Nous avons vu s'articuler une représentation de la traduction qui repose sur une distinction nette entre la traduction de textes religieux et la traduction dans d'autres domaines. En 1700, le journaliste offre un résumé des règles pour bien traduire publié par l'Abbé Regnier où est établi une distinction entre la pratique de la traduction dans le domaine sacré et dans les autres domaines (*Journal des savans*, 16 août 1700). Il dit :

> L'exactitude rigoureuse qui veut qu'on exprime jusqu'au moindre mot, jusqu'à la moindre particule ne regarde gueres que les Livres saints qui renferment quelque mystere de la Religion, ou quelque precepte de la morale. Dans les autres endroits on remplit le devoir de ce fidéle Traducteur, quand on donne une idée claire & distincte des faits dont il s'agit. (ibid.)

La fidélité est donc un critère évaluatif constant mais elle se réalise de manière différente dans les différents domaines.

L'insistance sur une éthique de la traduction qui repose sur la fidélité est compliquée encore plus par l'idée maintes fois répétée dans lc *Journal des savans* que la réussite de la traduction tourne autour d'un fin équilibre entre la beauté et la grâce des originaux qui les rendent inimitables, et le talent du traducteur qui réussit à les traduire. A plusieurs reprises, le journaliste reconnaît la difficulté de la tâche du traducteur tout en louant sa traduction. Discutant une traduction de Sapho et d'Anacréon, par exemple, il parle de « la delicatesse avec laquelle Mademoiselle le Fevre a imité [...] la naïveté presque inimitable de l'original » et la façon dont elle a fait « passer dans une prose fidelle toutes les graces que l'on trouve dans les vers Grecs » (*Journal des savans*, 16 février 1682). Ici l'on voit bien que c'est le paradoxe de pouvoir *imiter* ce qui est *inimitable* qui témoigne de la réussite de la traduction. Le fait d'insister sur la difficulté de cet art et la nuance qu'il exige souligne de nouveau son prestige et ce discours sur la traduction n'a pu ne pas avoir un effet sensible sur son statut. Ce fait n'est pas sans conséquence pour la langue elle-même car, comme nous l'avons vu dans l'introduction de cet article, le développement de la langue et la traduction sont intimement liés au XVIIe siècle. Renforcer le statut prestigieux de la traduction, c'est sans doute renforcer son usage comme modèle de style.

Conclusion

Pour conclure, nous voulons souligner l'intérêt de l'étude de la traduction dans le discours journalistique historique de la perspective de l'histoire de la langue. Il est évident que ce n'est pas aujourd'hui seulement que la traduction occupe une place centrale dans l'industrie de la presse : elle faisait partie intégrante de la production et de la diffusion périodique des informations à ses tout débuts aux XVIIe et XVIIIe siècles. Si un lien entre la traduction journalistique et l'innovation linguistique a déjà été établi pour la période contemporaine, il nous paraît urgent de déterminer si un tel lien existait dans le passé. Etant donné l'échelle des données, nous avons dû nous limiter ici à une évaluation de la possibilité que la traduction journalistique ait pu contribuer au changement linguistique aux XVIIe et XVIIIe siècles. La série de recherches ponctuelles présentées ici concernant la *Gazette* et le *Journal des savans* a suggéré que tel est le cas mais il est maintenant urgent de lancer de nouveaux projets qui permettront d'approfondir l'analyse en proposant des analyses systématiques et comparatives des différents types de changements linguistiques liés aux différents sous-genres journalistiques historiques.

Références bibliographiques :

Ayres-Bennett, Wendy. *A History of the French Language through Texts*. London: Routledge, 1996.

Ayres-Bennett, Wendy et Magali Seijido. *Remarques et observations sur la langue française : Évolution et histoire d'un genre*, Paris : Classiques Garnier, 2011.

Banks, David. « The Beginnings of Vernacular Scientific Discourse : Genres and Linguistic Features in some Early Issues of the *Journal des Sçavans* and the *Philosophical Transactions* ». *E-rea* 8(1) (2010) : DOI: 10.4000/erea.1334.

Barker, S. K. « 'News Lately Come' : European News Books in English Translation ». *Renaissance Cultural Crossroads : Translation, Print and Culture in Britain,* 1473–1640. Dir. S. K. Barker et Brenda M. Hosington. Leiden—Boston : Brill, 2013. 227–244.

Barker, S. K, et Brenda M. Hosington, dir. *Renaissance Cultural Crossroads : Translation, Print and Culture in Britain,* 1473–1640, Leiden—Boston : Brill, 2013.

Bellanger, Claude *et al.* dir. *Histoire générale de la presse française*. Vol. I : *Des Origines à* 1814. Paris : Presses Universitaires de France, 1969.

Bielsa, Esperança et Susan Basnett. *Translation in Global News,* London—New York: Routledge, 2009.

Burrows, Simon. « The Cosmopolitan Press, 1759–1815 ». *Press, Politics and the Public Sphere in Europe and North America,* 1760–1820. Dir. Hannah Barker et Simon Burrows. Cambridge : Cambridge University Press, 2002, 23–47.

Censer, Jack R. *The French Press in the Age of Enlightenment.* London : Routledge, 1994.

Chédozeau, Bernard. *Port-Royal et la Bible : un siècle d'or de la Bible en France,* 1650–1708. Paris : Nolin, 2007.

Chouillet, Anne-Marie et Madeleine Fabre. « Diffusion et réception des nouvelles et ouvrages britanniques par la presse spécialisée de France ». *La Diffusion et la lecture des journaux de langue française sous l'Ancien Régime, Actes du colloque international, Nimègue, 3–5 juin 1987.* Dir. Hans Bots, Amsterdam—Maarssen : APA—Holland University Press, 1988, 177–201.

Conway, Kyle. *Everyone Says No: Public Service Broadcasting and the Failure of Translation.* Montréal—Kingston: McGill-Queen's University Press, 2011.

De la Coste, M. *Lettre sur l'inoculation de la petite verole. Comme elle se pratique en Turquie & en Angleterre. Adressée à A. M. Dodart, Conseiller d'Etat, & Premier Medecin du Roy.* Paris : Claude Labottiere, 1723.

Duranton, Henir, Claude Labrosse et Pierre Rétat, dir. *Les Gazettes européennes de langue française : XVIIe et XVIIIe siècles.* Saint-Étienne : Publications de l'Université de Saint-Étienne, 1992.

Duris, Pascal et Joëlle Ducos, « Introduction », *Traduire la science. Hier et aujourd'hui.* Dir. Pascal Duris. Pessac : Maison des sciences de l'homme d'Aquitaine, 2008, 7–10.

Feyel, Gilles. *La Presse en France des origines à* 1944. Paris : Ellipses, 1999.

Feyel, Gilles. *L'Annonce et la nouvelle : La Presse d'information en France sous l'ancien régime (*1630–1788*).* Oxford : Voltaire Foundation, 2000.

Gough, Hugh. *The Newspaper Press in the French Revolution.* Chicago

IL : The Dorsey Press, 1988.

Haffemayer, Stéphane. *L'Information dans la France du XVIIe siècle : La Gazette de Renaudot, de* 1647 *à* 1663. Paris : H. Champion, 2002.

Kraemer, Gilles, dir. *Trois siècles de presse francophone dans le monde : hors de France, de Belgique, de Suisse et du Québec.* Paris : L'Harmattan, 1995.

Lüsebrink, Hans-Jürgen. « Transferts culturels transatlantique et circulation des savoirs dans les cultures populaires — le cas des almanachs de Benjamin Franklin ». *Tangence* 72 (2003) : 27–40.

Lüsebrink, Hans-Jürgen *et al. Les Lectures du peuple en Europe et dans les Amériques (XVIIe-XXe siècle)*. n.pl. : Editions Complexe.

McLaughlin, Mairi. *Syntactic Borrowing in Contemporary French: A Linguistic Analysis of News Translation.* Oxford: Legenda, 2011.

Popkin, Jeremy D. *News and Politics in the Age of Revolution : Jean Luzac's « Gazette de Leyde ».* Ithaca — London : Cornell University Press, 1989.

Raymond, Joad, dir. *News Networks in Seventeenth Century Britain and Europe*, London — New York : Routledge, 2006.

Riedel, Stefan. "Edward Jenner and the History of Smallpox and Vaccination". *Baylor, University Medical Center Proceedings* 18(1) (2005): 21–25.

Saada, Anne et Jean Sgard. « Tremblements dans la presse ». *The Lisbon Earthquake of* 1755 *: Representations and Reactions.* Dir. Theodore E. D. Braun et John B. Radner, Oxford : Voltaire Foundation, 2005, 208-224.

Sgard, Jean, dir. *Dictionnaire des journaux* 1600–1789. Oxford : Voltaire Foundation, 1991.

Trenard, Louis. « La Presse française des origines à 1788 ». *Histoire générale de la presse française*, Vol. I : *Des Origines à* 1814. Dir. Claude Bellanger *et al.*, Paris : Presses Universitaires de France, 1969, 17–102.

Vincent, Monique. *Le Mercure galant : présentation de la première revue féminine d'information et de culture,* 1672–1710. Paris : H. Champion, 2005.

Vittu, Jean-Pierre. « Diffusion et réception du *Journal des savants* de 1665 à 1714 ». *La diffusion et la lecture des journaux de langue française sous l'Ancien Régime, Actes du colloque international, Nimègue,* 3–5 *juin* 1987. Dir. Hans Bots. Amsterdam—Maarssen : APA—Holland University Press, 1988, 167–177.

Vittu, Jean-Pierre. « Du Journal des savants aux Mémoires pour l'histoire des sciences et des beaux-arts : l'esquisse d'un système européen des périodiques savants », *Dix-septième siècle* 228 (3) (2005) : 527–545.

Notes

1 Dans le domaine de la traductologie, l'étude la traduction journalistique est un champ de recherche émergeant mais l'histoire de sa pratique n'a pas encore été analysée à large échelle de ce point de vue (voir, par exemple, Bielsa et Bassnett 2009 et Conway 2011). Cela n'empêche que l'histoire de la traduction journalistique constitue un centre d'intérêt important pour les historiens. Voir, par exemple, les nombreux travaux de Lüsebrink sur la traduction des almanachs (e.g., Lüsebrink 2003, Lüsebrink *et al.* 2003) et la recherche sur les réseaux d'informations historiques (Haffemayer 2002 et Raymond 2006).

2 Sur l'histoire de cette hypothèse dans le domaine de la linguistique, voir McLaughlin (2011 : 1–2, 10–11).

3 Voir des histoires de la presse française comme celles publiées par Bellanger *et al.* (1969) et par Feyel (1999, 2000). Notons cependant avec Censer (1994 : 5) et avec Gough (1988) que l'on peut observer les débuts des changements associés à la Révolution dans les années qui la précèdent.

4 Citons à titre d'exemple l'histoire de la langue par Ayres-Bennett (1996) qui est motivée explicitement par le désir d'inclure une gamme plus large de types de texte.

5 Nous remercions un lecteur anonyme pour ses suggestions concernant la recherche dans ce domaine. Nous avons également pu profiter de suggestions données par des participants au colloque *Translating European Languages: History, Ideology, Censorship* (http://www.ehrc.ox.ac.uk/leafletp2).

6 La parution de la *Gazette* a été précédée par des publications non-périodiques, par un certain nombre de publications de parution irrégulière, et par certaines publications périodiques qui n'ont pas connu le succès qu'a eu la *Gazette*. Sur les débuts de la presse périodique de langue française et sur le débat concernant le statut de la *Gazette* comme premier périodique de langue française, voir Haffemayer (2002 : « Introduction ») et la discussion de la soi-disant « querelle de l'antériorité » dans l'article sur les *Nouvelles ordinaires de divers endroicts* dans le *Dictionnaire des journaux* (Sgard 1991).

7 Les histoires de la presse par Bellanger *et al.* (1969) et par Feyel (1999, 2000) fournissent des informations générales concernant ces titres. Voir Vincent (2005) et Vittu (1988, 2005) pour des études plus détaillées.

8 Sur l'histoire de la presse française extraterritoriale voir Duranton, Labrosse et Rétat (1992), Kraemer (1995) et Burrows (2002).

9 La *Gazette de Leyde* est un exemple de ce type de publication parce qu'elle avait d'abord été publiée sous le titre de *Traduction libre des Gazettes flamandes et autres* (Popkin 1989 : 10). Chouillet et Fabre (1988 : 183) citent également une

série de journaux publiés au XVIIIe siècle dont le seul but était de traduire la presse britannique (*Papiers anglais*, *Gazettes et Papiers anglais*, et *Analyse des papiers anglais*).

10 C'est surtout Feyel (1999 : 15, 2000 : 138–140, 172–190) qui fournit des informations sur le rôle de la traduction dans l'édition de la *Gazette.* Sur la répartition géographique des dépêches publiées par la *Gazette*, voir Haffemayer (2002).

11 Il n'est pas toujours possible d'identifier les articles et extraits traduits parce que ce n'est que récemment que les chercheurs ont commencé à comparer les dépêches publiées par les différentes gazettes. Voir, par exemple, Saada et Sgard (2005). Dans de rares cas, les journalistes signalent qu'il s'agit d'une traduction. Citons, à titre d'exemple, une nouvelle traduction d'une déclaration publiée dans la *Gazette d'Amsterdam* avec l'explication suivante : « La Traduction Authentique faite à *Berlin* par l'ordre du Roi, de la Déclaration de S. M. *Prussienne* du 8 Décembre dernier, nous étant parvenue par une voie très respectable, nous avons jugé à propos de la publier, d'autant plus qu'elle differe à quelques égards de celle que nous avons insérée dans notre Feuille du 18 du mois dernier. » (*Gazette d'Amsterdam*, 4 janvier 1782).

12 Voir Vittu (2005 : 531–532) qui parle d' « une seconde forme de mise en circulation dans un nouvel espace géographique ou culturel » (*ibid. :* 531) résultant de la traduction de numéros entiers de certains périodiques savants tels que le *Journal des savans* et les *Philosophical Transactions* entre 1665 et 1700.

13 Vittu (*ibid.*) souligne le rapport particulier entre le *Journal des savans* et les *Philosophical transactions :* « Le *Journal des savants* réalisa dès 1666 de tels transferts avec de très nombreux emprunts aux *Philosophical Transactions* dont une partie fut ensuite transposée en italien par le *Giornale de'letterati* de Rome, depuis cette traduction française. ». Citons à titre d'exemple un article intitulé *Extrait du Journal d'Angleterre* [sc. les *Philosophical Transactions*] *contenant une relation Chronologique des embrasemens du Mont Etna* (*Journal des savans,* 16 mars 1682).

14 Il n'est pas difficile de trouver des exemples de comptes rendus de traductions et d'ouvrages publiés en d'autres langues dans le *Journal des savans*. Les comptes rendus d'ouvrages qui traitent de la traduction comme thème sont plus rares mais nous discutons quelques exemples dans ce qui suit.

15 Les numéros discutés ici font partie de notre corpus linguistique qui se compose de cinq titres (la *Gazette de France*, le *Journal des savans*, le *Mercure galant*, la *Gazette d'Amsterdam* et le *Journal de Paris*). Nous avons construit un échantillon en utilisant le concept de la génération et celui de la semaine (ou de l'année) construite.

16 Nous nous concentrons sur les comptes rendus parce qu'ils représentent l'intérêt principal du *Journal des savans* tout au long de la période qui nous intéresse. Le même type de travail pourrait se faire pour les rubriques qui ne sont pas présentes au début telles que les *Nouveautés* ou les *Nouvelles de littérature* (voir Vittu 1988).

17 Les livres étrangers peuvent également être des traductions comme c'est le cas pour le livre *Pyratas de la America y luz a la defensa de las costas de Indias Occidentales (Journal des savans*, 11 mai 1682). Cela veut dire que l'importance de la traduction est légèrement sous-représentée dans le Tableau 1.

18 Lüsebrink (2003) semble également s'intéresser à la traduction dans son acception

plus large quand il présente *The Poor Richard's Almanack* (1733–1757) de Franklin, l'almanach qui est « de loin le plus traduit de l'époque moderne » (*ibid.* : 28). Il explique que l'almanach « s'approprie de nombreux textes en les citant, en les réécrivant et en les transformant » (*ibid.* : 34). Le recueil d'articles publié par Barker et Hosington (2013) a contribué également à un élargissement de la définition de la notion de la traduction dans la période pré-moderne.

19 Tous ces numéros font partie de notre corpus linguistique et nous les avons transcrits dans leur intégralité. Ils ont été publiés le 2, 9, 16, 23 et le 30 janvier 1632.

20 En dépit des difficultés entourant la notion du mot en linguistique, l'aspect comparatif de cette partie de l'étude permet d'utiliser un comptage du nombre de mots effectué par le logiciel *R* à la base de nos transcriptions en texte simple.

21 Sur la spécificité de la traduction journalistique, voir McLaughlin (2011 : 20–21, 112–113).

22 L'idée de l'emprunt stylistique comme effet de la traduction des nouvelles n'est pas nouvelle : Barker (2013) montre que les traducteurs anglais de nouvelles anglaises dans la Renaissance ont emprunté forme et contenu.

23 Il semble plus probable que la rédaction de comptes rendus mène à l'emprunt quand ils concernent des livres publiés dans d'autres langues que quand ils concernent des ouvrages qui ont déjà été traduits en français.

24 Voir l'article sur *alligator* dans le *Trésor de la langue française informatisée* (*TLFi*) (http://atilf.atilf.fr).

25 Faute de place nous ne pouvons décrire que l'exemple de *inoculation* ici mais voir un compte rendu de deux dictionnaires médicaux qui comprend plusieurs occurrences de termes techniques qui sont antérieures aux premières attestations citées par le *TLFi* : *absorbant, accelerateur* (dans son acception anatomique), *acme* et plusieurs variétés d'*agate* qui ne figurent pas dans le *TLFi* (*Journal des savans*, septembre 1732).

26 Voir Riedel (2005) sur l'histoire de l'inoculation.

27 Voir l'article sur *inoculation* dans le *Oxford English Dictionary*, http://www.oed.com.

28 Le compte rendu de la lettre anglaise a été publié dans le *Journal des savans* le 18 janvier, et le privilège n'a été accordé à l'auteur du livre que le 26 octobre (De la Coste 1723). Le mot d'*inoculation* a aussi été utilisé à de nombreuses reprises dans un autre périodique publié en 1723 (*Mémoires littéraires de la Grande Bretagne*) mais nous n'avons pas pu trouver la date exacte de sa parution. Selon une recherche basée sur le texte brut fournit par *Google Livres*, ce mot n'apparaît dans les *Mémoires de Trévoux* qu'au mois de décembre 1723.

29 Traduit par nous: « In the seventeenth century there were basically two ways of disseminating new knowledge. One, fairly obviously was books, but this was a lengthy and costly process. » (Banks 2010: §1).

30 Pour plus d'information voir Chédozeau (2007).

Réflexions sur quelques obstacles linguistiques en zoologie arabe : lectures de quelques traductions françaises du Kitāb al-Hayawān d'al-Djâḥiẓ (776–868)

Meyssa Ben Saâd, Mehrnaz Katouzian-Safadi, Philippe Provençal

Résumé

Cet article traite de la circulation des savoirs autour du bassin méditerranéen. C'est ici qu'eut lieu un important phénomène de traduction, de commentaires et de transmission du patrimoine grec en arabe, puis en latin et autres langues. Le *Kitāb al-Hayawān* d'al-Djâḥiẓ fait partie des œuvres qui n'ont pas été traduites en latin, et qu'on ne retrouve pas en intégralité dans une langue européenne. Les quelques extraits traduits existants ont été réalisés par des arabisants non-biologistes de formation. C'est un préalable indispensable à l'étude des textes biologiques afin de pouvoir les inscrire dans une histoire de la biologie.

Mots-clé : al-Djâḥiẓ (776–868), histoire des sciences arabes, traduction scientifique, zoologie arabe, *Kitāb al-Hayawān*, lexicographie

Abstract

In this article we look at how knowledge was circulated in the area of the Mediterranean Sea in the Middle Ages. Greek heritage texts were translated, commented upon and transmitted within this region, with translation first into Arabic and then into Latin and other languages. The *Kitāb al-Hayawān* [Book of Animals] by al-Djâḥiẓ is one of a number of books not translated into Latin, nor has the entire work been found in any other language. The few translated excerpts that do exist were done by specialists of Arabic with no scientific background, which is a prerequisite for the study of biological texts and for the inclusion of these texts in the history of biology.

Keywords: al-Djâḥiẓ (776–868), history of Arabic science, scientific translation, Arabic zoology, *Kitāb al-Hayawān*, lexicography

Introduction

La traduction est envisagée ici comme passerelle entre les Sciences et les Humanités. La Science est humanité ; la langue est savoir, le savoir est langue. Le savoir s'exprime en une langue, il se transmet par une langue, circule par une autre. La langue véhicule des savoirs, qui le long du chemin peuvent se voir altérés, modifiés, voire dans certains cas faussés par les aléas de l'exercice de traduction. La langue et sa complexité affrontent le traducteur, la discipline à traduire également. L'enjeu est de taille : comment être sûr de transmettre sans trahir la pensée originale ? Comment garantir l'exactitude de l'idée de départ ?

Les disciplines scientifiques ont toutes leurs logiques, leurs théorèmes, leurs termes techniques spécifiques, qui peuvent avoir des signifiants différents dans d'autres domaines (Rommevaux, 2009). D'où l'entreprise délicate et périlleuse qu'est la traduction scientifique. Au cours de l'Histoire des Sciences de la vie, les obstacles linguistiques ont été nombreux, précisément dans le cas de la zoologie arabe. Le *Kitāb al-Hayawān* d'al-Djâḥiẓ souffre d'une double peine : celle d'avoir été déconsidéré par les commentateurs arabes eux-mêmes qui en ont fait un ouvrage plus littéraire que scientifique, et par les traducteurs également qui sont partis de ce postulat qui a orienté leur traduction dans ce sens. Ainsi, les différentes lectures de la zoologie d'al-Djâḥiẓ ont été quelque peu désorientées, voire même déviées du champ même de la zoologie.[1]

La traduction des ouvrages scientifiques : une transmission des savoirs sans cesse remise en cause

Les traductions arabes au Moyen-Age

Le phénomène de traduction dans l'empire islamique aux VIII-Xe siècles revêt d'une importance majeure. En effet, ce sont les traductions qui ont orienté l'activité scientifique et créé une dynamique de recherche et d'innovation ; elles ont enrichi les savoirs, en ont révélé de nouveaux, et fait émerger une nouvelle langue scientifique : l'arabe. Bagdad, en ces temps-là était le lieu d'un extraordinaire éveil de la pensée philosophique, scientifique et linguistique, appuyé et encouragé par ce vaste mouvement de traduction.[2] Cette grande vague de traductions représente l'un des faits majeurs de l'Histoire des Sciences. En effet elle représente le pas décisif qui transmit le savoir de l'Antiquité au monde médiéval. Une partie de ces traductions furent effectuées au Bayt-al-Ḥikmah où étaient réunis un certain nombre de chercheurs et de traducteurs sous l'égide du calife al-Ma'mūn, mais elle n'était pas la seule institution à promouvoir les travaux de traduction.[3]

Al-Djâḥiẓ (776-868), basrien de naissance, ayant vécu à Bagdad et fréquenté la cour et les grands philosophes de la période d'effervescence scientifique et culturelle de la dynastie abbasside,[4] *adīb*,[5] humaniste, polémiste, théologien rationaliste *mutakallim muctazilite*,[6] est un polygraphe qui consacra une grande partie de son œuvre à l'étude du monde vivant, essentiellement le règne animal dans un ouvrage monumental : le *Kitāb al-Hayawān*, *Livre des animaux*. Il y entreprend une étude rigoureuse et précise des propriétés des animaux avec une méthodologie scientifique qui a été décrite (Aarab et al. 2003 ; Ben Saâd et al. 2010).

L'acte de traduction, qui est une étape majeure, si ce n'est essentielle à la transmission du savoir et donc d'une certaine manière à l'élaboration du savoir lui-même, est le phénomène révélateur qui démontre à quel point aucune discipline n'est indépendante ou autonome.

Le savant arabe al-Djâḥiẓ a été acteur et témoin privilégié de la science arabe. Dans ce mouvement prolifique de traductions, la qualité relative de chacune d'entre elles a été discutée au sein de la communauté scientifique de l'époque et al-Djâḥiẓ a soulevé ce problème dans son ouvrage. En effet, dans un passage du *Kitāb al-Hayawān*, il porte un regard intéressant sur la réception et la transmission des textes anciens via l'entreprise de traduction. Il tente d'évaluer les valeurs relatives des textes grecs transmis dans leur version arabe, tient à mettre en garde contre une lecture non critique et subjective des œuvres traduites et insiste sur le fait que plus les compétences du traducteur s'éloignent de la discipline du savant qu'il traduit, plus le risque d'incompréhension, d'erreurs, voire même de « trahison » est élevé. Voici le passage : *Ḥayawān*, I, 75–77 :

صعوبة ترجمة الشعر العربي

وقد نُقِلَتْ كتبُ الهند، وتُرجمتْ حكم اليونانيّة، وحُوِّلت آدابُ الفرس، فبعضها ازدادَ حُسناً، وبعضها ما انتقص شيئاً، ولو حوّلت حكمة العرب، لبطل ذلك المعجزُ الذي هو الوزن، مع أنّهم لو حوَّلوها لم يجدوا في معانيها شيئاً لم تذكرْه العجم في كتبهم ، التي وضعت لمعاشهم وفِطَنهم وحِكَمهم، وقد نُقِلَتْ هذه الكتبُ من أمَّةٍ إلى أمّة، ومن قَرن إلى قرن، ومِن لسانٍ إلى لسان، حتى انتهت إلينا، وكنّا آخرَ مَنْ ورِثها ونظَر فيها، فقد صحَّ أنَّ الكتبَ أبلغُ في تقييدِ المآثِر، من البُنيان والشعر.
ثم قال بعضُ مَنْ ينصر الشعر ويحوطه ويحتجُّ له: إنَّ التَّرجُمان لا يؤدِّي أبداً ما قال الحكيمُ، على خصائِص معانيه، وحقائق مذاهِبه ودقائق اختصاراته، وخفيَّاتِ حدوده، ولا يقدِر أنْ يوفيها حقوقها، ويؤدِّيَ الأمانة فيها، ويقومَ بما يلزمُ الوكيلَ ويجبُ على الجَرِيّ، وكيف يقدِر على أدائها وتسليمِ معانيها، والإخبار عنها على حقِّها وصدقها، إلاّ أنْ يكونَ في العلم بمعانيها، واستعمالِ تصاريفِ ألفاظِها، وتأويلاتِ مخارجِها ، ومثلَ مؤلّف الكتاب وواضعِه، فمتى كان رحمه الله تعالى ابنُ البِطرِيق، وابن ناعمة، وابن قُرَّة، وابن فِهريز، وثيفيل، وابن وهيلي، وابن المقفّع، مثلَ أرِسطاطاليس؟ ومتى كان خالدٌ مثلَ أفلاطون؟

قيمة الترجمة

ولا بدَّ للتَّرجُمانَ من أن يكون بيانهُ في نفس الترجمة، في وزْن علمه في نفسِ المعرفة، وينبغي أن يكون أعلمَ الناس باللغة المنقولة والمنقولِ إليها، حتَّى يكون فيهمِا سواءً وغاية، ومتى وجدناه أيضاً قد تكلّم بلسانين، علمنا أنّه قد أدخلَ الضيمَ عليهما، لأنَّ كل واحدةٍ من اللغتين تجذب الأخرى وتأخذَ منها، وتعترضُ عليها، وكيف يكونُ تمكّنُ اللسان منهما مجتمعين فيه، كتمكّنِه إذا انفرد بالواحدة، وإنّما له قوَّةٌ واحدة، فَإنْ تكلّمَ بلغةٍ واحدة استُفْرِغَتْ تلك القوَّةُ عليهما، وكذلك إنْ تكلّم بأكثرَ مِنْ لغتين، وعلى حساب ذلك تكون الترجمةُ لجميع اللغات، وكلّما كانَ البابُ من العلم أعسرَ وأضيق، والعلماءُ به أقلَّ، كان أشدَّ على المترجِم، وأجدرَ أن يخطئ فيه، ولن تجد البتّةَ مترجماً يفِي بواحدٍ من هؤلاء العلماء.

Traduction : [7]

Les difficultés qu'il y a à traduire la poésie arabe

Des ouvrages indiens ont été traduits ; de même des aphorismes grecs, des livres d'éthique et de littérature persanes. Certains ont gagné en beauté, d'autres n'ont rien perdu. Mais si on traduisait la sagesse (*hikma*) des Arabes, cet élément miraculeux (*mu'jiz*) qu'est le rythme (*wazn*) s'évanouirait. Cependant, si on avait essayé, on n'aurait certainement retrouvé aucun thème (*ma'ânî*) qui ne fût déjà traité dans les ouvrages des non-Arabes, qui rendent compte des modes de vie, de leur sagacité (*fitan*) et de leur sagesse (*hikam*). Ces ouvrages ont été, dans le passé, transmis d'une nation à une autre, d'une génération à une autre, d'une langue à une autre et sont parvenus jusqu'à nous. Nous avons été les derniers à en avoir reçu l'héritage et nous en avons fait un objet de réflexion. […]

La valeur de la traduction

[…] « L'interprète (*turdjumân*) ne restitue jamais intégralement ce que dit le poète (*hakîm*), ses thèmes (*ma'âni*) les plus

> spécifiques, ses nuances les plus intimes, ses raccourcis les plus subtils, les franges les plus imperceptibles. L'interprète, le traducteur, est incapable d'être totalement fidèle aux droits du texte, de restituer intégralement le dépôt qui lui est confié, les symboles qu'il contient. [...] Comment pourrait-il rendre les différences thématiques, les restituer dans toute leur pureté, leur vérité, leur authenticité, à moins que son savoir des significations, son usage des variantes lexicales, des interprétations, des réalisations articulatoires et des modes expressifs du poème en question ne soient comparables à ceux de l'auteur même qui a composé le poème ? Peut-on comparer un Ibn al-Bitrîq, un Ibn Nâ'imâ, un Abû Qurra, un Ibn Fihr, un Ibn Wahîlî, un Ibn al-Muqaffa' à Aristote ? Depuis quand Khâlid peut-il se mesurer à Platon ?
>
> *Les qualités exigées d'un bon traducteur*
> Il est indispensable que les qualités de *bayân* de l'interprète-traducteur se retrouvent dans la traduction elle-même ; qu'à son poids de connaissances, corresponde une égale compétence dans son œuvre de traducteur. Il est souhaitable en outre, qu'il soit d'une compétence hors du commun dans la langue de départ (*lugha manqûla*) et la langue d'arrivée (*manqûl ilayhâ*) au point que sa maîtrise soit dans les deux langues, également parfaite. [...]

Dans ce passage, al-Jāhiz essaie de mettre en lumière la difficulté de l'exercice de traduction et ses exigences, en insistant sur l'importance de prendre la question très au sérieux si l'on veut transmettre correctement un patrimoine scientifique qui passe d'une « sagesse » à une autre (*ḥikmah*),[8] d'un patrimoine à un autre, d'une nation à un autre, d'une culture à une autre, d'un siècle à un autre, et surtout d'une langue (sémantique, grammaire, stylistique) à une autre. Aussi, le traducteur doit être du même savoir que le savant à traduire, il doit maîtriser son savoir, et maîtriser à la perfection les deux langues, la source, et la cible ; il ne s'agit pas simplement de transcrire, mais de traduire, transmettre, interpréter. C'est ainsi que nous allons envisager la lecture de quelques extraits du *Kitāb al-Hayawān* traduits en français que nous avons pu consulter et qui démontrent l'importance de cette exigence.

Les obstacles épistémologiques et linguistiques en histoire de la zoologie

Dans le cas de l'histoire de la biologie, il y a un obstacle linguistique majeur : d'après les travaux de P. Provençal,[9] la difficulté se situe essentiellement dans la traduction des noms d'animaux et de végétaux, qui nécessite un travail d'investigation autant linguistique et philologique, qu'historique et épistémo-biologique.[10] En histoire de la biologie, il est indispensable d'avoir une connaissance assez solide en la matière pour pouvoir déterminer avec le plus de précision possible les noms d'espèces animales ou végétales, ou les phénomènes et mécanismes biologiques décrits dans les ouvrages anciens, et d'être également bon philologue et bon linguiste. La majorité des philologues arabisants n'ont pas de formation « universitaire » en sciences biologiques ; les textes botaniques et zoologiques arabes restent relativement opaques, la difficulté de la traduction des textes zoologiques arabes est renforcée par l'utilisation de nombreux dialectes et de la langue classique pour la détermination des noms zoologiques (Provençal, 1999, 2012).

Les travaux de Philippe Provençal sur Peter Forsskaal à ce sujet sont d'un intérêt majeur dans la relecture du corpus naturaliste arabe. P. Forsskaal (1732–1763) est un naturaliste suédois qui répond à la fois aux compétences du biologiste et du philologue. En effet, il est naturaliste, élève de Linné (1707–1778), mais également un philologue sémitique maîtrisant les langues arabes et hébraïques. Il sera envoyé en expédition scientifique en péninsule arabique et en Egypte par Frédéric V du Danemark, avec l'orientaliste et mathématicien Carsten Niebuhr (1733–1815). Il y constituera une collection de plantes et d'animaux de la région, tout en notant scrupuleusement les noms locaux des espèces.[11] Les études relatives à P. Forsskaal démontrent l'importance de la formation philologique du naturaliste dans la fiabilité de la détermination des noms d'animaux et de végétaux en arabe. En effet, les différents dialectes et l'utilisation de la langue arabe dite « classique » induisent facilement en erreur, créant de nombreux chevauchements, rendant ainsi la tâche du traducteur non biologiste approximative, et pour le biologiste non formé à la langue et à la philologie, la détermination de l'espèce (animale ou végétale) en devient plus laborieuse.[12] Cela rejoint les propos tenus par al-Djâḥiẓ lui-même dans son passage du *Kitāb al-Hayawān* cité plus haut.

Le cas du **Kitāb al-Hayawān** *et sa transmission en Occident*

Ces réflexions d'al-Djâḥiẓ sont d'une pertinence certaine en relation avec notre sujet ici, le phénomène de traduction, les difficultés de traduction concernant les textes zoologiques en particulier. Al-Djâḥiẓ soulève ainsi une préoccupation très importante dans une perspective historique et épistémologique de la transmission des savoirs via la traduction. Il est intéressant de souligner qu'à l'époque d'al-Djâḥiẓ, les premiers penseurs à s'être penchés sur l'étude du monde vivant et des animaux en particulier ont été des hommes de lettres, grammairiens, philologues, lexicographes. Al-Asmacī (740–831), Abu ʿUbayda (723–825), Abu Zayd al-Anṣarī (-215H), qui ont été les maîtres d'al-Djâḥiẓ, ont contribué à la zoologie arabe en écrivant de nombreux traités notamment sur les équidés, les camélidés, etc. On relève ainsi le lien étroit entre la naissance de la langue et l'établissement de ses règles syntaxiques, et le début des déterminations des noms d'espèces animales et végétales.

Le *Kitāb al-Hayawān*, vraisemblablement achevé vers 847, est une œuvre considérable où se mêlent considérations théologiques et littéraires, philosophie et descriptions zoologiques. Les références zoologiques dans le *Kitāb al-Hayawān* proviennent essentiellement de sources grecques traduites (essentiellement Aristote),[13] mais également de sources arabes préislamiques, ou encore persanes et indiennes. Le problème de la terminologie, des dénominations, et donc l'emploi d'une nomenclature claire et précise a posé problème dès les origines. Un autre problème important à résoudre, cette fois pour les traducteurs actuels du corpus arabe en langue européenne par exemple, c'est la recherche de néologismes (Troupeau, 1986) dans ces œuvres-là. Au-delà de quelques transcriptions phonétiques de mots étrangers, ou des emprunts, voire des calques, lorsque le terme est intraduisible ou l'espèce animale n'a pas son équivalent, on peut entrevoir l'utilisation de quelques néologismes, par exemple dans le *Kitāb al-Hayawān*: *yu'yu'*, mot d'origine persane désignant le faucon émerillon femelle, gardé tel quel en arabe; *marmāhi :* dérivé du persan, mot composé signifiant littéralement « poisson-serpent » (*mar*=serpent ; *mahi*= poisson) et désignant l'anguille, existant également sous sa forme grecque arabisée *ankilis*[14] qui fait qu'on en lit pas d'équivalent exact en arabe ; *šahamurġ :* dérivé du persan signifiant roi des oiseaux (*šah*=roi, *murġ*=oiseau), et désignant la poule vraisemblablement,[15] *ajdahāni,* se référant à l'hydre et ayant une origine persane également. Ceci peut malheureusement créer quelques chevauchements et redondances, ainsi qu'un manque d'éléments pour déterminer de manière certaine les espèces.

La culture scientifique des traducteurs et les interprétations des commentateurs[16]

De nombreuses œuvres d'al-Djâḥiẓ ont été traduites en français ou autres langues européennes.[17] Nous pouvons citer les travaux et les traductions du grand spécialiste d'al-Djâḥiẓ, Charles Pellat (1914–1992). Il fait partie de ces spécialistes qui ont essentiellement étudié la composante littéraire ou théologique d'al-Djâḥiẓ. À l'instar de nombreux arabisants, il a quelque peu mésestimé l'apport zoologique d'al-Djâḥiẓ, dont il évoque le « stade littéraire »[18] bien que lui accordant une place « honorable entre Aristote et Buffon ».[19] Est-ce que la zoologie connaît un « stade littéraire », comme une étape de son développement ou de son histoire ? Et est-ce que la dimension littéraire d'un ouvrage scientifique lui en enlève rigueur et scientificité ?[20] C'est en effet l'une des nombreuses interprétations de la zoologie d'al-Djâḥiẓ qui a diminué aux yeux des commentateurs la réalité de l'apport scientifique du *Kitāb al-Ḥayawān* dans l'Histoire de la biologie. Le *Kitāb al-Hayawān* n'existe pas en traduction française en texte intégral. L'aspect volumineux du corpus (7 vol. de 400 pages chacun) ainsi que la diversité des domaines étudiés, semble avoir ralenti l'entreprise d'une traduction complète. Il existe à ce jour deux anthologies rassemblant quelques extraits choisis et commentés,[21] et on retrouve également quelques extraits traduits en français ou en langues européennes dans quelques travaux sur la biologie d'al-Djâḥiẓ.[22] Après plusieurs lectures approfondies de quelques passages, on remarque des traductions des noms d'animaux et/ou des phénomènes biologiques qui ne sont pas les mêmes d'une traduction à l'autre, quelques approximations, voire erreurs de traductions des termes biologiques (noms d'animaux ou mécanismes biologiques) qui mènent immanquablement à de nombreuses fausses interprétations.

Détermination des noms d'animaux

– *Détermination incorrecte*

Le fennec, a par exemple été traduit par vison, alors qu'al-Djâḥiẓ n'avait certainement aucune connaissance de cet animal vivant en Europe ou aux Amériques. Le *fanak* est un mot arabe, signifiant fennec (*Vulpes zerda*), le renard du désert, mammifère de la famille des canidés, cousin du renard. Le fait qu'il soit utilisé aux côtés de la martre zibeline et de l'hermine, qui sont tous deux des carnivores de la famille des mustélidés, et dont l'auteur dit ne pas avoir d'informations suffisantes, peut faire penser à l'hypothèse du vison.[23] Mais dans ce cas précis, cela semble très peu probable sachant que le vison existe sous deux formes : vison d'Europe *Mustela lutreola* et le vison d'Amérique *Mustela vison* et qu'à priori, il n'y en avait pas en Asie, ni en Afrique du Nord; la question de savoir si al-Djâḥiẓ avait connaissance du vison européen est posée, et reste peu probable.

> Si je disposais d'une documentation sur l'anatomie et la morphologie (*abdân*) de la martre zibeline (*sammûr*), du **vison** (*fanak*) et de l'hermine (*qaqûm*) égale à celle dont je dispose sur les lièvres et les renards, sans parler de leurs toisons, je leur aurais, certes, consacré des développements relativement longs. (...)[24]
>
> A propos du rhinocéros (*himâr hindî*), je ne dispose d'aucune documentation le concernant. L'Auteur de la Logique l'évoque. Quant aux ours, aux rats musqués (*fa'ratu al-misk*), aux **visons** (*fanak*), à l'hermine (*qaqûm*), à l'écureuil (*sindjâb*), à la martre zibeline (*sammûr*), toutes ces bêtes sont des animaux à toison, au pelage abondant et moelleux, recherché, source de profits, car leurs fourrures sont extraordinaires.[25]
>
> Les animaux à toison (*dhawât al-wabar*) sont : les chameaux, les renards, les lièvres (*khuzaz*), les hases (*arnab*), les loutres (*kilâb al-ma'*), les martres zibelines (*sammûr*), les **visons** (*fanak*), les

> hermines (*qaqûm*), les petits-gris (*sindjâb*), les ours (*dibâb*).[26]

De même « *dîk al-hind* » associé à la dinde par simple analogie ou de manière grossièrement littérale en « dindon » révèle, au-delà de l'écart scientifique, l'absence de la dimension historique dans le processus de traduction lui-même. Il s'agit simplement d'une poule indienne, et non pas du « dindon », bien évidemment.[27] Il est inutile de rappeler, en effet, que la dinde vient de l'Amérique, et a été introduite en Europe par Christophe Colomb et les colons espagnols, et a été nommée poule de l'inde en référence aux Indes, puis par extension « dinde ».

> Chez les gallinacées (*dadjâdj*), pourtant, le *khilâsî*, produit du croisement des poules persanes métissées (*muwalladât*) et des **dindons** (*hindiyyât*), est visiblement une réussite : c'est une poule bien en chair, grasse et dodue.[28]

> De la même façon, les gallinacées (*dadjâdj*) présentent des variantes, ce qui ne empêche pas d'appartenir tous au genre gallinacé, ainsi le **dindon** (*dîk hindî*), le coq *khilâsî* (croisement d'un gallinacé d'Inde et de Perse), ou encore le coq nabatéen, la poule du Sind, le coq *zandjî*.[29]

Aussi, *djahl*, identifié comme la « reine des abeilles » (genre *Apis*) par Maalouf est traduit par « perdrix » (oiseau) dans une des anthologies.[30]

– Confusions, approximations

La dénomination *hašarât* désigne en arabe classique médiéval tous les animaux rampant sur le sol et regroupe les insectes rampants, les petits reptiles et quelques mammifères rongeurs. Aujourd'hui, le sens du mot a évolué, lorsqu'on parle de *hašarât* dans le langage courant ou dans les divers dialectes arabes, cela désigne les insectes (aussi bien ailés que non ailés). Or, pour al-Djâḥiẓ, et les naturalistes médiévaux, il ne s'agit pas uniquement d'insectes. Dans la plupart des traductions des extraits du *Kitāb al-Hayawān* (et d'autres traités zoologiques arabes), c'est par « insectes » que ce mot est traduit (Belhadj-Mahmoud, 1977) ; on peut ainsi lire des coquilles telles que « les serpents font incontestablement partie des insectes non-ailés ».[31] En soi, cette phrase peut être perçue par un lecteur non-arabisant comme une aberration et peut, par conséquent le faire douter du sérieux de la méthodologie scientifique de l'auteur.

Par ailleurs, nous remarquons différentes traductions pour le même terme arabe, et parfois un même nom d'animal pour traduire différentes appellations de la part d'al-Djâḥiẓ ; par exemple, *d̠arra*, traduite par petite fourmi la plupart du temps, se trouve curieusement sous la désignation « ciron »[32] alors que le ciron *Acarus siro* (Linné, 1758) est un acarien (Arthropode Chélicérate Arachnide) du même sous-embranchement que les araignées ; ce n'est pas du tout un animal proche de la fourmi qui est un Arthropode de la classe des Insectes et de l'Ordre des Hyménoptères,famille *Formicidae* (Latreille, 1809).

En outre, *sinǧāb* est traduit par « écureuil » et également par « petit-gris » Le petit-gris est la désignation de la fourrure d'hiver de l'écureuil roux (*Sciurus vulgaris*).[33] En effet l'écureuil d'Eurasie ou l'écureuil roux *Sciurus vulgaris* est roux en été (il y a aussi des spécimens sombres, voire noirs) mais en hiver les poils de la fourrure du dos prennent une nuance grise. C'est à dire quel l'écureuil en hiver a le ventre blanc, les flancs er la queue rousse et le dos gris. C'est ce pelage d'hiver que l'on nomme le petit gris et aussi le vair. C'est surtout la race nordique qui prend une nuance grise en hiver. Par extension, l'appellation petit-gris fut aussi appliquée à d'autres espèces d'écureuils au pelage gris au XVIIIe siècle. Nous savons qu'il y avait une grande exportation de fourrure d'écureuil vers le monde arabe. L'égyptien an-Nuwayrī écrit au XIVe siècle dans son *Nihāyat al-Arab fī funūn al-Adab* que l'écureuil (سنجاب) est connu (معروف) et qu'il a un beau pelage (حسن الوبر). Nous pensons qu'il décrit l'écureuil roux connu dans le monde arabe à travers l'importation de fourrures.

– Des espèces encore indéterminées

Les poissons ont été très peu décrits par al-Djâḥiẓ par manque, selon lui, de sources fiables et d'observations de sa part. Dans un chapitre sur les poissons migrateurs, il évoque les « *usbūr* », traduit par Sparidés (Maâlouf, 1932, Aarab, Provençal, 2000) ou par Mullidés (Souami, 1988) et les « *barastūǧ*», traduit par Sparidés (Souami, 1988),[34] ou gardé tel quel car supposé indéterminé (Aarab, Provençal, 2000)

Autres données biologiques

a. Les plumes des oiseaux

Dans le paragraphe de la classification des oiseaux, al-Djâḥiẓ évoque leur plumage : il parle des *qawādim*, *abāhir* et *ḫawâfī* notamment (dans d'autres passages du *Kitāb al-Hayawān*, d'autres comme les *manākib* et *kūla* seront décrites également).[35] Souami traduit *qawādim* par tectrices, *abāhir* par rémiges primaires, et *ḫawāfī* par rémiges secondaires. Les tectrices sont des plumes de couverture qui recouvrent le corps des oiseaux de la base des rémiges des ailes jusqu'aux plumes de la queue (rectrices). Elles ne jouent pas de rôle dans le vol. Les rémiges sont les grandes plumes des ailes dirigées vers l'extérieur et l'arrière, les primaires sont fixées au niveau de la main, les secondaires sont fixées au niveau de l'avant-bras (cubitus).

Cependant, selon F. Viré, les *qawādim* désignent chacune des quatre premières rémiges primaires, qui sont les plumes d'essor, dites « cerceaux »;[36] les *manākib* désignent les quatre rémiges primaires suivantes dites « couteaux » ; les *ḫawāfī* désignent les quatre premières rémiges secondaires, plumes cubitales situées au dos, dites « vanneaux »,[37] les *abāhir* désignent les quatre avant-dernières rémiges secondaires, les plumes de l'aile,[38] et les *kulā*, les quatre dernières rémiges secondaires. Ce genre de confusions amène immanquablement à de fausses interprétations, voire à une incompréhension totale du texte original, qui s'en voit diminué de valeur scientifique.

b. Propriétés biologiques.

Dans le chapitre sur la classification, al-Djâḥiẓ parle des oiseaux de nature « mixte » (*tab' muštarak*). Il s'agit d'oiseaux qui ont un régime alimentaire mixte et qui partagent certaines caractéristiques avec les oiseaux carnivores et / ou herbivores. On lit dans l'une des traductions les « animaux à nature amphibologique ».[39] Ce terme n'a pas de sens biologique et ne se réfère pas à la notion de nature mixte. Dans le langage courant, il dénote de quelque chose d'ambigu, d'équivoque. Il nous semble que cela ne peut se rapporter à une propriété biologique d'un animal. Nous sommes là face à une terminologie qui se veut biologique, mais qui ne l'est pas.

Petite comparaison entre les deux anthologies du Hayawân

La seconde anthologie existante en langue française ne reprend pas, de manière délibérée, les mêmes extraits choisis et traduits par Souami, donc on ne peut réellement faire une comparaison objective quant aux méthodes de traduction. Elle est relativement plus récente et a essayé de ne pas chevaucher l'ancienne afin d'apporter de nouveaux extraits traduits.[40]

Encore une fois, la *d̠arra*, a été traduite par ciron, également dans cette anthologie, alors qu'il s'agirait plutôt d'une petite fourmi.[41]

Il est intéressant de noter la traduction de «*fahd*» par guépard; c'est en effet plus juste,[42] car «*fahd*» a souvent été traduit par « léopard » ou « panthère ».[43] En arabe classique *fahd* désigne le guépard (*Acinonyx jubatus*) et *nimr* ou *namir désigne le léopard (Panthera pardus*).

Conclusion

L'acte de traduction, étape majeure de la transmission du savoir et d'une certaine manière de l'élaboration du savoir lui-même, est le phénomène révélateur qui démontre à quel point aucune discipline n'est indépendante ou autonome. En Histoire des Sciences, une lecture uniquement à travers le prisme technique est insuffisante, la traduction elle-même sans formation et références scientifiques est incomplète, et, si elle n'est pas inscrite dans un contexte socio-historique, l'analyse se trouve diminuée dans le sens, voire même faussée. La transmission d'un savoir dépend donc d'un ensemble de facteurs, d'informations et de compétences.

Lorsqu'il s'agit de textes zoologiques, il est indispensable de se référer aux compétences scientifiques aussi bien qu'à celles venant de la philologie, sinon le risque d'aboutir à un texte imprécis ou truffé d'approximations et/ou de contresens (par exemple en citant des espèces n'ayant jamais vécu ou n'ayant jamais été importées dans le pays d'origine) sera toujours présent. Le traitement des textes zoologiques et botaniques du monde arabe de l'époque médiévale requiert donc d'une façon absolue une approche interdisciplinaire, où le contenu de ces textes est sujet à une étude linguistique et historique et en même temps analysé à la lumière des connaissances biologiques. Ceci ne doit absolument pas aboutir à un « présentéisme », où l'on cherche le présent dans le passé, ni à une espèce de fausse hiérarchisation, où l'on essaye de juger les textes à la lueur du savoir actuel, mais bien à une détermination réelle de leur contenu scientifique afin de pouvoir les situer dans leur contexte historique. Fondamentalement, il faut essayer d'établir un lexique des termes techniques sans lequel le traitement de ces textes reste impossible. L'établissement même de ce lexique requiert une approche interdisciplinaire. Il faudrait soit reconnaître les espèces en question par les descriptions données par les textes mêmes, ou alors aller dans le pays arabophones afin de déterminer l'usage actuel des noms d'espèces, etc. Et en définitive, il faut intégrer toutes ces données pour pouvoir en tirer les renseignements nécessaires à l'établissement d'un tel lexique.

La pensée zoologique d'al-Djâḥiẓ s'inscrit pleinement dans une Histoire de la Biologie, ses observations, descriptions du règne animal et de ses propriétés, ses analyses de phénomènes biologiques, méritent d'être redécouverts, voire revisités et traduits dans une langue scientifique « intelligible » afin d'en saisir toute la rigueur et toute la pertinence dans une lecture historique des Sciences de la Vie.

Références bibliographiques

ابي عثمان عمر و بن بحر الجاحظ كتاب الحيوان، وضع حواشيه محمد باسل عيون السود، 2003 دار كتب العلمية، بيروت،

Al-Djâhiz, Kitâb al-Hayawân. Beyrouth : Editions Abdesselam Mohamed Harûn, (2ème edition), Beyrouth: Dar al-jîl, Dar al-fikr, 8 vol., 1988.

Al-Djâḥiẓ. *Le livre des Animaux, De l'étonnante sagesse divine dans sa création et autres anecdotes*. Traduit et préfacé par Mohamed Mestiri. Paris : Fayard, 2003.

Al-Djâḥiẓ. *Le Cadi et la Mouche, Anthologie du Livre des Animaux*. Extraits choisis, traduits de l'arabe et présentés par Lakhdhar Souami. Paris : E-ditions Sindbad, 1988.

Aarab, Ahmed. *Etude analytique comparative de la zoologie médiévale, cas du Kitâb Al-Hayawân de Al-Jâhiz*. Thèse, Abdelmalek Essaâdi, Faculté des Sciences, Tétouan (2001).

Aarab, Ahmed, Philippe Provençal & Mohammed Idaomar. "Eco-Ethological Data according to Jahiz through his work *Kitâb-al-Hayawân*". *Arabica* 47(2000): 278–86---. "La méthodologie scientifique en matière zoologique de Jâhiz dans la rédaction de son œuvre *Kitâb al-Hayawân* ». *Anaquel estudios arabes* 14 (2003) : 5–19.

Baccouche, Taieb. « La traduction dans la tradition arabe ». *Meta* 45, n°3 (2000) : 395–399. http://id.erudit.org/iderudit/001936ar

---, avec Mejri, Salah. « Terminologie et traduction (cas de l'ornithologie et de la linguistique) ». *Meta* 45, n°3 (2000) : 437–444. http://id.erudit.org/iderudit/001937ar

Balty-Guesdon & Marie-Geneviève. « Bayt al-Hikma de Bagdad ». *Arabica* 39 (1992): 131-150.

Ben Saad, Meyssa. « Ibn Khaldûn et la génération des êtres vivants : réception des textes et traductions françaises ». *Bulletin de la Société d'Histoire et d'Epistémologie des Sciences de la Vie* 15, N°1, Kimé (2008) : 71–111.

Ben Saad Meyssa, Katouzian-Safadi Mehrnaz. « Les insectes dans la classification des animaux chez al-Jâhiz (776–868) : entre mythe et raison ». *Explora International Conference Proceedings,* Toulouse Natural History Museum (2011) : 228–250.

---. « Raconter une Histoire naturelle : lorsque le verbe du conteur trace les observations du naturaliste (Le cas du *Kitāb al-Hayawān* d'al-Djâḥiẓ) ». *Arabic Biology and Medicine* I, N°1 (2013) : 77–102.

Cassarino, Mireille. « Traduire sans trahir chez les arabes du Moyen-Age ». *Studies in Arabic and Islam*. Eds., S. Leder, H. Kilpatrick, B. Martel-Thoumian, H. Schönig. Leuven: Uitgeverij Peeters, 2002.

Forskål, Peter. *Descriptiones Animalium—Avium, amphiborum, insectorum, vermium quæ in itinere orientali observavit Petrus Forskål, post mortem auctoris edidit Carsten Niebuhr*. København, 1775. [Forskål 1775a].

Gutas, Dimitri. *Pensée Grecque, culture arabe* [*Greek Thought, Arabic Culture*], *Le mouvement de traduction gréco-arabe à Bagdad et la société abbasside primitive (IIe-IVe/VIIIe-Xe siècles)*, trad. Abdesselam Cheddadi, Paris : Aubier-Flammarion, 2005

Maâlouf, Amin. *An Arabic Zoological Dictionary*. Beyrouth: Dar al-Ra'idal-'Arabi, 1932.

Provençal, Philippe. « Le problème de l'identité des espèces animales et végétales dans les textes arabes et les recherches faites en cette matière par Peter Forsskål (1732–1763) à ce sujet». *Circulations des Savoirs autour de la Méditerranée, philosophie et sciences (IX–XVIIe siècles).* Eds., G. F. Vescovini et A. Hasnawi, 2013

---. Enquête lexicographique sur les noms d'animaux en arabe, Thèse, Université Copenhague (2005).

Rommevaux, Sabine. « La constitution d'un vocabulaire mathématique dans la traduction des Eléments d'Euclide du XIIe siècle ». *Actes du Colloque « Sciences et Langues du Moyen-Age »*. Paris, 2009.

Salama-Carr, Myriam. "Translation into Arabic in the 'Classical Age,' When the Pandora's box of transmission opens." UCL (2002).

---. « L'évaluation des traductions vers l'arabe chez les traducteurs du Moyen-Age » . *TTR* 6, n°1, (1993) : 15–25. http://id.erudit.org/iderudit/037136ar

Troupeau, Gérard. « Les problèmes posés par la traduction de l'arabe ancien en français moderne ». *Meta* 31, n°1, (1986) : 11–15. http://id.erudit.org/iderudit/004511ar

Notes

1 Le mode de translittération arabe-français utilisé ici est celui de l'Encyclopédie de l'Islam (EI), à part pour la lettre « ق » gardée sous forme « q ».

2 Gutas, D., *Greek thought, Arabic Culture*, 1998. L'institution *Bait-al-Hikma* a réuni un certain nombre de chercheurs et de traducteurs sous l'égide d'al-Ma'mun, mais elle n'était pas la seule institution à promouvoir les traductions, Balty-Guesdon, M.-G., "Bait-al-Hikma de Bagdad"(1992) : 131–150.

3 Balty-Guesdon, M.-G., "Bait-al-Hikma de Bagdad" (1992), voir aussi Gutas, D. (2005)

4 Califat abbasside : 750 à 1258, capitale Bagdad, fondée en 762

5 *Adīb*, au-delà de la dimension littéraire, est une distinction sociologique et intellectuelle qui englobe toutes les connaissances acquises dans de nombreux domaines du savoir par le savant curieux, l'érudit, l' « honnête homme ». Le *adib* était un maître du verbe, de l'éloquence, du savoir, et aussi un homme courtois. De nos jours, et depuis le XIXe siècle, le mot *adab* - surtout dans sa forme plurielle *adâb*- concerne principalement la littérature, les « Belles Lettres». Pour plus de détails sur le *adab*, *Encyclopédie de l'Islam* vol. I (1986) : 175–76.

6 *Mutakallim* est le nom d'action de *Kalām* qui signifie littéralement « parole », ou « discours ». Il s'agit de la « théologie rationnelle ». cf. Rashed, M., *Les Grecs, Les Arabes, et Nous. Enquête sur l'islamophobie savante* (2009) : 121–169. Le *muctazilisme* est une école théologique, dont les principes fondamentaux sont essentiellement basés sur l'usage de la raison. Cf. *Encyclopédie de l'Islam* vol. VII (1993) : 783–793.

7 Traduction de L. Souami, *Le cadi et la mouche*, (1988) : 115–117

8 À l'époque 'abbāside le terme *ḥikmah* est souvent utilisé comme synonyme du terme de philosophie de l'Antiquité classique.

9 Provençal, P., *The Arabic Plant Names of Peter Forsskål's Flora Aegyptiaco-Arabica* (2010).

10 De nombreux travaux actuellement portent sur cette problématique : *Dictionnaire historique des termes zoologiques arabes*, projet lancé par le Professeur Ahmed Aarab, Université Malek Essaadi, Tétouan, Maroc ; Mouhajir, Y., *Etude analytique et comparative des termes zoologiques arabes médiévaux, cas du Kitāb Al Hayawan de Gahiz*, Thèse, Univ. A.Essaidi, Tanger (2010).

11 Niebuhr, seul survivant de l'expédition, se charge de la publication des manuscrits de Forsskål. Il fait paraître en 1775 *Descriptiones Animalium - Avium, amphiborum, insectorum, vermium quæ in itinere orientali observavit Petrus Forskål.* La même année, il fait aussi paraître un catalogue de plante du Yémen et de la basse-Égypte, *Flora Ægyptiaco-Arabica sive descriptiones plantarum quas per Ægyptum Inferiorem et Arabiam felicem detexit, illustravit Petrus Forskål.*

12 On peut citer également des travaux, certes plus anciens, mais intéressants, de l'orientaliste français Jean-Jacques Clément-Mullet (1796–1865) qui s'est penché sur l'Histoire de la zoologie arabe avec un regard de philologue, notamment sur al-Qazwīnī. Il se présente d'ailleurs lui-même comme un spécialiste des langues orientales et d'histoire naturelle. Il a travaillé sur Qazwīnī et Damīrī, ainsi que Maimonide et Avicenne, mais non sur al-Jāḥiẓ (par ailleurs, dans un article écrit par Jean Théodoridès [Théodoridès, J., « La zoologie dans l'œuvre de quelques médecins orientaux au Moyen-Age, Sezgin, F. (dir.), *Natural Science in Islam*, Vol. I., Zoology, Texts and Studies, I, Institute for the History of Arabic-Islamic Science, J. W. Goethe University, Frankfurt Am Main, (2000) : 617–621] sur la zoologie, il n'est pas fait mention d'al-Jāḥiẓ qui est cependant cité dans les extraits qu'il traduit de Qazwīnī et Damīrī: Clément-Mullet, J.-J., « Sur l'enchaînement des trois règnes de la nature : extrait de Kazwiny » (1840) : 421–431. Aussi, le dictionnaire zoologique arabe (anglais-arabe) du zoologiste irakien Amin Maalouf (Maalouf, A., *An Arabic zoological dictionary* (1932)), est une source riche et intéressante en termes de dénomination d'espèces animales arabes.

13 Les avis divergent quant à la fiabilité de la traduction du corpus aristotélicien par Yaḥyā Ibn al-Bitrīq, et au vu même de l'opinion d'al-Jāḥiẓ envers les traductions, on peut penser qu'il a lu ces traductions avec beaucoup de prudence. Ceci étant, on ne sait pas s'il a lu une autre traduction. Il en existe d'autres, mais rien ne nous permet d'affirmer actuellement avec certitude laquelle a été consultée de manière sérieuse par al-Jāḥiẓ.

14 *ankalīs* est une arabisation de la forme grecque qui désigne l'anguille (*Anguilla vulgaris*), appelé *thucbān al-mā'* (serpent de la mer) en Egypte, *marmarīj* en Iraq, et *ankalīs* en Syrie. Maâlouf, A., *Op. Cit.*, (1932) : 95.

15 Traduit par « poule sultane bleue » *Porphyrio porphyrio*, dans *Le Cadi et la mouche*, *Op. Cit.*, 91 et 333

16 Sur la réception des textes en arabe, les traductions françaises et les diverses interprétations, les obstacles linguistiques, et le risque de sur-interprétation, cf. : Ben Saad, M., « Ibn Khaldûn et la génération des êtres vivants : traductions des textes et réceptions françaises », *Bulletin SHESVIE*, Vol. 15 (2008) : 73–111.

17 Les principales œuvres d'al-Jāḥiẓ connues en Occident et traduites en langues européennes : *Kitāb al-buḫala*, trad. Fr « *Livre des avares* », par Ch. Pellat, Paris, G.P. Maisonneuve (1951), *Kitāb mufaḫarāt al-jawāri wa-l-ghilmân*, traduit sous le titre *Ephèbes et courtisanes* par Maati abal, préface et notes de Malek Chebel, Rivages poche Petite Bibliothèque, Paris (1997), et également traduit sous le titre *Le Livre des mérites respectifs des jouvencelles et jouvenceaux*, par Bernard Bouillon, éditions Philippe Picquier, Arles, (2000) ; *Kitāb al-tarbi' wa-l-tadwīr*, Damas (1955), *Kitāb al-Qiyān*, épître sur les esclaves chanteuses, J. Finkel, *Three Essays*, Le Caire (1926) ; *Risāla fi-l-Nābita*, traduction de Ch. Pellat, in AIEO, Alger, (1952) ; *Kitāb al-tāj* (Livre de la couronne), traduit par Ch. Pellat, Paris (1954) ; *Quatre Essais*, traduit par Charles Vial, *Excerpte Und Ubersetzungen aus der Schriften des Jâhiz*, Stuttgart (1931) ; *Nine Essays of Jâhiz*, éditions P ; Lang, American University Studies, série VII, vol. 53, New-York (1989).

18 Sur le discours naturaliste d'al-Jāḥiẓ empreint de verve littéraire, cf. Ben Saad, M., Katouzian-Safadi, M., « Raconter une histoire naturelle : lorsque le verbe du conteur trace les observations du naturaliste », *Arabic Biology and Medicine* (2013) : 77–102.

19 Pellat, Ch., *Hayawân*, EI2

20 Voir Ben Saâd, M., Katouzian-Safadi, M., *Op. cit.*

21 Le *cadi et la mouche*, *Anthologie du Livre des Animaux*, trad. L. Souami (1988), *Le Livre des animaux, de l'étonnante sagesse divine dans sa Création et autres anecdotes*, trad. M. Mestiri (2003).

22 Aarab, A. et P. Provençal, cf. références bibliographiques, Palacios, M.A., « el Libro de los animales de Jâhiz », *Isis*, 14, (1930) : 20–54 ; Kopf, L., « The book of animals (*Kitâb al-Hayawân*) of al-Jâhiz (ca. 767–868), *Actes 7ème Congrès International d'Histoire des Sciences*, Jérusalem, (1953) : 395–401 ; Pellat, Ch. *Le milieu basrien et la formation d'al-Gâhiz*, Adrien-Maisonneuve, Paris, (1953) et « Sur quelques noms d'animaux en arabe classique », *GLECS*, T. VIII, (1960) : 95–100 ; Wilson, W.G., *Al-Jâhiz and Arabic Zoology*, UMI Dissertation Services, Michigan, (1965) : 285 ; Ullman, M., *Die Natur-und Geheimwissenschaften im Islam, Die Tierkunde*, E.J. Brill, Leiden / Köln, (1972) : 5–60 ; Belhadj-Mahmoud, N., *La psychologie des animaux chez les arabes, le* Kitâb al-Hayawân *d'al-Jâhiz*, Klinksieck, Paris, (1977) ; Einsenstein, H., *Enführung in die arabische Zoographie*, Dietrich Reimer Verlag, Berlin, (1990) ; Ben Saad, M., *La Connaissance du monde vivant chez le savant al-Jāḥiẓ: les Sciences de la vie et le regard d'al-Jāḥiẓ dans l'Histoire des Sciences arabes*, thèse de Doctorat, CNRS Sphere-Chspam, UMR 7219-Université Paris Diderot, (2010).

23 *Le Cadi et la mouche*, *Op. cit.*, 46.

24 *Le Cadi et la mouche*, *Op. cit.*, 46, *Ḥayawān*, VI, 32.

25 *Le Cadi et la mouche*, *Op. cit.*, 81, *Ḥayawān*, VI, 27–28.

26 *Le Cadi et la mouche*, *Op. cit.*, 314, *Ḥayawān*, V, 483–484.

27 *Le Cadi et la mouche*, *Op. cit.*, 211 et 319

28 *Le Cadi et le mouche*, *Op. cit.*, 211, *Ḥayawān*, I, 156

29 *Le Cadi et la mouche*, *Op. cit.*, 319, *Ḥayawān*, III, 144–146

30 Maâlouf, 1932, « perdrix » *Le Cadi et la mouche*, *Op. cit.*, 90.

31 *Le Cadi et la mouche*, *Op. cit.*, 88-91- *Ḥayawān*, I, 26–31

32 Souami, *Le Cadi et la Mouche*, *Op. cit.*, 68, 319

33 Dans les parties montagneuses et boisées du Moyen Orient, c. à d. Turquie, Liban, Kurdistan, Caucase etc. mais non de la Péninsule Arabe il y a une espèce d'écureuil, l'écureuil de Perse ou du Caucase (*Sciurus anomalus*), qui est plus petite que l'écureuil roux et au pelage jaune et gris. Nous ne savons pas si c'est cette espèce- là qui est à l'origine du nom *sinj̱āb*, ou si ce nom ne s'appliquait à l'origine qu'aux fourrures importées d'Europe. Cependant la description donnée par ad-Damîrî décrit le *sinjāb* comme: un animal de la taille d'une gerboise parmi les [animaux du genre] souris (*min al-fa'r*), et dont le poil est des plus soyeux (*fī g̱hāyati-l-nu'ūmah*) (...)

34 "The zoological identities of these fish remain obscure, *usbūr* is a general name for *Sparidae* according to Maalouf (...)" Aarab, A., Provençal, P., Idaomar, M., « Eco-ethological data according to Gâhiz" (2000): 282

35 *Ḥayawān*, I, 26 et II, 355.

36 Viré, F., « Falconaria arabica : glanures philologiques » III, 167

37 Viré, F., *Op. Cit.*, I, 292

38 Viré, F., *Op. Cit* ;, I, 281.

39 *Le Cadi et la mouche*, *Op. cit.*, 90

40 Les auteurs se présentent comme ayant eu la volonté de ne pas traduire « les passages qui ont déjà fait l'objet de l'anthologie de L. Souami (1988) mais qu'ils ont cependant « à de très rares occasions, dérogé à cette règle », en précisant de même avoir « relevé certaines imprécisions dans la traduction de Souami, Mestiri, *Livre des animaux*, *Op. cit.*. 25.

41 Mestiri, *Op. Cit.*, 72, *Hayawân*, VII, 35

42 Aarab, A., *Ibid*

43 Mestiri, *Op. Cit.*, 122.123, *Hayawân*, VI, 471, et VII, 42

Interaction entre la sémiotique et la traduction littéraire

Sündüz Öztürk Kasar

Résumé

La sémiotique traitant de la production et de la saisie du sens se met en interdisciplinarité avec la traductologie étant donné que ces deux disciplines ont un souci majeur commun qu'est la construction du sens. Le présent article tâche d'illustrer la coopération entre la science des signes et la théorie de la traduction sur un exemple littéraire connu de tous: *Le loup et l'agneau* de La Fontaine et ses cinq traductions turques qui seront comparées dans une approche d'analyse sémiotique.

Mots-clé : sémiotique, sens, traduction turque

Abstract

Semiotics deals with the production and capture of meaning as its subject, and this discipline can be paired with translation studies in an interdisciplinary relationship since both disciplines focus heavily on the construction of meaning. In this article I seek to illustrate how both disciplines, the science of signs and the translation theory, can work together. Using the example of literary text that is well known, Jean de La Fontaine's fable, *The Wolf and the Lamb,* I apply the methodology of semiotic analysis to compare and contrast the five Turkish translations of this fable.

Keywords: semiotics, meaning, Turkish translation

Introduction

La science des signes, devenue une science de grande envergure qui ouvre ses portes à toutes les disciplines traitant de la production et de la saisie du sens se met en interdisciplinarité avec la théorie de la traduction étant donné que ces deux disciplines ont en commun une même visée qu'est le sens.

Dans notre étude, nous allons nous concentrer sur la contribution de la sémiotique à la traduction littéraire étant donné que le texte littéraire nous offre un *univers du sens*, autrement dit, un ensemble de significations actualisées et virtuelles. Dès qu'un lecteur participe au processus de la reproduction de cet univers, la *quête du sens* commence. Au même titre, le traducteur doit mener à bien cette quête avant de passer à la traduction tout comme le fait l'analyste sémioticien avant de contraster le texte original et le texte traduit.[1] La sémiotique leur offre une méthode de lecture, d'analyse et d'interprétation des signes et des significations. Ainsi, elle permet de mieux appréhender l'univers du sens d'un texte littéraire en même temps qu'elle fonde et légitime la traduction.

Mais, l'acte de traduire vu par le sémioticien pourrait aussi renouveler la théorie sémiotique car le sémioticien est en face d'un seul discours, d'un seul univers de signes, d'un seul processus de signification alors que le sémioticien de la traduction s'en occupe forcément de deux ou plus.[2] Donc, sémiotiquement parlant, la traduction est un acte langagier où les discours se superposent, les univers de signes se multiplient, les processus de signification se dédoublent, les instances d'origine des discours se rencontrent, les langues et les cultures se mettent en dialogue. En tant que tel, l'acte traduisant est une communication particulière qui nous incite à réfléchir sur l'interaction entre la sémiotique et la traductologie.

Nous allons essayer d'illustrer la coopération entre la théorie des signes et la théorie de la traduction sous le point de vue de la Théorie des Instances élaborée au sein de l'Ecole Sémiotique de Paris par les travaux de Jean-Claude Coquet. La sémiotique des Instances est une théorie qui met en avant la notion de *discours* fondé sur les coordonnées «*je-tu* ; *ici* et *maintenant*» qui assurent le lien à la réalité. Disciple fidèle d'Emile Benveniste et lecteur de Maurice Merleau-Ponty et de Paul Ricœur, Jean-Claude Coquet a su appliquer la perspective phénoménologique[3] à la perspective sémiotique.

La sémiotique des instances pose le principe selon lequel il n'est pas possible d'étudier le discours sans le rapporter aux instances qui le produit et qui le reçoit. Coquet fait aussi une typologie des instances suivant le critère de jugement : l'instance dotée de la capacité de juger est une instance *sujet* alors que celle qui en est privée s'appelle *non-sujet*. Entre les deux, il existe un état de passage où le jugement est suspendu momentanément ; il s'agit alors d'un *quasi-sujet*.

Nous allons donc aborder notre corpus d'analyse à la lumière de ces concepts. Notre analyse se fera sur un exemple connu de tous: *Le loup et l'agneau* de La Fontaine. Pour ce choix, nous nous sommes inspirée d'un article de Jean-Claude Coquet intitulé « Instances d'énonciation et modalités » (Coquet, 1997 147–158) où il démontre d'une manière succincte son approche au texte littéraire en prenant en main cette fable. Il existe des dizaines de traductions de *Le loup et l'agneau* en langue turque mais nous en avons choisi cinq exemples dont les trois sont traduits par trois grands poètes turcs Şinasi, Orhan Veli et Nâzım Hikmet et les deux autres par deux grands écrivains Sabahattin Eyüboğlu et Tahsin Yücel qui est en même temps sémioticien.

Apport de la sémiotique à la traduction littéraire

Nous pouvons envisager l'apport de la sémiotique aux différentes étapes de l'activité traduisante pour différents agents qui entrent en jeu: d'abord pour le traducteur avant qu'il ne s'engage à la traduction, elle lui offre une méthode d'analyse qui va fonder sa lecture et son interprétation ; le traducteur sert également de la science des signes dans le processus de l'acte de traduire puisqu'il rebâtit son texte sur l'analyse sémiotique qu'il vient d'effectuer. Ensuite, la sémiotique intervient lors de la publication du texte traduit afin de vérifier la tâche du traducteur ; ainsi, elle guide le relecteur qui doit saisir et comparer les deux univers du sens fondés dans l'original et dans la traduction. Enfin, après la publication du texte traduit, elle contribue à la fois à la quête du sens du lecteur de la traduction et au travail du critique ou de l'analyste qui établit un métadiscours sur le texte traduit. (*cf.* Öztürk Kasar, 2009a) Nous allons commencer à l'illustrer par l'étape « pré-traduction » où il s'agit d'analyser l'univers des signes de l'original.

Analyse sémiotique de la fable intitulée *Le loup et l'agneau* de La Fontaine

Pour mieux saisir l'univers du sens construit dans *Le loup et l'agneau*, nous allons entamer une analyse sémiotique à partir de l'analyse modale de Jean-Claude Coquet.

Segmentation du texte et instances d'énonciation

Dans une analyse sémiotique, la segmentation du texte est la première opération qui s'accomplit suivant les critères de disjonction temporelle, spatiale, actorielle, discursive, thymique, etc. Le but de cette opération est de diviser le texte en des séquences plus maniables dont chacune possède l'unité significative. La fable de La Fontaine est alors segmentée en quatre séquences qui se divisent à leur tour en des segments plus petits mettant en scène différentes instances énonçantes :

La première séquence (1–2), incipit du texte, se divise en deux segments ; le premier segment contient la morale de la fable[4] et se distingue du suivant à la fois par le ton d'une instance transcendante, une « divinité » (Coquet, 1997 156) qui annonce une vérité « universelle » (Coquet, 1997 156) ainsi que par le temps verbal qui y convient (présent dit *générique*). Quant au second segment, il pose tout d'abord, par le « nous », l'instance d'origine (IO) du texte qui se fait le sujet délégué du Destinateur qu'est l'instance transcendante. En tant que sujet délégué, il s'engage dans l'immédiat (d'où le futur proche) à illustrer la vérité universelle proférée par l'instance transcendante; et pour ce faire, il projette deux instances énonçantes.

La deuxième séquence (3–6) met en scène deux actants signalés déjà par le titre (le loup et l'agneau) en les localisant « au bord d'une eau pure » : elle se divise ainsi en deux segments dont chacun correspond à la présentation d'un actant.

Vient ensuite la troisième séquence qui est la plus grande (7–26) et qui se divise en onze segments. Cette séquence peut être appelé « Procès » et elle se trouve entre deux marques typographiques : des guillemets. Elle s'ouvre et se referme donc par des guillemets en mettant en

Le tableau des Instances et des Séquences dans Le loup et l'agneau

LE LOUP ET L'AGNEAU	**Instances**
La raison du plus fort est toujours la meilleure,	Instance transcendante
Nous l'allons montrer tout à l'heure.	
Un agneau se désaltérait	
Dans le courant d'une onde pure.	Instance d'origine (IO)
Un loup survient à jeun qui cherchait aventure,	
Et que la faim en ces lieux attirait.	

scène un débat. Nous sommes au tribunal et le procès dure tout au long de vingt vers. Pendant ce temps, la parole est détenue à tour de rôles par deux instances énonçantes projetées (IEP): d'une part, le loup qui est à la fois le procureur et le juge de ce procès, et de l'autre, l'agneau qui se trouve dans l'obligation de se faire l'avocat de lui-même. Le loup procureur accuse l'agneau « d'avoir troublé son breuvage », quant à l'agneau, il se défend à trois reprises contre les accusations du loup. La parole est répartie quasi équitablement entre les deux instances : le loup détient neuf vers et demi alors que l'agneau possède en sa faveur un minime avantage avec une ligne de plus, soit donc dix vers et demi en tout. Mais, comme le montre Coquet, le temps disposé par l'agneau pour sa défense diminue à chaque fois d'une manière sensible : la première argumentation (10 -17) contient huit vers, la deuxième (20–21) deux vers et la dernière ne contient qu'un demi vers (la moitié du 23). (Coquet, 1997 153) Car l'impatience du loup affamé augmente et il passe vite au verdict.

La quatrième et dernière séquence (27–29) comprend la sanction. A part les guillemets précédents qui la séparent de la troisième séquence, il y a aussi le changement de lieu « au fond des forêts » ainsi que le changement de voix (reprise de parole par l'instance d'origine) qui la justifient. (*cf. Le tableau des Instances et des Séquences dans* Le loup et l'agneau)

<table>
<tr><th>Séquences et segments</th><th></th><th>№</th></tr>
<tr><td>La « morale » de la fable</td><td rowspan="2">Incipit</td><td rowspan="2">1</td></tr>
<tr><td>Passage au récit</td></tr>
<tr><td>Présentation de l'Actant « l'agneau »</td><td rowspan="2">Mise en scène des actants</td><td rowspan="2">2</td></tr>
<tr><td>Présentation de l'Actant « le loup »</td></tr>
</table>

LE LOUP ET L'AGNEAU	Instances
« Qui te rend si hardi de troubler mon breuvage ?	1ère IEP (le loup)
Dit cet animal plein de rage :	IO
Tu seras châtié de ta témérité.	1ère IEP (le loup)
Sire, répond l'agneau, que Votre Majesté	2ème instance énonçante projetée (l'agneau)
Ne se mette pas en colère ;	
Mais plutôt qu'elle considère	
Que je me vas désaltérant	
Dans le courant,	
Plus de vingt pas au-dessous d'Elle,	
Et que par conséquent en aucune façon	
Je ne puis troubler sa boisson.	
Tu la troubles, reprit cette bête cruelle,	1ère instance énonçante projetée (le loup)
Et je sais que de moi tu médis l'an passé.	
Comment l'aurais-je fait, si je n'étais pas né ?	2ème instance énonçante projetée (l'agneau)
Reprit l'agneau, je tette encore ma mère.	
Si ce n'est toi, c'est donc ton frère.	1ère IEP (le loup)

Séquences et segments		№
Problématique : 1ère accusation de la 1ère IEP		
Description de l'Actant « le loup »		
Jugement avant procès de la 1ère IEP		
1ère argumentation de la 2ème instance énonçante projetée (l'agneau)	Proces	3
1er jugement de la 1ère IEP (le loup) lors du procès + Description de l'Actant « le loup » par l'IO		
2ème accusation de la 1ère IEP (le loup)		
2ème argumentation de la 2ème IEP (l'agneau)		
3ème accusation de la 1ère IEP (le loup)		

LE LOUP ET L'AGNEAU		Instances	
Je n'en ai point.	C'est donc quelqu'un des tiens :	2ème IEP (l'agneau)	1ère IEP (le loup)
Car vous ne m'épargnez guère,			
Vous, vos bergers et vos chiens.		1ère instance énonçante projetée (le loup)	
On me l'a dit : il faut que je me venge.»			
Là-dessus au fond des forêts			
Le loup l'emporte, et puis le mange		Instance d'origine	
Sans autre forme de procès.			

Modalités et programmes narratifs

Selon Coquet « une dimension modale caractérise chaque partition de l'univers de signification et [...] l'actant, pièce maîtresse du théâtre sémiotique, est défini lui-même par son mode de jonction modale. » (Coquet, 1997 149) La théorie des instances prévoit trois modalités pour un *actant autonome ;* ce sont les modalités du *vouloir*, du *pouvoir* et du *savoir*. Elle prévoit également une quatrième, le *devoir*, qui surdétermine ces trois modalités chez un actant *hétéronome*.

Nous allons étudier la compétence modale des actants de notre récit en fonction des programmes narratifs qu'ils poursuivent. En termes sémiotiques, le programme narratif (PN) est une fonction qui transforme un état initial de jonction[5] en un autre état final en visant la conjonction du Sujet (S) avec son Objet de valeur (Ov).

La fable de La Fontaine nous relate succinctement « la loi du plus fort ». Le texte nous invite à un procès au tribunal où les deux actants se présentent dans une position inégale. Le loup, représentant du plus fort dans la société, est affamé et il *veut* manger l'agneau. Quant à l'agneau, étant donné sa vie en danger, il *doit* éliminer ce danger, donc « sauver sa vie » (Coquet, 1997 152). La modalité du *vouloir* modèle

Séquences et segments			**№**
3ème arg. de la 2ème IEP (l'agneau)	2ème jugement de la 1ère IEP (le loup) lors du procès		
Dernière accusation de 1ère IEP (le loup)			
Le verdict et fin du procès			
Exécution		Sanction	**4**

la compétence du loup, *actant autonome* alors que celle du *devoir* détermine la compétence de l'agneau, *actant hétéronome*.

Nous pouvons également analyser cette scène en termes de « distance »: Le loup *veut* supprimer la distance entre lui-même et son objet quêté pour pouvoir le manger tandis que l'agneau projette une quête en sens inverse : il *doit* donc agrandir cette distance pour s'éloigner de son assassin potentiel. Face au danger de mort, l'agneau est incapable de se sauver au niveau *pragmatique* puisque le loup l'attrapera facilement. Il n'est donc pas sujet du *pouvoir*. De l'autre côté, le loup, bien que présenté comme une « bête cruelle » « pleine de rage », ne se comporte pas conformément à sa nature selon laquelle il pourrait sans peine « /capturer/, puis/dévorer sa proie/» (Coquet, 1997 152). Si c'était le cas, « il serait un *non-sujet* » [un] actant, privé de jugement [...] [qui] n'exécute que cela pour quoi il a été programmé ». (Coquet, 1997 153–154)

Or, le loup entreprend un *programme narratif* qui lui permettra de/manger *légitimement* l'agneau/en l'accusant d'« avoir troublé son breuvage ». Cette quête de légitimité fait de lui un être quasi-humain qui raisonne, et le place au niveau *cognitif* où il retrouvera son adversaire qui, lui, de son côté, entreprend un programme épistémique /prouver son innocence/ : il est donc sujet du *savoir.* Sur ce plan, l'agneau apparaît comme un actant très réussi : « Il réplique [...] aux attaques verbales de son adversaire d'une manière si parfaite que chaque fois le loup doit trouver une autre « raison » pour relancer le « débat » [...] » (Coquet, 1997 150)

Malgré la bonne performance de l'agneau comme avocat de lui-même, son programme narratif/prouver son innocence/se solde en échec car le loup, « piètre accusateur » (Coquet, 1997 151), voyant qu'il perd sur le plan cognitif passe au plan où il est « fort » en arrêtant sa quête de légitimité. Passé au plan *pragmatique* où il est « actant du pouvoir » (Coquet, 1997 151), il retrouve en fait sa nature originelle de *non-sujet :* il accomplit sans peine le « programme empirique [...]/ capturer/, puis/dévorer sa proie/» (Coquet, 1997 152) comme on attend de lui. Ce « programme réussi » (Coquet, 1997 151) vérifie finalement la morale de la fable.

Analyse sémiotique des différentes traductions turques de *Le loup et l'agneau*

Après avoir cerné, bien que partiellement, l'univers du sens de la fable, nous allons comparer les différentes versions turques sur deux exemples :

Exemple 1 :

Nous allons commencer par la morale de la fable en incipit : « La raison du plus fort est toujours la meilleure ». Dans cette proposition posée comme vérité universelle, c'est le mot « raison » qui crée difficulté en traduction. Etant donné qu'il s'agit d'un mot polysémique, il faut pouvoir saisir le sens qui s'actualise dans ce contexte. Effectivement, le mot « raison » signifie dans cette acception « argument pour convaincre, preuve pour démontrer, notamment dans le cours d'une discussion » (*Trésor de la Langue Française Informatisé ;* désormais, *TLFI*[6])

Dans notre corpus, le mot « raison » est traduit en turc de diverses façons : par des substantifs comme « *hüküm* » [jugement]; « *hak* » [droit]; « *kanıt* » [preuve] ou encore par des verbes comme « *haklı olmak* » [avoir raison] ; « *haklı çıkmak* » [remporter]. Quant à « le plus fort », il devient en turc « *gaalib* » [vainquer] ; « *daha güçlü* » [celui qui est plus fort] ; « *kuvvetli* » [le fort] et « *en güçlü* » [le plus fort]. Ainsi, la traduction de l'incipit de la fable actualise des interprétations différentes (*cf. Le Tableau de l'Exemple* 1). Nous remarquons également que la morale devient une question chez Şinasi : « Que signifie le jugement du vainqueur ? » ; cette question ne sera répondue qu'à la fin du texte. A part la morale du récit interprétée plus ou moins différemment, Eyüboğlu limite le public auquel la fable est adressée à « celui qui ne croit pas à ce précepte »! (*cf. Le Tableau de l'Exemple* 1).

Exemple 1 : Comparaison des traductions turques de l'incipit de *Le loup et l'agneau*

Textes	**Passage(s) soumis à l'analyse**	**Rétro-traductions en français**	**Elément(s) d'analyse**
Le loup et l'agneau, La Fontaine	La raison du plus fort est toujours la meilleure. Nous l'allons montrer tout à l'heure.		«raison» «le plus fort» «la meilleure»
Kurtla Kuzu, traduit par Şinasi, p. 17	*Nedir el-hükmi lil gaalib meâli* *Bilinmekçin getirdik bu misâli* (Version en turc moderne : *Galibin hükmü ne anlama gelir* *Bilinsin diye getirdik bu örneği*)	[Que signifie le jugement du vainqueur Pour qu'on le sache, nous donnons cet exemple.]	«*hüküm*» [jugement] ; «*gaalib*» [vainquer] ; La traduction pose une question qui sera répondue à la fin.
Kurtla Kuzu, traduit par Sabahattin Eyüboğlu, p. 23	*Kim daha güçlüyse hep odur haklı* *İnanmayan dinlesin bu masalı*	[Celui qui est plus fort a toujours raison Celui qui n'y croit pas écoute cette histoire]	«*haklı olmak*» [avoir raison] «*daha güçlü*» [celui qui est plus fort] La traduction s'adresse à un public limité.
Kurtla Kuzu, traduit par Orhan Veli, p. 20	*Hakların en güzeli kuvvetlinin hakkıdır* *İşte bu hikâye bunu anlatır :*	[Le plus beau des droits est celui du fort Voilà ce qui est raconté par cette histoire:]	«*hak*» [droit] ; «*kuvvetli*» [le fort] ; «*en güzel*» [le plus beau]

Kurtla Kuzu, traduit par Nâzım Hikmet, p. 24	*Kuvvetli her zaman haklı çıkar* *Dinleyin buna dair bir hikâyemiz var:*	[Celui qui est fort remporte toujours Ecoutez ; nous avons une histoire sur cela]	«*haklı çıkmak*» [remporter] «*kuvvetli*» [le fort]
Kurtla Kuzu, traduit par Tahsin Yücel, p. 23	*En güçlünün kanıtı en iyi, en üstün kanıttır. Az sonra göreceğiz bunu.*	[La preuve du plus fort est la meilleure preuve, la plus sublime. Nous allons le voir tout à l'heure.]	«*kanıt*» [preuve] «*en güçlü*» [le plus fort] «*en iyi, en üstün*» [la meilleure, la plus sublime]

Exemple 2 :

Le second exemple de notre étude concerne la partie finale de la fable où il s'agit de la sanction du procès. Nous avons vu lors de l'analyse des programmes narratifs que la quête de légitimité du loup a finalement succombé à son besoin d'assouvir sa faim ; aussi la bête a-t-elle coupé court le procès. Les trois derniers vers de la fable nous montrent la hâte du loup à dévorer sa proie et mettent fin au procès en toute vitesse : la séquence s'ouvre par un subite changement de lieu (« Là-dessus au fond des forêts ») et continue par les comportements mécaniques d'un loup « tenaillé par la faim » (Coquet, 1997 153) qui n'a plus besoin d'interrogation (« sans autre forme de procès »). La sanction exprimée d'un ton neutre dans l'original (« Le loup l'emporte, et puis le mange ») est interprétée par certains traducteurs d'une manière connotée : par exemple, Eyüboğlu le rapporte comme un « règlement de compte », de surplus, accompli « de belle » ! Il montre ainsi de façon quasi ironique la force du pouvoir dans l'ordre social. Quant à Hikmet, il nous fait assister à une scène de cruauté atroce face au loup qui dévore l'agneau en le craquant : « *çatır çatır yedi* ». Par le biais de cette onomatopée «*çatır çatır* », nous entendons le bruit des os de l'agneau qui se cassent ! Dans sa version pour les enfants, Yücel semble vouloir montrer la voracité du loup en dessinant une scène où la bête cruelle « mange [sa proie] avec appétit » et il y verse aussi du sentiment de la compassion pour la victime par l'ajout de « notre petit agneau » ! Ces trois interprétations infligent des connotations subjectives à la description objective de l'original. Or, dans les traductions de Şinasi et de Veli cette objectivité est respectée. Quant au dernier vers qui annonce le désistement de procès de la part du loup, il a aussi été sujet d'interprétations divergentes : Eyüboğlu continue sur le même ton ironique pour dire que, dans ce compte réglé, étaient comprises toutes les étapes d'une vraie justice avec le recours au Conseil d'Etat, à la Cour de Cassation, etc. Alors que dans les autres versions, le loup « ne respecte ni procès ni tribunal » (Hikmet) ou il « fait fi de la loi, de l'interrogation, de la justice et de tout » (Yücel) ou encore il « termine le procès » (Şinasi). Ces trois interprétations tournent autour du signe « procès » qui est la pièce maîtresse de cette fable alors que celle de Veli en fait économie puisque le loup y avale l'agneau « sans lui rien demander » ; mais cette dernière option est en fait une application illégitime. Car le « procès » constitue, dans cette fable, une unité marquée impossible à effacer puisqu'il a une fonction dans la production du sens : effectivement le mot « procès » sert à dénommer le processus pseudo-judiciaire précédant la sanction tout en invitant le lecteur à réfléchir sur la conformité de ce procès à la loi.

Lors de l'analyse du premier exemple, nous avons vu que Şinasi a rendu la morale par une question. Au dernier vers de sa traduction, Şinasi répond à cette question en faisant appel à son lecteur qui doit enfin « comprendre ce que signifie ⊠le supérieur vainc" ». Ainsi, il construit un processus de signification inductif à l'inverse de l'original et des quatre autres versions turques qui présentent un processus déductif. (*cf. Le Tableau de l'Exemple* 2)

Exemple 2 : Comparaison des traductions turques du final de *Le loup et l'agneau*

Textes	**Passage(s) soumis à l'analyse**	**Rétro-traductions en français**	**Elément(s) d'analyse**
Le loup et l'agneau, La Fontaine	Là-dessus au fond des forêts Le loup l'emporte, et puis le mange Sans autre forme de procès.		Sanction en ton neutre: « emporter et manger » [Fin du] « procès »
Kurtla Kuzu, traduit par Şinasi, p. 19	*Kaptı der-ân götürdü bişeye dek* *Yedi gitti bitirdi dâvâsın* *Anla men azze bezze mânasın* (Version en turc moderne : *Kaptı derhal götürdü ormana kadar* *Yedi gitti bitirdi davayı* *Anla 'üstün olan kazanır'ın mânâsını*)	Sur le coup, il l'emporta jusqu'à la forêt L'avala, et termina le procès. Comprenez [maintenant] ce que signifie « le supérieur vainc».	Sanction en ton neutre: « emporter et avaler » Terminer le « procès » La « morale » en induction

Kurtla Kuzu, traduit par Sabahattin Eyüboğlu, p. 24	*Kaptığı gibi kuzuyu doğru ormana* *Ve orada* *Görmüş hesabını güzelce ;* *Danıştayı, yargıtayı,* *hepsi içinde.*	En emportant l'agneau directement dans la forêt Et là Il lui a réglé son compte de belle manière; Y compris Conseil d'état, Cour de Cassation et tout.	Sanction en ton ironique : «régler son compte de belle manière » Critique sociale de la justice
Kurtla Kuzu, traduit par Orhan Veli, p. 20	*Bunun üzerine kaparak onu,* *Ormanın ta içlerine götürdü ;* *Hiçbir şey sormadan yedi, bitirdi.*	Et puis en le ravissant Il l'emporta dans les profondeurs de la forêt ; Il l'avala sans lui rien demander.	Sanction en ton neutre: « emporter et avaler » Signe Ø pour le « procès »
Kurtla Kuzu, traduit par Nâzım Hikmet, p. 25	*Kurt kaptı kuzuyu bunun üzerine, götürdü ormanın içerlerine,* *çatır çatır yedi,* *ne dâva ne mahkeme dinledi.*	Et puis le loup en ravissant l'agneau, l'emporta dans les profondeurs de la forêt, le mangea en craquant il ne respecta ni procès ni tribunal.	Sanction en ton naturaliste : « manger en craquant » Critique sociale de la justice
Kurtla Kuzu, traduit par Tahsin Yücel, p. 24	*Evet, işte böyle demiş kurt, sonra da kuzuyu kapmasıyla ormanın içlerine götürmesi bir olmuş ; yasaydı, soruşturmaydı, yargıydı, hepsine boş verip afiyetle yemiş bizim kuzucuğu.*	Oui, c'est ce que le loup a dit, et puis il l'emporta en le ravissant dans les profondeurs de la forêt; et en faisant fi de la loi, de l'interrogation, de la justice et de tout, il mangea notre petit agneau avec appétit.	Sanction en ton réaliste : « manger avec appétit » + compassion pour la victime : « notre petit agneau » Critique sociale de la justice

Conclusion : vers une sémio-traductologie

Le présent article tâche de résumer de quelle manière la théorie sémiotique des instances peut être appliquée à la traduction littéraire. Depuis une douzaine d'années, j'essaie de mettre la théorie sémiotique au service des futurs traducteurs dans mes cours à l'Université technique de Yıldız à Istanbul. Je leur propose un modèle de lecture et d'analyse pour mieux interpréter l'univers du sens créé dans un texte littéraire étant donné que l'analyse sémiotique sert à fonder et à justifier la traduction en même temps qu'elle permet de prouver ou désapprouver la traduction produite. Ainsi, nous avons mis à l'épreuve la contribution de la sémiotique à l'activité traduisante à l'aide des travaux pratiques en classe qui ont finalement confirmé cette contribution. (*cf.* Öztürk Kasar, 2002 ; 2003 ; 2005 ; 2006a ; 2006b ; 2007 ; 2009a ; 2009b ; 2009c et 2012) Mais cette contribution n'est en fait pas unidirectionnelle.

Toute langue naturelle, aussi riche qu'elle soit, nous offre une perspective imparfaite de la signification du monde puisqu'elle voit la réalité d'un seul point de vue qui occulte les autres. Alors la traduction vient combler cette lacune car elle multiplie les points de vue. Dans son analyse modale de *Le loup et l'agneau,* Coquet parle du « piège de ne réfléchir qu'à partir d'une seule langue naturelle » (Coquet, 1997 149). Les « structures de signification » (Coquet, 1997 157) sont « saturées » (Coquet, 1997 157) à différents degrés et de différentes façons d'une langue à l'autre et il pourrait qu'une langue soit plus apte à mieux exprimer une réalité. L'activité traduisante met en contact ces langues incomplètes de manière à leur permettre de se compléter en contribuant ainsi à la signification du monde et de l'être. La langue turque illustre merveilleusement ce fait par le verbe utilisé en turc pour dire « traduire » c'est-à-dire *çevirmek* qui signifie tout d'abord « tourner » au sens de « changer de direction »! Effectivement, dans l'acte de traduire, nous « changeons de direction » dans laquelle nous voyons la réalité. Le turc lexicalise alors cet aspect de l'activité traduisante ignoré et innommé par beaucoup de langues pratiquées sur notre globe.

Pour conclure, les langues et les cultures ont beaucoup à apprendre les unes des autres. Et les disciplines de recherche aussi. Aussi avons-nous essayé d'illustrer que l'interaction entre la sémiotique et la traductologie apportera beaucoup à la qualité des traductions littéraires.

Références bibliographiques :

Benveniste, Emile. *Problèmes de linguistique générale I-II.* Paris: Gallimard, 1966–1974.

Benveniste, Emile. *Dernières leçons.* Paris: EHESS-Gallimard-Seuil, 2012.

Constantini, Michel et Ivan Darrault-Harris. (Eds.). *Sémiotique, phénoménologie, discours. Du corps présent au sujet énonçant. En hommage à Jean-Claude Coquet.* Paris: L'Harmattan, 1996.

Coquet, Jean-Claude. *Sémiotique littéraire.* Paris: Mame, 1973.

Coquet, Jean-Claude. *Le Discours et son sujet I-II.* Paris: Klincksieck, 1984–1986.

Coquet, J.-C. « La Sémiotique de l'Ecole de Paris ». *L'état des sciences sociales en France.* Ed. M. Guillaume, Paris: La Découverte, 1986. 332–335.

Coquet, J.-C. *La Quête du sens. Le langage en question.* Paris: PUF, 1997.

Coquet, J.-C. *Phusis et logos. Une phénoménologie du langage.* Paris: PUV, 2007.

Coquet, Jean-Claude et Sündüz Öztürk Kasar. *Discours, Sémiotique et Traduction. Hommage à Emile Benveniste au centenaire de sa naissance.* İstanbul : Yıldız Teknik Üniversitesi Yayınları, 2003.

La Fontaine, Jean de. *Œuvres complètes, 1. Fables, contes et nouvelles.* Paris : Gallimard, Pléiade Bibliothèque numéro 10, 2005.

---. *Masallar* (traduit par Nâzım Hikmet). Ankara : Bilgi Yayınları, 1970.

---. *La Fontaine'in Masalları* (traduit par Orhan Veli). Istanbul: Yapı Kredi Yayınları, 2010.

---. *La Fontaine Masalları* (traduit par Tahsin Yücel). İstanbul : İş Bankası Yayınları, 2011.

---. *Masallar* (traduit par Sabahattin Eyüboğlu). İstanbul : İş Bankası Yayınları, 2012.

Öztürk Kasar, Sündüz. « Traduction de la ville sous le point de vue sémiotique : Istanbul à travers ses signes en trois langues ». N. Rentel, S. Schwerter, eds. *Les défis et les enjeux de la médiation interculturelle : perspectives plurilingues et transdisciplinaires.* Bern : Peter Lang, 2012. 267–285

---. « Pour une sémiotique de la traduction ». C. Laplace, M. Lederer, D. Gile, eds. *La traduction et ses métiers* (163–175). Caen: Lettres Modernes Minard, 2009a.

---. « Un chef-d'œuvre très connu: *Le chef-d'œuvre inconnu* de Balzac. Commentaires d'une traduction à l'autre laissant des traces ». *Les traces du traducteur.* Eds. M. Nowotna, A. Moghani. Paris: Publications de l'INALCO, 2009b. 187–211.

---. « Sens et intentionnalité en traduction ». *Synergies Turquie* 2 (2009c) : 187–195.

---. « Pour une typologie des non-sujets: au carrefour de la sémiotique et de la phénoménologie. » *Semio* 2007. *Rencontres sémiotiques: les interfaces disciplinaires, des théories aux pratiques professionnelles*. Le résumé de la communication se trouve au site web du colloque : http://semio2007.free.fr/spip.php?article43 date de création: 2007; date de derniere consultation: le 14 juillet 2013.

---. « Traducteur face à un texte énigmatique, essai d'illustration de la quête du sens ». , *Interdisciplinarité en traduction, Interdisciplinarity on Translation I*. Ed. S. Öztürk Kasar. İstanbul: ISIS Press, 2006a. 119–129.

---. « Contribution sémiotique à la quête du sens en traduction littéraire ». *Le sens en traduction*. Ed. M. Lederer. Caen: Lettres Modernes Minard, 2006b. 225–233.

---. « Trois notions-clés pour une approche sémiotique de la traduction: Discours, Sens et Signification dans *Mon nom est Rouge* d'Orhan Pamuk ». *D'une langue à l'autre*. Ed. M. Nowotna. Paris: Aux lieux d'être, 2005. 47–70.

---. « Apport des études sémio-axiologiques à la pédagogie de la traduction-interprétation ». *La Evaluación de la Calidad en Interpretación : Docencia y Profesión*. Eds. Collados Aís *et alii*. Granada : Editions Comares, 2003. 121–132.

---. « Comment franchir les obstacles rencontrés dans la traduction de *S/Z* de Roland Barthes et dans celle de *Sarrasine* d'Honoré de Balzac? ». *Aspects culturels de la traduction*. Eds. H. Anamur et *alii*. Istanbul : Publications de l'Université technique de Yıldız, 2002. 158–163.

Şinasi. *Terceme-i Manzume*. Ankara : Dün-Bugün Yayınevi, 1960 [1ère impression : 1859].

Notes

1 Ou les textes traduits s'il y en a plusieurs.

2 Lorsqu'il s'agit de plusieurs traductions dans une seule langue ou dans de différentes langues.

3 Le *Trésor de la Langue Française Informatisé* définie la phénoménologie dans le domaine des sciences sociales comme "étude des faits de l'expérience vécue, indépendamment des principes ou des théories (étude des rapports du sujet humain avec le monde, de la signification de la réalité sociale …)".

4 « La raison du plus fort est toujours la meilleure. »

5 conjonction (∩) ou disjonction (U)

6 Nous y avons trouvé de surplus la phrase de La Fontaine parmi les exemples qui illustrent ce sens : « *La raison du plus fort est toujours la meilleure*. V. *fort*2 I B. » (*TLFI*)

The Translation Tier in Interlinear Glossed Text: Changing Practices in the Description of Endangered Languages

Aimée Lahaussois

Abstract

For field linguists working on oral endangered languages, getting data into a written form can present challenges. Models such as Interlinear Glossed Text generally involve three tiers: transcription, glossing, and translation. The first two tiers follow IPA (International Phonetic Alphabet) and Leipzig Glossing Rules, but practical recommendations are scarce for the third one, the translation tier. Using examples found in an oral archive, I propose a typology of some of the features of these literal translations, as well as a hypothesis to explain why translation tiers are becoming more literal, specifically in the case of digital archives.

Keywords: language documentation, endangered languages, interlinearization, oral archives

Résumé

En tant que linguiste de terrain travaillant sur des langues en danger exclusivement orales, je suis régulièrement confrontée aux difficultés de mise à l'écrit de mes données. Il existe des modèles d'annotation, le système le plus commun étant de générer du *Interlinear Glossed Text* qui comprend trois niveaux : transcription, glose, et traduction. Des normes sont associées aux deux premiers niveaux, notamment l'alphabet phonétique international et les *Leipzing Glossing Rules*, mais il n'existe aucune recommandation pratique en ce qui concerne le niveau traduction. Dans cet article j'examine les traductions associées à des données de terrain recueillies dans une archive orale, et je propose une typologie des traits non-littéraux dans ces traductions, ainsi qu'une hypothèse sur les raisons pour lesquelles ces traductions sont de moins en moins libres.

Mots-clés : documentation linguistique, langues en danger, interlinéarisation, archives orales

Introduction

In documenting endangered languages in the course of fieldwork, the standard practice for presenting the data in writing is called interlinearization. The EMELD (Electronic Metastructure for Endangered Languages Data) website provides the following description of Interlinear Glossed Text (henceforth IGT): "The model typically used in IGT incorporates three tiers: a transcribed (either phonetically or orthographically) text, a gloss and a free translation." An example of IGT, to which I have added tier labels for clarity, is presented below:

(1)[1]	kʰuly	pʰeri	kʰrem-s-ɖa	ʔe	[transcription tier]
	earth	again	cover-mm-3sg.pst	hs	[glossing tier]
"The Earth covered (itself) up again					[translation tier]

As the above example illustrates, the transcription tier involves the rendering of oral source material into a written form. Depending on the linguistic tradition and country in which the documentation is taking place, this transcription tier can be rendered in any one among a number of different systems, the most common being phonetic (using the international phonetic alphabet), phonological (also based on the international phonetic alphabet but taking into account the phonological rules of the language), or orthographic, if the language has either its own written tradition or a tradition of using the writing system for the dominant language of the region.

The glossing tier involves the identification of each of the elements found in the transcription tier, typically on a morpheme by morpheme basis. Lexical items are translated and grammatical morphemes are signalled by abbreviations. The glossing tier, like the transcription tier, is governed by well-known standards, making it possible for readers encountering the data to interpret the content of the glossing tier.[2] A system which has become very widely used is the Leipzig Glossing Rules, a set of recommendations on how to align and present the tier and a suggested list of abbreviations for very common grammatical concepts. The adoption of such conventions for the glossing tier makes the data easier to compare cross-linguistically, as data from different languages is encoded in a similar way.

Thus both the transcription and glossing tiers are governed by standards, making the annotation of these tiers fairly straightforward (but only, of course, once an analysis of the language has led to an understanding of how to transcribe and gloss it). This is not, however, the case when it comes to the translation tier. It is generally acknowledged that the translation accompanying a glossed example should be a "free translation," which, according to Bow et al. (2003: 2), means a translation "in which more emphasis is given to the overall meaning of the text than to the exact wording". Yet a cursory look at language description materials suggests that in many cases, the translation tier is not free but instead reflects the structure of the source language.

Note for example the translation tier in example (2), taken from Shibatani's (1990:85) description of Ainu:

(2)	Kamuy	kat	casi	casi-upsor	a-i-o-resu
	god	build	castle	castle-inside	PASS-1sg/O-AppL-raise

"The god-built mountain castle, inside the mountain castle, I was raised."

Bow et al. (2003:5) note, referring to this segment of text: "The free translation doesn't always read fluently, which may be an attempt to reproduce the phrase structure of the source text in the English translation." This situation is of course not limited to the sample presented above, and one frequently encounters examples of translation tiers which do not read as free but instead seem to be written in such a way as to convey grammatical information about the source language, particularly in textual[3] material presented in isolation. The reason for this is that in text collections (appendices to grammars, volumes devoted to texts, oral archives), interlinearized material is disconnected from grammatical explanations that help the reader make sense of them. Mosel (2006:47), in discussing the format of grammars in an article on grammaticography, points out how collections of texts in grammars are often marginalized by their physical situation: "Corresponding to the back matter of dictionaries, the text collection does not fit into the organization of the content of the main part; it is an appendix which helps the reader understand how the language is used in various contexts." As a result of the commonly adopted structure for descriptive grammars, which relegates texts to an appendix, the glossing and translation tiers of these texts take on the role of explicating the material, not only semantically but also morphosyntactically.

This observation has led me to formulate the following hypothesis about the translation tier: the presentation of linguistic material on endangered languages in the form of interlinear glossed text in collections of texts (removed from grammatical description) makes it necessary for linguists to use the translation tier to explicate morphosyntactic features of the language. The result is a tendency towards a literal[4] translation in the translation tier.

In this paper, I explore the validity of the proposed hypothesis by looking at some of the ways the translation tier is used in IGT. I first consider what explicit instructions are provided for field linguists, in the absence of recommendations and standards such as those found for the transcription and glossing tiers, by looking at field manuals. I next consider the uses which are made of the translation tier, by both the resource producer and resource user, to examine how these uses influence the choices made in generating a translation tier. I then proceed with an investigation of a digital oral archive for endangered language materials, the Pangloss Collection. I look at the range and types of texts found in the archive, and set up, for those which are in three-tiered interlinear form, a typology of issues found in the translation tier making them examples of literal rather than free translation.

The translation Tier in Field Manuals

Mosel (2006: 50) points out that "[i]n spite of its long tradition and pervasive application, interlinear glossing has neither received attention in (meta-) grammaticography beyond Lehmann's (1982) article and the guidelines by editors, nor is it usually discussed in text books on grammatical analysis. The only exception I am aware of is Haspelmath (2002)."

It is indeed true that the practice of interlinearization is rarely discussed in books or manuals on morphological analysis, field methods or typology, all fields for which it is highly relevant to have an understanding of how to present language data. The following discussion is intended to show that the advice presently found in the literature is very limited.

Haspelmath (2002: 4, footnote 2) briefly lays out the basic principles of the translation ticr ("idiomatic translation") and the glossing tier ("literal translation"): "For each example sentence from an unfamiliar language, not only an idiomatic translation is provided, but also a literal ('morpheme-by-morpheme') translation." An appendix to Haspelmath's chapter on Basic Concepts (2002: 34) contains a description of some of the conventions usually applied to the glossing tier (one-to-one correspondence between elements in transcription and glossing tiers, use of abbreviations for grammatical categories, use of hyphens and periods, alignment), but does not explicitly state what is to be done with the translation tier.

Payne's popular field methods manual, *Describing Morphosyntax* (1997), makes absolutely no mention of what kind of translation to associate with IGT. An abundance of examples drawn from a variety of grammars provide (passive) pointers for readers, but the book does not address translation in descriptive situations. The omission is understandable considering the goal of the book is to present a typology of morphosyntactic features found in the world's languages, and propose a system which can be used to describe them. This is regrettable, however, because a field manual is a perfect venue for introducing students to techniques related to the physical presentation of data they aim to collect.

In *Studying and Describing Unwritten Languages* (1992^5), Bouquiaux and Thomas address the production of IGT. The advice is quite practical, providing examples of how to physically align transcription and translation on the page (63), and emphasizing the importance of getting glossing and translation done while the speaker is still available (58). Nonetheless, the term "free translation" is used with no clear explanation of what thi entails

Nida (1964: 159) is one of the rare linguists involved in endangered language description to clearly lay out the translation options, distinguishing between formal and dynamic equivalence, and connecting the former to glossing:

Formal equivalence focuses attention on the message itself, in both form and content. [...] The type of translation which most completely typifies this structural equivalence might be called a " gloss translation', in which the translator attempts to reproduce as literally and meaningfully as possible the form and content of the original. [...] A gloss translation of this type is designed to allow the reader to identify himself as fully as possible with a person in the source-language context. [...] In contrast, a translation which attempts to produce a dynamic rather than a formal equivalence is based upon "the principle of equivalent effect" (Rieu and Phillips, 1954). In such a translation, there is less emphasis on matching the receptor-language message with the source-language message, and more emphasis on the dynamic relationship [...], that the relationship between receptor and message should be substantially the same as that which existed between the original receptors and the message. A translation of dynamic equivalence aims at complete naturalness of expression, and tries to relate the receptor to modes of behavior relevant within the context of the receptor's own culture.

But these types of translation equivalence represent the extremes, and Nida (1964: 160) points out that "[b]etween the two poles of translating (i.e., between strict formal equivalence and complete dynamic equivalence) there are a number of intervening grades, representing various acceptable standards of literary translating. During the past fifty years, however, there has been a marked shift of emphasis from the formal to the dynamic dimension." While the shift from formal to dynamic may indeed be what is found in literary translation, this does not appear to hold true for translation for the purposes of linguistic research.

Use of the Translation Tier in Practice

The two main categories of linguists interacting with interlinearized materials are, unsurprisingly, resource users and resource creators, and in each case, the relationship with the translation tier is somewhat different. The resource user can be somewhat difficult to identify, particularly in the context of linguistic documentation projects, which aim to record a language as fully as possible with the idea that materials be used by specialists from fields such as anthropology, ethnobotany, religious studies. But in the context of linguistic research, we will consider that the most likely user will be a typologist or an areal specialist, in both cases researchers who probably do not know the language in question. If we consider the following example from that perspective, it gives us a sense of the use of the translation tier in IGT.

(3) Limbu[1] (Nepal): "On the Road"

pəhile	uhile	iŋga	cu:kt-aŋ-ɛllɛ	akkhɛn	bahrə	tehrə	bərsə
first	before	1SG	be.small-1SG.SO.PA-SUB	how.many	12	13	year

yor-aŋ	khɔmbhɛllɛ	kɔ	a-pa	sintola	lɛpt-ɛ
suffice.S2-1SG.SO.PA	then	TOP	1SG-father	tangerine	contract-PA

"Before when I was little—I was about 12 or 13—my father took a contract on some orange groves"

It is quite clear that a resource user with no knowledge of either Limbu or the contact language Nepali will not be able to make much of the example if only the transcription and glossing tiers are provided. In this context, the translation tier serves three important purposes: 1) It conveys the narrative content of the linguistic material in question; 2) It serves as a key to how the glossing tier works 3) It can help the resource user identify whether a certain construction is present. This last reason is of particular significance to linguists using the data for comparative purposes, as they will search the material for the presence of particular constructions, and this is precisely where the nature of the translation becomes relevant: in order for the constructions in a linguistic resource to be identifiable, the translation tier must reflect the characteristic features of the source language and therefore be literal rather than free.

Example (4) below from my own work on Khaling (Nepal)[6] will illustrate this point further. Generating the top two tiers of the IGT is, while challenging in its own way, not particularly problematic in any theoretical sense, once an analysis of the language has been carried out: the standards associated with these tiers make creating them a fairly objective matter. Generating the translation tier for the material is considerably more difficult, because of the multiple possibilities. In my work, I have four different translation tiers associated with the sentence below, each exemplifying different features of the language and produced according to what I needed to highlight for a given use of the data. The parentheses after each translation make explicit the reasons behind the choice made in the wording and word order of the sentence.

(4)	sô:-ʔɛ	mʌt-tɛ-na	kʉmîn-ʔɛ	mʌt-tɛ-na	ʔip-dɵk-tɛ-m
	hunger-INSTR	have.to-PST-after	thirst-INSTR	have.to-PST	sleep-AUX-PST-NMLZ

a) "He was hungry and thirsty and had fallen asleep." ("free")

b) "After suffering from hunger and thirst, he fell asleep." (highlighting instrumental case with " hunger" and " thirst")

c) "Obliged by hunger, obliged by thirst, he fell asleep." (highlighting use of verb " have to" in this construction)

d) "The fact is, he fell asleep from hunger and thirst." (highlighting nominalization of entire sentence)

Each of these translations was generated with a different purpose in mind: the most neutral translation tier is that in a), which I have labelled "free". Its sole purpose is to translate the narrative content into something close to natural English. This can be of use in comparing various forms of the same narrative, and identifying whether certain passages are found in all versions of a story. It can also be useful in order to identify the presence of certain lexical items, and to see how they are used in a natural context. It is less useful, linguistically speaking, than the three other translations I have used in various contexts for the same sentence, and which have specific goals, because they attempt to highlight unusual features of the language, all of which are found in the same sentence. Thus depending on the use I might make of a piece of IGT (whether, for example, the sentence is used to exemplify sentential nominalization, as in d), or the instrumental, as in b)), I have altered the translation to better suit my purposes. Within the context of papers or chapters describing specific aspects of a language system, the decision as to what kind of translation to use in the translation tier is not a particularly difficult issue to resolve, but within the context of text collections divorced from grammatical explanations, the choice of how best to use the translation tier—and what should be highlighted for any sentence-- becomes considerably more difficult.

Investigation of the Translation Tier in a Digital Archive of Endangered Languages

In order to test my hypothesis with respect to why translation tiers in the descriptions of endangered languages tend to be literal, I have examined materials found in the Pangloss Collection. The following is the description of the collection found on the Web site for this archive:[7] "The Pangloss Collection provides free access to documents of connected, spontaneous speech, mostly in "rare" or endangered languages, recorded in their cultural context and transcribed in consultation with native speakers." The materials in the collection are surprisingly varied, not only in terms of geographical coverage, but also in terms of time span and interlinearization practices. The earliest texts date from the 1960s, and new texts are being added regularly. Over this time span, practices in interlinearization appear to have changed, and these changes affect the use that is made of the translation tier. The IGT is either made up of a word for word translation in the glossing tier, essentially made up of lexical items, and accompanied by a free translation; or, in IGT prepared by younger researchers, the glossing tier uses technical morphosyntactic glosses and is accompanied by a more literal translation. Even in situations where the translation in the second type looks fairly free, there are traces of literalness in the form of the use of parentheses to add grammatical material, or alternative translations proposed. My explanation for this trend is that technical morphosyntactic glosses, which are found in more recent texts and presumably represent efforts to standardize abbreviations and glossing practices, render the glossing tier less accessible to the resource user and therefore tend to be accompanied by a more explicative rendering of the translation tier.

Typology of features of literal translations in the Pangloss Collection

Within the Pangloss collection's IGT texts with more literal translation tiers, I have identified a typology of features which result in the translations being classified as literal. These are exemplified in turn.

Word order issues

In sentences whose translations have word order issues, the translation tier reflects the word order of the source language. This is a very common issue found in the translation tier.

(5) Langi[8] (Tanzania): "Story"

transc	ma	dʒira	ŋgɔ	kara	katʃɪhɪ
gloss	then	dp10-dem.d	np10-clothes	dp12-dem.d	np12-bird
transc	kwɪɪrirɛ		ma	kakamʊwɛkɪra	
gloss	vp17-acc-darken-perf		then	vp12-narr-obj1-close-appl-appli-sfx	
transc	dʒira		ŋgɔ		
gloss	dp10-dem.d		np10-clothes		

transl "Then those clothes, the little bird landed and covered her with them."

(6) Thulung[9] (Nepal): Kakcilip

transc	hum-saɖ-ɖytsi-m	pətsʰi	ritsi		
gloss	spread-ASP-3DU/3SG.PST.NOM	after	sour.fruit		
transc	lat-tsi-m	pətsʰi	mɯrtsip	ri-tsip	dzyrpa-ku
gloss	see-3DU/3SG.PST-NOM	after	3DU	sibling-DU	bitter-GEN
transc	mina-ka	swaʈ-ka	gərdakʰeri	mɯrtsip	pʰeri
gloss	[filler word]-INSTR	taste-INSTR	doing	3DU	again
transc	dzʰuk-tsi	ʔe			
gloss	land-3DU.PST	HS			

transl "After she spread out the fruit, and after they saw it, the two, with the bitter taste, they landed again."

While a free translation would have rearranged the word order to reflect that of the target language, in (5) and (6) above, the translation reflects the order of segments found in the source language.

Tense concordance issues

Some texts have translations which show inconsistency in the tenses used within a same sentence, reflecting the fact that the use of tenses is different in the source language; the result of conveying this tense divergence in the translation tier is a literal translation.

(7) Araki[10] (Vanuatu): "The rat, the hawk and the octopus"

Hadiv	mo	dogo	mo	de	mo	m̈arahu		
Rat	3:R	feel	3:R	say	3:R	fear		
mo de	"Ale!	Codo	o	sna,	codo	o	sna	o vici!"
3:R say	alright	okay	2S:I	come	okay	2S:I	come	2S:I embark
Mo	lig-i-a		mo	vari-a	mo	v̈a		
3:R	embark-TR-3S		3:R	take-3S	3:R	go		

"The rat felt seized with fear and exclaimed "Okay! It's alright, come in, you may come aboard' takes them on board, carries them along..."

(8) Nepali, Accham dialect[11] (Nepal): "Tiger and Jackal"[12]

bag rə syalo satə bhəyapəchi nə əbə syal—bagəi khana—syaləkənə bagə bagə khanəinə rəechə. mama rəechə, syaləko. syal.

"When they were together the tiger doesn't eat the jackal, he's his maternal uncle—the jackal's—the jackal."

(9) Na-našu[13] (Italy): «Le voyage à Palata»

transc	Alor Tonin	Sa		vračaša	
gloss	Thus Tonin.NOM.SG.M	REFL		return.IPFV-IPRF-3SG	
transc	na	Mala	naza,	vidim	ka
gloss	ART.INDF-ACC.SG.N	little-ACC.SG.N	back	see-PRS-1SG	COMP
transc	biša	Profesor.			
gloss	be-IPRF-SG	professor-NOM.SG.M			
transl	"So Tonino drove back a bit, I see (=saw) that the professor was there."				

While we expect a free translation to smoothe out issues related to tense concordance, the translations in (7), (8) and (9) above reflect the actual tenses used, and give us a better sense of the oral nature of the data.

Morphosyntactic issues

In texts identified as having morphosyntactic issues, there are a number of translation choices that do not read as free, and as a result these reveal the structure of the source language.

(10) Romani[14] (Greece): "The louse and the Rom"

koleski	kor	tʃinen	kor	kirnisi	laʃen
that.one.DAT	neck	cut.3PL	neck	his	leave.3PL

"They cut this one's neck, that one's they leave."

In the above example, it seems that the choice of translation into English serves to highlight the expression of possession in Romani, something that cannot be rendered with a natural English translation.

(11) Araki (Vanuatu): "The rat, the hawk and the octopus"

Hede	na pa	p̈isu	cudug-i-a	aka-ca!
today	1S:I SEQ	prick	pierce-TR-3S	canoe-1IN:P

"I am going to prick and make a hole in your boat"

The Araki example above highlights, through an unusual translation, the fact that the verb in the sentence is a serial verb construction, something which would not come through if a more natural English translation were proposed.

(12) Nelemwa[15] (New Caledonia): "Kaavo Dela"

hla	ma	aaxiik kaari-n	xe	yaara-n	i
3PL	COMIT	un(e) soeur cadette-POSS.3SG	THEM	nom-POSS.3SG	REL
Hiixe,	na	aaxiik khia-hli	xe	bwaaxolat,	
Hiixe	CONTR	un(e) soeur ainée-POSS.3DU	THEM	infirme	
khabwe	kia	kua-n	bu u	fagaut hada	
c'est-à-dire	il n'y a pas	jambe-POSS.3SG	EXPL RESTR	corps seul	
xa	shit.				
et aussi	bras				

"Elles et sa soeur cadette du nom de Hiixe mais leur soeur ainée est infirme, elle n'a pas de jambes mais seulement un corps et un bras."

In the Nelemwa sentence, it appears that the source sentence is able to express existential predication not requiring copula, something which cannot be rendered naturally in French.

Alternative explanations for literal translations in corpus

I believe that the choices made in rendering the source language sentences into the target languages in all the cases above were conscious, and that the intent of the linguist was to use the translation tier to highlight typologically significant features of the language. But we must also raise the possibility that the literalness of the translation tiers may have been unintentional. One fact about descriptive linguistics is that linguists carrying out language documentation projects are inherently involved in translation, but without necessarily having received training in translation. It is thus possible, although I shall discuss why I do not believe this to be the case, that the overly literal translations found in some descriptive work are not intentional.

There are however clues in the translation tier as to the intentionality of translation choices. The use of parentheses to add material to the translation suggests that the linguist is aware that a completely literal translation is not always possible to convey all the data contained in the target language. The addition of linguistic material with parentheses (as in 13) and brackets (14), or alternative translations (15) are proof that the linguist in question is perfectly aware of the fact that a literal translation alone will not convey all the information needed by the resource user, and yet is still not willing to provide a free translation in its stead.

---

(13) Langi (Tanzania): "The Hyena and the lion"

εε	va-dʒʊkʊlʊ	va-a-nɪ	nɪ-mʊ-sim-ɪr-ε
Yes	np2-grand.child	dp2-det-poss1sg	pv1sg-obj1-tell-appl-sfx

"Hey, grandchildren, let me tell you (a story)."

---

(14) Hayu[16] (Nepal): "The merchant"

ã:ki-thik-mʊ	na	Siŋtoŋ-ha	ithara	beŋ-ta
1PL.IN-same-GEN	INTENS	man-ERG	this.much	wide-PASS.PART
noktshuŋ	po-yi			
ear	do-ACT.PART			

"[Go where there are] men like us but with ears this big—"

(15) Na[17] (China): "Sister: the sister's wedding"

ʈʂʰɯ˧ni˥	gɤ̩˧	tsɯ˥	mɤ̩˩
like.this	happen	°rep°	affirm

"c'est comme ça (que ça s'est passé), à ce qu'on raconte: / on dit que c'est ainsi"

The translation tier in (15) goes further than (13) and (14), actually providing both a literal and a free translation, suggesting a clear awareness of the need to both explain and translate the source structure.

Conclusion

An examination of the translation tier of IGT from the Pangloss Collection showed evidence of what I consider to be intentionally literal translations in the translation tier. This translation choice serves to highlight typologically unusual or interesting features of the language in question, by having the structure of the language reflected in the wording of the translation tier, even if the translation as a result deviates from what is considered "free." My argument is that the context of an oral archive, where language materials are presented independently of a reference grammar, where explanations for characteristic features might be found, increases the need for a mechanism to signal such linguistic elements. Such signaling is achieved using a style of translation which is literal as opposed to free, even though the manuals which address translation all seem to suggest that a free translation is required. I also suggest that recent trends in morphosyntactic glossing, while rendering data more informative in terms of linguistic analysis, in fact make it difficult to scan the material in search of specific constructions, because there are inevitably additional, nonstandard abbreviations that must be used and because of the difficulty in accessing glosses for a language one is not familiar with. In such a context, a literal translation in the translation tier facilitates the reading of the glossing tier and the identification of material of interest.

One question of interest is whether it might be useful to set up standards or recommendations regarding the translation tier of IGT. These recommendations might quite simply involve an additional tier of material, maintaining the transcription tier, a glossing tier involving all morphemes and grammatical information, and then two translation tiers, one where the words are rendered literally (to enable users to scan for particular constructions) and another involving a free translation, which can be used to look for narrative and semantic content. Recent work developing a system of Advanced Glossing (Drude and Lieb 2000, Drude 2002) points to the fact that some researchers are aware of the need for additional linguistic information in interlinearized texts, but this additional encoding comes at the cost of time and efficiency.

References

Adamou, Evangelia. Romani corpus, http://lacito.vjf.cnrs.fr/pangloss/. Accessed 2014-07-11.

Bouquiaux, Luc, and Jacqueline Thomas. *Studying and Describing Unwritten Languages. Dallas: SIL International,* 1992.

Bow, C., B. Hughes, and S. Bird. "Towards a General Model of Interlinear Text." In *Proceedings of EMELD Workshop:* 1–47, 2003. http://emeld.org/workshop/2003/bowbadenbird-paper.pdf

Breu, Walter. Na-našu corpus, Programme franco-allemand Euroslav 2010 : ANR(09-FASHS-025) - DFG(BR 1228/4-1), http://lacito.vjf.cnrs.fr/pangloss/. Accessed 2014-07-11

Bril, Isabelle. Nelemwa corpus, http://lacito.vjf.cnrs.fr/pangloss/. Accessed 2014-07-11

Dunham, Margaret. Langi corpus, http://lacito.vjf.cnrs.fr/pangloss/. Accessed 2014-07-1

Drude, Sebastian. "Advanced Glossing—A Language Documentation Format and its Implementation with Shoebox." In *Proceedings of the International LREC Workshop on Resources and Tools in Field Linguistics (Las Palmas* 26–27 *May* 2002*)*, Peter Austin, Helen Dry and Peter Wittenburg (eds.), 2002.

Drude, Sebastian, and Hans-Heinrich Lieb. "Advanced Glossing: A Language Documentation Format." Working paper, 2000.

EMELD website, http://emeld.org/school/classroom/text/levels.html

François, Alexandre. Araki corpus, CNRS / Fédération de recherche 2559: Typologie et universaux linguistiques, http://lacito.vjf.cnrs.fr/pangloss/. Accessed 2014-07-11

Haspelmath, Martin. *Understanding Morphology*. London: Arnold, 2002.

Leipzig Glossing rules, http://www.eva.mpg.de/lingua/tools-at-lingboard/glossing_rules.php

Lahaussois, Aimée. Thulung Rai corpus, http://lacito.vjf.cnrs.fr/pangloss/. Accessed 2014-07-11

Lecomte-Tilouine, Marie; Michailovsky, Boyd. Nepali corpus, Agence National de la Recherche ANR-06-CORP-030-01, http://lacito.vjf.cnrs.fr/pangloss/. Accessed 2014-07-11

Mazaudon, Martine; Michailovsky, Boyd. Hayu corpus, http://lacito.vjf.cnrs.fr/pangloss/. Accessed 2014-07-11

Michaud, Alexis. Na corpus, http://lacito.vjf.cnrs.fr/pangloss/. Accessed 2014-07-11

Mosel, Ulrike 2006. "Grammaticography," Ameka, Felix, Dench, Alan, and Evans, Nicholas (eds.) *Catching Language: The Standing Challenge of Grammar Writing, pp.* 41–68.

Nida, Eugene. *Toward a Science of Translating. Leiden: Brill,* 1964.

Pangloss Collection, http://lacito.vjf.cnrs.fr/archivage/index.htm

Payne, Thomas. *Describing Morphosyntax. Cambridge: Cambridge University Press,* 1997.

Shibatani, Masayoshi. *The Languages of Japan. Cambridge: Cambridge University Press,* 1990.

Notes

1 This example is from a story called Miyapma in Thulung (Nepal), http://lacito.vjf.cnrs.fr/archivage/languages/Thulung_Rai_en.htm

2 As will be shown in a later section, it can in fact be quite challenging to make sense of the glossing tier if one is not familiar with the language. Proposals for a more informative interlinearization system exist, such as Advanced Glossing (see Drude 2002, Drude and Lieb 2000.)

3 In using the term "text" I adopt the same definition as proposed in Payne (1997: 366): "any sample of language that accomplishes a non-hypothetical communicative task" and contrasting with elicitation data, which is hypothetical and non-spontaneous. For oral languages with no written tradition, spontaneous narrative is considered "text".

4 There is no judgment value whatsoever associated with the term " literal translation': it simply refers to a translation which is more closely aligned with the source language rather than the usual practices of the target language.

5 The 1992 edition is a translation of the 1976 second French edition

6 Work on Khaling in being carried out in collaboration with Guillaume Jacques via the ANR-funded HimalCo project.

7 http://lacito.vjf.cnrs.fr/archivage/index_en.htm

8 http://lacito.vjf.cnrs.fr/pangloss/languages/Langi_en.htm

9 http://lacito.vjf.cnrs.fr/pangloss/languages/Thulung_Rai_en.htm

10 http://lacito.vjf.cnrs.fr/pangloss/languages/Araki_en.htm

11 http://lacito.vjf.cnrs.fr/pangloss/tools/list_rsc.php?lg=Nepali&aff=nepali

12 Note that this resource is not glossed in the archive.

13 http://lacito.vjf.cnrs.fr/pangloss/tools/list_rsc_lieu_en.php?lg=Na-našu&aff=Na-našu&lieu=Montemitro

14 http://lacito.vjf.cnrs.fr/pangloss/languages/Romani_en.htm

15 http://lacito.vjf.cnrs.fr/pangloss/languages/Nelemwa_en.htm

16 http://lacito.vjf.cnrs.fr/archivage/tools/list_rsc_en.php?lg=Hayu&aff=Hayu

17 http://lacito.vjf.cnrs.fr/pangloss/tools/list_rsc_en.php?lg=Na&aff=Na

Relier la science à la littérature : la traduction de Jules Verne en chinois

Florence Xiangyun Zhang

Résumé

L'œuvre de Jules Verne est traduite et retraduite en chinois depuis plus d'un siècle. Intégrant la science à la littérature, elle a symbolisé le progrès et intéressé des intellectuels qui voulaient introduire en Chine une civilisation scientifique et technique. Convoité sur le plan idéologique il y a cent ans, connu et reconnu en différentes versions, le roman de Verne mérite pourtant une étude proprement traductologique. Le présent article étudie les caractéristiques de la traduction chinoise de Verne, et tente de jeter de la lumière sur les enjeux différents de ses traducteurs.

Mots-clés : Jules Verne, traduction chinoise, Lu Xun, science-fiction

Abstract

The novels of Jules Verne have been translated and retranslated into Chinese since the early 1900s. As they incorporated science into literature, Verne's novels were seen by Chinese intellectuals as symbols of human progress, and thus they were eager to introduce into China these new scientific and technical ideas from the West. In these early years, Chinese translators were attracted to the ideological features of Verne's novels. Today, however, these translations are of great interest to translation studies scholars. In this article I present an analysis of some of the major features of the Chinese translations of Verne's novels and attempt to shed light on what motivated the different translators.

Keywords: Jules Verne, Chinese translation, Lu Xun, science fiction

Introduction

Michel Serres compare schématiquement la science et la littérature : « Les sciences exactes parlent, en général, une langue qui a besoin d'un minimum de traduction. Il s'agit même d'une définition de la science : un message maximalement invariant par traduction. Inversement, la littérature fait circuler des messages maximalement variables par traduction. » (Serres, 100) Le langage de la science, selon Maurice Crosland, aspire à l'objectivité et l'universalité (Crosland, 19) ; tandis que le langage de la littérature se veut avant tout personnel. Mais quand l'œuvre associe la science à la littérature, et que le message invariant se fond dans les messages variables, que deviennent-ils dans la traduction ?

Dès lors que nous nous intéressons à la traduction comme une passerelle entre les sciences et les humanités, l'œuvre de Jules Verne nous semble incontournable pour relier ces deux univers. Figurant parmi les écrivains étrangers les plus traduits en langue chinoise, Verne nous fournit un terrain riche pour l'étude traductologique. Dès l'année 1900, *Le Tour du monde en* 80 *jours* est traduit[1], suivi rapidement par ses autres principaux romans ; et en une dizaine d'années, plus de quinze romans verniens sont traduits et publiés[2]. Parmi ses nombreux traducteurs, se trouvent de grands penseurs de l'histoire moderne de la Chine, tels que Liang Qichao[3] (1873–1929) et Lu Xun (1881–1936). Leur motivation et leur enthousiasme sont visibles : à cette époque d'inventions et de découvertes scientifiques en Occident, les intellectuels chinois croient profondément que l'avenir de l'humanité repose sur la science.

Lu Xun, dans son argumentaire précédant la traduction du roman *De la Terre à la lune*, ne cache pas son admiration pour l'auteur et son génie[4]:

> Il a à la fois de riches connaissances et de grandes idées. En anticipant les progrès futurs du monde, il expose son imagination dans les romans. Pour tisser le monde de ses fictions, il se sert de la science comme fils de chaîne, et de l'humain comme trame. […] Souvent les romanciers ont l'habitude de compter sur les personnages féminins pour charmer et attirer les lecteurs ; or dans ce roman (*De la Terre à la lune*) il n'y a que trois héros masculins sans aucune présence féminine, et il demeure spectaculaire et passionnant, ce qui est tout à fait extraordinaire.

En reconnaissant la difficulté de diffuser le savoir scientifique, Lu

Xun affirme que le roman de Verne constitue un moyen efficace en vue de cette fin :

> Les ouvrages scientifiques (de vulgarisation) ennuient les lecteurs, qui s'endorment facilement avant de finir leur lecture. [...] Il n'y a qu'en donnant au savoir scientifique la forme du roman et une parure littéraire, que les connaissances, même complexes, puissent pénétrer dans le cerveau des gens sans les ennuyer. [...] Le lecteur, qui comprend rapidement sans effort, acquiert de l'intelligence et rompt avec les vieilles croyances. Le roman scientifique a donc un pouvoir remarquable pour changer la mentalité et pour renforcer la civilisation (Lu Xun, Avant-propos, 5–6).[5]

Cet engouement pour Jules Verne n'a pourtant pas duré longtemps, et il ne revient qu'après 1950, avec de nouvelles traductions et d'une façon plus ordonnée, visant un public jeune et instruit. A partir des années 1980, la traduction d'autres romans verniens se développe. Une campagne de retraduction est entreprise par certaines maisons d'éditions chinoises spécialisées, ce qui suscite de nouvelles passions pour la littérature scientifique. En 2005, à l'occasion du centenaire de la mort de Verne largement commémoré, de nouvelles retraductions de romans verniens voient le jour et remplissent le marché.

A travers cet aperçu historique qui montre l'importance de la traduction vernienne en Chine, nous pouvons constater l'intérêt particulier pour le roman scientifique[6] chez les traducteurs comme chez les lecteurs. Les contextes historiques de chaque traduction sont certes différents, mais plusieurs questions peuvent se poser sur l'enjeu de ces traductions : s'agit-il de la démonstration d'un rêve (celui d'une civilisation scientifique)? Est-il question de la transmission de la connaissance scientifique? Est-ce un appel à l'innovation de l'espace littéraire? Enfin sommes-nous face à la présentation d'un univers littéraire particulier?

Début du XXe siècle : l'acte militant et le défi de la science

La plupart des traductions de romans de Verne du début du XXe siècle sont réalisées à partir de la traduction japonaise. En effet, au Japon de l'ère *Meiji*, les traducteurs japonais suivent de très près la parution de la traduction en anglais de romans verniens, et publient rapidement la version japonaise.[7] En exil au Japon, nombreux sont les étudiants et intellectuels chinois à vouloir suivre la voie de la modernisation japonaise, ce qui signifie avant tout l'ouverture à la science et à la technique de l'Occident.

Comme nous l'avons cité plus haut, Lu Xun, convaincu de la nécessité du progrès, voit dans l'œuvre de Verne un moyen efficace de diffuser le savoir afin de combattre les « vieilles croyances » et de « changer la mentalité ». Sa traduction est donc motivée par un engagement idéologique, plus que par passion pour le génie français. D'ailleurs il ne connaît pas, à cette époque, la vraie provenance de l'œuvre, puisque le traducteur japonais s'est trompé d'auteur[8]. Aussi se donne-t-il la liberté, dans sa traduction de *De la Terre à la lune*, de faire quatorze chapitres au lieu des vingt-huit de la version japonaise et de l'œuvre originale, supprimant des pages entières et de très nombreux passages[9] ; il adopte la forme du roman populaire traditionnel chinois (*zhanghui*) pour le titre et la fin des chapitres[10] ; il emploie un langage mélangeant le chinois classique et le vernaculaire[11] ; il cite de nombreux poèmes chinois pour commenter certaines situations du roman[12] ; et il ajoute même des informations qui ne sont pas évoquées dans l'œuvre française (Par exemple, il ajoute au chapitre V que la poudre explosive est inventée par les Chinois, ce dont Verne ne parle point).

Si nous regardons de près cette « prétendue » traduction qui ne totalise que cinquante-cinq pages de texte, il est difficile de la comparer avec le texte de Verne, tellement la différence est éclatante. Mais hormis les erreurs dues à une compréhension approximative, il serait imprudent d'attribuer à Lu Xun toute la responsabilité. D'après le chercheur japonais Yamada, le roman de Verne a déjà subi des modifications importantes dans la traduction anglaise sur laquelle sont basés les textes japonais, avant d'être remanié à nouveau par les traducteurs japonais, qui commettent également un certain nombre d'erreurs. En fait, dès que les explications scientifiques deviennent volumineuses, avec des chiffres, des faits complexes et des raisonnements techniques, les traducteurs japonais du XIXe siècle choisissent de les simplifier. Ensuite vient le tour de Lu Xun. On peut peut-être nommer son opération, non pas la retraduction, mais la ré-adaptation ou même la réécriture[13].

Lu Xun affirme d'ailleurs clairement, dans l'avant-propos de son texte, qu'il y a bien des parties de démonstration scientifique, inadaptées et sans intérêt pour le lecteur chinois, et qu'il convient de les raccourcir. En effet, cette déclaration n'est pas dépourvue de sens, car l'acquisition du savoir scientifique nécessite une accumulation progressive, et car le lecteur chinois de 1900 est certainement loin de pouvoir assimiler les connaissances de Verne.

Afin de justifier le bien-fondé de sa démarche, Lu Xun met également l'accent sur le manque d'une littérature scientifique en Chine :

> En Chine, si vous cherchez des fictions d'amour, des récits historiques, des romans de crimes et de monstres, vous êtes bien servi ; mais alors si vous voulez le roman scientifique, vous ne pouvez rien trouver. Le désert de la science, en voici la preuve. C'est la raison pour laquelle, nous devons commencer par la traduction du roman scientifique afin de remédier à ce défaut, et de guider le peuple chinois vers le progrès (Lu Xun 6).

Nous nous rendons bien compte ici que Jules Verne n'est qu'un prétexte au service du vaste projet de révolutionner la civilisation chinoise. Même si Lu Xun est conscient que la science structure l'œuvre vernienne, tenant compte de son éventuel lecteur, il la transforme pourtant en une sorte de décoration dans la traduction chinoise. En réalité, la précision de la connaissance importe moins que l'adhésion à l'idéologie du progrès. Tandis que de nombreux passages techniques détaillés et complexes sont supprimés, les explications scientifiques ponctuelles et succinctes ornent le récit. Par exemple, dans *De la terre à la lune*, pour la lettre de l'Observatoire de Cambridge qui répond aux interrogations du Gun-Club au sujet de la faisabilité du projet de lancer un projectile à la lune, la traduction est juste, claire, instructive et surtout attrayante.

Ce qui attire également notre attention, dans la traduction de Lu Xun comme dans celle de ses contemporains, c'est l'importance accordée au courage incroyable et à l'intelligence des héros savants, ce qui rapproche ces romans étrangers des fictions chinoises traditionnelles. La traduction n'omet jamais ni ne raccourcit les passages décrivant le physique et le caractère des héros. En général, il n'y a pas de coupures non plus dans les parties finales où le dénouement illustre bien le merveilleux des découvertes et le fantastique des inventions techniques.

La science est donc considérée comme décoration, qui se veut attrayante et surtout porteuse de rêve et du désir d'innovation. Traduire Verne, c'est montrer l'aspect fascinant de la science, l'avenir merveilleux promis par le progrès scientifique et technique, et en même temps appeler à créer une littérature scientifique pour arroser le désert de la science, voilà le rêve des traducteurs des années 1900.

Transportés par ce rêve, ces traducteurs et intellectuels relèvent un défi majeur mais ne sortiront pas vainqueurs. Les difficultés sont certes techniques, car non seulement ils ne disposent pas de savoir pointu relatif aux sciences représentées, il leur manque aussi tout un langage scientifique chinois pour accueillir les notions et concepts nouveaux. Le plus souvent, le mot japonais est repris sans modification ; ou alors les traducteurs ont recours à la transcription phonétique. Par exemple, dans la même traduction de *De la terre à la Lune*, on remarque la transcription phonétique de l' « Apogée » et de la « Périgée »[14] suivie de l'explication entre parenthèses, le terme standardisé n'étant créé qu'ultérieurement.

Mais malgré les efforts de ces intellectuels, la science ne semble pas s'enraciner dans le sol chinois et Lu Xun déplore ce résultat décevant :

> Cela fait dix ans que nous crions « la science pour sauver le pays », et tout le monde est conscient que c'est une cause juste. [...] Seulement on n'avait pas pensé que la Chine possédait bien sa propre civilisation, différente de celle du Japon. C'est-à-dire que la science n'était pas assez performante pour combler l'insuffisance de la culture chinoise, mais tout juste bonne pour illustrer la profondeur de celle-ci. Le Fengshui, est bien conforme à la géophysique ; les castes, conformes à la génétique ; l'alchimie, à la chimie ; la pratique du cerf-volant, à la science de la santé publique.[...][15]

Déçu par le sort de la science occidentale dans la Chine des années 1910, Lu Xun se tourne vers la création littéraire, afin de continuer sa mission de changer la mentalité. Ses contemporains vont choisir de traduire d'autres œuvres littéraires.

Après 1978, littérature de jeunesse et course commerciale

A partir de 1950[16], la vulgarisation et la diffusion de la science faisant partie du combat communiste contre l'ignorance et la superstition, les Éditions de la Jeunesse chinoise publient, entre 1957 et 1962, la nouvelle traduction des principaux romans verniens réalisés par des traducteurs de renom, et visent les lecteurs ayant reçu une instruction fondamentale en science. Ces traductions, faites le plus souvent à partir de l'anglais ou du russe que du français, respectent scrupuleusement la forme du texte étranger, et s'avèrent particulièrement complètes et rigoureuses vis-à-vis du contenu scientifique. Rééditées à partir de 1979, elles suscitent, en cette Chine à la sortie de la Révolution culturelle (1966–1976), la passion de la science et l'intérêt pour la littérature scientifique. De 1979 à 1982, on recense plus de cent cinquante publications par an de créations littéraires à caractère scientifique, et plus de 20 revues spécialisées en science-fiction. Or, la science-fiction chinoise ne survit pas à la campagne de lutte contre la « pollution morale » lancée en fin de l'année 1983, qui ordonne la fermeture de la plupart des revues spécialisées et l'interdiction de publier de la science-fiction[17].

Disparue de l'horizon littéraire, la science-fiction n'existe plus en Chine qu'en bibliothèque avec la traduction des quelques auteurs étrangers anciens (dont Verne), avant que le phénomène de création ne renaisse au seuil du XXIe siècle. En effet, depuis le milieu des années 1990, misant sur le renom du roman vernien, de nombreuses maisons d'éditions chinoises se ruent dans la course à la publication sans se soucier de la qualité des traductions. Il existe aujourd'hui plus de douze versions du *Tour du monde en 80 jours*, presque autant pour *Vingt mille lieues sous les mers*, *Voyage au centre de la terre*, et *L'Ile mystérieuse*, au moins cinq versions pour les autres célèbres romans de Jules Verne, dont des éditions remaniées des traductions de 1960, et de nombreuses nouvelles traductions à partir du français.

Si le militantisme de la génération de Lu Xun au début du XXe siècle détourne notre attention du problème de la traduction, la course commerciale un siècle plus tard nous force à nous concentrer sur les questions propres à la traduction de Jules Verne.

Science patente et science latente : raisonnement scientifique

Dans la phrase de Lu Xun que nous avons citée plus haut, la science constitue les fils de chaîne de l'œuvre vernienne, et l'humain en constitue les fils de trame. Pour Michel Serres, l'aventure humaine, dans l'œuvre de Verne, est conditionnée par la science. Selon lui, la présence de la science caractérise l'œuvre de Verne, et il y distingue deux sciences : la science patente, qui provient de la documentation de l'écrivain ; et la science latente, quand Verne applique son savoir scientifique pour inventer les circonstances et le développement de l'histoire (Serres, 93–109). Ainsi « le discours du savoir devient texte littéraire : l'assimilation des connaissances est source pour l'auteur d'une joie créatrice » (Compère, 1991 30). La science latente « travaille le texte », organise et produit le récit. D'après Irène Langlet qui cite *The Cambridge Companion to Science Fiction*, la science est cet élément de spéculation qui fait l'identité de la littérature scientifique :

> *Science fiction is simply fiction in which some element of speculation plays such an essential and integral role that it can't be removed without making the story collapse, and in which the author has made a reasonable effort to make the speculative element as plausible as possible* (Langlet, 166).

Autrement dit, le roman scientifique n'est crédible que lorsqu'il est fondé sur le savoir réel. Daniel Compère parle aussi de la « vraisemblance » à l'épreuve de laquelle Verne met ses romans (Compère 1996 145). Ayant assimilé les structures de la science, Verne les utilise dans un processus savant pour inventer, pour créer ses voyages extraordinaires. La science est bien le fil conducteur de l'œuvre vernienne. Michel Serres pose donc une question clé :

> Sans science, comment comprendre certains récits de Jules Verne, au sens où « comprendre » signifie reconnaître exactement l'endroit où il invente (Serres, 105)?

Sans science, comment les voyages extraordinaires peuvent-ils s'imaginer par un lecteur ? Irène Langlet parle d'une invitation à l'abduction que la science-fiction propose à la compétence cognitive du lecteur. Au lecteur qu'est le traducteur de Verne, nous pouvons poser la même question. Sans science, sans esprit scientifique, sans analyse et logique, est-on capable d'apprécier le monde imaginaire vernien et de le remontrer ?

Voyons un exemple tiré de *Cinq Semaines en Ballon*, lorsque la conception du ballon est présentée :

> *Mais le docteur, par suite de certain projet connu de lui seul, résolut de ne remplir son aérostat qu'à moitié, et puisqu'il lui fallait emporter quarante-quatre mille huit cent quarante-sept pieds cubes d'hydrogène, de donner à son ballon une capacité à peu près double* (Ballon 7 : 43).[18]

Traduction de 2008 :

> 但是，根据只有博士自己才清楚的谋划，又鉴于他要携带44847立方尺的氢气，而且还要让他的气球有双倍的容积，他决定只给气球填充一半的气体。(Traduction démonstrative en français du texte chinois[19] : *mais, selon le projet que seul le docteur connaissait, et puisqu'il devait emporter 44847 pieds cubes d'hydrogène, et qu'il voulait que son ballon ait une capacité double, il décida de ne remplir le ballon qu'à moitié.*)

Traduction de 1957 :

> 但是，博士根据只有他才知道的计划，决定只往气球里灌一半气体。不过，既然必须携带44847立方尺的氢气，他只好让气球具有几乎双倍的容积。(Traduction démonstrative du texte chinois : *mais, le docteur, selon le projet que lui seul connaissait, décida de ne remplir le ballon qu'à moitié. Seulement, comme il lui fallait emporter 44847 pieds cubes d'hydrogène, il devrait donner au ballon une capacité double.*)

Avant de les comparer au texte original, il nous semble nécessaire de faire la comparaison des deux traductions. Le raisonnement dans la traduction de 1957 est compréhensible et clair, alors que celle de 2008 laisse le lecteur perplexe. En effet, celle-ci déplace la partie « de donner au ballon une capacité à peu près double », la prenant pour un des arguments qui conduisent à la conclusion « résolut de ne remplir son aérostat qu'à moitié » à la fin. Or en se référant au contexte, la conclusion de ce passage n'est pas « de ne remplir son aérostat qu'à moitié », mais « de donner au ballon une capacité double » par rapport à la quantité d'hydrogène. La comparaison au texte original met en évidence la pertinence de la traduction de 1957, qui, par la modification de signes de ponctuation ainsi que l'ajout de certains mots conjonctifs, clarifie les liens logiques entre les propositions.

Le problème de la traduction récente est alors dû à une erreur de compréhension, mais aggravé par l'absence d'analyse scientifique. Ce même problème se répète dans cette traduction lorsqu'on explique le mécanisme qui permet au ballon de monter et de descendre :

> *Pour opérer l'ascension, je porte le gaz à une température supérieure à la température ambiante au moyen de mon chalumeau ; par cet excès de chaleur, il obtient une tension plus forte, et gonfle davantage le ballon, qui monte d'autant plus que je dilate l'hydrogène. La descente se fait naturellement en modérant la chaleur du chalumeau, et en laissant la température se refroidir* (Ballon 10 : 62).
>
> Traduction de 2008 : 如果要让气球上升，我可以用吹管将气体温度升高到高于周围的温度；依靠这股热力，吹管就会获得更强大的压力，从而将气球吹得更大，这样，<u>比起利用更多氢气让气球膨胀上升，能让它上升得更高</u>。<u>下降自然就是让温度降低，从而减少吹管的热量</u>。 (Traduction démonstrative du texte chinois : *Si je veux que le ballon monte en hauteur, je peux chauffer le gaz avec le chalumeau jusqu'à une température supérieure à la température ambiante ; avec cette chaleur, le chalumeau obtient une pression plus forte et gonfle donc davantage le ballon. <u>Ainsi, par rapport à gonfler le ballon avec plus d'hydrogène pour le faire monter, l'ascension est plus forte. La descente, c'est naturellement baisser la température, pour ainsi diminuer la chaleur du chalumeau</u>.*)
>
> Traduction de 1957 : 如果想升高，我就用喷嘴把氢气加热，使它的温度高于周围的气温。通过这种加热的办法，可获得更大的压力，使气球充得更大。

> 氢气膨胀得越大，气球便会升得越高。减少氢氧喷嘴的温度，让氢气冷却下来，气球自然就下降了。(Traduction démonstrative : *Pour monter, je chauffe l'hydrogène avec le chalumeau, pour que sa température soit supérieure à la température ambiante. Par cette action de chauffer, on obtient une pression plus forte pour gonfler davantage le ballon. Plus l'hydrogène se tend, plus le ballon monte. En baissant la température du chalumeau, l'hydrogène refroidit et le ballon descend naturellement.*)

En tant que lecteur attentif, nous ne voyons pas, avec la traduction de 2008, comment le héros contrôle l'ascension et la descente du ballon. Malgré la présence de nombreux conjonctifs (si, ainsi, donc, etc.) nous ne parvenons pas à déceler la logique de cette traduction, ni à comprendre le mécanisme. En réalité, les conditions et les conséquences sont souvent inversées, ce qui nous laisse supposer la compréhension insuffisante et l'absence totale de raisonnement de la part du traducteur. Sans cet élément de spéculation qu'est la science, le récit risque de s'écrouler. De son côté, la traduction de 1957 montre un réel visage de pédagogue qui explique.

En effet, s'il existait des lecteurs qui ne voulaient connaître que la vie ou la mort des personnages, ils auraient sans doute sauté ces passages étranges de la traduction et ne se seraient pas rendu compte du problème. Or, ces présentations techniques sont essentielles pour bien suivre le voyage en ballon. Car, chez Verne, comme le dit justement Daniel Compère, « [...] Le discours savant ne constitue ni un bruit de fond, ni du remplissage. Il appartient au texte vernien au même titre que les faits et paroles des personnages. Il sert à appuyer la démarche encyclopédique en donnant à chaque être et à chaque objet une place précise dans un savoir ordonné » (Compère 1991 22).

Pour un traducteur sans science, le roman vernien constitue réellement une épreuve particulière. Cependant comment entendre la citation suivante de Michel Serres ?

> Les sciences exactes parlent, en général, une langue qui a besoin d'un minimum de traduction. Il s'agit même d'une définition de la science : un message maximalement invariant

> par traduction. Inversement, la littérature fait circuler des messages maximalement variables par traduction (Serres, 100)?

En effet, le langage de la science, distingué du langage vernaculaire, est artificiel, impersonnel, et construit de façon à éviter les ambiguïtés. Il est vrai que le théorème de Pythagore ne perd rien de son sens, en passant du grec au chinois. Or il n'est compréhensible que pour ceux qui partagent les mêmes connaissances de la géométrie. Pour les autres, ce n'est pas une traduction, mais une explication et des illustrations qui seront nécessaires. Le style de Verne, aussi fluide soit-il, demande un bagage scientifique pour être apprécié.

Car dans le monde Vernien, la science devient de l'humain et il est indispensable d'en suivre la logique et le raisonnement. Le traducteur ne voyant qu'un décor à travers les passages scientifiques, reste définitivement en dehors de la démarche scientifique de Verne, et il lui est donc impossible de transmettre l'essentiel de l'œuvre et surtout l'enchantement que l'œuvre de Verne procure à son lecteur. Si Verne est nommé en France « grand instituteur » (Serres 135) qui fait grandir son lecteur, alors qu'en Chine il ne fait qu'embellir la bibliothèque, ou au mieux est considéré comme l'auteur des aventures insolites, la traduction a certainement trahi l'œuvre de Verne.

Verne trahi et le fossé entre la science et la littérature

Il n'est donc pas étonnant que dans les forums chinois de discussion[20] des lecteurs de Verne, la préférence soit largement affichée pour les traductions d'avant 1990. Si ce phénomène n'est pas réservé au roman scientifique de Verne, car tous les grands noms de la littérature mondiale subissent cette conséquence de la banalisation de la traduction en Chine, le problème de la traduction vernienne reflète surtout le fossé grandissant entre la science et le monde littéraire.

Le jeune auteur chinois de science-fiction, Liu Cixin[21], malgré le succès inespéré de sa trilogie *Santi*, se montre pessimiste pour l'avenir de la littérature scientifique en Chine. Quand il rencontre des écrivains célèbres qui ne savent pas ce que signifie « année-lumière », il croit avoir compris, avec ironie, le dédain de l'institution littéraire chinoise envers la littérature scientifique. De son côté, Irène Langlet évoque la méconnaissance de la science-fiction dans le cadre des études littéraires en France, en contradiction avec le succès de celle-ci auprès du lectorat ; elle cite également une position plus virulente de Gérard Klein qui, en observant la tendance dominante sociologique des études sur la science-fiction, reproche aux universitaires français leur « inaptitude à étudier *littérairement* » cette littérature (Langlet 157).

Pour Michel Serres, si le fossé existe aujourd'hui entre la science et la littérature, c'est qu'il nous manque des écrivains comme Jules Verne qui assurent l'interface entre la science et la société et qui puissent rendre la science culturelle (Serres, 109). Motivés par le vrai dédain ou par la simple méconnaissance, les traducteurs littéraires chinois reconnus d'aujourd'hui, comme les chercheurs littéraires, ne sont pas tentés par ce genre littéraire. Or, les traducteurs spécialisés, relevant d'un autre circuit, ne sont pas aptes à traduire la littérature. Si la science-fiction chinoise est encore immature au XXIe siècle, nous pouvons penser que la culture scientifique n'est toujours pas enracinée dans la société chinoise, ce qui aurait profondément déçu la génération de Lu Xun.

Conclusion

Phénomène mondial, la vogue de Verne s'est rarement démentie depuis son vivant. Pourtant l'œuvre du père de la science-fiction connaît des hauts et des bas en Chine.

Malgré l'engouement des intellectuels des années 1900 pour le roman vernien, la visée de leur traduction est profondément ethnocentrique. Texte raccourci, connaissance simplifiée, traits accentués, la traduction de Verne présente un exotisme occidental dans lequel la science symbolise le progrès.

Non plus comme symbole, mais en tant que connaissance, la science est arrivée au centre de toute attention dans une Chine communiste, moins grâce aux efforts des intellectuels que par la volonté d'un nouveau pouvoir politique. L'œuvre de Verne, de par son savoir scientifique, son optimisme et sa simplicité, correspond à un besoin spécifique de l'époque où très peu d'auteurs étrangers sont traduits.

Si la Chine possède aujourd'hui des recherches scientifiques de haut niveau, la société semble bien moins concernée et le roman de Verne en pâtit. Les nouvelles traductions publiées ces dernières années, d'ambition purement économique, ne placent pas la science au cœur de l'entreprise, et ne peuvent donc pas dépasser et remplacer les précédentes.

Ainsi, la traduction en chinois de Jules Verne ne relève-t-elle pas simplement d'une problématique du traduire ; intimement liée à l'histoire de la Chine, elle reflète l'évolution du rapport de la Chine moderne à la science, et nous pousse à y réfléchir, à l'avenir, sous des angles différents : idéologique, politique, sociétal et littéraire. En définitive, l'étude de la traduction de Jules Verne nous fournit une passerelle intéressante entre la science et les humanités.

Références bibliographiques:

Casanova, Pascale. *République mondiale des lettres*. Paris : Seuil, 2008.

Clamen, Michel. *Jules Verne et les sciences, cent ans après*. Paris : Belin, 2005.

Guo, Jianzhong. *Traduction de la littérature scientifique, théorie, technique et pratique*. Beijing : Société chinoise d'éditions de la traduction, 2004.

Compère, Daniel. *Jules Verne écrivain*. Genève : Droz. 1991.

Compère, Daniel. « Le Jeu avec les références scientifiques dans les romans de Jules Verne ». *De la Science en littérature à la science-fiction*. Ed. Jacquart, D. Paris : CTHS, 1996.

Crosland, Maurice. *Le Langage de la science, du vernaculaire au technique*. Traduction de Robert Lutz, Méolans-Revel : DésIris, 2009.

Fillon, Pierre (dir.). « Raisonner en science », *Aster* 14, 1992.

Guo, Yanli (郭延礼). « Ru le fan er na zai zhongguo de bainian zhilü (儒勒·凡尔纳在中国的百年之旅, Cent ans de voyage—Jules Verne en Chine) », Journal chinois de lecture, mis en ligne à http://culture.people.com.cn/GB/22226/45470/45475/3250765.html, consulté le 12 nov. 2012.

Jia, Liyuan (贾立元). « Lu Xun weishenme buxie kehuan xiaoshuo (鲁迅为什么不写科幻小说, Pourquoi Lu Xun n'écrit-il pas de science-fiction) », www.chinawriter.com.cn (site officiel de la Fédération des écrivains chinois), 23/06/2010.

Langlet, Irène. *La Science-fiction, Lecture et poétique d'un genre littéraire*.

Paris : Armand colin, 2006.

Lu Xun. *Traductions complètes*, Fuzhou : Fujian jiaoyu, 1987.

Serres, Michel et Jean-Paul Dekiss. *Jules verne, la science et l'homme contemporain*. Paris : Le Pommier, 2003.

Tadié, Jean-Yves. *Regarde de tous tes yeux, regarde!* Paris : Gallimard, 2005.

Vérine, Henri (dir.). *Les Sciences et leurs langages*, Paris : Éd du CTHS, 2000.

Zhao, Zhizhen (赵致真). « Zai kexue yu wenxue xiangyu de difang (科学与文学相遇的地方, Sur le lieu de rencontre entre la science et la littérature) ». *Quotidien du Peuple*, 20/01/2004, N°11.

Zou, Zhenhuan (邹振环). *Yingxiang zhongguo jindai de yibaizhong yizuo* (影响中国近代的一百种译作, Cent traductions qui ont influencé la Chine pré-moderne). Beijing : Société chinoise d'éditions de la traduction, 1994.

Zou, Zhenhuan (邹振环). *Yilin jiuzong* (译林旧踪, Trace ancienne de la forêt de traductions). Nanchang : Jiangxi Jiaoyu, 2000.

Notes

1 Le roman a intéressé plusieurs traducteurs et quatre traductions sont publiées entre 1900 et 1914 : *Bashiri huanyouji* (八十日环游记), de Chen Shoupeng et Xue Shaohui, éd. Jingshiwenshe, 1900; *Huanqiu lüxingji* (环球旅行记), de Chen Zeru, éd. Xiaoshuolinshe, 1906; *Huanqiu lüxingji* (环球旅行记), de Yuze, éd. Youzhengshuju, 1906; *Bashiri*(八十日), de Shuzi, éd. Commercial Press, 1914.

2 Parmi les romans verniens traduits en chinois entre 1900 et 1915 : *Vingt mille lieues sous les mers*, *Un capitaine de quinze ans*, *De la Terre à la lune*, *Voyage au centre de la terre*, *Cinq semaines en ballon*, *L'Ile mystérieuse*, *et Famille sans nom*, etc.

3 Liang Qichao (梁启超), un des trois auteurs du mouvement réformiste (1898) durant le règne de l'Empereur Guangxu (1871–1908, règne 1875–1908). Après la défaite sanglante du mouvement, Liang est exilé au Japon où il crée plusieurs journaux et notamment la revue *Xin Xiaoshuo* (新小说, Le Nouveau roman, 1902) pour publier le nouveau roman chinois qui se donne la mission de changer la mentalité des Chinois. Liang y publie en 1902 *Shiwu xiao haojie* (十五小豪杰), sa traduction de *Deux ans de vacances* de Verne.

4 Lu Xun (鲁迅), « Yuejie lüxing bianyan » (月界旅行辩言, Avant-propos de la traduction de De la Terre à la lune). *Traductions complètes de Lu Xun*, volume 1, éd. Fujian jiaoyu, Fuzhou, 1987, 5–6. La traduction en français est de nous.

5 La même idée est exprimée d'ailleurs par Verne à travers ses personnages dans Barsac : « il a pensé que, s'il racontait tout bonnement des faits véritables, on bâillerait à se décrocher la mâchoire, tandis que ces mêmes faits, racontés sous le voile de la fiction, auraient chance de distraire un instant le lecteur ». Voir Compère, 1991, 133.

6 Roman scientifique, ou roman d'anticipation, il s'agit de ce genre littéraire qui est nommé pour la première fois en 1926 « science-fiction » aux Etats-Unis. Ici nous utilisons indifféremment « roman scientifique », « littérature scientifique » ou encore « science-fiction ». Voir Roger Bozzetto, « Ecrits sur la Science-fiction », http://www.quarante-deux.org/archives/bozzetto/ecrits/bilan/genre.html, site créé en 1994, spécialisé en publication, critique et études de la Science-fiction, consulté 17 juin 2013.

7 Entre 1878 et 1897, ont été produites beaucoup de traductions japonaises de Jules Verne, appréciées avec ardeur par un lectorat d'intellectuels. En moins de dix ans, la traduction de *De la terre à la lune* a connu quatre éditions. Après la publication de la traduction de *Deux ans de vacances* en 1897, le phénomène s'estompe. Les intellectuels et étudiants chinois arrivant après 1898 (l'année de la défaite du mouvement réformiste en Chine) s'intéressent à leur tour aux romans de Verne. Voir Keizo Yamada, « *Lu Xun yu Fanerna zhijian (Entre Lu Xun et Jules Verne)* », *Lu Xun Yanjiu Yuekan* (鲁迅研究月刊，Mensuel d'études sur Lu Xun), N°6/2003, disponible sur http://www.douban.com/group/topic/9030249, consulté 17 juin 2013.

8 Lu Xun, comme le traducteur japonais Tsutomu Inoue, croyait que l'auteur de *De la terre à la lune* était un savant américain, puisque l'histoire dans le roman se passe en Amérique, et il se trompait de nom également. Pour *Voyage au centre de la terre*, il mettait la transcription phonétique de Verne, et l'Angleterre comme pays de l'auteur. Voir Lu Xun, « Didi lüxing (地底旅行, Voyage au centre de la terre) » (1906), *Traductions complètes de Lu Xun*, op. cit., 64.

9 Il ne s'agit pas de fusionner tous les deux chapitres, mais de couper et de raccourcir d'une manière libre certains passages, et d'en conserver intégralement d'autres.

10 La pratique consiste à terminer chaque chapitre par une coupure de l'action, marquée par la phrase « si vous voulez connaître la suite, merci d'attendre le chapitre suivant », et de commencer le chapitre suivant par présenter avec quelques mots l'action coupée.

11 Le chinois classique, langue écrite officielle jusqu'aux premières décennies du XXe siècle, ne peut être maîtrisé qu'après de longues années d'études. Le roman populaire des derniers siècles (XVe-XIVe), considéré comme une sous-catégorie de la littérature, utilise davantage la langue vernaculaire. Lu Xun explique dans son avant-propos : « j'avais l'idée de tout traduire en vernaculaire pour ne pas fatiguer le lecteur, mais par crainte de faire trop de pages, j'ai utilisé en même temps le chinois classique ». Voir Lu Xun, *op. cit.*, 6.

12 Il y a systématiquement un commentaire sous forme de poème ancien après chaque action. Cela peut être des poèmes des auteurs antiques connus, ou bien les propres poèmes de Lu Xun.

13 Lu Xun plus tard changera radicalement sa manière de traduire, voir F. Zhang, « Lu Xun: Traduction et révolution. Une lecture de la penséede la traduction de Lu Xun », in Antoine Cazé et Rainier Lanselle (éd.), Translation in an International Perspective: Cultural Interaction and Disciplinary Transformation, Bern, New York, Peter Lang, 2014, pp. 83–110.

14 « *Peiliqi* 胚利其» pour la Périgée et « *Aiboqi* 爱薄其» pour l'Apogée, suivis par les explications suivantes : le point de son circuit où la lune se rapproche le plus

de la terre ; le point où la lune s'éloigne le plus de la terre. Voir Lu Xun, « Yuejie lüxing 月界旅行» (De la terre à la lune), *op. cit.*, 14–15.

15 Lu Xun, « *Ougan* (偶感, Réflexion au hasard) », dans *Œuvres complètes de Lu Xun*, Tome 5, éd. Renmin wenxue, Pékin, 1981, 479. La traduction est de nous.

16 En 1949, le Parti communiste chinois prend pouvoir en Chine et entreprend une série d'actions visant l'alphabétisation massive et l'instruction obligatoire. Or, durant trente ans, la littérature occidentale est très peu traduite. Les seuls éditeurs publics coordonnent les traductions à tous les niveaux : du choix d'œuvres, à la sélection de traducteurs et de relecteurs, jusqu'à la diffusion.

17 La science-fiction chinoise souffre d'abord d'une confusion de la part du milieu des scientifiques qui lui reprochent de ne pas se concentrer sur la mission de la vulgarisation scientifique ; plus tard, elle se voit reprocher par les institutions littéraires et par les autorités d'avoir « tourné le dos à la réalité de la société chinoise », et de « promouvoir des idées du libéralisme capitaliste qui sont contre les quatre principes fondamentaux du socialisme chinois ». Fin 1983, elle fait partie de la « pollution morale » contre laquelle une campagne nationale de lutte est lancée : les auteurs principaux sont interdits de publier ; seules deux maisons d'édition littéraires publiques (Editions Renmin, Editions Renmin wenxue) sont autorisées officiellement à éditer des œuvres de science-fiction, et il ne reste plus qu'une seule revue spécialisée dans la province du Sichuan. Mais en réalité, malgré les autorisations officielles, plus aucune publication de science-fiction n'est possible à partir de 1984. Le dégel de la situation a lieu dans les années 1990. Voir Yang, Xujie, « Qinli kehuan shanshinian : gerenshi yu shehuishi (亲历科幻三十年：个人史与社会史) » (Vivre les 30 ans de science-fiction : histoire personnelle et histoire de la société), *Kepu Yanjiu* (科普研究，Etudes de la vulgarisation scientifique), Beijing, décembre 2009, 91–96.

18 Nous nous référons à l'édition 2000 de la Librairie générale française.

19 La traduction de 2008 est réalisée par Gu Yuanfen, éd. Yilin, Nanjing. La traduction de 1957 est signée par Wang Wen, éd. Jeunesse chinoise, Pékin. Nous choisissons de fournir une traduction littérale en français des traductions chinoises, afin de montrer la démarche de chaque traduction à ceux qui ne connaissent pas le chinois.

20 Le site *Douban* (parmi d'autres) crée systématiquement des pages pour les livres publiés en Chine, et réunit un grand nombre de lecteurs des livres d'éditions différentes. Les forums de lecteurs sont très actifs. Voir : http://book.douban.com.

21 Liu Cixin (刘慈欣), auteur de plusieurs romans de science-fiction, est plusieurs fois lauréat des prix de la science-fiction en Chine. Son dernier roman *San Ti* (三体, Problème à Trois corps), publié en 2010, grand succès, a suscité une vague d'intérêt d'un large public pour la science-fiction chinoise. Voir l'interview de Yao Haijun, le rédacteur en chef de la revue *Kehuan Shijie* (Monde Science-fiction), dans *Zhonghua dushubao* (Journal des livres en Chine) du 11 juillet 2012, p.6. Dans la même interview, Yao évoque également la difficulté de trouver des traducteurs de science-fiction pour sa revue.

Part 3 / Troisième Partie

Psychoanalysis and Theory / Psychanalyse et Théorisation

Traduire ce qui n'a pas pu se dire

JANINE ALTOUNIAN

Résumé

L'article considère la traduction dans la perspective inhabituelle d'une passerelle établie entre la traduction d'une langue à une autre et la traduction d'une transmission psychique en un langage partageable, c'est à dire entre les deux champs de mon activité de traductrice, soit en tant que germaniste, soit en tant qu'héritière d'Arméniens survivants au génocide de 1915. Co-traductrice des *Œuvres de Freud depuis 1970, j'ai par ailleurs cherché en effet, depuis 1975, à traduire dans mon écriture ce que les survivants à l'extermination de leur peuple n'ont pu transmettre en mots à leurs enfants.*

Mots clés : traduction psychique, survivants, transmission sans mots, dépossession, mutisme, traduire Freud

Abstract

In this article I look at translation from an unusual point of view, that of a bridge that connects translation from one language to another to translation of a psychological transmission into a language that can be shared. These represent the two main areas of my own translation activity, as I am both a scholar of Germanic languages and the heir of Armenian parents who survived the 1915 Genocide. I have been working as a co-translator of Freud since 1970, and since 1975 I have also been trying to translate into my own writing that which the survivors of the extermination of their own people were not able to transmit in words to their children.

Keywords: psychic translation, survivors, wordless transmission, dispossession, mutism, translating Freud

Introduction

Je me sens quelque peu embarrassée à devoir assurer la première intervention de ce colloque dans la mesure où, pour reprendre les termes de son argument, mon exposé considérera certes « la traduction [...] envisagée dans ses effets de passerelle entre disciplines », mais ce sera dans la perspective inhabituelle d'une passerelle établie entre la traduction d'une langue à une autre et la traduction d'une transmission psychique en un langage partageable, c'est à dire entre les deux champs de mon activité de traductrice, soit en tant que germaniste, soit en tant qu'héritière d'Arméniens survivants au génocide de 1915. J'ai en effet été depuis 1970[1] co-traductrice des Œuvres de Freud et, depuis 1975,[2] cherché à traduire dans mon écriture ce que les survivants à l'extermination de leur peuple n'ont pu transmettre en mots à leurs enfants puisque, comme l'écrit Shoshana Felman :

> Une victime, par définition, ce n'est pas seulement quelqu'un qui est opprimé, mais aussi quelqu'un qui n'a pas de langage propre, quelqu'un qui s'est fait voler le langage dans lequel il aurait pu articuler sa victimisation.[3]

Cette dépossession quant à la langue chez les survivants d'une catastrophe collective est le plus souvent occultée par les tenants d'une conception positiviste de l'histoire. Mais lorsque les messages non verbalisés de ces survivants se transmettent inconsciemment à un héritier susceptible de les élaborer et de les verbaliser, cette forme de traduction qui s'adresse à la subjectivité même des lecteurs et non à leur savoir, transforme cette expérience restée muette en un « objet du monde ».[4] Celui-ci ne peut plus être facilement refoulé comme l'est une connaissance purement historique, c'est pourquoi cette catégorie de traduction où un héritier / passeur traduit une expérience privée de mots et de visibilité en signifiants inédits jusque là dans une culture provisoirement non menacée de destruction est, en fait, un acte politique.

Mon article traitera de cette passerelle entre la traduction d'une langue et la traduction psychique sous trois aspects : la mise en parallèle de la traduction linguistique et de la traduction psychique, la traduction comme modèle d'interprétation du travail de l'inconscient, la posture du traducteur / transmetteur d'un héritage englouti.

La mise en parallèle de la traduction linguistique et de la traduction psychique

Pour justifier la passerelle établie entre mes deux activités de traductrice je m'appuierai sur un fait bien connu de la langue de Freud où le même substantif « Übertragung » désigne, en version française, à la fois « transfert » et « traduction »[5] et mettrai ainsi en parallèle les deux formes d'expérience du déplacement traductif que connaît chez moi ce « transfert ou traduction ». Cette pratique du déplacement s'exerce en effet aussi bien dans mon activité de traductrice de Freud que dans mon écriture d'analysante qui cherche à traduire ce qui du silence des survivants aux meurtres de masse s'est transmis sans mots à leurs enfants. Ces deux formes de pratique langagière sont habituellement étrangères l'une à l'autre mais elles présentent pourtant deux points de convergence : Dans chacune d'elles, la *pulsion à traduire* naît d'une nécessité à défier paradoxalement l'impossibilité d'une traduction : soit l'impossibilité à restituer un plaisir - d'un coté celui pris à la langue étrangère ignorée de son lecteur et, de l'autre, celui procuré par l'amour secret des ascendants vécu naguère dans le mutisme -, soit l'impossibilité à restituer une perte ou une douleur - d'un coté la perte de la polysémie des mots lors du passage d'une langue-source à la langue-cible et, de l'autre, la douleur partagée inconsciemment dans l'enfance avec ceux qui ont survécu à la perte de leurs proches, de leur pays et de leur foi en l'humanité.

Il s'agit en somme, dans ces deux situations, de chercher une voie de sublimation à l'inconfort ou à l'angoisse de se trouver au croisement de deux modes de réception du sens ou des émotions, deux codes délivrant de part et d'autre les déterminants de la pensée et de la vie affective. Dans chacune de ces postures, le traducteur est le seul à connaître la non-coïncidence des valences, soit entre deux systèmes de champ sémantique dans l'expression respective d'un rapport au monde, soit entre une impossible pensée survivant à la mort psychique d'une partie de soi et une pensée restée indemne de cet éclatement. Si le trauma opère une « détransitionnalisation »[6] entre la réalité psychique et la réalité factuelle, toute traduction de ce qui fut impossible à dire est, en fait, une entreprise de transitionnalisation qui offre une médiation, initialement absente, entre les lieux de l'extermination et le monde susceptible d'en accueillir les réalités. Comme le rappelle René Kaës, « Le trauma est [...] le résultat d'une mise en échec de la formation intermédiaire ».[7]

Ce qui encore justifie la mise en parallèle de ces deux mouvements traductifs, c'est que traduire est bien, dans le premier cas, *déplacer* la langue de l'*original* vers l'autre langue, parce que les mots de l'original ont un sens ignoré du lecteur étranger, et dans le second, *déplacer* vers le champ transférentiel de l'écriture un matériau *originel* ne disposant pas de mots pour se dire car, transmis sans mots, il doit se doter de mots entendables par les autres étrangers à cette expérience. Quant à ce qui *reste* difficilement traduisible, soit le plaisir ou la douleur - de teneur et de portée différentes dans l'une et l'autre des configurations - il a constitué, dans mon cas, un point de butée, aussi bien dans la traduction du corpus d'un texte fondateur que dans celui de la traduction d'un matériel transmis par une famille de survivants, notamment un témoignage paternel consigné dans un *Journal de déportation.*[8]

Si une pratique du sens à traduire, soit le *texte original,* soit le *matériau originel,* ne se fait qu'avec l'acceptation d'une limite, le consentement à la perte d'un *reste*, néanmoins, la préoccupation majeure dans ces deux configurations est de sauver le plus possible de ce qui se perd nécessairement dans cette mutation, étant donné que celle-ci conditionne, malgré tout, la possibilité d'une transmission. Dans le cas du texte original, ce *reste intraduisible*, qui révèle la différence irréductible entre un mode de penser dans une langue et celui dans une autre langue, offre au traducteur le privilège de jouir de cette différence, tandis que, dans le cas du matériau psychique originel, la récusation opposée par ce *reste* à une transférabilité totale garantit la distance interposée entre la langue d'un monde éteint et celle qui promeut une pensée vivante. Constater l'écart du non traduisible ne revient évidemment pas à l'effacer ni à renier sa fécondité. Je pourrais dire que, dans mon cas, la langue que m'apprit la défunte École de la République fut celle d'une première traduction laissant un reste évidemment *intraduisible*, une traduction douloureusement mais inévitablement castratrice qui me rendit ensuite possible, d'une part le plaisir à la traduction de Freud et d'autre part la traduction par l'écriture d'une transmission psychique.

La confrontation de ces deux champs de traduction s'impose d'autant plus, qu'il s'agit, en l'occurrence, de *traduire* un penseur dont la langue est celle d'un rapport au monde déterminé par un « emboitement » des cultures, comme l'a rappelé Didier Anzieu: « La culture d'appartenance de Freud est incontestablement germanique (de nombreux travaux ont montré qu'elle est également juive). Sa culture de référence est gréco-latine ... J'espère avoir montré que l'emboîtement d'une culture de référence dans une culture d'appartenance a été une des conditions de la découverte de la psychanalyse ... ».[9]

N'a-t-on pas affaire avec Freud à un innovateur qui, héritier sans doute des nombreux exils de son ascendance persécutée, a créé pour son investigation le dispositif de la cure comme celui d'un exil *agi*? Le processus à l'œuvre dans la cure est, entre autres, le déplacement des premiers liens affectifs dans le champ transférentiel visant à les reformuler dans ce nouvel espace psychique. Différentes figures du déplacement sont au service de la théorisation freudienne: Les métaphores sur la « migration » de la fonction libidinale et ses « migrants » semblent entretenir, dans « l'inconscient » du chercheur, une « inquiétante familiarité » avec les « détours », « déviations », « dérivations », « déplacements », « transferts », « traces », « clivages », « répressions », « persécutions », « refoulements » et autres « transpositions » sublimées dans son appareil conceptuel et dans la dynamique même de sa méthode exploratrice de l'inconscient.[10]

La traduction comme modèle d'interprétation du travail de l'inconscient

Avant d'aborder la tâche de l'héritier traducteur sur laquelle portera la troisième partie de cet exposé, je considérerai la traduction en tant qu'elle constitue un modèle d'interprétation de certains processus psychiques. Si, en effet, pour recueillir et transmettre *ce qui reste* d'une culture détruite, il faut le *traduire*, on ne peut traduire que ce qui a été symbolisé et le travail d'un héritier porteur des traces de cette destruction consiste précisément en ce travail que Freud nomme : travail culturel : « *Kulturarbeit* ». Or, dans le cas d'une transmission traumatique, la définition que Jean Laplanche donne de l'inconscient en se référant au processus de la traduction, peut être pour nous particulièrement éclairante. Voici l'ensemble de son argumentation que je vais ensuite résumer pour mon propos:

> La [...] tentative de traduction a pour fonction de fonder, dans l'appareil psychique, un niveau préconscient. Le précon-

scient [...] correspond à la façon dont le sujet se constitue, se représente son histoire. La traduction des messages de l'autre [...] est pour l'essentiel une historisation.

« L'inconscient est [...] ce qui a échappé à cette mise en sens que je désigne comme traduction.

[Quand] rien n'est traduit, le message originel reste tel quel dans l'appareil psychique [...] il constitue alors ce qu'on pourrait nommer "l'inconscient enclavé" [...] L'échec de la traduction peut se solder notamment par une transmission telle qu'elle, intergénérationnelle, sans aucune métabolisation.[11]

En résumé donc, « l'inconscient est [...] ce qui a échappé à cette mise en sens que [Jean Laplanche] désigne comme traduction »,[12] de sorte que le travail culturel aurait pour visée « de fonder dans l'appareil psychique, un niveau *préconscient »*[13] en exhumant le « non-traduit enclavé »[14] de l'héritage traumatique. Je mentionnerai ici un passage très intéressant de cette thèse de Laplanche qui souligne le rôle d'une « aide à la traduction, proposée par la culture ambiante » : « L'enfant doit faire appel à de nouveaux codes [...] Il a à sa portée, très tôt, de par son environnement culturel général [...] des codes, des schémas narratifs préformés. On pourrait parler ici d'une véritable « aide à la traduction », proposée par la culture ambiante».[15]

Ceci pour remarquer en passant que L'école laïque de la République proposait autrefois cette « aide à la traduction» de par le *colinguisme* qui structurait, comme l'explique Renée Balibar, le « français des instituteurs».[16] Partout où l'école ne peut plus assurer cette « aide à la traduction » qui, en fait, induit l'acculturation à « la culture ambiante», soit l'intégration des différents héritiers des catastrophes contemporaines, elle les expose aux tentations de la violence. La déprivation quant à la langue est un moteur puissant du recours à la violence.

Quant à «L'échec de la traduction» qui se solde, comme le rappelle Laplanche, « par une transmission telle qu'elle, intergénérationnelle, sans aucune métabolisation », elle fait penser à ce que Luba Jurgenson, traductrice de Chalamov, appelle «le brouillon perdu» constitué de traces non encore verbalisables de l'expérience immédiate chez les survivants des camps d'extermination. Il peut donner ensuite naissance au « livre I »[17] susceptible d'être rédigé ultérieurement, à partir de cet infra-texte perdu. En sa qualité de traductrice, elle précise :

> La question qu'énonce ici Chalamov est celle de la traduction, du passage de la langue de l'expérience vers celle du texte. On constate l'inadéquation des deux langues : celle de l'expérience est infiniment pauvre, mais, aussi absolument complète, elle ne connaît pas de manque ; la langue d'arrivée est riche au point de pouvoir dire sa propre insuffisance. L'expression du manque suppose, en effet, une grande complexité.[18]

On pourrait estimer que ce « brouillon perdu », puisqu'en deçà du langage, est semblable à l'expérience que les parents survivants ne peuvent ni ne doivent restituer à leurs enfants qui, l'ayant néanmoins perçue inconsciemment, peuvent accéder, grâce à leur acculturation à « la langue d'arrivée [...] riche » des normalement vivants, à cette « expression du manque » qui les rend apte à passer « de la langue de l'expérience vers celle du texte ».

Autrement dit, si l'on prend à la lettre la définition que Freud donne au refoulement dans sa lettre à Fließ le 6 décembre 1896: «Le refusement de la traduction (*Übersetzung*), voilà ce qui dans la clinique s'appelle refoulement »,[19] le terme *Übersetzung* (traduction) ayant en allemand le même radical que *Setzer* (typographe), on peut dire que ce « brouillon perdu » se « refuse » à la verbalisation des survivants mais que sa traduction (*Übersetzung*) devient par contre possible à leurs héritiers / typographes (*Setzer*) qui peuvent en constituer un livre I. Leur démarche qui cherche à sauver ce que recélait, dans le silence de leurs ascendants, ce «brouillon perdu» s'apparente à celle des traducteurs de textes anciens dont les originaux perdus ne nous sont parvenus que par leur traduction dans une autre langue.[20]

La posture du traducteur / transmetteur d'un héritage englouti

Ce que l'héritier / passeur a donc à traduire, c'est, comme l'écrit René

Kaës, « Ce qui se transmet, dans la transsubjectivité des générations, [...] ce qui fait défaut, ce qui manque, ce qui n'a pas reçu d'inscription, ce dont l'inscription a été empêchée, ce qui a été nié, refoulé, ou forclos ».[21]

Lors des relations infantiles précoces, une mère survivante n'est en mesure de transmettre à son enfant ni une expérience dialectisable en mots de ce qu'elle a vécu ni la vision du monde qui lui en est restée. Les paroles maternelles portent la saveur d'une secrète mélancolie et ne profèrent à l'enfant aucun savoir dispensateur d'altérité. Elles sont chargées de l'angoisse de nombreux affects incapables d'accéder à une secondarisation langagière. L'instance d'un ailleurs désirable ayant été destituée chez des parents survivants par leur relégation hors d'un monde vivable, ils ne peuvent introduire leur enfant au monde des autres ni à celui de leurs mots.

La perception d'un environnement clivé en deux espaces culturels et symboliques mutuellement exclus, la bipartition qui en résulte entre un monde qui semble ignorer ce que l'autre sait sans pouvoir en parler, réclament alors de cet enfant une mutuelle traduction pour que s'effectue *en lui* un quelconque travail de subjectivation. L'expérience traumatique que cette traduction cherche à apprivoiser est, en somme, celle du bâillon qui l'empêchait de dire à la maison, aux premiers objets mutiques, l'écartèlement qui se vivait au dehors, dans la langue de l'autre ignorant, puisque rien de ce dehors n'était présentifié dans l'espace de l'intimité. Mais pour celui qui cheminait ainsi d'un destinataire sourd à un autre, le dehors ne pouvait pas davantage recevoir, représenter les climats, les secrètes valeurs de la maison maintenue sous le sceau d'un non-lieu. En écho à l'expression « condamné à investir » avec laquelle Piera Aulagnier désigne la nécessité, pour l'être humain, d'œuvrer constamment au travail psychique d'élaboration, on pourrait donc dire, que l'enfant de survivants, « condamné à investir »[22] qu'il est comme tout un chacun, est pour ce faire «condamné à traduire ».

Le traducteur qu'il devient peut alors éventuellement, au cours d'une analyse et dans l'après-coup libérateur de l'écriture, tenter de dénouer, dissoudre une charge d'angoisse pétrifiée autrefois au lieu même de son ancienne impossibilité à parler. L'écriture après coup *traduit* alors une expérience archaïque en dévoilant violemment le lieu d'énonciation d'un sujet en souffrance, devenu traducteur pour reprendre à son compte des affects épars, demeurés si longtemps en quête d'auteur. Exploitant les avantages d'une posture filiale, l'écrivain passeur, œuvre en quelque sorte en traducteur *terroriste* car il conjugue en lui les deux modes de l'*accueil* : en légataire d'un parent *accueilli* au pays où il est né, parent naguère *exterminable* et privé de parole, il s'identifie à lui dont il est, dans le même temps, l'*accueillant*, prenant à tâche de l'héberger dans la langue des *non exterminables*. C'est ce biface qui détermine, chez l'héritier, la posture d'un traducteur : Être à la fois un *accueilli* par identification au parent survivant et un *accueillant,* de par sa compétence dans la nouvelle langue de la survie et ses identifications à une culture dominante, est ce qui conditionne sa propre accession à la parole. Toute accession à la parole se manifeste essentiellement par la capacité à énoncer le désastre d'en avoir été privé. Cet acte d'énonciation cherche à inscrire—au sein du langage acquis en dépit et au delà du désastre—l'événement effractant qui présida à la naissance de ce traducteur.

L'écrivant/héritier prête alors voix à son parent mutique et à l'aphasique qu'il fut lui-même enfant d'ici et d'ailleurs. En lui, la langue que *je* ne parl*ait* pas autrefois, faute d'exister, *je* la parl*e* aujourd'hui, mais en traducteur d'un lieu où *je* ne se trouve plus. Les apprentissages culturels sont venus enrober d'un langage autre les affects infantiles restés sans nomination, si bien que c'est la double désinence du *je* parl*e* à la première personne d'aujourd'hui et du je ne parl*ait* pas à la troisième personne d'un autrefois imparfait qui se fait entendre en creusant simultanément les deux sillons du paradigme, en réduisant enfin le clivage entre le ressenti *source* et les moyens d'expression *cible* du traducteur, en réconciliant quelque peu la voix toujours vivace de l'enfance et celle de l'analysant/écrivant.

Chassé naguère de sa langue maternelle, comme ses parents le furent de leur espace de vie, un tel traducteur sait d'expérience que comprendre l'autre, c'est d'une certaine façon s'expatrier.[23] Traduire, c'est finalement consentir à la rupture violente de l'exil[24] : s'il y a des similitudes entre l'expérience de l'exil et celle du transfert—dans le travail du traducteur et dans celui de l'analysant—c'est parce que l'exilé doit non seulement faire le deuil du terreau de ses investissements initiaux, mais il doit encore, pour ne pas totalement les perdre, assumer la douleur tout aussi déchirante de réinvestir—pour ainsi dire clandestinement en *marrane*—ces signifiants premiers dans les mots et les valeurs de la langue d'accueil.

Conclusion

En conclusion je rapporterai, en qualité non pas de traductrice mais de lectrice, une expérience des effets de lecture qu'a eus sur moi la traduction récente de deux témoignages de l'écrivain Aram Andonian,[25] publiés en arménien dans les années 1919–1920, intitulés en français: *Sur la route de l'exil (Souvenirs)* et *Dans le feu de cet enfer*.[26] Alors que j'avais travaillé, depuis de nombreuses années, à la réception d'un *Journal de déportation* de mon père[27] dont je n'avais pris connaissance que grâce à la traduction que j'en fis faire,[28] la lecture de ces deux témoignages me fut pourtant à ce point insupportable que je me refusai d'abord à en écrire la postface, à laquelle je m'étais engagée auprès du traducteur et de l'éditeur. L'hypothèse que j'avance pour expliquer cette réaction violente montre clairement l'importance capitale de la traduction lorsque celle-ci a pour objet les témoignages de survivants aux crimes de masse.

En effet, comme tout dans le monde, la première chose que j'ai apprise de mon histoire, c'est que le 24 avril commémorait la date anniversaire de la grande rafle qui, en 1915, avait déporté tous les notables et « têtes pensantes » des Arméniens de Constantinople vers les déserts de Mésopotamie pour les assassiner, souvent après les avoir suppliciés, décapitant ainsi la « nation » arménienne—pour reprendre l'expression d'Aram Andonian—devenue désormais orpheline de ses pères pratiquement tous disparus, à l'exception d'un très petit nombre d'entre eux qui, comme lui, avaient survécu. Alors pourquoi, malgré ce savoir, lire la traduction du récit de cette chasse aux Arméniens m'avait à ce point affectée jusqu'à susciter mon refus obstiné à ce qui était devenu pour moi une obligation persécutrice : écrire quelques pages au sujet de sa réception?

C'est que le discours historique se prête en nous au refoulement à l'œuvre après toute lecture oppressante, afin de nous laisser disponibles à la vie dont nous sommes redevables à la survie des ascendants. Par contre, la parole d'une expérience subjective s'adressant à nous en première personne, par le truchement du traducteur, parvient moins bien à être refoulée. Ce type de traduction, d'abord textuelle, promeut ensuite celle prise au sens plus large de traduction/élaboration psychique, car elle rend alors possible, dans un second temps, la lecture par les héritiers des documents jusque là ignorés de leur histoire. C'est en ce point précis que se manifeste l'importance capitale de la traduction, non seulement en raison de ses effets d'après-coup dans la transmission psychique mais aussi, en raison de son impact politique. Elle innove en effet, au sein des événements culturels de la cité, une instance d'énonciation inédite, au sens où l'entend Jacques Rancière pour le «litige politique».[29]

Notes

1 Co-traductrice de Freud depuis 1970, j'ai été également, depuis 1983, « responsable de l'harmonisation » dans l'équipe éditoriale des Œuvres complètes de Freud, publiées aux PUF sous la direction scientifique de Jean Laplanche. Cf. : J. Altounian, *L'écriture de Freud, Traversée traumatique et traduction*, PUF/ bibliothèque de psychanalyse, 2003.

2 Depuis mon premier article : "Comment peut-on être ? ", paru dans *Les Temps Modernes*, décembre 1975, n° 353, repris dans « *Ouvrez-moi seulement les chemins d'Arménie » Un génocide aux déserts de l'inconscient* (Préface de René Kaës), Les Belles Lettres/ Confluents psychanalytiques, 1990, 2003 (2° éd.); jusqu'à *La Survivance / Traduire le trauma* collectif (Préface de Pierre Fédida, Postface de René Kaës), Dunod / Inconscient et Culture, 2000, 2003 (réimp.) ; *L'intraduisible / Deuil, mémoire, transmission*, Dunod/ Psychismes, 2005, 2008 (réimp.); *Mémoires du Génocide arménien/ Héritage traumatique et travail analytique*, Vahram et Janine Altounian, avec la contribution de K. Beledian, J.F. Chiantaretto, M. Fraire, Y. Gampel, R. Kaës, R. Waintrater, PUF, 2009 ; et, récemment, *De la cure à l'écriture / L'élaboration d'un héritage traumatique*, PUF, 2012.

3 Shoshana Felman « À l'âge du témoignage : Shoah de Claude Lanzmann », in *Au sujet de Shoah*, le film de Claude Lanzmann, Belin, 1990, p. 24.

4 Je reprends ici l'expression de Luba Jurgenson dans son intervention: « Traduire et retraduire les témoignages du Goulag » au colloque : Traduire l'expérience au-delà de ses limites du 17 octobre 2012.

5 «übersetzen» s'emploie la plupart du temps pour signifier:«traduire», mais Freud emploie également «übertragen» dans ce sens-là. Le terme en usage dans la traduction française est donc, pour le substantif correspondant:«Übertragung», «transfert» alors qu'il inclut aussi le sens de «traduction».

6 Cf, Claude Janin, *Figures et destins du traumatisme,* Puf, 1996, p. 23–24.

7 René Kaës, « Le sujet de l'héritage », in *Transmission de la vie psychique entre générations*, Dunod, 1993, p. 54.

8 Sa version intégrale est accompagnée du facsimilé de l'original dans *Mémoires du Génocide arménien, op.cit.*

9 Cf. D. Anzieu, Influence comparée de la langue et de la culture française et germanique sur l'auto-analyse de Freud, in *Psychanalyse à l'Université,* 1987/12/48, p. 539.

10 On peut noter la double valence - psychique et territoriale - de nombreux concepts de la métapsychologie freudienne qui renvoient à un mouvement processuel non pas en droite ligne mais en différents types de déplacements: Voici dans l'ordre de l'énumération : « migration » (**Wanderung**) «détour »(**Umweg),** « déviation » (**Ablenkung**), « dérivation » (**Ableitung**), « déplacement (**Verschiebung**), « transfert » (***Übertragung***), « trace » (**Spur**), « clivage » (**Spaltung**), « répression » (**Unterdrückung**), « poursuites/persécutions» (**Verfolgung**), « refoulement » (**Verdrängung),** « transposition » (**Umsetzung**) ; de même les ruptures auxquelles renvoient les métaphores de la migration de la fonction libidinale, comparable à un peuple qui « quitte son territoire (**seinen Wohnsitz verläßt**) pour en chercher un nouveau [...], des petites bandes ou groupements de migrants (**Wanderer**) [faisant] halte en chemin [...], tandis que le gros de la troupe poursuivait sa marche », à « un peuple en mouvement (**ein Volk in Bewegung**) [qui] a laissé en arrière (**zurückgelassen**) de forts détachements aux stations de sa migration (**Wanderung**) », dont « ceux qui se sont avancés plus loin (**die weiter Vorgerückten**) courront d'autant plus le danger d'une défaite qu'ils auront laissé en arrière (**zurückgelassen**) un plus grand nombre d'entre eux au cours de la migration (**Wanderung**). « La libido migre et parcourt le chemin inverse (**wandert zurück**) jusqu'à ses propres points de fixation » (*Leçons d'introduction à la psychanalyse*, in *OCF/P* XIV, 2000, pp. 351, 353, 387; *G.W.* XI, pp. 351, 353, 388.) ; de même le symptôme qui est un « corps étranger » (**Fremdkörper**) jouissant du « privilège de l'extra-territorialité »(**Vorrecht der Exterritorialität**) (« Inhibition, symptôme et angoisse », in *OCF/P* XVII, 1992, p. 215; *G.W.* XIV, p. 125)

11 Jean Laplanche, « Trois acceptions du mot "inconscient" dans le cadre de la théorie de la séduction généralisée », in *Sexual, La sexualité élargie au sens freudien*, 2000–2006, puf, 2007, p. 200 à 203.

12 *Ibid,* p. 201

13 *Ibid,* p. 200

14 *Ibid,* p. 201.

15 *Ibid.* p. 208.

16 Renée Balibar, *L'institution du français / Essai sur le colinguisme des Carolingiens à la République*, PUF, 1985, p. 150. Voir aussi p. 4 : « Nous avons forgé un concept indispensable à notre étude. Le terme de colinguisme désigne l'association de certaines langues d'État dans un appareil de langues où elles trouvent leur légitimité et leur matière à exercices. Sans cette association (traduction, grammatisation)[...] la norme linguistique ne peut ni être instituée, ni fonctionner, c'est à dire qu'elle n'existe tout simplement pas ».

17 Elle le nomme « premier livre comme une mémoire prothèse » selon l'expression

de Primo Levi. Ainsi au Livre I de Primo Levi, Se questo è un uomo, 1947, correspond, d'après elle, le Livre II, I sommersi e i salvati, 1986. Cf. *L'expérience concentrationnaire est-elle indicible ? op. cit.*, p. 19 sq.

18 *Ibid. op. cit.*, p. 117.

19 « Die Versagung der Übersetzung, das ist das, was klinisch "Verdrängung" heißt «. Sigmund Freud, *Briefe an Wilhelm Fließ*, (1887–1904), J.M. Masson, M. Schröter, S. Fischer, 1986, p. 219 ; Sigmund Freud, *Lettres à Fließ* (1887–1904), Traduit de l'allemand par Françoise Kahn et François Robert, PUF, 2006, p. 265. Voir le commentaire de cette lettre par Jean Laplanche dans « Traumatisme, traduction, transfert et autres trans(es) », in *La révolution copernicienne inachevée, op. cit.*, p. 255 sq.

20 Ainsi, par ex., La Chronique d'Eusèbe de Césarée, dont l'original ne nous est parvenu que par sa traduction en langue arménienne. « Aucun peuple n'a étudié plus anciennement et avec plus d'ardeur les monuments littéraires de la Grèce, et la découverte de la traduction arménienne de la Chronique d'Eusèbe, dont l'original est perdu et dont il ne nous restait plus que de courts fragments, montre que s'il est permis de concevoir l'espoir de retrouver quelques traces de ces monuments que le temps a dévorés, c'est surtout dans les versions que les Arméniens en avaient faites. http://remacle.org/bloodwolf/historiens/michellesyrien/chronique1.htm

21 « Ruptures catastrophiques et travail de la mémoire » in *Violence d'État et psychanalyse*, Dunod, 1989, p. 173.

22 Piera Aulagnier, « Condamné à investir » in *Nouvelle Revue de Psychanalyse,* 25, *Le trouble de penser*, 309–330, Paris, Gallimard, 1982.

23 Cf. J. Altounian, « *Faute de parler ma langue » in « Ouvrez-moi seulement les chemins d'Arménie* », op. *cit.*, p. 147–150.

24 Cf. *L'écriture de Freud, Traversée traumatique et traduction*, op.cit., p. 92.

25 Introduction du traducteur Hervé Georgelin: « Aram Andonian est un homme mûr et reconnu quand il est arrêté lors de la grande rafle du 11 avril 1915 au soir — selon le calendrier julien alors en usage chez les Arméniens ottomans — dans la capitale impériale. Par le hasard ou plutôt grâce à la chance qu'il sait aider de sa ruse, de son courage, de son intelligence et de son envie de survivre, Aram Andonian ne connaîtra pas le sort de ces centaines de premiers exilés, déportés vers l'Anatolie centrale pour disparaître à jamais. Il saura s'échapper, se blesser, se grimer, mentir, se dissimuler pour échapper à la machine de destruction ottomane. Il parviendra tant bien que mal à descendre vers Alep et le Liban et à être encore en vie quand la région sera libérée ou conquise, selon le point de vue de chacun, par les Britanniques puis les Français »

26 Publiés en feuilleton dans le journal arménien de Paris : Renaissance du 31 juillet 1919 au 24 avril 1920. Traduits par Hervé Georgelin, ils vont paraître incessamment aux Editions Metis Presses à Genève.

27 Intitulé « Terrorisme d'un génocide » dans *Les Temps Modernes* en 1982, il a été repris intégralement dans « *Ouvrez-moi seulement les chemins d'Arménie* », *op. cit.* p. 81 à 119, et *Mémoires du Génocide arménien, op. cit.*, p. 13 à 97, en extraits dans *L'intraduisible, op. cit.*, p. 19 à 91, et dans *De la cure à l'écriture, op. cit.* p. 75 à 87.

28 Je l'avais fait faire en 1978, huit ans après la mort de son auteur. Il était écrit en caractères arméniens mais en langue turque, un grand nombre d'Arméniens ayant été turcophones dans L'empire ottoman. Cf. la contribution du traducteur Krikor Beledian : « Traduire un témoignage écrit dans la langue des autres », in *Mémoires du Génocide arménien, op. cit.* En voici quelques passages significatifs :

« Nous étions fatigués et nous avions très faim. [...] Quand nous sommes arrivés à Akhtarine, nous étions harcelés d'un côté par la faim, de l'autre par les saletés. Les chiens déchiquetaient les morts, personne ne les enterrait. Tout alentour sentait mauvais [...] Après six heures de marche, nous sommes arrivés à Hamam. Là nous avons été surpris: les gens mangeaient des sauterelles. Quant aux mourants, on ne pouvait pas les compter. [...] Mon père était très malade, il ne pouvait plus se déplacer [...] Alors l'un d'eux s'est mis frapper mon père à la tête. [...] Mais à quoi bon? Que devient un homme gravement malade qu'on bat à coups de bâton? Six jours plus tard, le jour du décès de mon père, ils ont de nouveau déporté [...] Ils ont dit à ma mère : "Ton malade est mort". Et ma mère:" Nous partirons quand nous aurons enterré le mort." Ils ont répondu: " Non, vous ferez comme les autres. " Les autres, en fait, abandonnaient les morts et la nuit les chacals les dévoraient. [...] J'ai vu que ça n'allait pas et qu'il fallait faire quelque chose. J'ai pris un flacon de 75 *dirhem* , je l'ai rempli d'huile de rose et je suis allé voir tout de suite le chef du convoi de déportation. Je lui ai dit : "Laisse-nous aujourd'hui, nous partirons avec le prochain convoi avec les autres". Heureusement il n'a rien dit. Nous sommes restés encore un jour. Nous avons creusé une fosse long de deux *archines* et ayant payé cinq *kourouchs* au *derder* nous avons enterré mon père [...] À Racca, [...] les gens mourraient partout de faim, on ne pouvait pas rester à l'intérieur de l'auberge, tout sentait la pourriture [...] Nous n'avions plus d'argent, c'est pourquoi nous avons commencé à manger des herbes. Nous avons essayé de continuer ainsi pendant un mois, on a vu qu'on allait mourir. On faisait à peine deux pas et on tombait par terre. Ma mère a réfléchi. « Moi, pour mourir, je mourrai, vous, il ne le faut pas. » C'est ainsi qu'elle nous a donnés, nous deux, aux Arabes», *Mémoires du Génocide arménien, op. cit.* pp. 21, 24–25, 28.

29 Cf. Jacques Rancière, *La Mésentente / Politique et Philosophie*, Galilée, 1995. 140/141 : « le litige politique se différencie de tout conflit d'intérêts entre parties constituées [...] puisqu'il n'est pas une discussion entre partenaires mais une interlocution qui met en jeu la situation même d'interlocution »

La traduction comme stratégie subjectivante en contexte de rééducation auditive post-implantatoire

Rémy Potier, Olivier Putois*

Résumé

Dans cet article, on s'appuie sur la prise en charge d'orientation psychanalytique d'une patiente psychotique dotée d'implants cochléaires, pour souligner une facette inconsciente de la traduction, comprise comme passage de la langue maternelle à une langue étrangère. En insistant sur le nœud liant le contexte linguistique de son suivi (en langue étrangère) et son utilisation remarquable des implants, nous montrons que la traduction interroge la séparation inconsciente entre le sujet et ce que nous proposons d'appeler le corps de la langue.

Mots-clés : psychose, psychanalyse, implantation cochléaire, subjectivation, traduction

Abstract

In this paper, we draw on the psychoanalytically-oriented therapy of a psychotic patient with cochlear implants to draw attention to an unconscious facet of translation, understood as the passage from mother tongue to foreign language. Focusing on the knot between the foreign-language context of her follow-up and therapy, and her excellent use of the implants, we show that translation brings into play the unconscious separation between the subject and what we propose to call the body of her mother tongue.

Keywords: psychosis, psychoanalysis, cochlear implantation, subjectivization, translation

Introduction

Notre propos sera ici de contribuer à préciser le noyau de vérité que la psychose, dès lors qu'on la ressaisit au prisme de la psychanalyse, nous enseigne quant à l'enjeu subjectif inconscient de la traduction, entendue comme *passage de la langue maternelle à une autre*. Une telle contribution a des précédents : la mobilisation de la pluralité des lan-

* Ces deux auteurs ont participé à ce travail dans les mêmes proportions. Le travail d'Olivier Putois a été réalisé dans le cadre du LABEX portant la référence ANR-11-LABX-0071, qui a bénéficié d'une aide de l'Etat gérée par l'Agence Nationale de la Recherche au titre du programme Investissements d'avenir portant la référence n° ANR-11-IDEX-0005-01.

gues dans la psychose a trouvé, avec le cas Wolfson, son représentant sans doute le plus célèbre—rencontrant un écho aussi bien chez Deleuze qu'auprès des psychanalystes.[1] La nouveauté de la contribution que nous nous proposons d'apporter à cette question tient au fait qu'elle articule, aux deux paramètres croisés de la psychose et de la mobilisation d'une langue étrangère, un troisième : une intervention (en l'occurrence chirurgicale) dans le réel du corps, visant à implanter un dispositif de substitution auditive, qui permet d'entendre à condition d'effectuer une rééducation, laquelle s'effectue en langue étrangère.

L'introduction de ce troisième paramètre nous permettra, en partant du cas d'une patiente de langue maternelle arabe que nous appellerons Sibylle, suivie par l'un d'entre nous (R.P.) en français (qu'elle parle depuis longtemps) après une implantation cochléaire, de souligner :

—en quoi ce passage à une langue autre que la langue maternelle exhibe la *facture charnelle du rapport du sujet à la langue maternelle ;*

—et corrélativement, la *perte dans son corps* que représente ce passage traductif d'une langue à l'autre.

C'est ce double versant, qui nous semble receler la vérité biface de l'enjeu de la traduction pour le sujet de l'inconscient, que nous nous attacherons ici à mettre en évidence.[2]

La spécificité de la contribution que nous inspire Sibylle, patiente psychotique dont le suivi thérapeutique a suscité ces réflexions, tient en effet à ce qu'elle a été prise en charge dans un dispositif hospitalier consécutivement à une *implantation cochléaire*. Il s'agit d'une procédure chirurgicale destinée aux sourds et aux malentendants graves qui consiste à implanter un dispositif de haute technologie (fréquemment surnommé « oreille bionique ») dans l'oreille interne, au niveau de la cochlée, à laquelle il se substitue. On cherche ainsi par là à *pallier l'absence d'ouïe* en substituant cet appareil au premier segment de l'appareil auditif, afin de transmettre un signal sonore substitutif aux nerfs de la rampe tympanique, qui relaient ce signal jusqu'au cerveau.

Une telle implantation fait apparaître à ciel ouvert, conformément à la structure psychotique, *un nœud inconscient habituellement refoulé*—en l'occurrence, celui qui *lie le passage de la langue maternelle à une autre par la traduction,* et la *séparation d'avec le corps maternel dont fait partie la voix qui parle la langue maternelle.* Ce nœud est celui de l'emprise sur le corps, et en particulier l'oreille, de celui que Lacan appelait l'Autre primordial (la mère ou son tenant-lieu), ici arabophone; ledit nœud se révèlera être le négatif de l'implantation, qui s'avèrera constituer une tentative de séparation de cet Autre dans le réel du corps par la substitution, à l'oreille qu'il contrôle, d'un dispositif technologique étranger. Dans ce cadre, le fait que le dispositif de prise en charge post-implantatoire mobilise une langue étrangère nous permettra de mettre en évidence que ce *corps étranger qu'est l'implant* ne peut remplir sa fonction séparative *qu'à s'étayer sur un dispositif en langue étrangère*, c'est-à-dire sur un espace aménagé par la traduction comme passage à une autre langue.

De ce cas, nous tirerons ensuite des conclusions théoriques à l'endroit du rapport inconscient du sujet au corps de la langue que mobilise la traduction.

Le cas Sibylle

Nous partirons donc du cas clinique de Sibylle, suivie dans un cadre hospitalier en psychothérapie d'orientation psychanalytique, au Centre de Réglage des Implants Cochléaires (CRIC) de l'Hôpital Rothschild (Paris). La souffrance de Sibylle, qu'elle a cherché à dépasser au moyen de l'implantation cochléaire en contexte de prise en charge francophone, nous est en effet apparue révéler par contraste, au décours des manifestations cliniques liées à sa structure psychotique, quelque chose de la vérité du rapport inconscient de tout sujet à sa langue maternelle.

Pour mettre en relief cette vérité, il faut insister sur le fait que son rapport spécifique à la langue maternelle n'a pu se manifester que dans le cadre d'un dispositif clinique particulier, propre à la prise en charge hospitalière suite à une implantation cochléaire—qui comprend deux versants : de rééducation orthophonique et cognitive, et de suivi psychothérapeutique d'orientation psychanalytique. Un tel dispositif biface vise, de manière générale, à prendre en charge la surdité et son traitement par implantation cochléaire en ses deux dimensions complémentaires, cognitive et relationnelle. Mais il représentera dans le cas de Sibylle un véritable dispositif de subjectivation, en raison de la signification que pourra revêtir pour elle, en raison de son histoire, le couplage entre *implantation et dispositif de prise en charge en langue étrangère*. Un tel couplage, en introduisant un fragile écart avec la position à laquelle l'Autre familial l'assignait, l'ouvrira à un nouvel espace d'élaboration psychique que nous qualifierons d'espace de subjectivation, où s'illustreront les avancées et les reculs de la prise en charge.

Il faut donc situer les éléments cliniques de l'histoire de cette patiente afin de ressaisir les manifestations cliniques survenues à l'occasion de sa prise en charge post-implantatoire.

Atteinte d'une surdité dégénérative depuis l'enfance, Sibylle a grandi au Maroc. Elle a d'abord entendu et parlé l'arabe, puis a appris le français durant sa scolarité. Si cette dernière langue est parfois parlée à la maison, elle l'est peu, car son père ne la parle pas, et sa mère imparfaitement—elle a clairement un statut de langue étrangère, et sa présence dans le foyer ne se substitue pas à celle de l'arabe. Dans les années quatre-vingt dix, toute la famille émigre ; Sibylle a 21 ans, et sa surdité continue à évoluer.

Dans l'équilibre familial, la place assignée à Sibylle est celle d'une handicapée : le discours communément partagé est que *Dieu l'a voulue ainsi*, et qu'on l'aime comme cela chez elle. Concrètement, avant d'entrer dans le protocole médical, Sibylle ne s'exprime pas, elle ne remet rien en cause de ce discours familial ; parallèlement, elle s'affaire pour toute la famille mais n'émet aucun souhait pour elle-même, n'exprime aucun désir en son nom propre. Dans ce cadre, sa surdité est parfaitement intégrée à l'économie familiale, qui se redouble de la justification divine invoquée devant ce symptôme organique. En d'autres termes, *en tant que sourde*, elle occupe, pour reprendre la manière dont Lacan a pu thématiser la psychose dans sa « Note sur l'enfant » (2001), la *position d'objet de la mère, ou de l'Autre primordial*, ici élargi à l'échelle d'une famille arabophone fédérée (aux dires mêmes de la patiente) par son adhésion commune à la représentation de Sibylle comme handicapée voulue de Dieu.

Ce n'est que quelques d'années plus tard, à 27 ans, qu'elle décide par elle-même de se faire implanter. C'est à l'occasion de cette implantation que se manifesteront des éléments cliniques propres à éclairer le rapport inconscient de tout sujet à la langue maternelle, que la psychose présente à ciel ouvert. Car ce choix, où s'ébauche un mouvement dont la portée subjective exacte reste à interroger mais qui inscrit une rupture avec son positionnement univoque comme objet de l'Autre, rencontre l'opposition ferme de ses parents, très religieux. Les paroles reçues sont en effet profondes et inquiètes: « Ne fais pas ça, tu brûleras en enfer », « Dieu ne l'a pas voulu ainsi » (il s'agit là de propos rapportés et traduits, qui ont été proférés dans le contexte de la langue maternelle et familiale, en arabe). C'est Dieu même, voix sans visage de l'interdit par excellence, qui serait offensé par une implantation remettant en question l'inéluctabilité et la fatalité de Ses choix, devant lesquels chacun(e) doit s'incliner.

La violence des réactions à l'annonce de sa saisie de l'opportunité d'une implantation cochléaire indique assez la rupture de l'équilibre familial qu'engage un tel choix, où affleure un désir singulier de *s'approprier une des possibilités de son corps* par le truchement étranger d'une prothèse technologique. Éclate ici, dans l'opposition familiale qui mobilise le signifiant religieux et son cortège de châtiments à venir, la *prétention à la jouissance du corps de Sibylle revendiquée par l'Autre familial arabophone appuyé sur un discours religieux*, qui ne supporte pas qu'elle prétende s'affranchir de sa surdité pour retrouver l'exercice érogène de l'ouïe—tentative de reconquête d'un auto-érotisme, insupportable aux yeux de cet Autre?

La radicalité de sa tentative d'affranchissement de ce dispositif symbiotique d'emprise corporelle apparaît par contraste dans le type d'investissement dont elle dote le service hospitalier, qu'elle considère selon ses dires « comme une nouvelle famille » : voilà douze ans qu'elle vient chaque semaine, cumulant divers rendez-vous qui constituent aujourd'hui sa seule activité extra-familiale. Notons en particulier que ses rendez-vous avec le psychologue, initiés à sa demande, se déroulent sans que sa famille soit au courant. Elle verbalise au sujet de cette discrétion qui confine, pour elle, au secret—juxtaposition de deux espaces qui atteste du type de défenses psychotiques mobilisées face à l'Autre jouisseur qui menace toujours de faire retour.

Car en effet, l'histoire de son parcours de soin est jalonnée, dès les suites de la première opération, de nombreuses complications—en particulier somatiques—qui laissent l'équipe médicale perplexe. Ainsi, malgré de nombreuses investigations, aucune explication médicale ne permet de mettre en évidence de cause physiologique pour la brûlure qu'elle arbore au niveau de l'implant. On ira même jusqu'à changer celui-ci, mais la brûlure réapparaîtra. Voici dix ans déjà qu'elle est implantée, des deux côtés. Elle présentera souvent des crises similaires, notamment lorsqu'au sein de sa famille les reproches fusent à l'endroit de cette implantation, exigeant le *retour à une surdité synonyme de repli sur la position exclusive d'objet de l'Autre familial primairement arabophone, visant à apaiser ce dernier*. Dans ces moments, dit-elle, « elle brûle » : le signifiant religieux interdicteur de l'« Enfer », qui lui était brandi par sa famille au moment de son choix de se faire implanter, revient dans le réel de son corps.

Ainsi, durant les vacances, quand son suivi psychothérapeutique s'interrompt, déstabilisant le *contre-investissement de l'implant en contexte francophone* par lequel Sibylle tente de se réapproprier son corps entendant contre l'Autre familial arabophone qui la veut sourde, des crises brûlantes lui imposent régulièrement de retirer l'implant, seul geste qui pacifie cet Autre. Là-contre, durant les moments de crise, l'hôpital est le seul endroit où elle parvient à remettre ses implants : l'ébauche de triangulation que permet l'espace francophone du suivi psychothérapeutique, des consultations et des discussions autour de problèmes médicaux, soutient son investissement de l'implant comme protection vis-à-vis de l'Autre arabophone qui la blesse en la consumant littéralement de l'intérieur.

Au bout de quelques années, elle décide d'abandonner son travail, et de se consacrer exclusivement à sa prise en charge en contexte hospitalier, qui acquiert alors un statut de plus en plus central dans sa tentative de subjectivation. Les liens entre ses crises et sa situation familiale sont évidents, mais il n'est possible de les lui faire saisir que patiemment, dans la diachronie que déploie un suivi thérapeutique appuyé sur le transfert multifocal envers cette « nouvelle famille » francophone qu'est l'équipe—qui s'attache à contrebalancer sa mise en position d'objet sourd de l'Autre en portant sa revendication narcissiquement d'une position d'entendante.

Dès lors, la rééducation orthophonique et cognitive, menée en parallèle du suivi psychodynamique, bénéficiera du transfert sur le dispositif thérapeutique comme lieu d'une langue étrangère : Sibylle arrive à des performances de rééducation qui émerveillent l'équipe. Alors qu'en famille, elle ne comprenait rien, conformément à son statut d'handicapée voulue par Dieu, elle comprend désormais tout au sein de cette « nouvelle famille » qu'est l'hôpital. Le dispositif de prise en charge biface rééducation/psychothérapie fonctionne ici de manière à contrecarrer l'injonction à occuper une place voulue par le seul Autre, face auquel elle n'aurait pas son mot à dire.

Mais, on l'a tout juste indiqué, cet investissement de la « nouvelle famille » de langue française a un prix, indexé sur la défense archaïque contre les retours de l'Autre dans le corps : l'interruption de son travail, des vertiges inexplicables du point de vue médical, et plus généralement des somatisations qui reviennent de manière cyclique. Petit à petit cependant, dans le cours du travail thérapeutique, elle se permet de nouvelles associations, et des liens auparavant interdits. Elle se permet de critiquer, de remettre en question et de questionner son désir — facettes différentes de la subjectivation qui s'ébauche dans le cadre du suivi. Elle conquiert ainsi une forme rudimentaire de subjectivité en se séparant de l'Autre envahisseur par le truchement d'une stratégie d'écart linguistique, en aménageant un espace propre et secret, préservé de la langue maternelle.

Pour autant, la tentative de séparation qui a échoué au sein de la langue maternelle, et que permet de rejouer l'ouverture d'un espace transférentiel d'interlocution en langue étrangère à l'occasion de l'implantation, demeure incomplète : *la séparation corporelle ou charnelle n'est pas totale*. En effet, l'identification de l'équipe francophone à une « nouvelle famille », dans son discours, signifie aussi bien qu'elle reconduit, dans la fragile symbolisation que permet sa relation à l'équipe, un rapport de *séparation charnelle inaccomplie* à l'Autre : elle témoigne en effet d'une grande dépendance à l'endroit d'un suivi à la fois chronique et pérenne, seul à même d'alimenter sa symbolisation. Le point d'évolution tient à une défense améliorée vis-à-vis de l'envahissement par l'Autre, qui rend possible un espace de relative séparation subjective dans son corps—c'est-à-dire une sortie partielle du statut d'handicapée auquel elle s'est initialement trouvée assignée, en aménageant l'espace d'une libidinalisation de l'ouïe.

Ainsi, aujourd'hui, l'autonomie locale que lui permet cette séparation subjective partielle débouche sur une subjectivation par investissement de l'hébreu, langue étrangère dans laquelle elle écoute des chansons qu'elle fredonne ; suite à cet investissement, elle effectue des voyages réguliers en Israël.[3] Dernièrement, après plus de dix ans de thérapies hebdomadaires et un accompagnement psychiatrique mensuel, elle a mis en acte sa liberté acquise dans l'espace de la langue: agissant la séparation, elle est partie seule pour la première fois de sa vie, à Tel Aviv. Cette expérience de quinze jours constitue pour elle une référence subjectivante, car elle a pu s'éloigner réellement de sa famille et expérimenter une autonomie dans les échanges dans une langue autre, en l'absence du cadre médico-hospitalier, armature étayant jusqu'alors sa fragile séparation avec la langue maternelle.

Notre hypothèse est donc que ce dispositif thérapeutique a pu être subjectivant en soutenant sa tentative de reconquête de son corps pulsionnel, en étayant sa *séparation réelle* avec un Autre familial arabophone vécu dans un registre symbiotique—c'est-à-dire éprouvé dans une *continuité corporelle, qu'est venu interrompre le corps étranger de l'implant*. Mais la leçon de cette prise en charge est que ce corps étranger qu'est l'implant ne peut remplir sa fonction séparative qu'à *s'étayer sur un dispositif en langue étrangère, dont le noyau est un transfert sur le thérapeute comme interlocuteur de cette langue étrangère*. C'est ce transfert qui fait du dispositif hospitalier un espace de possible subjectivation, aménagé par la traduction comme passage à une autre langue ; en atteste le fait qu'en l'absence de cet étayage hospitalier, les somatisations font retour avec violence—autrement dit, *c'est bien du côté du réel du corps de Sibylle que se jouera cet essai de subjectivation, qui ne semble pas pouvoir se poursuivre indépendamment du contexte thérapeutique dans sa réalité concrète*.

Comment rassembler les conséquences de ce parcours clinique à l'endroit du rapport inconscient du sujet à sa langue maternelle—et corrélativement, à la traduction comme passage hors de cette langue ?

Traduire : se séparer du corps de la langue ?

Pour préciser l'apport théorique que nous pouvons tirer du cas Sibylle afin de répondre à cette question biface, nous partirons de l'apport que constitue la constitution par Wolfson d'un délire psychotique, qui mobilise la traduction pour se défendre contre la prise de possession de son oreille par l'Autre maternel anglophone. Nous contrasterons cette solution délirante avec celle qu'a choisie Sibylle en élisant l'implantation pour faire barrage à la jouissance de l'Autre, afin de faire ressortir sa spécificité.

Les différentes configurations subjectives que présente la clinique psychopathologique mettent toutes en évidence que la fonction psychique de la langue maternelle ne peut être ressaisie qu'à considérer celle-ci non seulement comme langue du pays d'origine, mais bien comme la langue de la mère, c'est-à-dire de l'Autre primordial qui introduit l'*infans* au langage. Mais la psychose a ceci de particulier que, dans la mesure où les représentations de mots y fonctionnent comme des représentations de chose, mettant directement en présence de l'Autre réel, la langue maternelle peut y être éprouvée par le sujet comme *envahissement ou appropriation effective de son corps par cet Autre*, dont la voix sera vécue comme le prolongement réel jusque dans la chair du sujet, ainsi mis en position d'objet de jouissance de l'Autre. C'est cet impact charnel de la langue maternelle que la psychose offre à saisir hors du refoulement, dans sa vérité, comme le cas Sibylle nous l'a montré.

Un précédent célèbre existe, où le délire remplace l'implantation. En 1970, dans un ouvrage directement écrit en français et intitulé *Le schizo et les langues ou la phonétique chez le psychotique. Esquisses d'un étudiant de langues schizophrénique*, Wolfson—alors jeune étudiant—offre l'occasion de saisir sur le vif, dans la vitalité du témoignage, la violence traumatique interne de la langue maternelle. Celle-ci est littéralement insupportable, pour lui au sens où elle le blesse, le pénètre et résonne dans le réel de son corps—les mots rebondissent en lui, en échos dans sa tête. Il écrit ainsi par exemple, dans une déclaration particulièrement frappante, que sa mère semblait :

> si remplie d'une espèce de joie macabre par cette bonne

> opportunité d'injecter en quelque sorte les mots qui sortaient de sa bouche dans les oreilles de son fils, son seul enfant,—ou, comme elle lui avait de temps en temps dit, son unique possession—, en semblant si heureuse de faire vibrer le tympan de cette unique possession et par conséquent les osselets de l'oreille moyenne de la-dite possession, son fils, en unisson presque exact avec ses cordes vocales à elle, et en dépit qu'il en eût. (Wolfson, 1982, 183)

L'insupportable est ici clairement qualifié : il tient à l'appropriation, à la prise de possession quasi-démoniaque du corps de Wolfson par sa mère par l'entremise de l'impact vibratoire de sa voix à travers le tympan et jusque dans la cochlée de son fils—par quoi on retrouve bien la dimension de jouissance dont parle Lacan, qui entend déployer une relation de *propriété*. Wolfson s'éprouve, au plan auditif, *non séparé d'elle ;* son oreille joue bien plutôt le rôle de *lien de continuité avec le corps maternel proférant*, comme en atteste l'usage du terme *unisson*—qui renvoie non seulement à *l'accord* de deux sons (ici, métaphoriquement, du proféré et de l'entendu), mais aussi à leur *simultanéité* : au moment de leur profération, les paroles de la mère sont quasi-immédiatement dans le corps de l'enfant. En l'absence de *limitation* par une instance tierce qui produirait un effet de séparation, l'oreille devient le canal d'un envahissement hallucinatoire qui dépossède le sujet de lui-même, c'est-à-dire qui *l'aliène*.

L'originalité du cas Wolfson tient à ce que le type de défense contre cet envahissement auditif, visant à se décoller de l'Autre réel, passe par une *stratégie de traduction*, qui se réalise sous la forme d'un délire linguistique. Il s'agit en effet pour lui de construire une langue nouvelle composée d'éléments de toutes les langues, dans laquelle il traduit des mots proférés en langue maternelle suivant une *ressemblance de son et de sens*. Dans un article intitulé « Louis Wolfson, ou le procédé », Gilles Deleuze commente la stratégie de Wolfson sur l'expression « don't trip over the wire » (qui signifie littéralement « ne trébuche pas sur le fil électrique ») :

> Ce que fait l'étudiant [de langues schizophrénique], c'est de traduire suivant certaines règles. Son procédé est le

> suivant : un mot de la langue maternelle étant donné, trouver un mot étranger de sens similaire, mais ayant des sons ou des phonèmes communs (…)

Tel est le procédé général : la phrase *Don't trip over the wire,* Ne trébuche pas sur le fil, devient *Tu'nicht tre*bucher *uber eth he Zwirn*. La phrase de départ est anglaise, mais celle d'arrivée est un simulacre de phrase empruntant à diverses langues, allemand, français, hébreu : « tour de babil ». (Deleuze, 1993, 18–19)

Il s'agit donc de tenter de se séparer de la mère, Autre primordial omniprésent dans la langue maternelle, en mobilisant, face aux mots qui pénètrent son oreille, un principe d'altération qui limitera leur emprise, et que Wolfson appelle le père. Celui-ci contrecarrera, dans le théâtre de la jouissance maternelle qu'est son corps, la présence exclusive de la voix maternelle, en opérant sa traduction suivant cette langue nouvelle, comme le résume Deleuze :

> Ce qu'on appelle Mère, c'est la Vie. Et ce qu'on appelle Père, c'est l'étrangeté, tous ces mots que je ne connais pas et qui traversent les miens, tous ces atomes qui ne cessent d'entrer et de sortir de mon corps. Ce n'est pas le père qui parle les langues étrangères et qui connaît les atomes, ce sont les langues étrangères et les combinaisons atomiques qui sont le père (Deleuze, 1993, 30).

La nature délirante—au sens psychopathologique du terme—d'une telle tentative de séparation se marque cliniquement dans la fidélité du schizophrène à la sonorité originale des mots prononcés en langue maternelle. Alors que dans la traduction ordinaire d'une langue à l'autre, on conserve le sens en faisant le deuil du son, il cherche à conserver les deux, et atteste ainsi du caractère *inachevé* de sa séparation avec l'Autre maternel, *dont la voix*, à peine transfigurée par une néo-traduction qui en conserve le noyau phonique, *reste fantomatiquement présente dans l'idiolecte multi-lingue qui lui sert de défense*.

Là-contre, Sibylle a au fond fait le choix, en se faisant implanter, d'une tentative de subjectivation par séparation réelle du corps de l'Autre parlant la langue maternelle — non dans le réel du délire, mais dans le réel de son corps –, auquel la liait le pacte aliénant de sa surdité, et duquel la protège désormais en partie le couple de l'implant et de l'espace auditif francophone dont il est l'interface. Apparaît donc avec Sibylle, en une radicalisation corporelle de la défense traductive mobilisée par Wolfson, le point auquel *la traduction, au plus loin d'un primat du sémantique, engage le somatique* dans sa dimension pulsionnelle (l'entendre). En d'autres termes, la dimension de la mobilisation psychotique de la traduction que permet de souligner ce cas de défense par implantation et suivi en français — dimension qu'on trouvait déjà chez Wolfson, mais qui apparaît ici au grand jour — tient au fait que cette mobilisation *semble toujours en son fond, pour le sujet, viser une séparation dans le réel du corps* (Wolfson cherche par son délire traductif à s'extraire de l'envahissement de sa cochlée par la voix maternelle).

Le fait que l'ouverture à un dispositif de prise en charge en langue étrangère soit avec Sibylle médiatisé par un organe prothétique fait ainsi entrevoir que c'est en termes *d'affranchissement du corps de la langue maternelle* que se dit l'affranchissement de la jouissance de l'Autre réel par la traduction. Ce qui exhume à ciel ouvert un enjeu central de la traduction : elle est *tentative de séparation du sujet de ce corps de la langue, duquel fait partie cette voix maternelle qui en constitue le prolongement jusque dans la chair du sujet.*

C'est à cette aune que la psychanalyse peut contribuer à faire saisir l'envers inconscient de l'innovation, c'est-à-dire de la créativité, sur laquelle fait fond toute traduction : nommément, l'arrachement au corps de la langue maternelle. *N'est-ce pas là la patrie à laquelle tout traducteur est traître*, du point de vue du locuteur de la langue maternelle ? À suivre cette hypothèse, c'est rien moins que la musique de la langue maternelle qui aura originairement baigné ses oreilles bien avant toute séparation subjective, et qu'il ressent de ce fait comme son corps, dont l'écrivain éprouve la perte au moment d'être traduit ?

Références bibliographiques

Deleuze, Gilles. « Louis Wolfson ou le procédé », dans *Critique et Clinique*. Paris : Minuit, 1993.

Lacan, Jacques. « Note sur l'enfant », dans *Autres Écrits*. Paris : Le Seuil, 2001.

Pontalis, Jean-Bertrand, éd. *Dossier Wolfson ou L'affaire du « Schizo et les langues »*. Paris : Gallimard, 2009.

Uriburu, Maria-Eugenia. « L'opposition à la langue maternelle. Introduction à la bibliographie du dossier Wolfson ». *Recherches en Psychanalyse*, 2013/1, 15. 80–92.

Wolfson, Louis. *Le schizo et les langues ou La Phonétique chez le psychotique (Esquisses d'un étudiant de langues shizophrénique)*. Paris : Gallimard, 1982.

Notes

1 Deleuze (1993) ; Pontalis éd. (2009) ; pour une bibliographie récente sur Wolfson, cf. Uriburu (2013).

2 Insistons donc d'emblée sur le fait que notre propos n'est pas de présenter ce cas dans toute sa complexité, ni de produire des indications thérapeutiques de suivi clinique de patients psychotiques dans un cadre bilingue, ce dont le présent volume, à vocation et lectorat interdisciplinaires, ne saurait être le lieu. On cherchera plutôt à indiquer ce que cette prise en charge psychothérapeutique d'orientation psychanalytique a pu nous évoquer au titre de contribution psychanalytique à un examen interdisciplinaire des différentes facettes de la traduction, quant à l'enjeu inconscient engagé par la traduction que nous localisons dans le rapport charnel du sujet à sa langue maternelle.

3 Même s'il n'est pas à l'heure actuelle possible d'apprécier définitivement la portée mutative de cet investissement, on peut se demander dans quelle mesure il ne signe pas un approfondissement de la mobilisation de la langue étrangère dans l'évolution subjective, dans la perspective d'une tentative de triangulation des identifications : l'hébreu est à la fois une langue étrangère et celle de la religion de ses pères.

Déplacement territorial, traduction et maternité. Quand la traversée des frontières favorise les phénomènes traductifs chez la femme

Elise Pestre

Résumé

Les effets du déplacement territorial seront envisagés à partir de l'économie psychique et pulsionnelle du sujet depuis les passerelles établies entre psychanalyse et traduction. L'exil engage le sujet à entrer dans une véritable « position traductive », perspective clinique qui s'observe notamment à l'occasion de l'avènement du processus gestatif chez la femme en état migratoire. Le travail du psychothérapeute consistera à accompagner les phénomènes traductifs à l'œuvre entre corps et subjectivité afin de faciliter la création d'une nouvelle demeure à celle qui est en puête de lieu.

Mots-clés : psychanalyse, déplacement, migration, gestation, position traductive

Abstract

This article examines the effects of migration on the subjective economy and drives, based on the connections between psychoanalysis and translation. Exile requires the subject to assume a "translating position;" the incidence of pregnancy among migrant women is a clinical manifestation of this phenomenon. The psychotherapist's work consists in facilitating the translation processes between the psyche and the soma, in order help the subject create a new home.

Keywords : psychoanalysis, exile, migration, pregnancy, translation position

Introduction

Le déplacement territorial et l'installation dans un nouveau lieu de vie engagent le sujet étranger à expérimenter des modalités de traduction aussi multiples que singulières. Pour se reterritorialiser — c'est-à-dire se recréer un territoire propre — et se façonner une nouvelle demeure, subjectivité et corps vont faire, l'objet d'importants réaménagements psychiques et pulsionnels. Nous emprunterons ici les « voies de traverse » (Michaud, 1998, 9-37) initiées par Freud entre psychanalyse et traduction, afin de considérer la façon dont le déplacement territorial invite le sujet à entrer dans une « position traductive » (Oustinoff, 2003, 64). C'est à partir d'une population de femmes migrantes enceintes rencontrées à l'occasion d'une recherche en psychanalyse conduite en Argentine (à Buenos Aires) que nous envisagerons la traduction comme un acte tout autant psychique que corporel.

Injonction à traduire et levée du refoulement

La traduction opère constamment chez l'homme et en ce sens, excède la langue. C'est parce que le langage est structurel, qu'il est indétachable de l'humain que nous sommes *condamnés* à être des traducteurs. A l'occasion du déplacement territorial, l'impulsion traductive se déploie tout particulièrement chez celui qui a migré. Il est en effet mis en demeure de traduire, et en permanence, tout ce qui l'entoure. Ce nouveau contexte crée un rapport au sensible particulier, dont la clinique auprès de patients exilés rend compte. Le sujet est ainsi réceptif, comme le décrit J. Kristeva, à une langue sensible qui « n'est pas une langue de signes : elle est une « langue » entre guillemets, un chaos et un ordre de battements, d'impressions, de douleurs et d'extases aux frontières de l'informulable biologie. Cette « langue » — là est la véritable « étrangeté » — plus étrangère que tout idiome déjà constitué — (...) » (Kristeva, 1997, 23).

L'immersion dans un nouveau bain culturel et l'entrée dans des modalités langagières inédites acheminent le sujet vers une position subjective, à fleur de refoulement. C'est-à-dire que dans ce contexte d'exil, les matériaux habituellement maintenus refoulés se voient comme encouragés à remonter plus aisément à la surface, vers le conscient. Ce qui était resté jusque-là entravé et non-traduit — voire ce qui était de l'ordre de l'intraduisible (Altounian, 2005) — va être plus facilement révélé avec l'environnement nouveau. Les matériaux tapis seront prêts à surgir dans le conscient, au risque de multiplier les « rejetons » de l'inconscient, notamment par le bais de la formation de symptômes. Ce qui était enseveli psychiquement sera alors susceptible de provoquer des soubresauts dans le corps, conditionnant ainsi les avatars pulsionnels du sujet, qui sont déjà en partie déterminés par les « vicissitudes contingentes » (Assoun, 1997) relatives à l'exil. Les enjeux inconscients et pulsionnels liés à l'avènement de la maternité chez la femme migrante, nous permettront d'envisager en particulier les modalités traductives qui se déploient de part en part des topos psychiques et du soma.

Processus gestatif et mise en traduction des nœuds inconscients refoulés jusqu'alors

Une recherche clinique menée auprès de patientes migrantes enceintes en situation de précarité, a livré des articulations fécondes entre déplacement et processus gestatif en terre étrangère.[2] Observée avec récurrence chez la population envisagée, la grossesse se révèle être un événement imprévu, mentionné comme involontaire, qui surgit au détour du déplacement.[3] Il convient de souligner que presque la moitié des femmes rencontrées ont en effet débuté une grossesse lors de leur première année de présence sur le sol argentin,[4] alors même que le contexte migratoire mentionné—qualifiée d'« économique » pour la majorité—n'apparaissait guère propice à cet événement. Ces propos pourraient être synthétisés par: « je ne veux pas tomber enceinte, moins encore juste après mon arrivée dans un nouveau pays dans lequel je dois trouver du travail ». Relevons qu'avec l'avortement interdit en Argentine, une telle annonce revêt un caractère d'irréversibilité, de l'ordre du Réel : il va falloir assumer la charge de cette gestation et l'enfant à venir.[5]

Cette sorte *d'empressement inconscient* à enfanter a retenu toute notre attention : qu'est-ce qui pousse ainsi ces femmes à procréer *si vite* en terre étrangère?

C'est comme si le franchissement des frontières territoriales, -représentées par des lignes symboliques et imaginaires dont la traversée matérielle et fantasmatique rend compte -, avait une influence directe sur les coordonnées biologiques de la femme, favorisant et accélérant, à son insu, l'éveil de la matrice par la gestation.[6] A la suite de l'analyse des entretiens de recherche, il est en effet ressorti de façon significative que l'avènement de la grossesse émergeait chez beaucoup de femmes comme opérant tel un traducteur de nœuds refoulés qui avaient jusqu'alors été maintenus hors du conscient.

Des travaux scientifiques ont exploré les liens entre migration et fertilité, mais l'orientation de cette littérature porte rarement sur les phénomènes inconscients en jeu et les modalités traductives singulières suscitées par le déplacement. Aussi ne développerons-nous pas plus en avant ces perspectives.[7]

Il est intéressant de voir que peu après leur migration, les femmes interviewées semblent littéralement *tomber* enceintes. Comme en français, on retrouve en espagnol l'expression « tomber enceinte » avec le signifiant tomber (caer) qui introduit la dimension de chute inattendue et soudaine, que provoque ici l'annonce de la gestation. Mentionnons que ce terme renvoie aussi au fait d' « être entraîné vers le bas sous le poids de la pesanteur »,[8] ainsi qu'à une multitude de significations qui seront éclairantes dans la suite de nos développements, notamment dans le fait de « commettre une faute, céder au péché ».[9]

On s'interroge ainsi sur ce qui amène ces femmes à s'*embarrasser*, à leur insu, peu après leur arrivée dans ce nouveau pays. Là encore le signifiant *embarrassé* est riche de sens. Si en espagnol on l'emploie pour désigner le fait d'être *enceinte* (*embarazo, embarazada*), ce terme renvoie à l'expression *embarrassée* autrefois utilisée en France, généralement lorsqu'une femme tombait enceinte alors qu'elle n'était pas mariée. Ce terme fait appel, sans équivoque, à la dimension passive et gênante que semble revêtir ici cet état transitoire et à l'embarras qu'il suscite.

Rencontre avec le sexuel

Le franchissement des frontières semble receler une portée émancipatrice qui fait du déplacement un événement propice à la rencontre avec le sexuel, et à la mise en acte des désirs qui lui sont liés.

On perçoit, surtout chez les jeunes femmes migrantes, comment le corps pulsionnel, qui était initialement régulé par la culture d'origine, se trouve soudainement « décadenassé ». En termes oedipiens, la culture du père, dont les référents traditionnels présents au sein de la population interviewée sont imprégnées de catholicisme—avec tous les interdits sur la sexualité que cette religion implique—semble être reléguée au second plan.

Ce « dévérouillage » de la sexualité s'avère être tout aussi symbolique que réel: que les jeunes femmes s'ouvrent à la sexualité, voire passent à l'acte dans la réalité. Ce vécu est d'ailleurs ressenti et exprimé, avec une certaine lucidité chez les femmes les plus jeunes, qui formulent d'une manière ou d'une autre que « ça ne serait pas arrivé »—cette grossesse accidentelle donc—dans leur pays d'origine.

Par exemple Sandra, une jeune adolescente bolivienne dira : « C'est certain, je ne serai pas tombée enceinte là-bas. C'est une autre culture, on ne sort pas autant. Ici les filles sont folles et c'est contagieux! ». Ou encore Maria : « Au Pérou je crois que je ne serai pas tombée enceinte. Je crois que je n'aurai pas eu de copain. Ici j'ai été un peu relâchée».

L'éloignement de la terre d'origine semble produire une chute de l'autorité surmoïque et une redistribution pulsionnelle est ordoné. La libido peut désormais circuler sans frontières, loin des regards réprobateurs rattachés à la terre des ancêtres. En ce sens, l'exil, représente un effacement du regard paternel, celui même qui réfrène la jouissance et favorise une une nouvelle configuration de la situation: le « tombé enceinte », avec toute la dimension transgressive et parfois punitive que cette grossesse implique chez la fille.

Dans ce contexte, les signifiants *caer et embarazada* qui renvoyaient au fait de « *tomber dans le péché,* commettre une faute » endossent une signification nouvelle. L'expression en argot: « Tomber sur le dos et se faire une bosse au ventre »[10] apparaît aussi très évocatrice. Certaines de ces gestations n'auraient-elle pas comme dessein ultime celui de maîtriser la formidable poussée des pulsions sexuelles par le truchement de ce corps enceint, qui apparaît désormais autrement *cadenassé,* par la grossesse? En effet, la gestation obstrue la pulsion et semble venir en place du sexuel irrépressible et inconciliable.

Le cas de Mariana : le déplacement suivi d'une gestation inattendue

Plusieurs femmes interviewées ont témoigné du fait qu'elles ne réussissaient pas à enfanter sur « leur » terre natale, mais qu'elles y étaient parvenues, à leur grand étonnement, peu après leur migration en Argentine. La traversée des frontières, et la multiplicité de déplacements qu'elle engendre—topiques, physiques, etc.—exercerait-elle une influence sur la capacité à procréer de la femme? Le modèle traductif freudien revêt ici tout son intérêt pour penser les blocages de la traduction au niveau des procédés de traduction/détraduction/retraduction, et de leur remise en mouvement à la suite d'un déplacement. Le cas de l'une d'entre elle, Mariana, rendra compte des variations subjectives révélées à l'occasion du changement territorial et de ses effets inédits sur la matrice.

Mariana était encore « sous le choc » de l'annonce de sa grossesse quand je l'ai interviewé dans la salle d'attente de la maternité où elle attendait pour une consultation de contrôle. Agée de vingt-sept ans, une stérilité lui avait été diagnostiquée dans son pays d'origine, en raison, me dit-elle, d'une malformation utérine.[11] « Je ne peux toujours pas y croire » exprima-t-elle à ce propos. Quand je la questionnais sur son ressenti, elle précisa: « Je ne m'y attendais pas du tout. Là-bas [au Paraguay] ils me disaient que je ne pouvais pas en avoir. Que je n'avais pas l'utérus suffisamment développé ».

C'est seulement à quatre mois de gestation qu'elle s'est rendue compte de sa grossesse. Lorsque je la rencontrais, elle était enceinte de plus de cinq mois et son ventre était très petit. Cette situation semble nous donner à voir toute la dimension psychique de l'infertilité[12] et souligne l'inéluctable condition psycho-biologique de l'être humain. Le fait que peu après le déplacement territorial ce symptôme s'évanouisse sans prévenir, interroge les remaniements inconscients liés à la capacité biologique à enfanter. D'ailleurs Mariana, encore sidérée par cette annonce, trouve comme seule réponse à cette énigme biologique, un présage divin. Quand je la questionne sur cette grossesse Mariana dit en effet : « Puisque dieu le veut, c'est comme ça ». Elle dort mal et souffre de cauchemars de pertes très envahissants, qui démontrent à quel point elle tâche de faire sienne la réalité de cette grossesse qui a surgi contre toute attente, engendrant des tentatives psychiques d'élaborations intenses.

La chute mystérieuse du symptôme d'infertilité dévoile la force extraordinaire que l'inconscient exerce sur le corps : le diagnostic de stérilité médicale est balayé au profit d'une *fertilité médicalement inexpliquée* (on parle en général d'*in*fertilité médicalement inexpliquée). C'est une fois qu'ils sont déportés dans une autre réalité, que soma et psyché se *dé-figurent* et se reconfigurent, autrement donc. Le corps sort d'une impasse d'engendrement, d'un « défaut de traduction »[13] comme le désignait Freud, autorisant le déploiement de nouveaux nouages libidinaux dans la mise en corps du sujet par l'avènement de la gestation.

En terre nouvelle, la subjectivité s'ouvre aux transformations pulsionnelles : le possible transfigure l'impossible et donne à voir la façon dont la déterritorialisation du sujet a « défait tout ce qu'une territorialisation antérieure avait pu faire» comme Deleuze le formulait (Deleuze, 1991, 66). Chez Mariana, comme chez d'autres, il aura fallu ce changement de pays pour que la grossesse soit spontanément *mise en route*.

La capacité à procréer prend un nouvel envol une fois la migration accomplie, le changement de territoire agissant ici à la manière d'un *accélérateur de traduction* qui se manifeste par le biais du corps. Ce déplacement semble en effet opérer tel un véritable « fertilisateur » chez les femmes en état migratoire.

La quête d'une nouvelle demeure passerait-elle par celle d'un corps enfanté ?

Pour certaines femmes migrantes, la grossesse se profilerait telle une façon de fabriquer de l'autre, un *alter ego* qui l'accompagne en terre d'exil. *Créer, procréer un autre en devenir en soi* aurait - fantasmatiquement tout du moins - des vertus protectrices et de contention qui permettrait à la femme parfois isolée de se blottir imaginairement dans ce lieu que peut constituer la grossesse.

La migration suivie d'une gestation, donnerait à voir cette maternité comme ayant une signification essentiellement *nostalgique.* L'éloignement du pays natal engendrerait en effet la dimension du *nostalgos,* une tristesse liée au regret de la terre quittée. Dans le nouveau lieu, l'enfant porté se matérialiserait en tant que « preuve d'amour, comme un cadeau » (Freud, 1997) disait Freud, offert au père éloigné, et à sa patrie.[14]

En-deçà du père c'est un double mouvement qui est ici en jeu : il s'agirait aussi pour la femme enceinte de retrouver la mère des temps pré-oedipiens,[15] car si la terre est *pater* (père) elle est avant tout *mater,* terre mère.

La « bosse au ventre » marque le retour du refoulé qui surgit dans le corps de la fille, comme symptôme. C'est précisément là que se situent les *rejetons* de l'inconscient, terme freudien qui prend toute son acuité dans cette situation de grossesse. Avec l'exil, les « messages énigmatiques »[16] qui ont parfois été transmis au cours de l'enfance visitent plus aisément la subjectivité. Ils tachent en vain de trouver des traductions possibles, pour écrire des versions nouvelles du passé, et ce quel qu'en soit le coût pour l'appareil psyché-soma.

Enfin, soulignons que cette grossesse se profile également comme potentiel vecteur d'autonomisation et de lien social. La nationalité échue à l'enfant à sa naissance dans le pays d'accueil vient incarner cette inscription territoriale nouvelle.[17] Une forme de recodification juridique se produit alors au sein de la famille: avec l'enfantement naît la possibilité de construire une demeure, voire, et par effet de ricochet, générer une forme de réhabilitation familiale, sociale et subjective pour tous ses membres. La maternité garantit l'hospitalité psychique et politique de la mère, mais aussi du couple, leur offrant la possibilité d'un enracinement juridique et social nouveau. C'est en quelques sortes une vie qui est à donner en réponse à la quête d'un lieu.

De quelques éléments conclusifs

Alors que la « mutation de structure subjective par l'exil de la langue » (Peraldi, 1982, 9-25) s'observe tout particulièrement à l'occasion du déplacement territorial, on constate cliniquement combien les « tentatives de traduction de l'Inconscient » dont parlait Freud sont continues dans l'appareil psyché-soma. Au-delà et en deçà de la langue, ces tentatives ont parfois le pouvoir de mettre en branle les fondations subjectives, impliquant dans certains contextes psychiques des formations psychopathologiques conséquentes. « Une série de métamorphoses continues » s'engage alors chez le sujet par « le passage d'un langage dans un autre » (Benjamin, 2000, 157) mais également au-delà, par le biais de tout ce que le déplacement génère comme modalités traductives diverses. De la même manière que la langue se recrée avec la traduction (Benjamin, 2011, 109-137), les variations subjectives et pulsionnelles s'avèrent consubstantielles à la condition d'exilé.

Les hypothèses avancées sur les liens entre déplacement et maternité nous amènent à songer que le déplacement d'un territoire à un autre produit des effets inédits sur l'économie inconsciente de la femme, dont l'impact sur la réalité corporelle peut s'avérer puissant et déstabilisant. La femme en état de déplacement semble parfois convoquée par des modalités traductives qui se manifestent en acte, muées par l'entrée précipitée dans la maternité.

Quand des impasses à la traduction sont présentes, des *refusements*[18] liés aux restes enkystés intraduisibles émergent par le biais du symptôme. Ces empêchements à la traduction vont se donner à entendre tout particulièrement dans ce contexte de grossesse advenue peu après un déplacement territorial, et parfois conduire le sujet à consulter un thérapeute.[19] C'est par les seuls effets de la parole déployés à l'occasion des entretiens cliniques, que le travail élaboratif instauré par le lien transférentiel pourra se développer. L'engagement dans des processus de traduction qui se rellent au au langage aura la capacité de fluidifier les mouvements psychiques et les remettre dans une circulation signifiante pour le sujet. Ainsi favorisés, les mouvements subjectifs ne seront plus seulement actés mais symbolisés et le sujet sera en mesure de s'approprier le monde du sensible au sein duquel il est immergé.

A partir des matériaux psychiques remis en circulation par la parole, et de l'exploration des signifiants laissés dans le creux de la langue par le patient, l'analyste ou le psychothérapeute aidera à la traduction, sans précipiter les tentatives singulières mises en œuvre par le sujet lui-même.

C'est parce que le déplacement produit de l'écart, de la différence, que des innovations subjectives peuvent se produire. Car la traduction pose fondamentalement la question de l'interstice et de la chute. C'est avec cet écart que travaille aussi l'analyste, celui dont la tâche s'apparente à celle du traducteur, nécessaire opérateur qui interprète les dires du sujet en rendant possible « le passage d'une rive à une autre de ce qui était resté exclu psychiquement » (Pestre, 2011, 29).

La clinique de l'exil qui s'intéresse aux populations migrantes invite les cliniciens et les analystes à être innovant dans leurs pratiques afin que le sujet puisse être en capacité de s'ajuster à ses modalités traductives pour ainsi habiter un nouveau lieu, et étré en mesure de se créer une demeure propre.

Références bibliographiques

Altounian J. *L'intraduisible, Deuil, Mémoire, transmission.* Paris : Dunod, Coll. « Psychismes », 2005.

Assoun P.-L. *Psychanalyse.* Paris : PUF, Coll. Premier cycle, 1997.

Benjamin W. (1923). « La tâche du traducteur ». *Expérience et pauvreté.* Paris : Petite Bibliothèque Payot, Paris, 2011. 109–137.

Benjamin W. (1916). "Sur le langage en général et sur le langage humain en particulier". *Oeuvres I.* París : Gallimard, coll. Folio, 2000.

Bydlowski M. *La dette de vie, Itinéraire psychanaytique de la maternité.* Paris : PUF, 1997.

Deleuze G. *Qu'est-ce que la philosophie ?* Paris : Ed. de Minuit, 1991.

Faure-Pragier S. « Stérilité féminine. Aspects psychiques des stérilités féminines ». *Dictionnaire du corps.* Ed. M. Mzrzano, Paris : PUF, 2007. 903–906.

Freud S. (1917). « Sur les transpositions de pulsions plus particulièrement dans l'érotisme anal ». *La vie sexuelle*, Paris : PUF, 1997.

Freud S. « Lettre 52 à Fliess ». *Lettres à Wilhelm Fliess*, 1887–1904. Paris : PUF, 2007.

Greil AL. "Infertility and Psychological Distress: a Critical Review of the Litterature". *Soc Sci Med* 1977; 45:1679–1704.

Kristeva J. « L'Autre langue, ou traduire le sensible ». *l'Infini* 57, printemps 1997.

Kulu, H. "Migration and Fertility: Competing Hypotheses Re-examined," *European Journal of Population* 21 (2005). 51–87.

Michaud G. « Psychanalyse et traduction: voies de traverse ». *Traduction, terminologie, rédaction* 11, n° 2 (1998). 9–37. Consultable sur www.erudit.org.

Oustinoff M. *La traduction.* Paris : PUF, coll. Que sais-je, 2003. 64.

Peraldi F. « Psychanalyse et traduction ». *Meta : journal des traducteurs,* 27:1, mars 1982. 9–25.

Pestre E. "Maternidade do exílio. Quando o deslocamento favorece a fertilidade" (trad. Portuguais F. Baptista). *Revista Agora, Instituto de psicología de UFRJ*, (à paraître 2013).

Pestre E. « Expérience, traduction et modernité ». Préface à *Expérience et pauvreté*. Benjamin W. Paris : Petite Bibliothèque Payot, 2011.

Stoléru & al. « Psychological characteristics of infertile patients: discriminating etiological factors from reactive changes ». *J. Psychosom Obstet Gynaecol* 17 (1996) : 103–118.

Notes

1 Glasson-Deschaumes G., intervention orale à l'occasion de la synthèse de la conférence « Traduction et innovation. Une passerelle entre les sciences et les humanités », 13–15 déc. 2012.

2 Cette recherche intitulée : « Les effets subjectifs de l'exil chez les femmes enceintes en situation de précarité», s'est déroulée en 2009, à Buenos-Aires (Argentine). Elle a été réalisée en collaboration avec le CRPMS (Centre de Recherches Médecine Psychanalyse et Société, EAD 3522), l'équipe du service de santé mentale de l'hôpital Ramon Sarda (Pr. S. Naddeo), la direction de l'établissement (Pr E. Andina) et l'Université de Psychologie de Buenos-Aires (UBA). La population accueillie au sein de cette maternité publique était généralement en situation de grande précarité (les femmes vivaient dans logements insalubres, des bidonvilles de la ville de Buenos Aires ou ses alentours). Plus de 40% des femmes accueillies étaient étrangères, généralement issues des pays limitrophes de l'Argentine (Bolivie, Paraguay, etc.) Les femmes interviewées s'exprimaient toutes en espagnol, même si leurs langues premières étaient parfois des dialectes régionaux (quechua, guarani). Nous avons interviewé ces femmes en espagnol à partir d'un guide d'entretien de recherches essentiellement basé sur leur vécu subjectif de grossesse en terre étrangère.

3 Ce total représente plus de la moitié des quarante femmes interviewées.

4 Il s'agit de 42%, 18 femmes sur 40 la première année, et 9/40 la seconde année.

5 Au-delà des situations conjugales diverses, si la contraception s'avère être peu utilisée par les femmes interviewées qui pratiquent, pour beaucoup, la contraception « naturelle », c'est la temporalité en jeu dans le déclenchement gestatif qu'il nous intéresse ici d'explorer.

6 Pestre E., "Maternidade do exílio. Quando o deslocamento favorece a fertilidade" (trad. Portuguais Baptista F.), *Revista Agora*, Instituto de psicología de UFRJ, (à paraître 2014).

7 Le démographe anglais Hill Kulu (Kulu, H., 2005, "Migration and fertility: competing hypotheses re-examined", *European Journal of Population*, 21: 51–87), a par exemple montré que les taux de fécondité apparaissaient plus élevés après changement de lieu de résidence. Cependant, cet auteur démontre que les études portant sur ce thème sont divergentes. Soulignons également qu'elles s'inscrivent pour la majorité d'entre elles dans le cadre d'études démographiques, ethniques, souvent empreintes d'une dimension néo-malthusienne de la fécondité, qui prône des restrictions démographiques. Ce sont finalement les travaux des *migrations studies* et *gender studies* portant sur la thématique « migration et sexualité » qui

s'avèrent être, à notre sens, les plus pertinents. Pourtant là encore le paradigme psychanalytique reste peu exploité.

8 *Dictionnaire TLFI*, Cnrtl, CRNRS Edition, http://www.cnrtl.fr

9 Huitième édition du dictionnaire de l'Académie française (CNRS / ATILF) version électronique: http://atilf.atilf.fr / academie.htm

10 Expression qui signifie se laisser séduire et se retrouver enceinte.

11 La patiente précisa: "j'avais un utérus trop petit". Diverses analyses médicales auraient conclu à une hypoplasie utérine relativement grave, d'après le dossier médical que j'ai consulté. Cependant guère plus d'éléments y étaient mentionnés, les analyses n'ayant pas été adjointes au dossier médical.

12 Depuis les années 1970 d'importantes études cliniques ont proposé des liens entre infertilité et psychisme à partir de paradigmes différents, l'auteur Greil en propose une revue : Greil AL, (1977), « Infertility and psychological distress: a critical review of the litterature », *Soc Sci Med* 1977; 45:1679–1704. On citera parmi ces travaux actuels : Bydlowski M. (1997), Stoléru & al : « Psychological characteristics of infertile patients: discriminating etiological factors from reactive changes », *J. Psychosom Obstet Gynaecol* 1996; 17:103–118, Faure-Pragier S. (2007).

13 Freud S., Lettre 52 à Fliess (06/12/96), *Lettres à Wilhelm Fliess*, 1887–1904, PUF, « Bibliothèque de psychanalyse », Paris, 2007.

14 Patrie est dérivée de *pater*, père et signifie "pays où l'on est né", Rey A. (sous la dir. de) *Le grand Robert de la langue française,* Dictionnaire Le Robert, Paris, 2001, p.353.

15 Monique Bydlowski a démontré le double versant pré-odipien et oedipien du désir d'enfant et du processus de maternité dans ses écrits, notamment dans Bydlowski M., *La dette de vie, Itinéraire psychanaytique de la maternité,* PUF, Le fil rouge, Paris, 1997.

16 Laplanche J., « Entretien avec », par Danon G. et Lauru D., *Enfance & Psy*, Érès

17 Le droit du sol en Argentine amène les enfants nés sur son territoire à accéder de fait à la nationalité du pays.

18 Le terme de « refusement » employé par Janine Altounian pour traduire le terme « Versagung » semble ici tout à fait opportun. Cons. Altounian J., « Traduire ce qui n'a pu se dire », conférence au colloque « Traduction et innovation. Une passerelle entre les sciences et les humanités », 13–15 déc. 2012

19 Ceci lorsque les consultations avec un clinicien sont facilitées comme c'est le cas au sein de la maternité Ramon Sarda où l'équipe de santé mentale est compose d'une équipe de plus de vingt de psychologues qui se propose de rencontrer les patients au sein de l'hôpital.

La traduction de la psychanalyse en cinghalais : simple intérêt ou véritable défi?

Elizabeth Kaluaratchige

Résumé

Traduire Lacan en cinghalais incite à réfléchir sur la traduction de la psychanalyse en langues indiennes. Pourquoi traduire directement du français les textes déjà traduits de l'anglais ? Comment introduire le mot juste dans le vocabulaire psychanalytique cinghalais dérivé des concepts hindouistes et bouddhiques ? La traduction de l'universel inconscient, au-delà d'un modèle européen ou indien, a besoin d'être soutenue par des recherches en anthropologie psychanalytique.

Mots clés : psychanalyse, Freud, Lacan, traduction en cinghalais, bouddhisme, hindouisme, anthropologie psychanalytique

Abstract

Translating Lacan's writings into Sinhala encourages us to think about Indian translations of psychoanalysis. Why should we translate directly from French a text already translated from English? How to introduce an exact equivalent of the original term to the sinhala psychoanalytic vocabulary dérived from Hindu and Buddhist concepts? Beyond European or Indian model, translation of universal unconscious will need to be supported by researches in psychoanalytic anthropology.

Keywords: psychoanalysis, Freud, Lacan, translation in Sinhala, Buddhism, Hinduism, psychoanalytic anthropology

Introduction

Après la réception d'une statuette de Vishnou offerte par Girindrashekhar Bose, de la part de la Société psychanalytique indienne, Freud écrit dans son carnet intime: « La statuette est charmante et je lui ai donné la place d'honneur sur mon bureau. Aussi longtemps que je vivrai, elle gardera présentes à mon esprit les fières conquêtes que la psychanalyse a réalisées dans les pays étrangers, et les sentiments positifs qu'elle m'a valu, au moins de la part de quelques-uns de mes contemporains » (Freud, 1929–1939, 114). Freud est heureux d'avoir réussi une expansion de la science de l'inconscient, par une « conquête » et d'avoir reçu un signe de reconnaissance de la part du monde indien. C'est à partir de ces paroles freudiennes que nous souhaiterions réfléchir à notre problématique. La psychanalyse « inventée » par Freud, un juif « athée », écrite en allemand et reprise par Lacan et les post-freudiens en français et en anglais, restera-t-elle toujours étrangère au monde indien ? Point de question plus élémentaire, ni plus fondamentale qui survient à un traducteur de langue indienne, dès qu'il pense à traduire les sciences sociales ou psychologiques germées en Europe. Nos interrogations sur cette question seront abordées à partir d'une étude de cas ; un projet de traduction de la psychanalyse en cinghalais, la langue de la communauté cinghalaise du Sri Lanka. Cette langue, utilisée dans les études universitaires et dans les publications littéraires, philosophiques et scientifiques, a des racines remontant jusqu'aux S*anskrit* et *pali*, les langues anciennes de la culture indienne.[1] Comment rendre la psychanalyse saisissable par une langue proche et familière au lecteur cinghalais sans déformer ni « indianiser » le sens véhiculé par la théorie et la clinique ? Il est évident que pour une chercheuse en psychanalyse opérant dans deux sphères culturelles, il s'agit d'un *challenge* inévitable.

Le retour à Freud et à Lacan

Il n'existe aucune traduction cinghalaise d'une œuvre psychanalytique faite directement de l'allemand et du français, sauf une traduction de *Introduction à la psychanalyse* faite par P. Kodikara, à partir de la traduction russe, et quelques études, essais et commentaires sur la psychanalyse. Parmi les plus récents on peut mentionner *La psychopathologie* (1996) de D.S. Ranawaka et G. Hapuaratchi, *Councelling* (2003) de R.M. Jayatunga, *L'hypnothérapie* (2009) de R.M. Jayatunga et la traduction de N. Malagoda, du livre de Rachel Baker *Sigmund Freud for Every Body* (2003) et notre propre publication *Freud, Lacan et Dolto : l'image et le réel caché* (1998). Notre projet de traduction directe des œuvres psychanalytiques sera inaugural. De futurs collaborateurs se sont déjà fait connaître, ce qui permettra d'éviter la solitude dans notre travail de traduction. Notre projet d'une traduction complète des œuvres freudiennes ou lacaniennes doit en conséquence passer par la formation d'une équipe de traducteurs ayant de l'intérêt pour la psychanalyse et la maîtrise suffisante du cinghalais, français et allemand. Notre démarche est de commencer par quelques œuvres freudiennes telles que *Au-delà du principe de plaisir* (*Jenseits des Lustprinzips* (1920) de Freud. La deuxième étape sera *Freud et les sciences sociales* de P.-L. Assoun. Enfin, la troisième sera consacrée au Séminaire *La formation de l'inconscient* de Lacan. Ce projet sera complété d'une « édition critique », ouvrant sur un débat à partir des colloques et séminaires qui auront lieu à l'occasion des sorties de ces publications. Les raisons de cette procédure seront traitées dans cet article sous les thèmes suivants : « La traduction et les recherches », « L'intérêt de l'anthropologie psychanalytique », « Pourquoi traduire les recherches actuelles en France ? » et « Traduction et lacanisme ».

Notre chantier de traductions vise en effet les lecteurs, soit les universitaires, connaisseurs des traductions anglaises, soit les « profanes », lecteurs des commentaires cingalais faits principalement à partir des textes anglais. On pourrait s'interroger alors sur l'intérêt de traduire les textes de Freud, de Lacan et les recherches en psychanalyse menées en France actuellement. On pourrait nommer ce projet *Un retour à Freud et à Lacan dans sa dynamique temporelle en France*. Ce projet se caractérise par l'union de l'autonomie et de l'hétéronomie dans la traduction y compris pour la pré-analyse des textes au sens où l'entend A. Berman (Berman, 1995, 76). Il s'agit également d'un pas nécessaire pour sortir la psychanalyse de la sphère littéraire et philosophique cinghalaise et pour y introduire la clinique du symptôme et du social. En effet, c'est l'intérêt scientifique de ce travail qui à maints égards semble constituer le défi. Nous pensons que la traduction directe de la langue d'origine—de l'allemand pour Freud, du français pour Lacan et les publications récentes—à une langue indienne devrait être « impérative » pour le succès des échanges scientifiques entre ces deux mondes. Selon l'adage de Freud, si l'exemple est la chose même, ce projet nous permettra-t-il d'aborder la vaste question de la traduction de la psychanalyse en Asie ?

Le désir de traduction chez le psychanalyste vise un transfert vers le lecteur, mais il vise finalement une situation transférentielle entre Freud et le lecteur ; un retour aux racines mêmes de la pratique analytique. Le transfert déjà, en un sens très général « implique un déploiement de valeur, de droit, d'entité plutôt qu'un déploiement matériel d'objets » (Laplanche, Pontalis, 1967, 492). *A priori*, dégager les points faibles des traductions existantes permettra de lever, en premier lieu, non seulement les barrières de la langue à la compréhension, mais aussi les obstacles à l'entente entre le texte, l'auteur, sa science et le lecteur. Le traducteur, au sens étymologique du terme, *traducere* du latin, *trans* (à travers) et *duco* (conduire), nous fait penser à un passeur ; le traducteur pourra passer la parole freudienne à travers le texte traduit, qui a son tour devient l'*avatar* freudien face au lecteur. Dans ce cas, si on accepte l'idée de W. Benjamin selon laquelle « la version interlinéaire du texte sacré est le prototype ou l'idéal de toute traduction », la traduction de nos textes pourra s'éloigner plus ou moins de cet idéal laissant une marge de liberté au traducteur (W. Benjamin, 2011, 137). Notre but est ainsi de rester « sourcière » (source-oriented),—sans être arrogant et violent refusant tout compromis avec la langue cible—avec une touche nécessaire pour assouplir et oser davantage respecter le lecteur. Nous éviterons ainsi l'adaptation et la « naturalisation » des œuvres freudiennes ou lacaniennes permettant aux futurs chercheurs et praticiens cinghalais de mener leurs recherches et rédiger leurs propres textes sans trahir la théorie ni la pratique psychanalytique.

Cependant, dans la pratique le traducteur est avisé que, comme le note M. de Launay, à l'instar d'un déménageur qui abandonne quelques éléments de mobilier, la traduction fait perdre en quelque sorte quelque chose de l'original. Autrement dit, vu « sous l'angle à la fois spatial et substantiel, l'opération de traduction semble toujours vouée à l'échec » (M de Launay, 2006, 39). Sans devenir un « traître », le traducteur, en dépit de sa rigueur, trahit malgré lui le sens « exact » que l'auteur voudrait transmettre. En parlant des traductions françaises, Lacan ajoute : « Je vous laisse à juger quelle sorte de maléfice il faut admettre dans le sort fait aux textes de Freud en français, si l'on refuse à croire que les traducteurs se soient donné le mot pour les rendre incompréhensibles, et je ne parle pas de ce qu'ajoute à cet effet l'extinction complète de la vivacité de son style » (Lacan, 1954, 387).

Peut-on dire autant du cas des traductions cinghalaises ? Ces dernières seraient-elles aussi affectées d'une « tare originaire » ou bien de leurs « secondarités » en tant que textes traduits ? On sait que la critique et la traduction vont structurellement ensemble. Elles contribuent à enrichir la langue et la littérature « traduisantes » (A.Berman, 1995, 42). En effet par-delà l'hommage qu'on pourrait rendre aux lexicographes et aux commentateurs pionniers du pays, on peut noter à quel point les traductions cinghalaises de concepts ont rendu « incompréhensibles », enfin presque, la science de l'inconscient. La traduction à partir de l'original serait-il « un mythe cachant la frayeur devant la langue cible et sa nudité échappant entre les doigts de ceux qui traduisent » comme le note P. de Oliveira (Oliveira, 2010, 22). Il apparaît nécessaire au traducteur d'abandonner son vouloir « tout traduire » ou rendre tout le texte au lecteur (Laplanche, Bourguignons, Cotet, Robert, 1989, 15), sans pour autant négliger les termes et les styles des textes d'origine et introduire une langue proche des lecteurs de la langue cible. La traduction directe des œuvres originales qu'on envisage servirait en premier lieu de nouvelle boussole aux lecteurs cinghalais du 21e siècle, dans la préhension de la science psychanalytique, de ses origines jusqu'aux développements plus récents. Pour autant, notre projet de traduction ne prétend en rien mettre un point final aux traductions du passé ni de l'avenir. Il ne sera qu'une incitation aux traducteurs et aux éditeurs de progresser vers les traductions, de la langue d'origine à la langue visée, évitant l'alternative de seconde main qui risque d'introduire les déformations à la science de l'inconscient.

Inventer ou reformuler les « mots » ?

En premier lieu, le souci du traducteur de Freud est de trouver les termes ou les concepts pour harmoniser et articuler la rigueur du vocabulaire freudien en sa scientificité et sa souplesse, sans pour autant détruire le vocabulaire psychologique de la langue d'arrivée. Il est toujours soumis à la langue déjà utilisée dans les traductions d'antan, qui semble faire barrage à un véritable débat théorique et clinique. Ainsi souhaitons-nous que les jeunes lecteurs enthousiastes, qu'ils soient familiers ou non de la psychanalyse, puissent la ressaisir en cinghalais à partir du lexique en vigueur pour avancer vers les termes introduits par la nouvelle traduction.

Comme le note W. Benjamin, « la fidélité dans la traduction du mot individuellement ne peut presque jamais restituer entièrement le sens qu'il a dans l'original ». Le tissage doit se faire à partir non seulement de la littéralité mais aussi du sens (Benjamin, 2011, 129). Quels sont alors les véritables défis que rencontre un nouveau traducteur cinghalais ? Citons pour exemple, (*Das*) *Unbewusste* traduit dans les lexiques par le mot *aviññānaya*. Ce terme relève de la conception bouddhique de l'inconscient. Il élimine en quelque sorte le facteur sexuel de l'inconscient freudien, et le sens lacanien du langage dans le fait inconscient. Le terme est en revanche plus proche du concept inconscient de Jung. Si nous voulons garder ce terme *aviññānaya*, il serait prudent d'aborder la différence à partir d'un travail scientifique. Ouvrir un débat scientifique sur cette question facilitera la restitution du sens freudien de l'inconscient sans introduire un mot nouveau. Pourquoi ne pas traduire notre article écrit en français sur le freudisme et le jungisme (Kaluaratchige, 2011a)? Au contraire, certains concepts exigent des mots nouveaux incitant le traducteur à retravailler les significations freudiennes plus attentivement. Comment chercher et trouver le mot « juste » pour traduire un tel terme ou un tel concept ? Le concept *Es* est traduit en cinghalais *Id*. Emprunté aux traductions anglaises, le terme *Id* a été utilisé par les créateurs de lexiques, sans aucun effort d'introduire un mot proprement cinghalais. On aurait pu, nous semble-t-il, introduire le mot *eka* du sanskrit pour désigner le *Es* freudien. Ce n'est pas sans raison que nous avons introduit le mot cinghalais *eka* pour le rendre plus compréhensible et pour être plus fidèle au sens que Freud a voulu lui accorder en utilisant un terme simple tel que *Es*. *Id* vient de l'anglais ancien et classique remontant aux sources latines. Les traductions anglaises ont négligé le terme *it*, et trahit en quelque sorte, le sens freudien du terme. En effet la langue allemande que Freud utilise a sa spécificité d'être une langue « populaire »,[2] que les traductions anglaises ont perdue la plupart de temps en cours de route. Il n'est pas étonnant que les traductions cinghalaises de deuxième main portent ainsi en elles les mêmes séquelles. D'après G.-A. Goldschmidt, les gens peuvent lire Freud en allemand, à condition de savoir lire, mais les traductions françaises présupposent une certaine

« initiation » linguistique (Goldschmidt, 2006, 38). Ce propos, nous semble-t-il, est aussi valable pour les traductions cinghalaises.

Le *Ich* de Freud a rencontré un autre destin en cinghalais. Il est traduit avec le terme *Ahama*, un terme tiré de la philosophie bouddhique,[3] désignant une entité d'un soi existant, en tant qu'aggloméрat de cinq agrégats. Autrement dit, *Aham* introduit une conception bouddhique qui déforme le concept du moi freudien, portant en lui une part inconsciente et une autre consciente. De surcroît, ce terme alourdit le *Ich*, terme simple et populaire que Freud utilise pour expliquer le développement du moi à partir du *ça* et des couches identificatoires. Le moi freudien est loin d'être un moi qui pourrait disparaître et se désagréger, comme le *Ahama* ou le soi de la pensée bouddhique. Notre effort était dès le début de trouver les mots cinghalais les plus simples, les plus proches de *Es* et *Ich* allemands. Introduire dans nos traductions, le terme *eka* à la place de *Id,* et *mama* (je en cinghalais) *y(a)* (cette lettre introduit le sens d'une instance) à la place de *Ahama* rencontre une autre problématique. Nous avons alors proposé notre néologisme, sans remplacer brutalement ces termes pour le lecteur déjà habitué à entendre les termes anciens, mais en plaçant le mot nouveau entre parenthèse ou à côté du mot ancien. Le terme entre parenthèse réveille déjà chez le lecteur une autre manière de saisir ce concept.

La traduction et les recherches

On sait que c'est dans la langue allemande que la science de l'inconscient est née et se développe. Freud, « inventeur de langue » (Laplanche, 1991, 402), lance lui-même des investigations à travers la grammaire, la littérature, la mythologie et les sciences. Pour être sûr d'introduire le terme le plus pertinent pour désigner ou pour comprendre tel ou tel phénomène psychique, il étudie les textes, comme dans le cas de *Unheimlich* le texte de E. T. A. Hoffmann, et des expressions des langues étrangères (Freud, 1919). La traduction des processus psychiques et des concepts métapsychologiques exige, nous semble-t-il, un véritable travail de recherche. La raison principale de la traduction de *Au-delà du principe de plaisir* concerne l'introduction à la métapsychologie, dans le « continuum des créations des concepts freudiens » qui se situent depuis les phrases du texte jusqu'aux autres textes antérieurs, y compris « l'œuvre dans son entièreté et sa diachronie » (Laplanche, 1991, 402). C'est à partir du principe de *Nirvãna* que nous voudrions situer les recherches nécessaires venant faire écho dans notre projet de traduction. Le principe de *Nirvãna* comme le dit Lacan, entre dans la métapsychologie et dans le vocabulaire de la psychanalyse en tant que l'apogée de la théorie freudienne (Lacan, 1954–1955, 131). Pour la première fois, un terme religieux (bouddhique), en passant par la physiologie, nomme une instance de la métapsychologie freudienne, la discipline entre la physique, la métaphysique et la psychologie (Freud, 1937, 240). Dans son *Au-delà du principe de plaisir,* Freud ajoute qu'il emprunte le terme « principe » de *Nirvãna* à Barbara Low (Freud, 1920, 51 ; 1924, 287), un concept physiologique utilisé pour expliquer le principe qui pousse l'homme vers le repos, vers la mort, pour atteindre l'inanimé, le degré zéro de tension. Il étudie la théorie quantitativiste de Fechner depuis ses débuts, déjà dans *Esquisse* (1895), et trouve le lien et la différence entre « une donnée physique et un phénomène psychique » (Assoun, 1981, 151). La discussion que Freud a menée avec le traducteur japonais témoigne de l'influence du bouddhisme dans la réflexion freudienne (Freud, 1929–1939, XXIII, 5). Mais ces deux concepts, le *Nirvãna* et le principe de *Nirvãna*, l'un bouddhique, l'autre psychanalytique, apparemment contradictoires, se situent en fait sur deux niveaux différents dans leurs fondements théoriques aussi bien que dans leurs pratiques.[4] Freud assimile le roc de la pratique analytique, - la résistance des patients à la guérison-, à la soumission au principe de *Nirvãna,* tandis que le Bouddha suggère l'aspiration *nirvãnique,* comme solution à la souffrance (Rahula, 1961). La traduction du terme « le principe de *Nirvãna* » renvoie automatiquement chez un lecteur bouddhiste, à la conception bouddhique du *Nirvãna.* C'est au traducteur d'introduire l'historique et la signification de ce terme métapsychologique, en note de bas de page et dans un glossaire commenté.

Citons encore pour exemple le terme *Mutterleibphantaisie,* le fantasme du retour, régi par le principe de *Nirvãna. Leib* est un terme qui crée des confusions de sens chez les traducteurs anglais. *Mutterleib* est traduit le plus souvent en *maternal womb* à la place de *maternal bossom.* Les traducteurs français rencontrent une problématique spécifique à la langue française. Dans la plupart des traductions françaises, *Mutterleib* est présent en tant que sein maternel. Comme le note Lacan, la langue française crée en effet une confusion entre le sein, cet objet *a* qui chute entre l'enfant et la mère, et le giron maternel auquel le sujet voudrait faire le retour. Il ne s'agit pas non plus du ventre maternel qui renvoie à une conception biologique. Le *Mutterleib* chez Freud n'est pas un concept proprement biologique telle que la matrice, mais il désigne un vécu dans l'infantile, comme « la masse des sensations » (Freud, 1930, 8). Quant à nous, nous pourrons traduire *Mutterleib* par le *mavthurula,* plus proche du terme *Leib* au sens de giron, non pas par mav*kusa, mavgeba* désignant le ventre ou utérus, pour rester fidèle au sens freudien du mot composé *Mutterleibphantaisie,* « le fantasme de retour au giron maternel », qui ne sera pas le même que le retour au ventre maternel. On peut s'interroger avec J. Laplanche, A. Bourguignons, P. Cotet et F. Robert, sur le questionnement : « De quel droit substituer l'explication à l'explication ? ». Ces derniers pensent qu'il sera préférable d'ajouter, sans apporter des déformations aux textes, « les notices, les notes réduites au minimum », qui « comprennent, volontairement, aucun commentaire de fond, rapprochement de textes, historiques des concepts etc. » (Bourguignons, Cotet, Laplanche, Robert, 1989, 15; 66). En effet, Laplanche admire malgré quelques réserves, *le Strachey model,* pour avoir réalisé une édition critique sans *misinterpretations* (Laplanche, 1991,401). Nous pensons situer notre projet entre *Strachey model* et le modèle récent d'édition critique française.[5]

L'universel inconscient : l'intérêt anthropologico psychanalytique

On sait que Freud renvoie ses concepts psychanalytiques à un phénomène « universel inconscient », à ce savoir originaire existant déjà chez l'enfant avant même d'apprendre sa langue, et à une symbolique persistante, qui est la même chez tous les peuples, en dépit des variétés des langues et des cultures (Freud, 1939, 238). C'est par cette position freudienne que notre chantier de traduction prend une dimension plus large : aller au-delà de la traduction de textes psychanalytiques. Si la psychanalyse aborde l'universel inconscient, elle traiterait des phénomènes qui échappent aux langues ; c'est la raison par laquelle, la traduction pourrait être épaulée par l'anthropologie psychanalytique.[6] La langue de l'inconscient, ce qui échappe à la langue porte en elle, le langage universel ou la langue du refoulé (Kaluaratchige, 2014). Freud ajoute qu' « En réalité, on n'a perçu, de la symphonie du devenir universel, que la partie chantée par la civilisation, mais on est resté sourd à la mélodie des instincts, malgré son intensité primitive » (Freud, 1904,149). Freud renvoie à la phylogenèse en liaison avec le complexe parental, le refoulement originaire et le surmoi remontant vers l'ancêtre originaire (Freud, 1923, 278–280). Les langues sont donc pas un même « langage », (la langue du mythe de Babel), fragmenté en une multiplicité des langues portant en lui, ce qui est compréhensible, « ce même » qui passe autrement de langue en langue ? (Goldschmidt, 2006, 18–19). Une traduction porte-t-elle avec elle un fragment du refoulé du collectif à la lumière pour démasquer ce qui cache les mythes ?

On sait que chaque langue est articulée à une forme de pensée du peuple qui la parle, donc la pensée de l'individu est faite de représentations, mythologies et religions. Contrairement à Jung qui pense que les mythes font fonctionner dans le réel les créations endopsychiques et les projections vivantes, Freud trouve l'universel inconscient caché derrière le mythe que la psychanalyse peut démasquer (Assoun, 2003). La psychanalyse, à partir des études de cultures, met en relief la structure mythique de la *Kultur* au sens large du terme que Freud utilise. La « langue » intervient comme illustration de la coutume et complément du mythe (au sens cerné) : c'est dire que pour Freud, la *Sprache* est tout d'abord un concept de la *Kulturtheorie*, avant d'être objet de la linguistique (Assoun, 2008, 49). L'infantile est ainsi renvoyé, par la psychanalyse, à la préhistoire de la culture humaine. Nous pourrons saisir ces traces que l'enfant porte comme « déjà là », qui peuvent être relevées dans la clinique, et aussi dans les mythes, légendes, traditions et coutumes laissant passer « entre les lignes ». En deçà des mots, des paroles et des mécanismes conscients et préconscients, on peut démasquer les phénomènes inconscients universels.

Freud parle de la transposition, *übertragung*, de la conception psychanalytique acquise par le rêve aux produits de l'imagination populaire comme les mythes. La mythologie est l'idéologie du rite et il met en scène l'ontogénétique et la phylogénétique (Assoun, 2003, 174). Quand Eduardo Weiss, psychanalyste italien traduit dans sa langue *L'interprétation des rêves*, *Traumdeutung,* il remplace un certain nombre de rêves de Freud par les siens propres. Freud approuve cette démarche et lui écrit : « la manière dont vous traduisez rêves et actes manqués en remplaçant les exemples par des exemples qui vous sont propres, est naturellement la seule exacte. Malheureusement, je n'ai pas la garantie que ce procédé sera suivi dans les autres traductions ... » (Freud, Weiss, 1920). Or, nous proposons un exemple de la mythologie de la communauté cinghalaise, qui nous permet de situer le complexe d'Œdipe dans l'enveloppe culturelle cinghalaise. Ce mythe fait surgir les concepts tels que le parricide, l'interdit de l'inceste et la fonction paternelle. Le fait inconscient qu'on voudrait traduire toucherait la mythologie et les légendes propres à la culture de la langue visée. Cela facilitera au lecteur l'entrée dans le vif du sujet, le parricide.

Dans le mythe d'origine de la communauté cinghalaise, le prince *Sinha ba* (qui a les bras d'un lion) est le fils d'une femme et d'un lion. Le lion emprisonne sa femme et ses enfants dans une grotte et ramène de quoi nourrir la famille. *Sinha Ba,* frustré par la puissance paternelle, profite de l'absence du père-lion pour ouvrir la porte de la grotte et prend son envol en libérant sa mère et sa sœur. *Sinha ba* retourne au royaume de sa mère et prend comme épouse sa sœur. Selon la perspective psychanalytique, ce mythe est un rêve de la communauté cinghalaise ayant un rapport à la vérité historique de l'inconscient. Le mythe de *Sinha Ba* est masqué, du moins dans la communauté cinghalaise, sous forme d'histoire d'un amour paternel ou de la bravoure d'un fils héros. Notre travail servirait à démasquer l'universel du complexe paternel et du désir de l'inceste. Il importe de noter que, dans ce mythe, le fils retourne au royaume de sa mère et épouse sa sœur. Le fils tue le père-lion qui vient dévaster le royaume. A la différence du mythe d'Œdipe, ce mythe épargne au fils un mariage avec la mère et lui permet de prendre sa sœur comme épouse; la transgression de l'interdit de l'inceste serait ainsi adoucie dans le mythe cinghalais. Fidèle à Freud, nous évitons une étude du mythe en son entier. Par les vignettes, on pourra ressaisir le mythe scientifique freudien du père originaire, *Urvater* (Freud, 1913a), le désir et l'interdit d'inceste. Il nous servira ainsi à aborder l'Œdipe qui peut être tout à fait « normal » dans les deux sens : d'une part en tant que « normalisant », et d'autre part, en tant que « dénormalisant » (son effet névrosant par exemple) (Lacan, 1957–1958, 168).

Pourquoi traduire les recherches actuelles en France ?

La deuxième étape de notre projet concerne la traduction des textes écrits récemment en français. Le premier *Freud et les sciences sociales* (2008) de P.-L. Assoun sera traduit afin d'ouvrir un débat sur l'universel inconscient dans la diversité culturelle et sur le thème du symptôme dans le social. C'est ainsi que nous souhaitons poursuivre notre hypothèse que la traduction de la psychanalyse est synonyme de recherche fondée sur des expériences cliniques et des objets sociaux. Certains thèmes seront privilégiés dans ce chantier de recherches. Par exemple comprendre le névrosé dans l'individuel et le collectif permet de saisir la figure paternelle du contexte cinghalais. Penser entre les langues, c'est donc se situer aussi entre la philologie et la philosophie. « Les cultures comme les langues sont des grammaires », écrit H. Wismann. Si le traducteur cesse d'être ennemi d'une autre (langue ou culture), « la quête de l'altérité » deviendra une ressource (H. Wismann, 2012, 48–52). Cette approche permettra de rencontrer « l'anti-paternel » des promoteurs et des passionnés du sentiment océanique et de la spiritualité indienne (Kaluaratchige, 2008). En revanche, c'est à partir d'un débat autour de nos recherches sur le Bouddha-le-Père, *Budu piya* cinghalais (Kaluaratchige, 2011b), que nous pourrons avancer vers les recherches sur ce sujet avec la collaboration des chercheurs cinghalais. Le désir de traduire les textes sur le complexe paternel vient-t-il de cette « part échappée », ce qui « traverse les langues » selon les termes de Goldschmidt ? Le cinghalais attend-il que la traduction parle de ce qu'il n'a pas voulu « énoncer » ou ce qu'on a voulu masquer jusqu'à maintenant ? L'expérience de deux univers est-elle éclairante et profitable (Goldschmidt, 2006, 14, 211)? Le père refoulé ressortirait de nouveau chez les lecteurs cinghalais, sous condition de le penser à partir non seulement des textes traduits mais aussi des mythes, légendes, coutumes et des formes de symptômes propres au pays. Pour Freud, « un universel de la culture qui répond à un besoin anthropologique structurel, celui-ci ne vaut pas pour tous et ne garantit pas à tous le même statut » (Assoun, 2013, 21). Les symptômes parlent en effet des failles dans le processus culturel dans la singularité du sujet. Dans un pays où la psychanalyse n'entre pas encore dans le cadre de la clinique, ce sont le monde éducatif, le « councelling », l'anthropologie et la littérature qui sont concernés par la clinique du social. Cordélia dont parle Freud est-elle la seule qui a déclaré son funeste amour au père? Iphigénie était-elle la seule qui s'est sacrifiée pour sauver le royaume du père ? Nous essayons de saisir la question de l'Œdipe au féminin, par exemple dans les mythes tels que *Vihara* de la tradition cinghalaise, qui pourrait témoigner du sacrifice de la fille pour sauver le royaume du père ? (Kaluaratchige, 2010). Pénélope dont parle Freud lorsqu'il traite du travail culturel de la femme, le tissage et le tressage, et Médée mentionnée par Lacan nous renvoient au mythe de Kuweni, cette princesse autochtone qui trahit son peuple pour l'amour d'un prince venu d'un pays étranger. Elle attend le prince en faisant le tissage. Après la naissance de deux enfants, le prince l'abandonne et la chasse de son royaume pour épouser une princesse de sa communauté lors de son couronnement. Elle se transforme en un démon pour se venger des rois successifs en rendant stériles leurs épouses. Ces mythes ne renvoient-ils pas en effet à quelques vignettes cliniques des figures féminines dont parlent Freud et Lacan ?

C'est par ce biais de l'universel que nous poursuivons nos traductions des œuvres littéraires. Il faudrait donc relever au passage, notre traduction de *Nadja* d'André Breton, suivie d'une introduction sur le rapport entre le surréalisme et la psychanalyse.[7] On sait que le personnage du roman pourrait être pris pour une figure ou un cas clinique, comme le souligne Freud dans l'analyse de la Gradiva de W. Jensen (Freud, 1907). La littérature classique est toujours utilisée par Freud pour aborder les phénomènes inconscients. « Le monde représenté par l'écrivain, note Freud, peut coïncider avec la réalité qui nous est familière, ou il peut s'en éloigner d'une façon ou d'une autre. Dans tous les cas, nous le suivons », ajoute Freud (Freud, 1919, 259). Les expériences de vie de ces écrivains telles qu'elles se réfléchissent dans leurs pensées sont des phénomènes démonstratifs de certaines réalités cliniques. Freud se ressource dans la littérature depuis Shakespeare, Goethe, Hoffmann, Ibsen et les poètes Schiller et Heine, et il montre que le fantasme met en écriture sous forme d'œuvre littéraire. Freud écrit, « Sur l'exemple d'une petite nouvelle, sans grande valeur par elle-même en soi, la *Gradiva* de W.Jensen, j'ai pu montrer que les rêves inventés par un poète se prêtent aux mêmes interprétations que les rêves réels, donc que dans la production littéraire les mécanismes inconscients qui nous sont connus à partir du travail du rêve est également à l'œuvre » (Freud, 1925, 111).

La rencontre avec les autres disciplines

En effet, Freud dans *L'intérêt de la psychanalyse* (Freud, 1913b), montre que la psychanalyse, « dans la mesure où il s'agit d'un rameau de la psychologie, d'une méthode de traitement des troubles névrotiques et d'une série de conceptions psychologiques susceptibles d'extension—donc 'd'application' [...] il va s'agir de son intérêt en général et en particulier pour les autres domaines de savoir ». Autrement dit, il est question de l'intérêt à la psychanalyse : donc de l'intérêt que les autres « disciplines » sont en droit d'avoir pour la psychanalyse (Assoun, 2009, 676). Lorsqu'on lit la traduction française de *Das Interesse an der Psychoanalyse* en « L'intérêt de la psychanalyse », on doit comprendre que, c'est d'elle que l'intérêt émane, mais c'est l'intérêt pour les autres (domaines). Donc la périphrase ajoutée dans l'œuvre complète française, « L'intérêt que présente la psychanalyse » est encore plus explicite. La question est de savoir à quoi la psychanalyse est-elle « bonne » pour les autres domaines ? Cela n'explique pas que la psychanalyse domine les autres domaines, biologie, physiologie, psychologie, science du langage, philosophie, sociologie, éducation, mais elle est impliquée dedans et réciproquement. En effet, Freud rédige ce texte à la demande d'une revue italienne *Rivistia di Scienzia*, une activité plutôt éditoriale destinée aux chercheurs « étrangers », qui n'est publié en Autriche qu'en 1924, « un article d'exportation » (Assoun, 2009, 677) pour expliquer l'importance du dialogue avec les autres domaines du savoir.

La traduction et le lacanisme

La troisième partie de notre projet concerne les textes lacaniens. Lacan est travaillé par les chercheurs cinghalais dans les travaux-recherches sur Durkheim, Lévi-Strauss, Saussure et Frege, et en traversant la philosophie, l'anthropologie, la linguistique et la mathématique. L'absence presque totale de traduction des textes lacaniens en cinghalais ne prive pas les chercheurs cinghalais de débattre sur le lacanisme, à partir de quelques traductions anglaises. Traduire Lacan en cinghalais est une nécessité pour reprendre son retour à Freud, sa relation étroite et sa prise de distance avec les post-freudiens très connus du monde anglophone, tels que Winnicott, Klein, Bion, Erikson. Malgré la difficulté évidente de traduire certains concepts lacaniens, il s'agit d'un terrain encore vierge pour introduire les termes cinghalais aux explications lacaniennes en français. Cependant, Lacan par son retour à Freud, introduit une reprise des termes allemands en langue française, et invente des termes et un style spécifiquement français et lacanien. En effet il crée un malaise même chez les traducteurs anglais. On le sait déjà, comme le note le traducteur anglais de *Fonction et champ de la Parole et du langage en psychanalyse*, A. Wilden, on doit prêter attention au sens caché des termes et il est nécessaire d'introduire une convention pour que le lecteur puisse le trouver en index ou en notes de bas de page. Les traducteurs anglais ont trouvé des solutions. Par exemple pour désigner la différence entre la connaissance et le savoir, A. Wilden se satisfait d'un ajout, L ou K majuscule et l ou k minuscule (Language = Langage ; language = la langue ou Knowledge = le savoir ; knowledge = la connaissance).[8] Citons les exemples les plus frappants dans notre traduction cinghalaise. La différence entre le petit « autre » et le grand « Autre » introduit en quelque sorte une impasse ; dans le cinghalais les lettres majuscules sont absentes. Dans nos traductions, il s'agit d'introduire la lettre qui représente le A (majuscule) comme un simple agrandissement de quelques points dans le texte imprimé.

On sait qu'il n'existe presque pas de psychanalystes dans le pays. S'il y en a, ce sont des jungiens, les « counsellors » ou des psychiatres qui sont sensibles à certains aspects de la psychanalyse. Certains praticiens du milieu thérapeutique et propédeutique sont demandeurs de traductions cinghalaises. Dans ce monde de la médecine indienne, *Ayurvédique,* prédominée par la pensée brahmanique, hindouiste et bouddhique, la fierté de la tradition thérapeutique locale est à surmonter sans pour autant la déprécier ni sous-estimer. Les psychiatres formés selon la tradition anglaise ont peu de contacts avec le monde latin de la psychanalyse, à part quelques concepts winnicottiens ou kleiniens. Cependant on observe plutôt une véritable demande des lecteurs qui ne sont pas des praticiens de santé. Malgré la prédominance de la tradition anglaise de « councelling », les professionnels de santé et d'éducation questionnent l'énigme de la psychopathologie et des concepts psychanalytiques. La psychose aussi bien que la névrose, tant dans les formes anciennes que nouvelles, font du bruit dans ce monde indien où la modernité destitue la pensée ainsi que les techniques traditionnelles. Les psychoses sortent du contexte du chamanisme ou de l'animisme, et elle entre dans le milieu hospitalier. La psychiatrie continue à les traiter par les camisoles ou les substances chimiques. Nous nous questionnons toujours, faut-il adresser les traductions aux praticiens ou aux universitaires ? La technique aura-t-elle une place un jour si le débat est ouvert dans les universités ? Face à la psychiatrie qui résiste contre la pratique psychanalytique, nous visons le milieu universitaire et les jeunes non universitaires intéressés par les énigmes de l'inconscient. Sans entrer dans une logique d'une ethnopsychiatrie ni d'une clinique ethnocentrique, il s'agit d'introduire la clinique psychanalytique sans changer l'essentiel. Rappelons l'histoire de ce fameux couteau de Lichtenberg que Freud cite au sujet des modifications que Jung voulait apporter à la psychanalyse freudienne. Comme le note Freud, si on change le manche et remplace la lame, on ne possèdera plus le même instrument, malgré la marque ancien qu'il porte (Freud, 1914, 154–155).

Références bibliographiques

Assoun P.-L. *Introduction à l'épistémologie freudienne.* Paris : Payot, 1981.

Assoun P.-L. « Topique freudiennes du mythe. Thèses sur la *Mythenforschung* analytique ». *Topique, Mythe et anthropologie, n*°84. Paris : Esprit du temps, 2003. 173–184.

Assoun P.-L. *Freud et les sciences sociales. Psychanalyse et théorie de la culture*. Paris : Armand Colin, 2008.

Assoun P.-L. « Freud et la religion. Une illusion et son avenir ». *L'avenir d'une illusion,* Paris : Cerf, 2013. 6–94.

Assoun P.-L. *Dictionnaire des œuvres psychanalytique*. Paris : PUF, 2009.

Benjamin W. *Expérience et pauvreté suivi de Le conteur et La tâche du traducteur*, trad. Fr. Paris : PBP, 2011.

Berman, A. *Pour une critique des traductions : John Donne*. Paris : Gallimard, 1995.

Bourguinon A., Cotet P., Laplanche J., Robert F. *Traduire Freud.* Paris : PUF, 1989.

Freud S. *Chronique la plus brève, Carnet intimes (*1929–1939*)*. Paris : Albin Michel, 1992.

Freud S. *Cinq leçons sur la psychanalyse(*1904*)*. Paris : PBP, 1982.

Freud S. *Le délire et les rêves dans la Gradiva de W. Jensen (*1907*)*. Paris : Gallimard, 1986.

Freud S. *Totem et Tabou (*1913*a*). Paris : PBP, 2001.

Freud, S. *L'intérêt de la psychanalyse(*1913*b)*. Paris : RETZ, 1981.

Freud S. « Contribution à l'histoire du mouvement psychanalytique » (1914). *Cinq leçons sur la psychanalyse.* Paris : PBP, 1982.

Freud S. « L'inquiétante étrangeté » (1919). *L'inquiétante étrangeté*, Paris : Folio, 1985.

Freud S. « Au-delà du principe de plaisir » (1920*),* « Le moi et le ça » (1923). *Essais de psychanalyse*. Paris : PBP, 1981.

Freud S. « Le problème économique du masochisme » (1924). *Névrose, psychose et perversion*. Paris : PUF, 1999.

Freud S. *Le Malaise dans la culture (*1930*)*. Pais : PUF, Quadrige, 2000.

Freud S. « L'analyse avec fin et l'analyse sans fin » (1937). *Rés. Id. prob. II*. Paris : PUF, 1998.

Freud S. *L'homme Moïse et la religion monothéiste* (1939). Paris : Gallimard Folio, 1986.

Freud S., et Weiss E. *Lettres sur la pratique psychanalytique*, Paris : Privat, 1970.

Freud, S. *Freud présenté par lui-même(*1925*)*. Paris : Gallimard, Folio-Essais, 1984.

Goldschmidt G.-A. *Quand Freud attend le verbe*. Paris : Buchet/Chastel, 2006.

Kaluaratchige E. « Protection d'un père exalté ou refuge dans le sentiment océanique … ». *Psychologie Clinique* 26, 2008. 55–71.

Kaluaratchige E. « La violence, le don symbolique et l'adolescente ». *Psychologie Clinique* 30, 2010. 114–126.

Kaluaratchige E. « Freud versus Jung : Analyse versus Synthèse ». *Recherches en Psychanalyse* 11, 2011.

Kaluaratchige E. « Le rapport au père dans le bouddhisme : du lien à l'identification ». *L'Inde de la psychanalyse*. Ed. Livio Boni. Paris : - Campagne Première, 2011.

Kaluaratchige E. « La langue " maternelle ", l'exil et l'adolescente ». *Adolescence*. Paris : GREUPP, T.32, 1, 2014. 139–149.

Lacan J. « Réponse au commentaire de Jean Hyppolite sur la 'Verneinung' de Freud » (1954). *Ecrits*. Paris : Seuil, 1966.

Lacan J. *Le Séminaire, Livre II* (1954–1955). Paris : Seuil, 1978.

Lacan J. *Le Séminaire, Livre V* (1957–1958). Paris : Seuil, 1998.

Laplanche J., et Pontalis J.-B. *Vocabulaire de la psychanalyse*. Paris : PUF, 1967.

Laplanche J. "Specificity of Terminological Problems in the translation of Freud". *The International Review of Psycho-Analysis* 18 (1991). 401–406.

Launay de M. *Qu'est-ce que traduire ?* Paris : Vrin, 2006.

Oliveira de P. *Les meilleurs amis de la psychanalyse, Ce que l'on en fait*. Paris : L'Harmatan, 2010. 22.

Rahula W. *L'enseignement du Bouddha*. Paris : Seuil, Folio Sagesse, 1961.

Wilden A. *Speech and Language in Psychoanalysis, Jacques Lacan*. Trans. with notes and commentary. London: John Hopkins paperback edition, 1981.

Wismann H. *Penser entre les langues*. Paris : Albin Michel, 2012.

Notes

1 Nous présentons cet article après plusieurs années d'expérience dans l'enseignement et la recherche universitaires au Sri Lanka et en France. Depuis plusieurs années nous sommes engagée dans un travail de traduction de la psychanalyse en cinghalais.

2 Goldschmidt note que Deutsch vient également de *tiuts, dud,* c'est-à-dire le peuple. L'allemand était bel et bien la langue du peuple contrairement à la langue française. (Goldschmidt, 2006,48)

3 A Sri Lanka selon les statistiques 2012 de Census Department, 74% environs sont de la communauté cinghalaise et environs 7% seulement de la religion catholique, avec 1% environs des autres chrétiens.

4 Voir notre thèse de doctorat intitulée « *Le principe de Nirvãna et la jouissance dans la clinique du sentiment océanique - les formes de la jouissance dans l'auto thérapie corporelle et spirituelle du sujet bouddhiste occidental moderne* » soutenue en 2008, à l'Université Paris Diderot, Paris 7.

5 Nous faisons référence à la première édition critique de L'avenir d'une illusion de Freud, faite par P.-L. Assoun, avec la nouvelle traduction de C. Gillie, Pais, Cerf, 2012.

6 Ce projet fait partie des activités scientifiques de l'équipe interne « Corps, Pratiques Sociales et Anthropologie Psychanalytique » du CRPMS (Centre de Recherches Psychanalyse, Médecine et Société) de la faculté d'Etudes Psychanalytique, de l'Université Paris 7, France.

7 C'est avec la traduction de *Nadja* d'André Breton en cinghalais que nous avons vu l'intérêt d'adresser aux lecteurs les thèmes de la psychanalyse. Notre introduction de Nadja intitulée « Le surréalisme, la politique et la psychanalyse » traite de l'articulation entre le mouvement surréaliste, non seulement avec la politique mais également avec le mouvement psychanalytique. Il s'agit également d'une occasion de reprendre la question de la psychose au féminin. C'est l'anthropologie psychanalytique que nous avons saisie pour travailler dans les sillons tracés par Freud, et ceci avec P.-L. Assoun pour introduire une préface intitulée « La passante considérable. Breton, la folie et le féminin » que nous avons traduite en cinghalais.

8 "It has further nécessary to establish certain conventions for this pupose (for example, "Word " for parole) which the reader will find elaborated in the notes and listed in the indexe. I have also employed capitalization elsewere to distinguish or emphasize certain words or concepts: "Language" for langage ("language" for langue); "Knowledge" for savoir ("knowledge" for connaissance); "truth" for vérité; "the Symbolic", "the Imaginary" and "the Real" for le symbolique, l'imaginaire, and le réel". Because of its special meaning in Lacan , however , "Imaginary" is always capitalized, even as an adjective, whenever it is a question of the Imaginary order" (Wilden, 1968, xv)

Sommes-nous des laquais de l'impérialisme ? De l'apport du tournant culturel en traduction pragmatique[1]

NICOLAS FROELIGER

Résumé

Le tournant culturel a changé profondément la traductologie : on ne l'ignore aujourd'hui qu'au péril de sa propre pertinence. Mais qu'en est-il de son impact sur la traduction pragmatique, sujet que ses tenants ont tendance à ignorer, voire à mépriser ? Après un aperçu synthétique de ce courant, cet article cherche, pour la traduction pragmatique, un autre rôle que celui de repoussoir qui lui est généralement réservé dans ce contexte.

Mots-clés : tournant culturel, traduction pragmatique, Belles infidèles, études sur le genre, marché de la traduction.

Abstract

The cultural turn truly deserves its name since it has left few stones unturned in translation studies: casting it aside today often amounts to flirting with irrelevance. What is, however, its impact on pragmatic translation, a field it often ignores and sometimes despises? After an overview of the cultural turn (postcolonial studies, gender studies in translation, most notably) and its sources of inspiration, this articles aims at finding, for pragmatic translation, a more positive role than that of scarecrow in that context.

Keywords: cultural turn, pragmatic translation, Unfaithful Beauties, gender studies, translation market.

Introduction

Deux phénomènes parmi d'autres sont de nature à faire dresser l'oreille du traducteur et palpiter la narine du traductologue : lorsqu'un terme est repris tel quel dans une langue étrangère et lorsqu'il invite à des imitations formelles. C'est bien le cas de ce que l'on appelle le *cultural turn*. D'une part, en effet, cette appellation, popularisée par Mary Snell-Hornby (1990), mais due à Susan Bassnett et André Lefevere

(1990), est souvent citée en version originale, ce qui dénote une prise de distance et une difficulté d'insertion dans le paysage intellectuel du pays d'arrivée, comme pour les *gender studies* ou les *post-colonial studies,* qui lui sont d'ailleurs liées. D'autre part, certains s'en sont inspirés pour proposer un tournant sémiotique, un tournant de la mondialisation, un tournant empirique, un tournant sociologique, un tournant œcuménique (Ladmiral, 2008), et même un tournant linguistique, voire, pour les plus hardis, sans doute, un tournant traductif ou traductionnel (Bassnett, 1998, Snell-Hornby, 2006, pp. 146–160) ... Ce refus de traduire conjugué à cette postérité zigzaguante montrent bien que nous tenons là un sujet bien réel pour la recherche. Je me propose donc, dans un premier temps, de revenir brièvement sur les problèmes soulevés par ce courant (que, en tant que traducteur, je n'aurai nulle vergogne à franciser), et dans un second temps, de le pousser au bout de sa logique en le repliant sur le champ de la traduction pragmatique, objet premier de mes préoccupations.

Du tournant culturel en général

Tout comme la théorie interprétative et la théorie herméneutique, cette école de pensée s'inscrit d'abord en réaction à la domination de la linguistique en traductologie. Déjà en 1978, Gideon Toury écrivait : « *However highly one may think of Linguistics, Text-Linguistics, Contrastive Textology or Pragmatics and of their explanatory power with respect to translational phenomena, being a translator cannot be reduced to the mere generation of utterances which would be considered "translations" within any of these disciplines. Translation activities should rather be regarded as having cultural significance.* » (Toury, 1978/1992 198). Ce courant a donc pour principe que le contexte culturel (au sens large) joue un rôle essentiel pour déterminer, d'une part, ce qu'est une traduction dans un univers donné et, d'autre part, quels en seront les critères d'acceptabilité (d'où la définition digne de Ponce-Pilate donnée par Toury : « *any target-language utterance which is presented or regarded as such within the target culture, on whatever grounds* [...] » [Toury, 1985 20].) Le tout en gardant en mémoire cette observation : « *On every level of the translation process, it can be shown that, if linguistic considerations enter into conflict with considerations of an ideological and/or poetologi-*

cal nature, the latter tends to win out. », Lefevere, 1992 39). Même si Mary Snell-Hornby (2010, pp. 366–370) inclut dans cet ensemble les travaux des fonctionnalistes allemands, au motif que la visée d'un texte est clairement un élément culturel, on peut considérer que le tournant culturel comporte deux subdivisions principales.

Les études postcoloniales

On trouve tout d'abord les théories postcoloniales, avec une argumentation en quatre temps :

— la traduction a joué un rôle actif dans le processus de colonisation (mais aussi, précise Lori Chamberlain [1988 459], qui ne serait pas démentie par Anne-Marie Thiesse [2001], dans la constitution des identités nationales), notamment par la diffusion d'une image idéologisée du colonisé ;

— après la décolonisation a émergé une littérature écrite dans la langue des ex-puissances impériales et qui donne une place centrale à des phénomènes jusqu'alors périphériques (identité, genre, ethnicité, immigration, oralité, notamment) ;

— la traduction va alors servir de modèle aux études consacrées à cette littérature : « *the representation of cultures of orality in colonial language writing is viewed as a double transposition process involving translating oral narrative cultures into written form and translating between distant or alien language cultures.* » (Bandia, 2010 265) ;

— il s'agira enfin de faire accéder les cultures en question, minoritaires, à une plus grande reconnaissance par la traduction, en s'attachant (Spivak, 1993) à préserver l'altérité que fait entendre cette littérature.

Traduction et féminisme

Un autre pan du tournant culturel porte sur la relation entre traduction et genre. La traduction et les femmes, dira Sherry Simon (1996 1, notamment) se rejoindraient en effet dans leur secondarité par rapport à un modèle dominant (le texte original et l'homme, en l'occurrence), qui serait le siège de la puissance et de la création, tandis qu'elles devraient se contenter de l'imitation et de la reproduction (d'où un riche assortiment de métaphores dépréciatives). À partir de ce socle, certaines traductologues féministes vont se battre pour un renversement des normes d'écriture et en particulier du genre, grammatical cette fois (voir Binard, 2008). C'est une théorie (et une pratique) militante, qui renvoie entre autres à Benjamin : « l'erreur fondamentale du traducteur est de conserver l'état contingent de sa propre langue au lieu de la soumettre à la motion violente de la langue étrangère » (Benjamin, 1923/1971 274). Il y a donc, dans cette approche, un rejet de toute velléité d'acclimatation, mais aussi un désir de transformation sociale à travers la langue et la traduction : « *My translation practice is a political activity aimed at making language speak for women. So my signature on a translation means: this translation has used every translation strategy to make the feminine visible in the language* » (Suzanne de Lotbinière-Harwood, citée par Simon, 1996 15). Ou, pour paraphraser les paroles de George Clinton, « *Free your language … and your mind will follow* » (1970).

On recense également, dans cet ensemble, des féministes, parmi lesquelles Sherry Simon ou Luise von Flotow, qui vont mettre en cause le discours sur la traduction elle-même, notamment chez Steiner dans sa description en quatre actes, disons virils, de « l'élan herméneutique » (1975/1978, pp. 278–275, notamment) :

— « l'élan de confiance », qui doit permettre la compréhension ;
— « une étape d'incursion et d'extraction », qui consiste essentiellement en une « agression » du texte, par laquelle « le traducteur envahit, extrait et rapporte », et qui peut prendre la forme d'une « pénétration-annexion » ou d'un « transfert-appropriation » ;
— « l'incorporation », qui consiste à intégrer le texte dans son contexte d'arrivée ;
— « la mise en œuvre d'une réciprocité qui recrée l'équilibre » et que Steiner compare à un « retour de piston » (p. 280).

Effectivement, n'est-il question que de traduction, dans cette description ? Quelle est la métaphore sous-jacente ? La même question pourrait être posée à Valery Larbaud : « Même dans nos rapports quotidiens avec l'œuvre que nous traduisons nous reconnaissons les conditions du couple humain … » (Larbaud, 1946 87, dans un chapitre intitulé « L'amour et la traduction ») ; ou encore : « traduire un ouvrage qui nous a plu, c'est pénétrer en lui plus profondément que nous ne pouvons le faire par la simple lecture, c'est le posséder plus complètement, c'est en quelque sorte nous l'approprier. » (Larbaud, 1946 22). Quant à Jean-René Ladmiral, faut-il rappeler qu'il a écrit « La langue violée ? » (1991). D'où la tentation d'une question plus culturelle : James Brown, lorsqu'il a écrit « *It's a Man's Man's World* » (1966), pensait-il aussi à la traductologie ? Et bien sûr, une cible toute trouvée pour ces critiques est une tradition qui présente l'intérêt d'être attaquable à la fois en tant que domesticatrice et que machiste : les *Belles infidèles*.[2]

Références communes à ces deux courants

Études postcoloniales et études sur le genre ont donc pour point commun d'employer la traduction à la fois comme sujet scientifique et comme outil pour mettre au jour des phénomènes d'ordre socioculturel, ce qui cadre assez bien avec les préoccupations de cet ouvrage et, plus généralement, du Centre d'études de la traduction qui en est à l'origine. Elles s'appuient en particulier sur la notion d'altérité et se rejoignent aussi dans leurs références à Venuti, Berman et Meschonnic.

Le premier se fait l'avocat d'une résistance de l'étranger dans la langue d'arrivée, et s'oppose à l'impérialisme de la langue anglaise, responsable d'une répartition inégale des traductions entre l'économie dominante (les États-Unis, au centre en termes d'influence culturelle) et celles, périphériques, qui en subissent l'influence, tout en dénonçant « *the ethnocentric violence that every act of translating wreaks on a foreign text* » (Venuti, 1995 212[3]). La domestication qui tend vers l'invisibilité selon cet auteur procède d'un principe sous-jacent : la traduction et le traducteur doivent rester cachés, car ils sont de rang inférieur. C'est à la fois l'étranger et le traducteur qui sont ainsi rendus invisibles. Ce qui se constate d'ailleurs aussi sur le plan universitaire, où l'on voit que l'institution a encore du mal à considérer la traduction comme une activité de plein droit plutôt que comme l'annexe d'une discipline qui serait jugée plus noble.

Antoine Berman (1984), pour sa part, s'oppose à la « *naturalisation* », et incite à « accueillir l'Étranger comme Étranger » (Berman, 1985 68, allusion à Levinas) et à lutter, là aussi, contre l'ethnocentrisme. Ce qui passe, sous sa plume, par une « traduction de la lettre », qui fasse ressortir l'altérité dans le texte d'arrivée là où celui-ci est à même de l'accueillir (point essentiel qui fait toute la subtilité de son approche). Et de décrier 13 procédés qui sont pour lui des erreurs graves parce qu'elles dévient de ce principe : rationalisation, clarification, expansion, anoblissement, appauvrissement qualitatif, appauvrissement quantitatif, destruction des rythmes, destruction du réseau sous-jacent de signification, destruction de la trame linguistique, destruction ou exoticisation des réseaux vernaculaires, destruction du caractère idiomatique, effacement de la superposition des langues (Berman, 1999, *passim*).

La même préoccupation pousse Henri Meschonnic à expliquer pourquoi la traduction a aujourd'hui un rôle plus important à jouer qu'hier dans la façon dont on peut penser le langage : « La traduction depuis toujours tient une place majeure comme moyen de contact entre les cultures. La communication y consiste à faire passer un énoncé d'une langue dans une autre. C'est la notion encore la plus répandue. Elle peut suffire pour certains objectifs. Elle n'est plus la seule. Pour des raisons qui tiennent à la transformation en cours des rapports interculturels. Transformations liées aux diverses décolonisations et à la planétarisation de ces rapports, et à la transformation des conceptions du langage [...]. » (Meschonnic, 1999 13).

Quel emboîtement avec la traduction pragmatique ?

Comme toute pensée polémique, celle qui se déploie sous le nom de tournant culturel a vocation à être critiquée. On pourra ainsi reprocher à son aile féministe une tendance à l'essentialisme qui consiste à figer des identités au lieu de les considérer comme des entités dynamiques, en évolution. On pourra déplorer sa propension à poser les conditions du débat en termes de victimes et de coupables, ce qui, transposé à l'échelle de la société (mais c'est bien cela qui est ici en jeu), aboutit à une segmentation du corps social qui fait passer à l'arrière-plan toute lutte pour l'universel. On pourra lui objecter que le masculin n'a pas le monopole de la violence. On pourra observer qu'on n'y lit guère d'auteurs hommes, et ajouter que la cause en question aura fait bien des progrès lorsque ce sera le cas. On pourra, enfin, faire valoir que l'opération de traduction ou son résultat ne sont, pour une partie de ces auteurs, qu'un faire-valoir au profit d'idées et de combats autres. Et bien sûr, chacune de ces critiques pourra appeler des réponses, qui auraient pour point commun de sortir du cadre de ce document.

Ceux qui s'intéressent à la traduction professionnelle et à ses métiers pourraient néanmoins formuler un autre grief. Tous les tenants du tournant culturel semblent en effet avoir un ennemi commun dans la sphère traductologique : la traduction pragmatique. Celle-ci, en effet, est considérée comme le repoussoir absolu soit parce qu'elle est le véhicule de l'idéologie capitaliste américaine dominante ; soit parce qu'elle obéit aux stéréotypes du centre, empreint d'une vision machiste de la langue et de la société ; soit parce que son orientation cibliste la conduit à nier l'altérité dont le texte source est l'expression. Ainsi, tout ce qu'écrit Venuti tend à défendre l'insularité de la sphère littéraire par rapport au marché. On sait en effet que cet auteur reproche aux traductions ciblistes (qui ne datent pas d'hier, certes, même si l'expression est récente) de faire disparaître le traducteur, sous la contrainte des éditeurs, en écrivant en anglais dans une langue qui coule, qui se lise, et qui soit idiomatique, avec pour effet de créer une « *illusion de transparence* » (Venuti, 1998 1). Ce qui, effectivement, constitue l'idéal d'une traduction pragmatique, précisément parce que celle-ci se doit de tenir compte de la réception adéquate de son destinataire, et donc d'un cahier des charges. En somme, comme le dramaturge Christophe Honoré (2012) a pu faire dire à Alain Robbe-Grillet au sujet de Balzac, la traduction pragmatique, « *C'est un très bon ennemi !* »

Nous sommes ici en présence d'un profond paradoxe : un des apports majeurs du tournant culturel est bel et bien d'intégrer les conditions socio-économiques de réalisation des traductions dans le champ scientifique. Cependant, cette logique relègue du mauvais côté de la ligne de démarcation, parmi ceux que l'on aurait qualifiés, dans les années 60 et 70, de laquais de l'impérialisme, tout le champ pragmatique, là où s'effectuent pourtant l'essentiel des traductions.

Il serait tentant, alors, pour ceux qui s'intéressent à ce domaine, de faire l'impasse sur un courant qui le condamne et le méprise. C'est d'ailleurs ce que fait Jean-René Ladmiral (1999) dans sa typologie des quatre âges de la traduction. Je compte néanmoins proposer une autre approche. D'abord parce que, comme le fait dire Vladimir Nabokov à un de ses personnages, « nous avons l'habitude d'être insultés » (Nabokov, 1940/1979 150). Ensuite, parce que rien ne nous oblige à accepter des clivages qui procèdent de préoccupations étrangères aux nôtres : comme le dit Bob Dylan, « *The ghetto that you build for me is the one you're living in* » (1981). Il me semble au contraire éminemment souhaitable de réactualiser certaines des approches de la traduction pragmatique à la lumière des apports du tournant culturel. On pourra en particulier s'en servir pour opérer un retour sur les *Belles infidèles*, pour nous demander si les critiques adressées à certains traductologues qualifiés de machistes sont totalement disqualifiantes et pour réfléchir aussi bien à la sociologie de la profession qu'aux positionnements de ceux qui en vivent par rapport à la norme dominante.

Des vertus de l'éclairage indirect

Retour sur les Belles infidèles

Pourquoi évoquer les *Belles infidèles* au sujet de la traduction pragmatique ? Tout simplement parce que cette école, on ne le dit pas assez, préfigure ce qui sera la localisation et la transcréation à partir de la fin du XXe siècle et qu'elle est plus généralement une des matrices de ce que l'on appellera plus tard le *ciblisme*. Ce préalable étant posé, on peut revenir sur ses critiques féministes, notamment celles de Lori Chamberlain, (1988, pp. 454–472), pour se demander si elles sont totalement justifiées. On peut en effet observer que ce sont les reproches d'une chercheuse contemporaine sur un phénomène survenu trois siècles auparavant. Et qui font fi de l'Histoire. Or, si l'un des mérites des théories féministes consiste à exposer le discours machiste comme parole située, on peut faire à cette auteure exactement la même remontrance : elle met en cause avec sa conscience politique d'aujourd'hui un phénomène qui procède lui-même d'une dynamique historique. Il faudrait au contraire replacer les *Belles infidèles* dans leur contexte, qui est celui du libertinage, d'abord philosophique, au XVIIe siècle, puis sexuel, au siècle suivant : l'infidélité, y compris de la part des femmes, commence ici à être admise, du moins dans les couches supérieures de la société. C'est un moment où naît, dans l'élite lettrée, une forme de liberté dans les rapports entre hommes et femmes, et qui marque l'émergence de ces dernières comme sujets à part entière. Sans donc constituer un idéal social, ces *Belles infidèles* sont le signe que les relations d'inégalité entre les genres étaient en train de changer pour un mieux. Dans ces conditions, les traductions ainsi métaphorisées ne sont pas *belles mais infidèles :* elles sont *infidèles parce que belles.* Elles peuvent maintenant et désormais se le permettre ! On observe d'ailleurs que les traductions anglaises de ce concept français hésitent entre ces deux options : on trouve tantôt « *beautiful but unfaithful* » (voir par exemple DeLater, sous la direction de, 2002), ou, beaucoup plus neutre, et à mon sens beaucoup plus proche de l'esprit initial, « *unfaithful beauties* » (voir par exemple Hatim et Munday, 2004 104[4]). Chacune de ces deux traductions procède d'une vision idéologique — et c'est le tournant culturel qui nous permet de le voir de la manière la plus éclatante ! Ce qui me semble manquer à la lecture de théoriciennes comme Lori Chamberlain, c'est donc une pensée dialectique : la métaphore, tant pour les femmes que pour les traductions, n'est peut-être pas si dépréciative qu'on a voulu le croire.

De la centralité problématique du machisme en traductologie

Il est par ailleurs impossible de nier que certains chercheurs du XXe siècle ont une vision sexuée et machiste de la traduction. Cette seconde critique est donc plus justifiée et mieux étayée que la première. Reste à déterminer si ce rapprochement est central dans la posture théorique des auteurs en question, ou s'il ne trahit qu'un phénomène banal, à savoir la tendance, y compris pour les esprits les plus novateurs, à s'exprimer, à l'occasion, en arrière de leur époque. On peut, à l'appui de la deuxième option, estimer avec Cornelius Castoriadis qu'« Un grand auteur, par définition, pense au-delà de ses moyens. Il est grand pour autant qu'il pense autre chose que ce qui était déjà pensé, et ses moyens sont le résultat de ce qui était déjà pensé, qui n'a jamais fini d'empiéter sur ce qu'il pense, ne serait-ce que parce qu'il ne peut pas annuler tout ce qu'il a reçu et se placer devant une table rase même lorsqu'il en a l'illusion. » (Castoriadis, 1975 242). Le véritable problème est donc plutôt ici dans l'actualité des métaphores que l'on se choisit. Et certaines métaphores vieillissent plus vite que les concepts qu'elles ont permis de faire apparaître. La composante phallocrate des œuvres en question montre ainsi avant tout que leurs auteurs sont les produits de leur éducation et de leur psychisme ; elle n'invalide pas forcément ce qu'ils ont à dire par ailleurs sur la traduction.

On peut donc reprendre ces critiques féministes de la traductologie pour séparer les questions de fond et les références que l'on a pu utiliser pour exprimer celles-ci. Plutôt que d'opposer les unes (traductologues féministes) aux autres (traductologues phallocrates sans la conscience de l'être), il paraît souhaitable de procéder, là aussi, dialectiquement. Le discours féministe peut en effet libérer la traductologie d'une partie de son caractère machiste, lié à un système de représentation qui a fonctionné, mais qui n'est plus valide : on ne gagne rien à jeter Steiner, Larbaud ou d'autres avec l'eau de la domination masculine. En procédant de la sorte on s'empêche en outre de porter sur leur œuvre des critiques qui seraient sans doute plus centrales …

De la sociologie du marché de la traduction et de l'écriture y afférente

Le tournant culturel mérite donc bien son nom en ceci qu'il fait apparaître comme des observables des phénomènes qui passaient jusqu'ici pour naturels, et permet de faire la part, dans les théories qui l'ont précédé, entre l'ancien et le véritablement nouveau. On voit ici toute son utilité pour la traduction pragmatique. C'est peut-être grâce à lui que l'on peut s'interroger aujourd'hui sur l'évolution de la répartition entre les genres dans le secteur de la traduction : il y a 50 ans, les traducteurs étaient essentiellement des hommes ; aujourd'hui, ce sont en grande majorité des traductrices—et qui sont actives pour l'essentiel dans le champ pragmatique, ce qui influe sur la sociologie et sur l'image de la profession. Il nous faut réfléchir à partir de cette réalité et il est sans doute possible de le faire en s'aidant, par exemple, des travaux de Sherry Simon, qui visent à « *identify and critique the tangle of concepts which relegates both women and translation to the bottom of the social and literary ladder* » (Simon, 1996 1).

Cette problématique se déployant dans le rapport à la norme, on pourra alors revenir à l'ambition d'une féminisation du discours par la traduction telle que proposée par Suzanne de Lotbinière-Harwood. La pratique militante visant à changer la perspective sur les rapports entre hommes et femmes (et dont la forme la plus anodine est l'emploi du vocabulaire épicène) est-elle envisageable en pragmatique? On pourrait oser une réponse positive en établissant un parallèle avec le rôle des traducteurs vis-à-vis de la néologie et de la préservation d'une langue (française) dynamique, ouverte à la nouveauté et apte à résister au calque. Mais cet optimisme est sans doute hors de propos. On sait en effet que les traducteurs pragmatiques se doivent bien souvent de se comporter en normopathes, c'est-à-dire d'adhérer en tout point aux formes stylistiques les plus communément admises chez leurs lecteurs. Cette nécessité les amène en bonne logique à produire des textes qui sont conformes aux canons conservateurs du système institué. Elle les expose *ipso facto* au reproche d'agir comme des serviteurs fidèles de l'ordre établi.

Le tout, néanmoins, est d'avoir saisi que cette tendance est contingente. Elle ne procède pas d'un état de nature, mais d'un fait de culture et à ce titre elle ne saurait engager absolument ceux qui se doivent d'y adhérer pour de simples raisons économiques. En somme, la prise de conscience, grâce notamment au tournant culturel, de nos aliénations est un pas important vers l'émancipation, quand bien même cette libération serait condamnée à n'être qu'intellectuelle (et donc à ne pas déboucher sur des traductions substantiellement différentes). Poser la problématique dans ces termes peut sans doute contribuer à alléger certaines des souffrances dues à deux sentiments très prégnants chez les traducteurs professionnels : l'imposture et l'insécurité linguistique.

Tout est ainsi dans la prise de distance. On rejoint alors le concept d'ironie : le traducteur doit être conscient que ce qu'il produit n'a pas à l'engager personnellement—ni sur le fond ni sur la forme. Il devient ainsi libre de manier son outil d'une manière qui ne soit pas innocente. On sait bien que l'essentiel, en effet, est de ne pas avoir un rapport naïf à la langue, au texte, à la demande. On sait bien que la traduction, loin de ne concerner que la langue, est une affaire de société, d'échange, de discours, le tout teinté d'idéologie. On sait qu'elle emprunte au moins autant à la civilisation qu'à la linguistique. Le tournant culturel le confirme de manière éclatante. Grâce lui en soit rendue.

Il est donc important, en traductologie aussi, de dessiner des lignes de partage afin de permettre l'éclosion de réflexions cohérentes et collectives, mais ce n'est qu'un premier temps de l'exercice. En effet, une fois les champs et les sous-domaines délimités, il faut s'attacher à établir des circulations. Dans le cas présent, on s'apercevra alors non seulement, en reprenant les 13 procédés décriés par Berman dans *La traduction et la lettre ou l'auberge du lointain* (1999), que ceux-ci sont bel et bien à la base d'une bonne traduction pragmatique, mais aussi que les stratégies qu'il propose, en se servant notamment de Chateaubriand, pour réaliser à la place une traduction respectueuse de la lettre ont bel et bien cours en traduction pragmatique. L'espace nous manque pour une telle démonstration détaillée, qui devra donc attendre une publication ultérieure. En tout état de cause, cet auteur se révèle ainsi comme un sagace théoricien de la traduction pragmatique, non seulement en attaque, mais aussi—quoi qu'il ait pu en penser - en défense. Les meilleurs observateurs d'un champ quelconque sont bel et bien ceux qui le considèrent avec un œil critique, car ils l'envisagent du dehors. Grâce au tournant culturel, les traducteurs pragmatiques peuvent eux aussi se doter d'un tel mode de vision—et fournir ainsi, ajouteront les cyniques, des traductions encore plus conformes aux attentes du système.

Références bibliographiques

Bandia, Paul. "Post-colonial literatures and translation". Eds. Yves Gambier et Luc van Doorslaer. *Handbook of Translation Studies, volume* 1. Amsterdam: John Benjamins Publishing. 2010.

Bassnett, Susan et André Lefevere, dir. *Translation, History and Culture.* Londres : Pinter. 1990.

Benjamin, Walter. « La tâche du traducteur ». Œuvres, tome I (Mythe et violence). Préface à la traduction des Tableaux parisiens de Baudelaire, traduit par Maurice de Gandillac. Paris : Denoël. 1923/1971 : 261–275.

Berman, Antoine. *Pour une critique des traductions : John Donne.* Paris : Gallimard. 1995.

Binard, Florence. « Limites linguistiques du genre grammatical et féminismes ». Nicolas Froeliger, éd. *Stratégies normalisatrices et traduction. Traductologie de plein champ, deuxième édition.* Perros-Guirec : La Tribune internationale des langues vivantes, n° 45, novembre 2008 : 49–59.

Castoriadis, Cornelius. *L'Institution imaginaire de la société*. Paris : Éditions du Seuil, collection Esprit. 1975.

DeLater, James Albert, dir. *Translation Theory in the Age of Louis XIV. De Optimo Genere Interpretandi of Pierre Daniel Huet (1630–1721)*. Manchester : St Jerome Publishing. 2002.

Hatim, Basil et Jeremy Munday. 2004. *Translation: An Advanced Resource Book*. Londres : Routledge. 2012.

Honoré, Christophe. *Nouveau roman (pièce de thétre)*. Créé au festival d'Avignon. 2012.

Ladmiral, Jean-René, « Les quatre âges de la traductologie – Réflexions sur une diachronie de la théorie de la traduction », in *L'histoire et les théories de la traduction*. Les actes (colloque de Genève en l'honneur de Louis Truffaut, 3-5 octobre 1996), Berne et Genève, ASTTI et ETI, 1999.

Ladmiral. Jean-René. « La langue violée ? » *L'étranger dans la langue*. Paris : Palimpsestes n°6. Presses de la Sorbonne Nouvelle. 2008 : 23–33.

Ladmiral, Jean-René. « Pour un tournant œcuménique en théorie de la traduction ». Christian Balliu, éd. *Traduire : un métier d'avenir, Actes du colloque du 50e anniversaire de l'ISTI*. 14–15 octobre 2008. Bruxelles : Les Éditions du Hazard. 2008.

Larbaud, Valery. *Sous l'invocation de Saint Jérôme*. Paris : Gallimard, Tel. 1946/1997.

Lefevere, André. *Translation, Rewriting and the Manipulation of Literary Fame*. Londres et New York: Routledge. 1992.

Lotbinière-Harwood, Suzanne de. *Rebelle et infidèle. La traduction comme ré-écriture au féminin. The Body Bilingual*. Montréal et Toronto : Les éditions du remue-ménage/The Women's Press. 1992.

Meschonnic, Henri. *Poétique du traduire*. Lagrasse : Verdier. 1999.

Nabokov, Vladimir. *The Real Life of Sebastian Knight*. New York : New Directions. 1940. *La vraie vie de Sebastian Knight*, traduction de Y. Davet. Paris : Gallimard, 1962.

Simon, Sherry. *Gender in Translation. Cultural identity and the politics of transmission*. Londres et New York: Routledge. 1996.

Snell-Hornby, Mary. "Linguistic Transcoding or Cultural Transfer? A Critic of Translation Theory in Germany". *Translation, History and Culture*. Eds. Susan Bassnett & André Lefevere. London: Pinter, 1990. 79–86.

Spivak, Gayatri Chakravorty. "The Politics of Translation". *Outside in the Teaching Machine*. New York et Londres: Routledge. 179–200.

Steiner, George. *After Babel. Aspects of Language and Translation.* New York et Londres: Oxford University Press. 1975. Traduction française de L. Lotringer. *Après Babel.* Paris : Albin Michel. 1978.

Thiesse, Anne-Marie. *La création des identités nationales—Europe. XVIII*[e]*–XX*[e] siècle. Paris : Seuil. 2001.

Toury, Gideon. "The Nature and Role of Norms in Translation". John Biguenet et Rainer Schulte, dir. *Theories of Translation: An Anthology of Essays from Dryden to Derrida.* Chicago: University of Chicago Press.1978/1992 : 198–211.

Venuti, Lawrence. *The Translator's Invisibility. A History of Translation.* New York: Routledge. 1995.

Von Flotow, Luise. "Feminist Translation : Contexts. Practices and Theories". *TTR* 4 n°2 (1991): 69–84.

Accompagnement musical

Brown, James et Betty Jean Newsome. "It's a Man's Man's World". Cincinnati: King Records. 1966.

Dylan, Bob. "Dead Man, Dead Man (When Will You Arise?)." *Shot of Love.* New York: Columbia Records. 1981.

Clinton George, Ray Davies, Eddie Hezel. "Free Your Mind … and Your Ass Will Follow." Detroit : Westbound Records. 1970.

Notes

1 Les considérations qui suivent sont la lointaine conséquence d'échanges répétés et parfois polémiques avec Jane Wilhelm, qui mérite d'en être remerciée. Cette contribution a également bénéficié de la relecture sagace de Sophie Azzopardi, qui mérite tout autant de gratitude.

2 D'où le brillant jeu de mots qui donne son titre au livre-programme de Suzanne de Lotbinière-Harwood : *Rebelle et infidèle. La traduction comme ré-écriture au féminin […]* (1992).

3 Notons que cette opposition entre centre et périphérie se trouve déjà, nous dit Mounin (1963 240) dans les premiers écrits de Nida, qui la formule en termes d'opposition entre « *cultures simples* » et « *cultures complexes* ».

4 Cette confusion a au demeurant été alimentée, en français, par Edmond Cary, qui va déformer la phrase de Gilles Ménage à l'origine de cette appellation : « *Elle me rappelle une femme que j'ai beaucoup aimée à Tours, et qui était belle mais infidèle* » (selon Cary, 1963 29). En réalité, Gilles Ménage avait écrit : « *Lorsque la version du Lucien de M. d'Ablancourt parut, bien des gens se plaignirent de ce qu'elle n'était pas fidèle. Pour moi je l'appelai la belle infidèle, qui était le nom que j'avais donné étant jeune à une de mes maîtresses.* » (cité par Ballard, 1992 147.)

Traduction pragmatique et complexité

Patricia Minacori

Résumé :
Notre étude examine les relations entre communication technique et traduction pragmatique. Dans ce cadre, notre objectif est d'analyser ces domaines sous l'aspect de la complexité. En se basant sur les principes préconisés par E. Morin et en partant des éléments constitutifs, de la pratique professionnelle et des compétences du traducteur, cet article tente d'analyser la traduction pragmatique pour déterminer s'il s'agit d'un objet complexe.
Mots-clés : traduction pragmatique, complexité, communication technique, méthodologie

Abstract
In this article we look at the relationship between technical communication and pragmatic translation. With this in mind, our goal is to analyze these areas from the perspective of complexity as defined in France by E. Morin. Using the four methodological principles put forth by Morin, we analyze pragmatic translation to determine if it is a complex object, based on its components, professional practice and the translator's skills.
Keywords: pragmatic translation, complexity, technical communication, methodology

Introduction

Notre objet de recherche est la complexité des opérations qui vont de la conception de documents techniques à leur traduction. En effet, la communication technique et la traduction sont des activités différentes et parfois complémentaires. Elles font partie d'une chaîne de communication au cours de laquelle un communicateur technique crée une documentation, parfois *ex nihilo* qui sera par la suite bien souvent traduite. Lorsque l'on examine la situation du communicateur technique qui doit recueillir les informations auprès de spécialistes, créer des documents, les sédimenter pour les diffuser à des destinataires particuliers sur des supports et avec des outils spécifiques, on comprend que cet acteur est confronté à une myriade de difficultés. Il est en effet à l'interface d'un grand nombre d'intervenants. Par la suite, cette documentation peut être traduite dans une multitude de langues. Dès l'instant qu'un document technique est conçu par un communicateur technique dans une langue donnée, on peut aisément imaginer que la documentation sera traduite dans d'autres langues pour répondre aux exigences de la mondialisation. Dans certains cas, comme pour les notices des médicaments, il y a en France par exemple, une obligation légale de traduction. Il en va de même pour les nouvelles technologies où la documentation technique accompagnant tout matériel ou tout logiciel offre des potentialités de traduction.

L'objectif de cet article est de circonscrire nos propos à la traduction pragmatique à travers laquelle nous tâcherons d'explorer la notion de « complexité ». Il convient tout d'abord de passer en revue les origines de ce concept ainsi que ses principes fondateurs.

Les origines de la notion de complexité

En Occident, jusqu'au début du XXe siècle, la pensée analytique avait guidé les théories scientifiques. En effet, de Platon à Aristote, de Galilée à Descartes et à Newton, la culture scientifique a eu pour habitude de se placer dans une doctrine positiviste selon laquelle l'objet à connaître est la réalité. Dans ce cadre, le critère universel qui permet de légitimer les connaissances enseignables, est celui de la vérité objective. Ainsi, il n'existe pas de relation entre le sujet et l'objet. Les faits découlent de façon exclusive de l'observation et de l'expérimentation et peuvent ainsi être analysés de façon neutre et objective (Cambien 2007 : 10).

D'après A. Comte (2002 : 125), une discipline scientifique, c'est-à-dire un champ de connaissances, se définit par son objet, ainsi que le morceau de réalité objective qu'elle va décrire puis expliquer en appliquant une méthode d'investigation. Cette dernière repose sur l'observation, la mesure et la répétitivité des faits. Les méthodes de description étaient parfaitement adaptées à l'étude de systèmes stables, constitués d'un nombre limité d'éléments que l'on arrivait à séparer en se fondant sur la raison et l'analyse pour en expliquer les causes et le fonctionnement.

Or, vers les années 1930, nombre de scientifiques ne parvenaient plus à comprendre, expliquer, voire agir face à la complexité du monde en se fondant sur les principes de la pensée analytique (Bériot 2006). Dans ce contexte, trois disciplines, entre autres, vont apporter des solutions face à ce que l'on nomme désormais la complexité, à savoir :

— la théorie des systèmes élaborée par biologiste Ludwig Von Bertalanffy, en 1947 ;
— la théorie de la communication mise au point par l'ingénieur Claude Shannon et le philosophe Warren Weaver, en 1948 ;
— la cybernétique, provenant notamment des travaux du mathématicien Norbert Wiener en 1950.

La théorie des systèmes

En 1947, Ludwig Von Bertalanffy (1993) introduit *la notion de système*. Selon lui, pour comprendre des ensembles, il importe d'étudier non seulement les éléments constitutifs mais aussi leurs relations et plus encore leurs interactions avec l'environnement. Son objectif est de formuler des principes valables pour tout système, indépendamment de la nature de ses éléments et des relations qui les relient à d'autres systèmes. La démarche systémique est dominée par une logique qui permet de relier les différents éléments constitutifs. Centrée sur le but à atteindre, elle cherche toujours une finalité. Son approche est globale puisqu'elle prend en compte la diversité des réalités. De plus, elle est orientée vers la recherche d'une pluralité de solutions, dans un objectif de faire émerger des nouveautés et de favoriser l'innovation.

La systémique a eu une influence notable sur les recherches en biologie en permettant de mieux comprendre le fonctionnement des cellules. Son influence s'étendit également au domaine de la médecine, à travers l'étude des relations entre les organes du corps humain mais aussi à d'autres domaines tels les sciences sociales, l'économie et même celui de l'entreprise, puisqu'elle sert à éclairer les décideurs et à orienter leurs actions. Nous tenons à souligner finalement que ce sont les recherches en systémique qui ont permis de réaliser des études sur la modélisation et sur la simulation.

La théorie de la communication

Dans ce bouillonnement d'idées de la première moitié du siècle dernier, une autre théorie a fortement nourri les spécialistes de la complexité. Il s'agit de *la théorie de la communication.* Mise au point en 1948 par l'ingénieur Claude Shannon et le philosophe Warren Weaver (1998), cette théorie stipule qu'une source d'information émet un message. Celui-ci sera codé par un émetteur qui l'acheminera à travers un canal vers un récepteur. Le message sera ensuite décodé par un récepteur qui doit le reconstituer en partant d'un signal, pour le transmettre au destinataire. Enfin et surtout, ce message peut être brouillé ou déformé par un bruit (Shannon, Weaver 1998).

Comme nous pouvons le constater, ce schéma de la communication ne prend pas en considération les éléments constitutifs de l'information et il n'intègre pas la notion de boucle de rétroaction. Il est désormais considéré comme un modèle très statique, même si en son temps, ce schéma a eu beaucoup de retentissement, car il avait pour fonction première l'étude de la cryptographie.

Harold Lasswell (1948) a décrit les différents éléments de l'information avec précision. Ce sociologue américain s'est intéressé à l'importance des moyens de communication pour la diffusion des idées politiques et de la propagande. Pour ce faire, il propose de répondre aux questions : Qui dit quoi ? Par quel canal ? A qui ? Avec quel effet ? Aussi les principaux axes de recherche vont-il s'orienter sur la description des émetteurs, l'analyse du contenu, l'étude des canaux de transmission, l'identification des récepteurs et l'évaluation des effets de la communication. Ces éléments sont fort intéressants pour le traducteur.

La cybernétique

La troisième discipline sur laquelle nous nous penchons pour suivre l'évolution de la notion de *complexité*, est celle de *la cybernétique.* Venant du grec « *kubernêtiké* », dérivé de «*kubernan* » qui signifie «diriger, gouverner» (Dictionnaire culturel Le Robert, 2005 : 2065) la cybernétique est liée à « l'art de diriger ». Norbert Wiener (1971) élabore en 1950, la science des systèmes autorégulés qui permet de contrôler et aussi de faire communiquer l'homme, l'animal et la machine, car, pour lui, l'humain et la machine sont de purs organismes de relations et de communication. Dans ce cadre, l'approche de N. Wiener cherche d'abord à reconnaître la structure et l'intérieur d'une machine ou d'un animal, puis à décrire les relations entretenues avec son environnement et enfin, à prévoir son comportement et son évolution au fil du temps. Il s'est beaucoup penché sur ce qu'il a appelé le *feedback*, ou *rétroaction* selon laquelle un élément interagit avec un second, et par là même, crée en retour une réponse du second vers le premier élément (Wiener 1971). Si un système cybernétique est équilibré, il a pour propriété de s'autoréguler et il manifeste une grande stabilité dans le temps. Il s'agit alors d'une autorégulation. L'idée fondamentale véhiculée par Wiener est que l'être vivant ne peut plus être considéré comme une entité biologique qui agit, mais comme un être doué de communication qui réagit. La cybernétique est donc la science de la régulation et de l'information. Son objectif est la connaissance et le pilotage des systèmes. Il est à souligner qu'aujourd'hui, de nombreux secteurs scientifiques découlent des applications de la cybernétique et notamment la robotisation de la production, les réseaux informatiques de communication, les nouvelles méthodes de management des organisations, etc.

Au milieu du XXe siècle, les conférences de Macy ont aussi été à l'origine de la création de cette nouvelle discipline, la cybernétique. En effet, en 1942 et entre 1946 à 1953, des scientifiques, ingénieurs, philosophes, neurologues, anthropologues, psychologues, et économistes ont réfléchi aux idées naissantes dans le cerveau. Neuf conférences ont en effet été organisées à New York et une dixième dans le New Jersey, sous l'égide de la Fondation Macy. D'après J. P. Dupuy (1993 : 132) les travaux de ces conférences vont fonder les sciences cognitives.

Le creuset de la complexité était prêt, notamment grâce aux travaux que nous venons de décrire et qui ont tous pour dénominateur commun l'interdisciplinarité.

La complexité dans la pensée d'Edgar Morin

J.L. Le Moigne (2002 : 48) fait remonter à 1948 la date à laquelle le monde scientifique allait prendre un tournant dans son rapport avec la science. En effet, un article fondateur de W. Weaver (1948) appelait le monde scientifique à traverser le continent de l'irréductible, de l'indécomposable, de l'inanalysable. Si la science devient irréductible à ses composants, elle peut être modélisable si la compréhension humaine s'en charge.

J.L. Le Moigne (2002 : 11), considère que les deux chefs de file de la complexité sont Herber Simon aux États-Unis et Edgar Morin en France. Ce dernier va créer « la méthode de la complexité » (1977 : 386). Son œuvre principale, forte de 2500 pages, fournira de multiples éclairages sur un projet central : celui de *la connaissance.* Il résume son propos dans la célèbre phrase : « *Toute connaissance acquise sur la connaissance devient un moyen de connaissance éclairant la connaissance qui a permis de l'acquérir* » (1986 : 232).

A travers ses travaux, E. Morin donne le sens étymologique du mot *complexité* et présente sa propre vision pour cet objet de recherche :

> Au premier abord, la complexité est un tissu (complexus : ce qui est tissé ensemble) de constituants hétérogènes inséparablement associés : elle pose le paradoxe de l'un et du multiple. Au second abord, la complexité est effectivement le tissu d'événements, actions, interactions, rétroactions, déterminations, aléas, qui constituent notre monde phénoménal. Mais alors la complexité se présente sous les traits inquiétants du fouillis, de l'inextricable, du désordre, de l'ambigüité, de l'incertitude ... D'où la nécessité, pour la connaissance, de mettre de l'ordre dans ce phénomène en refoulant le désordre, d'écarter l'incertain, c'est-à-dire de sélectionner les éléments d'ordre et de certitude, de désambiguïser, clarifier, distinguer, hiérarchiser... Mais de telles opérations, nécessaires à l'intelligibilité risquent de rendre aveugle si elles déterminent les autres caractères du complexus ; et effectivement, comme je l'ai indiqué, elles nous ont rendus aveugles (2005 : 21).

La complexité concerne des phénomènes de l'ordre du quantitatif comprenant un grand nombre d'interactions et d'interférences entre un grand nombre d'unités (Morin, 2005 : 92). Elle apparaît au départ de l'ordre de la confusion, du désordre, de la difficulté. Or, raisonner en termes de complexité permet de faire apparaître l'incertitude et la multidimensionalité : « La conscience de la complexité nous fait comprendre que nous ne pourrons jamais échapper à l'incertitude et que nous ne pourrons jamais avoir un savoir total : la totalité c'est la non-vérité » (Morin, 2005 : 93). L'objectif n'est pas d'isoler les éléments, car si l'on agit ainsi, on arrivera à connaître ces derniers, mais pas leurs relations. Ce nouveau paradigme permet de penser qu'il n'est guère possible d'atteindre la complétude, il n'est pas possible d'avoir une vision globale sur tous les éléments constitutifs des objets analysés.

Par ailleurs, E. Morin fait la différence entre *complexité* et *complication*. Avec un peu de persévérance, on arrive à résoudre un phénomène compliqué. Il considère que la complication est un élément de la complexité. La complication peut se résoudre, mais non la complexité : « *La complexité est un mot problème et non un mot solution* » (Morin, 2005 : 10). Si l'on considère ce paradigme, il ne s'agira pas de résoudre des difficultés, mais au contraire, de les comprendre, de les anticiper pour les contourner. On est obligé de composer avec la complexité, mais la complication peut trouver à plus ou moins long terme une résolution.

Pour ce faire, il faut utiliser des outils pour relier les connaissances et cet impératif consiste à relier la connaissance des parties à la connaissance du tout et inversement. Morin a repris cet impératif déjà formulé par Pascal : « Toutes choses étant causées et causantes, aidées et aidantes, médiates et immédiates, et toutes s'entretenant par un lien naturel et insensible qui les lie les plus éloignées et les plus différentes, je tiens impossible de connaître les parties sans connaître le tout, non plus de connaître le tout sans connaître les parties » (2004 : 83).

Cela dit, quatre principes méthodologiques serviront à relier les connaissances et à penser à l'aune de la complexité :

—*le dialogique,* défini par Morin comme le dialogue entre plusieurs (ou différentes) logiques qui peuvent apparaître à la fois contradictoires et complémentaires ;

—*la récursion organisationnelle,* principe qui s'illustre par les boucles de rétroaction dans lesquelles les produits et les effets sont à la fois cause et producteur de ce qui est produit. Il illustre ce principe par l'image du tourbillon, processus qui est à la fois produit et producteur ;

— *l'hologrammique* selon lequel le tout et les parties sont liés. Morin reprend le principe de l'hologramme dans lequel la moindre partie de celui-ci contient la quasi-totalité de l'information. Ce principe permet de considérer que le tout ne peut se réduire à la somme des parties, car dans un système complexe, il est primordial de prendre en considération les interactions entre ces parties ;

— *le méta-point de vue* permet de prendre en considération l'observateur, la chose observée et leur environnement. On pourrait voir dans ce dernier principe un héritage du constructivisme qui permet ainsi de prendre en considération une pluralité de points de vue. La complexité d'un phénomène n'est plus une de ses caractéristiques, elle émane aussi du regard de l'observateur et de son interaction avec ce phénomène.

Ces quatre principes énoncés, il convient de voir s'ils peuvent être appliqués à l'opération traduisante.

Le traducteur pragmatique face à la complexité

La traduction est une opération axée plutôt sur le sens que sur les mots. L'opération traduisante est avant tout un apprentissage. Elle n'est donc pas spontanée et on le voit bien à travers les longs cursus offerts par les différentes écoles de traduction. Il faut en effet cinq années au moins pour former un apprenti traducteur.

Pour déterminer les éléments constitutifs de l'opération traduisante, il faudra analyser les différentes phases par lesquelles doit passer la traduction d'un document, à savoir : *la compréhension*, *l'expression, la recherche* et *la révision.*

La compréhension est une activité qui se déroule dans la boîte noire de notre cerveau. Elle fait intervenir de multiples facteurs, comme, par exemple, le travail sur les différents types de mémoire et tout particulièrement sur la mémoire de travail. Les opérations sont multiples et imbriquées. Citons entre autres la lecture d'un texte dans une langue étrangère, la prise en considération des collocations, des expressions figées, des sous-entendus et des métaphores et surtout la compréhension d'un technolecte spécifique à une discipline.

Une fois que le traducteur appréhende le sens d'un message exprimé dans une langue qui n'est pas la sienne, il va pouvoir exprimer ce sens. *L'expression* dans sa langue maternelle est une opération qui va être guidée par la rigueur, pour exprimer le sens voulu par l'auteur, par la précision et aussi par la concision.

Par ailleurs, s'il existe un différentiel de connaissances entre l'auteur du texte de départ et le traducteur, ce dernier va mettre en place des activités de *recherches* notionnelles, documentaires, terminologiques, etc. pour combler ce différentiel. Par ailleurs, toute contradiction entre le message de l'auteur et les connaissances du traducteur, doit amener ce dernier à rétablir la cohérence logique du texte afin de dissiper toute confusion. Par exemple, face à une contradiction qui se révèle entre un texte et l'illustration qui l'accompagne, le traducteur se doit de faire *les recherches* nécessaires pour rétablir la logique voulue par l'auteur.

Nous allons revenir plus loin à la phase de *révision* qui est une opération fondamentale dans l'opération traduisante.

Nous avons détaillé ces quatre différentes phases (Minacori 1999) et nos travaux de docimologie en traduction ont permis d'offrir un panorama des difficultés de traduction analysées sur 545 copies sur une période de presque un an, d'organiser ces difficultés en un arbre facile à utiliser pour l'évaluateur, facile à comprendre par les étudiants et respectant les différentes éléments de la traduction professionnelle, dont la phase de *révision* (Minacori 2006). Ces recherches se sont notamment fondées sur les compétences du traducteur.

Les compétences requises en traduction pragmatique

Parmi toutes les recherches sur les compétences en traduction, nous avons retenu celles du groupe PACTE (*Process of Acquisition of Translation Competence and Evaluation* 2003). Ce groupe de recherche de l'Universita Autŏnoma de Barcelona en Espagne, a élaboré un modèle selon lequel, pour réussir une opération de traduction, il convient de mettre en place un système de connaissances doté de certaines caractéristiques. Tout d'abord, l'expertise du traducteur ne peut se résumer à celle d'un bilingue. Elle est constituée de cinq sous-compétences liées les unes aux autres et qui peuvent se résumer ainsi :

— *la sous-compétence bilingue* : le traducteur a des connaissances pragmatiques, socio-linguistiques, textuelles, lexicales et grammaticales dans au moins deux langues, la langue du texte de départ et celle de la traduction, en général la langue maternelle du traducteur;
— *la sous-compétence extra-linguistique* selon laquelle le traducteur a des connaissances encyclopédiques, thématiques dans deux cultures;
— *la sous-compétente de traduction* permet à l'expert de connaître les processus, les méthodes et les procédures propres à la profession ;
— *la sous-compétence instrumentale* permet d'acquérir des connaissances sur l'utilisation d'un ensemble de sources documentaires et d'outils informatiques spécifiques du métier ;
— *la sous-compétence stratégique* est la plus importante car elle permet au traducteur de comprendre les difficultés rencontrées et de les résoudre, en visant une grande efficacité dans les méthodes. Il s'agit de planifier, de réaliser et d'évaluer les méthodes mises en œuvre.

Enfin le Groupe PACTE ajoute des éléments psycho-physiologiques concernant tous les mécanismes cognitifs et comportementaux (mémoire, attention, persévérance, esprit critique) et psychomoteurs. On remarquera le caractère systémique de ces sous-compétences qui sont le fruit d'un apprentissage et d'une longue pratique.

Toutes ces constatations nous renvoient à la problématique de notre recherche et nous amènent à poser la question suivante : la traduction pragmatique est-elle un objet complexe ? Pour répondre à cette interrogation, nous nous appuierons sur les quatre principes suscités définis par Morin (2005) permettant de relier les connaissances, pour analyser la possibilité de les appliquer à la traduction pragmatique.

La traduction à la lumière de la complexité

L'idée de relier les connaissances concerne tout particulièrement les activités mises en œuvre en traduction pragmatique. Le rôle du traducteur est d'associer le texte à traduire à ses connaissances antérieures, mais aussi aux informations concernant les paramètres discursifs de tout texte, à savoir auteur, destinataire, support de publication, date de publication, objectifs. Le traducteur va également acquérir de nouvelles connaissances lors de l'opération traduisante, tout en établissant des ponts avec ses propres connaissances. S'il éprouve des difficultés de compréhension ou d'expression, il aurait la possibilité d'avoir recours aux experts du domaine.

Il est désormais important de mettre en relation l'opération traduisante aux quatre grands principes édictés par Morin.

a) Le premier principe est dit *dialogique*, il s'agit d'établir un dialogue entre des logiques qui peuvent apparaître à la fois comme contradictoires et complémentaires. Ce premier principe peut trouver une illustration sur un point fondamental qui a fait couler beaucoup d'encre et qui est lié au degré de spécialité d'un traducteur. Par exemple, pour réaliser une traduction médicale faut-il être médecin ? Dans les faits, il est rare qu'un traducteur et l'auteur du texte aient le même degré d'expertise sur les informations présentes dans un texte. En effet, dans la grande majorité des cas, il existe une différence fondamentale de connaissances entre l'auteur et le traducteur. La fonction de ce dernier va donc consister, entre autres choses, à identifier ce différentiel de connaissances entre l'expert, en l'occurrence l'auteur, et lui-même afin de le combler. Le traducteur professionnel sait prendre conscience qu'il ne comprend pas certaines parties du texte. Ce qui le conduit à mettre en place une stratégie tout à fait adaptée à son propos, pour combler ce différentiel. D'un autre côté, il est sommé de prendre en considération le facteur temps dans ses recherches et appliquer un grand principe : être le plus efficace possible dans le minimum de temps possible pour satisfaire à des contraintes professionnelles, car le client n'attend guère.

Le traducteur sait adapter sa méthodologie à son propos. On ne lui demande pas d'être l'expert du domaine, car cette activité est dévolue à l'auteur. Il sait « juste » adapter ses capacités cognitives à son savoir-faire professionnel qui consiste à : comprendre le texte, l'exprimer, si besoin faire des recherches adéquates, réviser et appliquer des règles de méthodologie.

Dans ce contexte, la logique du traducteur est complémentaire à celle de l'auteur, puisque l'objectif est le même : l'auteur communique un message à un expert de son domaine, le traducteur a pour mission de faire comprendre ce message à un expert d'une autre langue, si l'on s'en tient aux exemples décrits ci-dessus. Par contre, on voit que les niveaux d'expertise de ces deux acteurs sont fort différents, voire contradictoires. L'un est le spécialiste du domaine, l'autre de l'opération traduisante.

Il est aussi intéressant d'examiner la collaboration établie entre des apprentis traducteurs et un expert. Par exemple, les étudiants en traduction pragmatique de l'Université Paris Diderot, du Master 2 Industrie de la langue et traduction spécialisée (M2 ILTS) doivent réaliser un mémoire de traduction, de terminologie et de documentation dans le cadre de leurs études. Une étudiante, (Leroy 2012) dont nous étions le directeur de mémoire, a choisi de traduire un texte sur un système de convertisseur d'énergie de la houle conçu par une société écossaise, Pelamis Wave Power. La houle est un mouvement ondulatoire à la surface de la mer, causé par les vagues. Après avoir constitué un corpus en français, l'étudiante a fait des recherches notionnelles et terminologiques, notamment en se fondant sur la riche documentation en ligne de l'ADEME (Agence pour l'environnement et de la maîtrise de l'énergie), de l'IFREMER (Institut français de recherche pour l'exploitation de la mer). Elle a ensuite contacté un expert du domaine de l'énergie houlomotrice pour valider ses recherches. En effet, l'étude du corpus ne lui permettait pas de faire un choix univoque dans sa traduction. Elle se retrouvait face à différentes collocations et elle voulait valider ses choix. Par exemple, elle pensait traduire « *wave cycle* » par « *cycle de vagues* », mais l'expert lui a proposé de choisir « *cycle de houle* » ; elle a traduit « *a range of incident power* » par « *des puissances incidentes très variées* » et l'expert a proposé « *des houles très variées* ». Par ailleurs, une partie du texte mentionnait : « *The primary transmission, consisting of the hydraulic cylinders and their controls, converts the work done by the waves on the structure to stored energy* ».

Elle pensait traduire "*the work done by the waves*" par une formule assez proche du texte : "le travail fait par les vagues". Mais l'expert lui a proposé la formule suivante : « *La transmission primaire, qui repose sur les vérins hydrauliques et leurs commandes, convertit le travail des forces exercées par les vagues sur la structure, en énergie stockée.* » Dans cette solution proposée, on note que l'expert a explicité le type de forces en action par « *le travail des forces exercées par les vagues* ». Ces quelques exemples illustrent bien les propos analysés par Lagarde (2009) dans sa thèse. En effet, cet auteur détaille l'activité traduisante de textes techniques par des traducteurs professionnels et il a notamment fait une enquête quantitative sur les démarches d'acquisition de connaissances des traducteurs auprès des experts.

b) Le deuxième principe est celui de *la récursion organisationnelle* qui s'illustre par les boucles de rétroaction. Or, la révision est fondée sur la rétroaction. Le traducteur doit appliquer des principes d'objectivité sur son texte. Il va en effet, mettre en œuvre une méthode pour lui permettre de réviser son propre texte afin d'en faire un objet fini et vendable. Nous pensons que la révision peut s'articuler en trois phases :

— la première durant laquelle il faut comparer le texte de départ et le texte d'arrivée, pour vérifier que rien ne manque à la traduction, notion, mot, paragraphe, page, chapitre, etc. ;
— la deuxième phase va permettre au traducteur de retravailler sur la formulation de sa traduction, pour améliorer le fond ;
— la troisième a pour objectif de vérifier qu'il n'existe plus aucune difficulté d'ordre orthographique, morphosyntaxique, etc. Loin d'être une action cosmétique sur le texte, cette phase est tout aussi primordiale que les deux autres.

Ces différentes phases peuvent, en fonction des traducteurs, du temps imparti, de la longueur de la traduction, se dérouler dans un ordre différent de celui indiqué. Cette phase de révision est la cerise sur le gâteau. En effet, tout texte destiné à être communiqué est sans aucun doute soumis à des révisions, et les traductions ne peuvent déroger à cette règle.

Cette boucle de rétroaction permet d'éviter la subjectivité en traduction, lorsqu'il s'agit de réviser son propre texte. En effet, rien de plus difficile pour un esprit humain de juger de ces propres choix de traduction. Parfois, notamment dans les procédures mises en place dans les organisations internationales, la révision par un tiers est prévue pour les documents traduits et l'on comprend bien que l'activité de réviseur vise l'objectivité.

Cette boucle de rétroaction est aussi appliquée par le traducteur lorsqu'il réalise des recherches pour combler le différentiel de connaissances dont nous parlions plus haut. En effet, le traducteur sait faire des recherches et aussi soumettre celles-ci à l'épreuve de l'enquête en effectuant des boucles de rétroaction, pour vérifier si les informations qu'il recherche sont fiables et il valide ainsi ses choix.

c) Le troisième principe concerne *le principe hologrammique* selon lequel le tout est bien plus que la somme des parties et selon lequel, la moindre partie d'un hologramme contient la quasi-totalité de l'information (Morin, 2005 : 101).

Pour illustrer ce principe en utilisant les caractéristiques de l'opération traduisante, on peut avancer que, dans tout texte à visée pragmatique, il existe une potentialité de traductions. Il est possible d'établir un parallèle avec les sculptures de Michel-Ange intitulée « les Esclaves » exposées à la *Galleria dell'Accademia* à Florence, en Italie. Le travail réalisé sur ces sculptures a été qualifié de *non finito* et Michel-Ange l'a fait volontairement. Certaines parties des « Esclaves » sortent de la pierre alors que d'autres y restent enfouies. Ces figures font penser à la potentialité de traductions qui pourrait émerger de tout texte. C'est pourquoi, on peut voir dans tout texte la projection vers des traductions possibles, dans différentes langues, au gré de la volonté de communication. Si l'on part d'un texte et que l'on en envisage des traductions, on peut aboutir à différentes représentations de cet élément. Celles-ci seront élaborées par des acteurs différents, avec des critères d'évaluation qui leur sont propres. On retrouve alors ce principe hologrammique dans tout texte offrant une infinie potentialité de traductions.

Les opérations de localisation répondent aussi au principe de l'hologramme selon lequel le tout est bien plus que la somme des parties. Pour démontrer ce principe, nous avons tout d'abord retenu ces deux définitions du terme « localisation » :

Localization is the process of adapting a product, in our context

> *a software program, to a specific locale, i.e., to its language, standards and cultural norms as well as to the needs and expectations of a specific target market. A properly localized product also meets all the legal requirements in force in the user's region.* (Dolher, 1997 : 3)

Cette définition semble assez peu complète dans la mesure où la traduction pragmatique est déjà orientée vers une cible particulière comprenant les aspects culturels et langagiers.

Une seconde définition plus complète a été rédigée lorsque ce phénomène de localisation avait pris pied dans le monde de la traduction :

> *The processes by which digital products and content developed in one locale (defined in term of geographical area, language and culture) and adapted for sale and use in another locale. Localization involves: (a) translation of textual content into the language and textual conventions of the target locale; (b) adaptation of non textual content (from colors, icons and bipmaps to packaging, form factors, etc.) as well as input, output and delivery mechanisms to take into account the cultural, technical and regulatory requirements of that locale. In sum localization is not so much about specific tasks as much as it is about the processes about which the products are adapted.* (Dunne, 2006 : 4)

Il y a lieu de signaler ici que les exigences culturelles, techniques et légales sont particulièrement intéressantes à étudier dans des phénomènes de localisation. Au cours du processus de localisation d'un site internet, elles peuvent concerner les couleurs utilisées pour véhiculer un message. En France, il n'est guère étonnant de voir un site dont la dominante sera la couleur verte pour défendre l'environnement, la lutte contre la pollution. En revanche, en Thaïlande, le vert est associé à la jungle et aux maladies que l'on peut y contracter. C'est pourquoi, si l'on veut promouvoir des produits qui respectent l'environnement, le vert sera à proscrire dans un site destiné à un public thaïlandais.

Dans un autre registre, en France, une responsable d'une entreprise qui a pour mission de réaliser des modules de formation de *E-learning* spécialisés dans les langues, explique que dans certains cas, elle a dû faire changer les photos qui accompagnent ces modules de formation pour satisfaire aux exigences culturelles de publics diversifiés. Cette entreprise réalise aussi des cours d'anglais pour débutants francophones. Les sujets traités sont adaptés à ceux des enseignements dans les collèges en France et ils reprennent les thématiques que les collégiens abordent dans leurs enseignements. Or, cette société qui devait localiser ces cours pour un public de grands débutants américains, aux États-Unis, a dû revoir tous ses modules pour les adapter aux thèmes abordés par les collégiens de ce pays. Dans ce dernier cas, la localisation va jusqu'à la création de contenu.

Les exigences techniques peuvent concerner le système des mesures internationales. Si dans le texte de départ figurent des mesures appartenant au système dit « impérial » en vigueur au Royaume Uni, mais aussi aux États-Unis (avec des valeurs différentes notamment pour les volumes) et si, dans la culture de la langue d'arrivée, le système international d'unités est utilisé, il faudra alors convertir ces mesures pour respecter les usages dans la langue d'arrivée. Les opérations de conversion de ces mesures sont d'une importance primordiale, comme c'est le cas par exemple du matériel médical de radiothérapie.

Enfin, concernant les exigences légales, on peut citer la création de mentions légales dans la localisation de sites. En effet, lorsqu'une entreprise décide de localiser un site internet en français pour vendre ses produits en France, il est important de respecter la loi pour la confiance dans l'économie numérique (LCEN) de juin 2004. L'objectif de cette loi est de protéger les internautes et de leur permettre d'établir un contact avec les éditeurs de tout site internet, pour le respect de leurs droits. La loi prévoit donc de mettre à disposition des internautes une page facilement identifiable contenant les mentions légales, dont des informations sur la raison sociale, le siège social, le numéro de téléphone, le nom du directeur de la publication ou du responsable de la rédaction, ainsi que le numéro d'inscription au registre du commerce des sociétés (RCS). Par ailleurs, pour un site de vente en ligne, il faut aussi publier les conditions générales de vente, mentionnant le délai de rétractation ou de réclamation, le délai moyen de livraison, les conditions de remboursement. Le respect de cette loi devra permettre au traducteur de créer un contenu qui ne figurait pas dans le texte original. La localisation passe par cette création de contenu qui correspond à un tout constitué de bien plus que la somme de ses parties.

d) Le quatrième et dernier principe concerne *le méta-point de vue*. Il permet de prendre en considération l'observateur, la chose observée et l'environnement. La complexité d'un phénomène émane aussi du regard de l'observateur et de son interaction avec ce phénomène.

Toute traduction est l'œuvre d'un traducteur et elle lui est spécifique. Ce qui pourrait ressembler à une tautologie ayant pour simple objectif de définir le traducteur à la fois comme un concepteur et comme un observateur. Or, dans ce cas-là, « sujet et objet sont inéluctables l'un à l'autre » (Morin, 1994 : 309). En effet, si le sens est bien transféré d'un texte de départ vers un texte d'arrivée, l'expression de ce sens est intimement mêlée au traducteur. Nous avons tous un idiolecte, soit une façon spécifique de nous exprimer à l'écrit. On voit bien lorsque nous enseignons à des classes de 30 étudiants d'apprentis traducteurs, on peut presque trouver autant de propositions différentes pour un même texte qu'il y a d'étudiants, si tant est que l'on reste dans un sens voulu par l'auteur.

Par ailleurs, tout le travail des réviseurs consiste justement à vérifier que la traduction réalisée par un tiers est en bonne adéquation avec le sens voulu par l'auteur dans le texte de départ. Il applique une vision externe à une opération traduisante faite par autrui. En ce sens, il s'agit de mettre en place une boucle de rétroaction dans ce processus pour viser plus d'objectivité dans la réalisation de cette opération. La révision permet de ne plus être juge et partie dans l'opération mais de pouvoir avoir un expert externe qui va pouvoir évaluer la traduction.

Conclusion

Les quatre principes qui permettent de relier les connaissances sur la traduction à l'aune de la complexité servent à penser des stratégies qui mènent à l'innovation : « La complexité appelle la stratégie. Il n'y a que la stratégie pour avancer dans l'incertain et l'aléatoire » (Morin, 1990 : 178). La traduction assistée par ordinateur (TAO) pourrait être le fruit de cette réflexion. On peut ainsi supposer qu'à l'avenir, on pourrait tenter d'améliorer encore le confort du traducteur grâce à des outils conçus par lui, ouverts à tous sur des plateformes. Ces outils collaboratifs commencent à voir le jour, leur objectif est de bien relier les connaissances sur la traduction pour contourner la complexité.

Références bibliographiques

Bériot, Dominique. *Manager par l'approche systémique.* Paris : Eyrolles, 2006.

Cambien, Aurore. « Une introduction à la pensée systémique, Appréhender la complexité ». *CERTU*, 2007. Consultable : http://lara.inist.fr/bitstream/handle/2332/1431/CERTU-RE_08-09.pdf?sequence=1 (15.12.2013)

Conte, Auguste. *Discours sur l'esprit scientifique.* Paris : Vrin, 2002.

Dictionnaire culturel en langue française. Direction Alain Rey, Paris : Le Robert, 2005.

Dohler, Per. "Facets of Software Localization: A Translator's View", *Translation Journal* 1 (1997), no 1.

Dunne, Keiran. *Perspective on Localisation.* ATAS Scholarly Monograph Series, Vol XIII. Amsterdam and Philadelphia: Benjamins Publishing, 2006.

Dupuy, Jean Pierre. *Aux origines des sciences cognitives.* Paris : Editions la Découverte, 1994.

Lagarde, Laurent. *Le traducteur professionnel face aux textes techniques et à la recherche documentaire.* Thèse, Université Paris III Sorbonne Nouvelle, Paris, 2009. Consultable http://tel.archives-ouvertes.fr/docs/00/79/70/32/PDF/2009PA030085.pdf (15.12 2013)

Lasswell, Harold. "The Structure and Function of Communication in Society." *The Communication of Ideas. Ed. Bryson, Lymon. New York: Institute for Religious and Social Studies,* 1948. 37–51.

Le Moigne, Jean-Louis, *Le Constructivisme—Tome 1 : les enracinements.* Paris : Ed L'harmattan, 2002.

Minacori, Patricia, « L'évaluation en traduction pédagogique, technique et scientifique : première partie », *Forum* 4 n°1 (2006). 113–138.

Minacori, Patricia, « L'évaluation en traduction pédagogique, technique et scientifique : seconde partie », *Forum* 4 n°2 (2006). 139–169.

Minacori, Patricia. « La compréhension en traduction ; aspects professionnels et pédagogiques », *French Studies in Southern Africa* 28 (1999) : 92–108.

Morin, Edgar. *Introduction à la pensée complexe*. Paris : Seuil, 2005.

Morin, Edgar. *Les Idées*. Paris : Seuil, 1999.

Morin, Edgar. *La complexité humaine*. Paris : Flammarion, 1994.

Morin, Edgar. *Science avec conscience*. Paris : Seuil, 1990.

Morin, Edgar. *La Connaissance de la connaissance*. Paris : Seuil, 1986.

Morin, Edgar. *La Nature de la nature*. Paris : Seuil, 1977.

PACTE, "Building a Translation Competence Model," *Triangulating Translation: Perspectives in process oriented research*. Ed. Alves, Fabio. Amsterdam: John Benjamins, 2003: 43–66.

Pascal, Blaise. *Pensées*. Paris : Folio Classique, 2004.

Von Bertalanffy, Ludwig. *Théorie générale des systèmes*. Paris : Dunod, 1993.

Weaver, Warren. "Science and Complexity." *American Scientist*, 36, 1948: 536–544.

Weaver, Warren, Shannon, Claude E., *The Mathematical Theory of Communication, IU Press*, 1998.

Wiener, Norbert. *Cybernétique et société*. Paris : 10/18, 1971.

Sur la recherche en traduction

Jean-René Ladmiral

au regretté Jean-Bertrand Pontalis

Résumé

Si le principe de la traduction n'est pas changé depuis son origine, la recherche en traduction qui la prend pour objet a profondément changé. Au delà des quatre âges de la traductologie (à savoir : la traductologie normative ou prescriptive, la traductologie descriptive, la traductologie productive et la traductologie scientifique ou inductive), auxquels il faut ajouter le tournant culturel et le tournant sociologique, la discipline se situe bien dans une interdisciplinarité à la fois interne et externe.

Mots-clés : fondements épistémologiques, interdisciplinarité, philosophie, linguistique, psychologie

Abstract

The principles of translation have not changed since its beginnings, however, research which takes translation as its subject has profoundly changed. In addition to the four phases of translation studies, i.e., normative, descriptive, productive, scientific or inductive translation studies, we also need to account for the cultural turn and the sociological turn. The discipline today is clearly an interdisciplinary one, and its interdisciplinarity is both internal and external.

Keywords: epistemological foundation, interdisciplinarity, philosophy, linguistics, psychology

Introduction

Comme je me plais à le répéter, la traduction est le plus vieux métier du monde! On va donc faire comme on a toujours fait ...[1] N'y a-t-il pas dès lors quelque chose d'un oxymore dans le rapprochement accouplant «traduction et innovation» qui fait l'intitulé du colloque dont ce sont ici les Actes? En définitive, que peut-on espérer trouver de vraiment neuf en la matière ?

On touche là à une sorte d'amphibologie propre au statut épistémologique des sciences humaines en général. Autant une science exacte comme la chimie, par exemple, pourra isoler un élément nouveau, complètement inconnu jusqu'alors, autant les sciences humaines ne vont-elles qu'à renouveler et approfondir un pan de l'expérience humaine qui nous était connu à travers les brouillages qu'il leur revient de dissiper. Pour faire bien voir cette différence épistémologique, je dirai que l'objet des sciences humaines est un objet *méconnu* à mettre en lumière, plutôt qu'un objet *inconnu* à découvrir. Dans cette perspective, on conçoit que la psychanalyse représente un paradigme déterminant qui va contribuer à éclairer, de près ou de loin, la logique des sciences humaines, ainsi que l'avait noté d'emblée Claude Lévi-Strauss au début des *Tristes Tropiques* (Lévi-Strauss, 1955 : 47–51). Ainsi en va-t-il aussi bien sûr de cette discipline encore jeune que constitue la traductologie.

Mais s'il est vrai que la traduction est une activité bien connue de tout temps, et au demeurant comme engoncée dans les exigences de la pratique, il semble qu'on soit fondé à douter qu'il y ait place pour une *recherche* en traductologie et, à tout le moins, à s'interroger sur le contenu qui peut bien être le sien. La difficulté ne tient pas seulement aux apories épistémologiques inhérentes aux sciences humaines, sur lesquelles il y aura lieu de revenir : c'est l'objet lui-même de la recherche qui semble faire défaut.

Dans la mesure où il est indéniable que ce qui fait le cœur de la traduction reste pour l'essentiel inchangé, c'est pour ainsi dire à la marge et dans ses prolongements périphériques qu'on trouvera la nouveauté qu'a pour fonction d'apporter la recherche. Ainsi l'informatique met-elle à la disposition du traducteur tout un ensemble d'outils, permettant notamment l'accès presque instantané à des ressources documentaires quasiment illimitées. D'une façon générale, la traduction va maintenant de pair avec l'utilisation des nouvelles technologies de l'information et de la communication (NTIC). Quant à l'utilisation du traitement de texte (TDT), elle touche au cœur de l'activité traduisante, qu'elle facilite grandement; elle n'en change toutefois pas la nature. Il reste que les développements récents de la traduction automatique (TA) et, plus précisément, de la traduction assistée par ordinateur (TAO) ont ouvert des perspectives encore incertaines mais déjà «prometteuses» (ou menaçantes?) quant à l'exercice réel de la pratique traduisante elle-même[2]. Ces données nouvelles et, plus encore, l'évolution du marché ont déterminé un élargissement et une diversification de la profession de traducteur aux dimensions de ce qu'il y a lieu d'appeler maintenant les métiers de la traduction. - Sans parler du tournant culturel de la traduction dont on fait grand cas depuis quelques années.[3]

De tout cela, je ne saurais traiter ici, parce que ce serait sortir des limites de l'épure et aussi parce que, encore une fois, je tiens que cela n'affecte pas le cœur de l'activité traduisante. Cela dit, si j'en reviens à la perspective de l'amphibologie épistémologique évoquée plus haut, il apparaît que ce n'est certes pas le principe même de la traduction qui s'est trouvé changé, mais la description et l'analyse théorique qu'en fait la discipline traductologique qui la prend pour objet.

Pendant plusieurs décennies, la traductologie s'est astreinte à une méthodologie strictement *linguistique* (et ce, avant même qu'elle n'existe en tant que discipline *sui generis*). La traduction était pensée en termes de langues, de «langues en contact» (pour faire écho à la formule d'Uriel Weinreich). De fait, la traductologie était l'une des deux branches principales de la Linguistique Appliquée (particulièrement outre-Rhin). Ce n'est en somme qu'assez récemment que le traducteur et son aperception du sens ont été remis au centre des préoccupations. Cela impliquait d'enfreindre le tabou épistémologique que constituait l'interdit du «mentalisme» (si ce n'est de la sémantique elle-même). Au terme de ce qui fait figure rétrospectivement de changement de paradigme, certains traductologues ont pris conscience qu'il convenait de partir de l'activité *psychique* et du travail intellectuel (ou, si l'on veut, cognitif) qui est au principe de la démarche de traduire.

C'est cette rupture épistémologique (pour reprendre un concept de Bachelard) qui est à mes yeux l'essentiel. En outre, il m'est apparu qu'il y avait lieu de la re-situer dans le cadre un peu plus large de l'esquisse d'une histoire de la discipline distinguant «quatre âges de la traductologie», à savoir : la traductologie normative ou prescriptive, la traductologie descriptive, la traductologie productive et la traductologie scientifique ou inductive.[4] À quoi il conviendra d'ajouter le tournant culturel (mentionné plus haut), mais aussi bien d'autres tournants comme le tout récent tournant sociologique de la traductologie. Sans parler des dérives idéologiques auxquelles sont sujettes les sciences humaines en général et la traductologie en particulier (et tout spécialement en Amérique du Nord).

C'est d'entrée de jeu que la question de *l'interdisciplinarité* était «au programme», puisque le sous-titre que s'est donné le colloque dans le cadre duquel s'inscrit la présente étude allait à rien de moins qu'à penser la traduction comme «une passerelle entre les sciences et les Humanités». Encore pourra-t-on distinguer ici deux formes d'interdisciplinarité : une interdisciplinarité interne et une interdisciplinarité externe.

L'interdisciplinarité interne

Avant tout, je veux évoquer une interdisciplinarité interne à la traductologie. D'une façon générale, on s'accorde à voir en elle une *interdiscipline* (comme le rappelle un Yves Gambier). Dans la mesure où elle n'est n'apparue que tardivement, la traductologie se situe nécessairement en aval des grandes disciplines des sciences humaines. Il lui a fallu puiser les éléments de sa méthodologie et de ses conceptualisations dans le vivier de ce que j'ai défini comme le *triangle interdisciplinaire* de la traductologie.[5]

S'il est vrai qu'elle ne saurait se réduire à une simple «linguistique appliquée», ainsi que je me suis attaché plus haut à en poser le principe, il est bien évident que c'est quand même et d'abord à la *linguistique* que la traductologie a dû faire ses premiers emprunts fondateurs, puisqu'elle a affaire à des langues, des mots, des textes et autres réalités langagières. C'est d'autant plus vrai que ladite linguistique s'est entre temps affranchie des interdits méthodologiques qui en bridaient la capacité d'innovation et qu'elle a intégré des approches comme la pragmatique, une sémantique renouvelée, la théorie de l'énonciation, la sociolinguistique, etc. Si l'on peut encore dire que la traductologie constitue une sous-discipline autonome de la linguistique, ce n'est pas tant au sens où elle serait une partie autonome *au sein de* la linguistique qu'au sens où c'est une sous partie autonome *par rapport à* la linguistique. Ce qu'en usant de la procédure d'un parenthésage logique on pourrait formaliser ainsi : (x(yz)) plutôt que (xy(z)).

Pour l'essentiel, il convient de rappeler que la traduction part du sens et qu'en somme la «gestion» interlinguistique (et interculturelle) du sens est sa fonction principale. Cela dit, en dépit du développement des recherches récentes, la sémantique linguistique ne nous fournit pas les outils conceptuels adéquats à la pratique traduisante. Aussi m'est-il apparu qu'il y a lieu de définir une sémantique descriptive à visée pratique qui soit spécifiquement au service de la traduction, à la différence de la sémantique linguistique à visée «scientifique» (Ladmiral 2006 : 118–122).

Cette *sémantique pratique,* je l'appelle aussi une «sémantique sauvage» (un peu comme on parle de psychanalyse sauvage) dans la mesure où elle n'est pas enfermée dans les limitations méthodologiques qui définissent telle ou telle discipline constituée, comme la linguistique par exemple. C'est là un point commun avec la *philosophie* (en quelque sorte par défaut). Mais surtout, et pour ainsi dire par excès, l'immense trésor réflexif, théorique et culturel dont est porteuse la tradition philosophique vient fournir la traductologie de tout un arsenal précieux de concepts qui lui permettent de thématiser le sens que précisément il s'agit de traduire dans toute sa multiple et délicate complexité, telle que nous la révèle le travail de la traduction. Plus fondamentalement encore, ce qu'apporte la philosophie à la corbeille de cette jeune mariée qu'est la traductologie, c'est aussi l'héritage de *l'herméneutique* qu'elle a elle-même reprise de la théologie en la sécularisant, avec des penseurs comme Heidegger et Gadamer.[6] En effet, il s'agit bien au bout du compte d'interpréter des textes, aux différents sens que peut revêtir le concept d'interprétation. On ne saurait ignorer qu'il faut «interpréter pour traduire» (Seleskovitch/Lederer, 2011).

Au sein de ce vaste ensemble de sous-disciplines diversifiées qui constitue la *psychologie* aujourd'hui, la traductologie va aussi chercher son bien du côté des approches que je range (faute de mieux) sous la rubrique de la psychologie de la personnalité. Ces dernières sont essentiellement marquées par la méthode clinique (et il y a là un point important sur lequel il y aura lieu de revenir). C'est bien évidemment la psychanalyse qui figure au tout premier plan des disciplines psychologiques mises à contribution au profit de la traductologie que je défends. Mais j'entends ne pas négliger d'autres apports plus anciens que peut nous offrir la psychologie, qui a déjà toute une histoire et une tradition. Je mentionnerai en passant la psychologie de la forme *(Gestaltpsychologie)*, ou même, les vieilleries de la psychologie associationniste, et puis bien sûr ce qu'on appelait encore la psychologie de l'intelligence du temps où j'étais étudiant en psychologie et qu'on rangera maintenant dans le rayon de la cognition ... J'ajouterai la psychologie sociale, où il y a des éléments à puiser pour le traductologue (Ladmiral, 1982), etc.

Ce n'est bien sûr qu'une liste indicative. Au demeurant, l'ambition n'est pas de se mettre à l'école de la psychologie comme mode de connaissance. Il s'agit seulement d'en appeler, plus modestement, à *culture psychologique*; à tel enseigne que j'ai parlé à ce propos d'une «psychologie de non-psychologues» (Ladmiral 1992: 122). Le premier bénéfice qu'on peut en attendre est un peu le même que celui de la philosophie (cf. *sup.*): la culture psychologique va nous apporter un ensemble de concepts permettant de verbaliser les problèmes de la traduction. De fait, il y a là en effet des acquis de pensée comparables—et ce d'autant qu'une part importante de la psychologie s'inscrivait dans le prolongement de la philosophie, en même temps qu'elle s'est attachée à s'en séparer. De même, la clinique procède elle-même d'un travail d'interprétation, non plus des signes verbaux seulement, mais plus globalement des symptômes au sein desquels ils prennent leur sens. Ainsi peut-on voir dans la psychanalyse une «herméneutique des profondeurs».

En outre, une approche psychologique est aussi de nature à aider le traducteur à opérer un retour réflexif sur son propre travail et sur les difficultés qu'il y rencontre. Il arrive que la pression d'impératifs contradictoires, qu'il ne parvient pas à hiérarchiser, induisent chez lui, une forme de «blocage» psychologique. Plus généralement, la tension inhérente au bilinguisme en lui-même et l'exercice de la traduction peuvent déboucher sur l'expérience temporaire d'une perte des moyens d'expression extrêmement frustrante (cf. Ladmiral 2010a: 25). J'irais presque jusqu'à hasarder l'idée d'une «castration linguistique». En permettant de verbaliser et de conceptualiser les difficultés vécues par le sujet, le discours traductologique pourra contribuer à lever ce type d'inhibitions. C'est pourquoi je me suis cru fondé à proposer le concept de *champ traductologique* par analogie avec le concept de «champ psychanalytique» (cf. notamment Ladmiral, 1987: 194–195). Corollairement, dans un contexte de formation, je considère qu'une part de ma tâche pédagogique est d'assurer des séminaires de «clinique traducto-thérapeutique» ... (Ladmiral, 2006: 117, 123).

Pour être complet, il faut bien dire que l'interdisciplinarité interne dont procède la traductologie ne se limite pas au triangle qui réunit la linguistique, la philosophie et la psychologie. Je rappellerai que, pour moi, la démarche traductive s'articule essentiellement en deux phases : (I) la lecture-interprétation du texte-source (To) et (II) la réexpression produisant un texte-cible, qu'on appelle la «traduction» (Tt). D'une part, le traducteur est donc un lecteur privilégié. D'autre part, la traduction est un travail *d'écriture*—d'écriture seconde, mais d'écriture quand même! Dans les deux cas, il y faut une certaine culture *littéraire*, qui fournit le terreau de *l'écriture de précision* que se doit de maitriser un bon traducteur. Au reste, il est à noter que la traduction était déjà classiquement un chapitre de la littérature comparée, qui est donc venue rejoindre la traductologie. C'est pourquoi j'ai dû «carrifier» mon triangle! et en faire un carré interdisciplinaire.

En fait, on n'en reste pas là. De proche en proche, c'est l'ensemble des sciences humaines (SH) ainsi que des études littéraires et culturelles (ÉLC) dont les apports se trouvent finalement convoqués par une traductologie qui tend à devenir ce que j'ai appelé une anthropologie interdisciplinaire de la traduction (AIT) inchoative (Wilhelm 2012).

L'interdisciplinarité externe

Au-delà d'une interdisciplinarité interne à la traductologie, qui en assure les bases méthodologiques et conceptuelles, il y a aussi une *interdisciplinarité externe* de la traduction. Si l'on considère la traduction et la traductologie comme constituant une discipline, c'est donc les rapports qu'entretient cette dernière avec d'autres disciplines qui est en cause.

En premier lieu, pour des raisons de fond (et aussi pour des raisons tenant au contexte institutionnel du colloque), on pense à la psychanalyse. Ainsi récemment encore l'immense entreprise de la retraduction des Œuvres complètes de Freud a conduit à mettre la traduction au centre de discussions dont la polémique n'était pas absente et contribuait par là même à nourrir toute une réflexion portant non seulement sur la traduction, mais encore sur le discours psychanalytique lui-même.[7]

Entre traduction et psychanalyse, l'échange interdisciplinaire se fait dans les deux sens. On peut en faire la constatation d'emblée, à un niveau élémentaire. Comme on sait, Freud lui-même assimilait l'interprétation du rêve à une «traduction», du texte-source des contenus latents au texte-cible des contenus patents. Inversement, le concept freudien de *déplacement* est un concept extrêmement puissant, qui pourra notamment être considéré comme un équivalent synonymique de la traduction, non pas seulement en un sens très général et plus ou moins superficiel, mais comme un outil conceptuel qui va permettre à la traductologie de traiter des problèmes importants et délicats comme la traduction des connotations (Ladmiral, 2010a : 115–248) ou les écueils de la communication interculturelle.[8] Je m'en suis tenu là à illustrer mon propos de façon élémentaire par ce que j'ai envie d'appeler la migration interdisciplinaire des concepts. Il reste qu'on a affaire en l'espèce à une problématique dont les enjeux sont beaucoup plus considérables et qui méritera d'être traitée en profondeur …

Pour me situer dans le sillage de mon triangle interdisciplinaire, je peux prendre aussi un exemple de migration des concepts dans le domaine de la philosophie. Dans le même esprit de simplification pédagogique (et conférant un sens élargi au concept de traduction), il n'est pas interdit de voir le transcendantal chez Kant comme une traduction des idées innées de Descartes, elles-mêmes étant une traduction de la Réminiscence platonicienne. Il n'est pas jusqu'aux «petites perceptions» de Leibniz où l'on ne puisse voir comme une traduction par anticipation de l'inconscient de la psychanalyse, etc.

D'une façon générale, on est fondé à rechercher l'incidence que peut avoir la traduction sur la logique des disciplines dans le cadre desquelles elle intervient. Dans une perspective encore plus englobante, André Clas a organisé à l'Université de Montréal en octobre 1989 un grand colloque international sous le titre aussi énigmatique que suggestif : la traduction *proligère* (Cormier/Lethuillier 1990), plongeant tout le Gotha de la traductologie mondiale dans la perplexité! Ainsi la traduction pourra-telle servir de paradigme interdisciplinaire permettant de penser les conjonctures ethno-sociologiques, les relations interculturelles, d'éventuels invariants anthropologiques, la communication, la sexualité elle-même …

Au départ, j'entendais consacrer la présente étude (comme la conférence dont elle procède) à des questions spécifiquement traductologiques. Mais il m'est apparu dans le contexte du colloque que le projet de ce dernier était beaucoup plus vaste et ambitieux. Aussi ai-je cru devoir renoncer à mon propos initial et l'infléchir dans le sens d'une anthropologie de la traduction. Soit que j'inscrive la présente étude dans le prolongement de mes travaux voués à une philosophie de la traduction et que, par exemple, je reprenne la question du littéralisme en traduction.[9] Soit que je développe l'anthropologie psychanalytique de la traduction à laquelle j'ai commencé à travailler. Mais le virage m'est paru excessif par rapport au titre que j'avais initialement proposé : il y aurait eu tromperie sur la marchandise! J'ai donc opté pour une solution de repli intermédiaire; et j'ai choisi de prendre ma casquette d'épistémologue, plutôt que ma casquette de traductologue (renouant en cela avec mes enseignements de philosophie à l'Université de Paris-X Nanterre et avec les cours d'épistémologie que j'y ai dispensés notamment en psychologie et en sociologie).

C'est pourquoi je me suis attaché à traiter la question l'interdisciplinarité (qui faisait partie de la «commande») en la spécifiant, dans un premier temps, comme un cas d'interdisciplinarité interne, déterminant les fondements épistémologiques qui se trouvent au principe de la traductologie. Cependant il m'est apparu par la suite que c'est l'interdisciplinarité externe qui semblait surtout retenir l'attention. En somme : l'interdisciplinarité externe, c'est l'interdisciplinarité tout court! Dès lors, le champ d'étude est illimité. On conviendra que c'est un vaste programme ...

Sans aller plus avant, je voudrais faire le lien entre ces deux modalités de l'interdisciplinarité et une problématique où se manifeste une sorte de pesanteur à la fois thématique et institutionnelle qu'on retrouve couramment dans les contextes où il est traité assez largement de la traduction, comme les colloques et autres recherches collectives. En cette affaire, on a tendance à mélanger deux choses bien différentes, comme je m'efforce de le rappeler en maintes occasions. (cf. notamment Ladmiral, 2003).

Soit on aborde la traduction comme un *objet* de recherche. C'est-à dire qu'on en traite comme telle, pour elle-même. Ça, c'est l'affaire de la traductologie. L'interdisciplinarité interne y a sa place dans la mesure où, comme je me suis attaché à le montrer, elle est pour ainsi dire constitutive de la discipline. On pourrait même dire que les apports d'autres disciplines basculent dans l'interdisciplinarité interne dès lors qu'ils sont intégrés au sein de la logique de recherche et de réflexion qui est celle de la traductologie. Telle est la perspective qui a été le plus souvent la mienne.

Soit on invoque la traduction comme un *dispositif* de recherche. C'est-à-dire qu'elle sert à autre chose. La traduction peut être utilisée comme un «outil d'investigation» pour la recherche en linguistique (cf. Mejri, 2003). Il arrive qu'elle soit considérée comme un paradigme de réflexion pour la philosophie.[10] Elle a pu servir d'opérateur analogique pour le travail de la psychanalyse (cf. *sup.)*. Finalement, comme il a été indiqué, la traduction pourra être évoquée de façon plus ou moins métaphorique dans bien des domaines. Tel est le programme ouvert par ladite interdisciplinarité externe, qui pourra faire l'objet de développements thématiques selon des axes multiples ...

Conclusion

Les limites quantitatives légitimement imparties pour les Actes d'un colloque m'imposent de conclure. En sorte que, par rapport à la conférence dont elle est issue, la présente étude se doit de «tourner court» (au sens propre). À l'expérience, en effet, la forme écrite se révèle paradoxalement astreinte à une logique de l'explicitation, puisqu'elle ne peut plus faire fond sur l'implicite ambiant qui sous-tendait la communication orale dans un contexte déterminé. À l'écrit, on doit donc souvent renoncer à développer l'ensemble des idées qui avaient pu être évoquées lors d'une présentation orale en situation pour un public donné.[11] C'est le cas ici. Je me vois donc dans l'obligation de m'en tenir à quelques remarques conclusives qui resteront nécessairement elliptiques et programmatiques, certaines d'entre elles faisant écho à des considérations évoquées plus haut.

1°) Aussi ne puis-je reprendre la question épistémologique fondamentale de la spécificité des sciences humaines au regard des sciences exactes, à laquelle j'ai consacré déjà plusieurs publications (cf. notamment Ladmiral, 2003). Et pourtant, je dirai que c'est l'essentiel : il n'est que trop évident que cela concerne très directement le problème particulier du statut épistémologique de la traductologie (ou même de la psychanalyse elle-même) qui nous occupe ici. Mais il n'est pas moins évident qu'il y faudrait toute une étude *sui generis* dont l'ampleur excèderait très largement les limites de la présente publication.

2°) Avant tout, je rappellerai que la dimension *clinique* de nos recherches est essentielle (cf. *sup.).* Comme on sait, elle trouve son origine en médecine et, pour ce qui nous occupe, en psychologie ainsi qu'en psychothérapie. Outre le lien essentiel qu'elle entretient avec la psychanalyse, j'entends souligner deux ou trois points (d'inégale importance) qui en sont le prolongement. D'abord, la psychologie que j'ai convoquée dans le cadre de mon triangle interdisciplinaire de la traductologie est bien sûr à dominante clinique. Et puis il y a l'analogie que j'ai thématisée en d'autres lieux entre traduction et psychothérapie (Ladmiral, 2008 : 23–26).

Surtout : la clinique acquiert plus fondamentalement une pertinence épistémologique générale pour l'ensemble des sciences humaines, dont le paradigme fondateur a sa source dans l'histoire de la psychologie, qui a été la plus précoce des sciences humaines (au sens moderne de ce concept). Le clivage méthodologique opposant les cliniciens et les expérimentalistes en psychologie préfigure la dichotomie épistémologique dont je pose le principe à partir duquel devront être définies la spécificité des sciences humaines et les modalités ce que j'ai appelé leur amphibologie épistémologique.

3°) Tout cela rejoint un principe plus général, qui est de toute première importance: la *critique du positivisme.* Le positivisme est en effet l'idéologie délétère et sournoisement dominante de la modernité; et ses méfaits vont bien au-delà de ses inconvénients épistémologiques majeurs pour des sciences humaines comme la traductologie.[12]

4°) Corollairement, je plaide donc pour que la *subjectivité* soit résolument remise au cœur du travail intellectuel, en sciences humaines comme en philosophie, en traductologie comme en psychologie. S'agissant de la traduction, il conviendra donc de remettre le traducteur au centre de la démarche, d'adopter une attitude centrée sur le sujet traduisant. On conçoit aisément qu'il en résulte des conséquences essentielles au niveau de la pratique (Ladmiral, 2012c).

5°) Il s'ensuit sur le plan du travail intellectuel et de la recherche (en sciences humaines) que *l'égo* du chercheur fait problème. La logique publicataire à laquelle il est soumis (*publish or perish*) le contraint à investir son propre nom, comme signataire de ses publications, à la manière d'«une *marque*» publicitaire. En somme, on glisserait du publicataire au publicitaire![13] Mais derrière cette mise en avant constante d'un moi onomastique, il y a l'égo du chercheur qui se trouve donc très sollicité, et de façon *ambivalente*. Il y a certes des gratifications narcissiques, mais il y a aussi des coups à prendre. Le discours de la recherche est en effet très souvent polémique. Il y a aussi tout un travail du doute, ainsi que des échecs personnels, des phases de «sécheresse» (un peu comme chez les mystiques). En tout cas, il est parfois difficile de faire la part des choses entre le moi existentiel, le moi «scientifique» et le moi publicataire : en sciences humaines, en philosophie et en littérature, plus encore sans doute qu'en sciences exactes. Et ce n'est pas toujours bien compris, ni bien accepté, dans l'entourage. Ainsi ma mère me mettait-elle en garde, avec une indulgence affectueuse, d'une formule : Attention! Jean-René: le nom des fous est écrit partout ...

Références bibliographiques

Bourgignon, André, Pierre Cottet, Jean Laplanche et François Robert. *Traduire Freud.* Paris : PUF, 1989.

Cercel, Larisa, éd. *Übersetzung und Hermeneutik /Traduction et herméneutique.* Bucarest : Zeta Books, 2009.

Cormier, Monique C. et Jacques Lethuillier, dir. « Hommage à Jean Darbelnet (1904–1990) », *Meta* 35 (1990).

Ladmiral, Jean-René. «Traduction et psychosociologie», *Meta* 27 (1982) : 196–206.

Ladmiral, Jean-René. «Sourciers et ciblistes», *Revue d'esthétique* 12 (1982) : 33–42.

Ladmiral, Jean-René. «Technique et esthétique de la traduction». *Encrages* 17 (1987) : 190–197.

Ladmiral, Jean-René. «La traduction : philosophie d'une pratique». *Les gens* du *passage*. Ed. Christine Pagnoulle. Liège : Presses Universitaires de Liège, 1992 : 120–136.

Ladmiral, Jean-René. «Les quatre âges de la traductologie - Réflexions sur une diachronie de la théorie de la traduction». *L'histoire et les théories de la traduction.* Genève : ASTTI/ETI, 1997. 11-42.

Ladmiral, Jean-René. «Le prisme interculturel de la traduction». *Palimpsestes* 11 (1998) : 15–30.

Ladmiral, Jean-René. «La traductologie au XXIe siècle : de la linguistique à la psychologie». *Traduire au XXIème siecle : Tendances et perspectives.* Ed. Tania Nenopoulou. Thessalonique : Faculté des Lettres de l'Université Aristote de Thessalonique, 2003: 336–346.

Ladmiral, Jean-René. «La traduction entre en philosophie». *La Traduzione fra filosofia e letteratura/La Traduction entre philosophie et littérature.* Ed. Antonio Lavieri. Turin : L'Harmattan Italia, 2004. 24–65.

Ladmiral, Jean-René. «L'empire des sens». *Le sens en traduction.* Ed. Marianne Lederer. Paris-Caen : Lettres modernes Minard, 2006. 109–125.

Ladmiral, Jean-René. «Pour un tournant œcuménique en théorie de la traduction». *Traduire : un métier d'avenir*, Ed. Christian Balliu. Bruxelles : Hazard, 2008. 11–32.

Ladmiral, Jean-René. *Traduire : théorèmes pour la traduction.* Paris : Gallimard, 2010.

Ladmiral, Jean-René. «Sur le discours méta-traductif de la traductologie», *Le parcours du sens : d'une langue à l'autre. Mélanges offerts à André Clas*. Eds. SaJah Mejri et Gaston Gross. *Meta* 55/n° 1 (2010). 4–14.

Ladmiral, Jean-René. «Approche méta-théorique». *La traduction : philosophie et tradition. Interpréter/traduire.* Ed. Christian Berner & Tatiana Milliaressi. Villeneuve d'Ascq : Presses Universitaires du Septentrion, 2011. 23–40.

Ladmiral, Jean-René. «Esquisse herméneutique». *Unterwegs zu einer hermeneutischen Übersetzungswissenschaft. Radegundis Stolze zu ihrem* 60. Eds. Geburtstag, Larisa Cercel et John Stanley. Tübingen: Narr Verlag, 2012. 21–30.

Ladmiral, Jean-René. « Note sur la médiation interculturelle». *Défis et enjeux de la médiation interculturelle.* Eds. Nadine Rentel & Stephanie Schwerter, Francfort-sur-le-Main : Peter Lang, 2012. 77–85.

Ladmiral, Jean-René. « De la subjectivité du traducteur aux conceptualisations de la traductologie». *Au cœur de la démarche traductive : dé-*

bat entre concepts et sujets. Ed. Nadia D'Amelio. Mons : Éditions du CIPA, 2012. 15–27.

Ladmiral, Jean-René & Edmond Marc Lipiansky. *La Communication interculturelle.* Paris : Armand Colin, 1995.

Lévi-Strauss, Claude. *Tristes Tropiques*. Paris : Plon, 1955.

Mejri, Salah. « La traduction linguistique : problème terminologique ou construction conceptuelle ? ». *Traduire la langue, traduire la culture.* Paris : Maisonneuve et Larose, 2003. 177–191.

Ricoeur, Paul. *Sur la traduction*. Paris : Bayard, 2004.

Seleskovitch, Danica & Marianne Lederer. *Interpréter pour traduire.* Paris : Didier Érudition, 2011.

Wilhem, Jane. « Jean-René Ladmiral - une anthropologie interdisciplinaire de la traduction ». *Meta* 57 / n°3 (2012). 546–563.

Zins, Céline, Jean-René Ladmiral et Marc de Launay, dir. *Traduire Freud : la langue, le style, la pensée. Actes des Cinquièmes Assises de la Traduction littéraire*. Arles : Actes Sud-ATLAS, 1989.

Notes

1 Si j'ai tenu à reprendre cette formule qui m'était venue en 1976 et que j'ai remise dans mon livre (Ladmiral, 2010a : 89), c'est qu'au-delà de son caractère plaisant cette boutade pointe vers une isotopie associant de façon inattendue la traduction et la sexualité, comme en témoigne aussi d'autres formules comme les «belles infidèles », la «pulsion de traduire» et d'autres. On dirait presque que cela fait allusion par anticipation à la collaboration entre traductologie et psychanalyse qui est au principe de notre colloque.

2 Sur l'informatisation et la traduction en général, la bibliographie est maintenant très étendue. Il y a quelque vingt ans, j'avais moi-même coordonné un Numéro de la revue *Langages :* Ladmiral (1994). Mais je veux souligner l'intérêt des travaux de Daniel Gouadec et d'Yves Gambier ... A quoi viendra s'ajouter le livre Nicolas Froeliger : *Les Noces de l'analogique et du numérique—De la traduction pragmatique* (à paraître très prochainement aux Editions des Belles Lettres).

3 Là encore, il y a maintenant sur le sujet une bibliographe très importante que je ne peux pas citer ici. Je cède toutefois à la tentation de renvoyer à quelques-uns de mes propres travaux touchant cette vaste problématique : voir notamment Ladmiral / Lipiansky (1995) et (2012b).

4 Il ne m'est guère loisible d'expliciter ici les termes de ce «quatrain traductologique» (dont les termes riment deux à deux). J'en ai abondamment traité ici et là et je dois me contenter de renvoyer aux études que j'ai publiées sur la question : voir notamment Ladmiral (1997) et (2010b).

5 Là encore, je reprends ici une thématique que j'ai abordée en maintes occasions : voir notamment Ladmiral (2006) : 113–118.

6 On conçoit aisément qu'il y ait là matière à tout un développement que je ne peux qu'évoquer au passage dans la présente étude. J'ai abordé cette vaste problématique dans un article encore programmatique : Ladmiral (2012a) ; mais cela fera l'objet d'un prochain ouvrage consacré à une herméneutique de la traduction. Cf. aussi Cercel (2009).

7 Sur les principes de traduction adoptés pour ces «OCF.P» (*Œuvres complètes* de Freud : Psychanalyse), cf. Bourguignon / Cottet / Laplanche / Robert, 1989 ; voir aussi les débats dont a été l'occasion la Journée d'Arles en 1988 (ATLAS) : Zins / Ladmiral / de Launay, 1989.

8 Je tiens que la communication interculturelle et la traduction proprement dite constituent deux domaines de recherche distincts, même s'il est vrai qu'il y a de nombreux recouvrements et qu'on a trop souvent tendance à les identifier, sinon même à les confondre! Cf. notamment Ladmiral / Lipiansky, 1995 et Ladmiral, 1998.

9 Mais j'ai craint d'être en cela trop répétitif, dans la mesure où j'ai déjà publié plusieurs textes sur le rapport entre traduction et philosophie. Je n'en citerai ici qu'un seul (que j'ai considéré, pour un temps, comme mon testament philosophique en la matière) : Ladmiral (2004). Quant à la question du littéralisme, la parution de mon étude opposant les ciblistes et les sourciers (Ladmiral, 1986) a déclenché toute une polémique dont il est bien évidemment impossible de rendre compte ici. J'y consacrerai un prochain ouvrage.

10 Outre le livre de Paul Ricœur, qui traite de la question (Ricœur, 2004), la traduction semble être devenue pour bien des philosophes (et autres intellectuels) l'occasion de développer tout un discours métaphorisant dont il conviendra un jour d'entreprendre la critique ...

11 Sur cette problématique de l'explicitation et la double logique qu'il y a lieu d'en dégager : Ladmiral (2011 : 23–26).

12 C'est un principe fondamental auquel je ne cesse de me référer dans l'ensemble de ma recherche, tant en traductologie qu'en philosophie, en sorte qu'il est présent, plus ou moins expressément, dans la quasi-totalité de ceux de mes travaux que j'ai cités ici.

13 *Post-Sriptum :* On voudra bien excuser le nombre élevé des références à mes propres travaux. Au demeurant, c'est un usage qui est de plus en plus répandu dans les publications en sciences humaines, et qu'on peut trouver agaçant. Mais il y a à cela une bonne raison. La présente étude ayant pris une orientation épistémologique, elle ne pouvait manquer d'être assez largement programmatique et d'accumuler les renvois ouvrant sur des problématiques trop vastes pour être présentées comme il aurait convenu, mais dont j'avais traité dans des publications antérieures (auxquelles j'ai pu faire allusivement référence lors de ma conférence présentielle au colloque). J'ai donc cité expressément ces dernières dans la présente étude, à la fois pour illustrer mon propos et pour en argumenter concrètement le bien-fondé; et puis c'était une façon d'alléger la présente étude qui menaçait de prendre une ampleur excessive. Dans le prolongement de ce qui a été ma dernière remarque conclusive, touchant la sollicitation ambivalente dont est affecté l'égo des chercheurs, on voudra bien ne pas voir dans ce *post-scriptum* qu'un plaidoyer *pro domo* subreptice ...

Index

Contributor Biographies / Liste des auteurs

Janine Altounian
(Keynote Speaker/Conférence plénière)

French translator of the complete works of Sigmund Freud and member of the editorial team in charge of harmonization of this translation at Presses Universitaires de France (PUF). Born in Paris, she is the child of parents who survived the 1915 Armenian Genocide. She also works on the issue of "translation" of the collective trauma that these survivors transmitted to their heirs.

Traductrice de Freud et responsable de l'harmonisation des traductions dans l'équipe éditoriale des Œuvres Complètes de Freud aux PUF sous la direction de Jean Laplanche. Née à Paris de parents arméniens rescapés du génocide de 1915, elle travaille sur la « traduction » de ce qui se transmet d'un trauma collectif aux héritiers des survivants

Meyssa Ben Saâd

Researcher in the SPHERE Laboratory of the Centre National de Recherche Scientifique and a member of the CHSPAM team at Université Paris Diderot. She is a founding member of the Tunisian Association of Epistemology and of Didactics and the History of Science and Techniques (ATEDHist). She teaches courses in the history of science at the University of Tunis. Her research areas include the history of medieval Arabic zoology, al-Djâsea (776–868) and the *Kitāb al-Hayawān.*

Chercheur associée au CNRS Laboratoire SPHERE, équipe CHSPAM-Université Paris Diderot. Membre fondateur de l'Association Tunisienne d'Epistémologie, des Didactiques et d'Histoire des Sciences et des Techniques (ATEDHiST), enseignante en Histoire des Sciences à l'Université de Tunis. Parmi ses domaines de rercherche on peut conter l'histoire de la zoologie arabe médiévale, al-Djâḥiẓ (776–868) et le *Kitāb al-Hayawān.*

Jean-Michel Benayoun

Director of the Department EILA (Intercultural and Applied Language Studies) at Université Paris Diderot, and member of the Research group CLILLAC.

Directeur de l'UFR EILA (Etudes Interculturelles et Langues Appliquées), Université Paris Diderot, et membre du centre de recherche CLILLAC.

Danielle Candel

Researcher in the History of Linguistic Theories Laboratory at the Université Paris Diderot. Her research interests include: analysis of theories, practices and usages in prescriptive terminology that deal with the experience and results of general lexicography; studying terminographical, terminological and lexicographical orientations and methods, looking at "equivalents" or "translations" tailored either to audiences of specialists or generalists.

Chargée de recherche au CNRS et membre du UMR HTL, Université Paris Diderot. Parmi ses domaines de recherche on peut citer : Analyse des théories, pratiques et usages terminologiques prescriptifs, en relation avec l'expérience et les résultats de la lexicographie générale ; réflexion sur les orientations et les méthodes terminographiques, terminologiques et lexicographiques, dans le choix d' « équivalences » ou de « traductions » adaptées à des publics de spécialistes et de généralistes.

Pascaline Dury

Associate Professor in the Department of Applied Languages at the Université Lumière Lyon 2 and researcher with the Centre de Recherche en Terminologie et Traduction (CRTT). Her research interests include specialized languages, specifically medical, environmental and urban planning languages. Her research mainly consists of a diachronic approach to these issues.

Enseignant-chercheur au Département LEA (Langues Etrangères Appliquées), Faculté des Langues à Université Lumière Lyon 2. Elle s'intéresse aux langues de spécialité, notamment dans le domaine médical et dans celui de l'environnement et de l'urbanisme. Ses recherches se placent principalement dans une perspective diachronique.

Nicolas Froeliger

Professor, head of the ILTS translation program, co-director of CET (*Centre d'études de la traduction*) at Université Paris Diderot. He is president of AFFUMT (*Association française des formations universitaires aux métiers de la traduction*). His research mainly deals with pragmatic translation, as exemplified by the *Traductologie de plein champ, or Field-Grown Translation Studies* conferences and the *Tralogy* (translation and technology) conferences. He is also the author of *Les Noces de l'analogique et du numérique, De la traduction pragmatique,* [The marriage of analog and digital, on pragmatic translation] Paris, Les Belles lettres, 2013.

Professeur, responsable du master 2 ILTS de l'université Paris Diderot, Paris (75). Il est président de l'AFFUMT (*Association française des formations universitaires aux métiers de la traduction*). Sa recherche est principalement axée sur la traduction pragmatique, notamment via la création et l'organisation des colloques de *Traductologie de plein champ* et *Tralogy* (*translation and technology*). Il est également auteur d'un livre sur la traduction, *Les Noces de l'analogique et du numérique, De la traduction pragmatique,* Paris, Les Belles lettres, 2013.

Christopher Gledhill

Professor of English Linguistics and Specialized Translation and a member of the Research group CLILLAC-ARP / Department EILA (Intercultural and Applied Language Studies) at Université Paris Diderot. His current research interests include English as a lingua franca, systemic functional grammar, constructed languages, interlinguistics and phraseology.

Professeur des universités en linguistique anglaise et traduction spécialisée et membre du Groupe de recherche CLILLAC-ARP / UFR EILA (Etudes Interculturelles et Langues Appliquées), Université Paris Diderot. Orientations de recherche actuelles : anglais lingua franca, grammaire systémique fonctionnelle, langues construites, interlinguistique, phraséologie.

John Humbley

Emeritus Professor of English Linguistics and Specialized Translation and a member of the Research group CLILLAC-ARP / Department EILA (Intercultural and Applied Language Studies) at Université Paris Diderot. His current research interests include relationships between terminology, neology and specialized translation.

Professeur émérite en linguistique anglaise et traduction spécialisée et membre du Groupe de recherche CLILLAC-ARP / UFR EILA (Etudes Interculturelles et Langues Appliquées), Université Paris Diderot. Sa recherche est axée sur les liens entre terminologie, néologie et traduction spécialisée.

Elizabeth Kaluaratchige

Associate Professor in the Department of Psychoanalytical Studies at Université Paris Diderot. Her research activities focus on psychoanalytical anthropology, psychoanalysis and religions, specifically Buddhism, adolescent girls and social issues, feminity and women's issues, psychoanalytical practice and children in the 21st century.

Enseignant-chercheur, UFR d'Etudes Psychanalytiques, Université Paris Diderot. Elle est membre du Centre de Recherches en Psychanalyse, Médecine et Société, Université Paris Diderot. Ses recherches sont axées sur l'anthropologie psychanalytique, psychanalyse et religions, en particulier le Bouddhisme, l'adolescente et le social, la question du féminin, l'enfant et la pratique psychanalytique au 21e siècle.

Mehrnaz Katouzian-Safadi

Researcher in the SPHERE Laboratory of the Centre National de Recherche Scientifique and teaches courses in the history of science at Université Paris Diderot. Her research focuses on the history of Arabic and Persian pharmacy in the medieval period and specializes in the medical therapy of the 11th-century physician Râzî.

Chargée de recherches au CNRS, Laboratoire SPHERE, et Chargée de cours en Histoire des Sciences Université Paris Diderot. Ses recherches portent sur l'histoire de la pharmacie médiévale arabe et persane, spécialisée sur la thérapie médicamenteuse chez le médecin Râzî (IXe siècle).

Douglas Kibbee

Emeritus professor of French linguistics at the University of Illinois, Urbana-Champaign. His current research focuses on the history of French grammatical writings and the invention of a standard language. Two editions of seventeenth-century remarks on the French language are in preparation, as well as a study of the intersection of law and language in the United States.

Professeur émérite à l'Université de l'Illinois, Urbana-Champaign. Ses recherches actuelles portent sur l'histoire de la grammaire française et l'invention de la langue standard. Deux éditions de remarques sur la langue française au XVIIe siècle sont en préparation, et une étude des droits linguistiques aux États-Unis.

Jean-René Ladmiral
(Keynote Speaker / Conférence plénière)

German language scholar, translator and philosopher. He is a professor at the Institut de management et de communication interculturels (ISIT) in Paris. Translator of Immanuel Kant, Jürgen Habermas and of Theodoro Adorno, he is also the author of *Traduire : théorèmes pour la traduction* [Translating: theorems for translation]: He has published seminal articles in translation studies and is known as one of the founders of the discipline.

Germaniste, traducteur et philosophe. Il est aujourd'hui professeur à l'ISIT (Institut de management et de communication interculturels de Paris). Traducteur de Kant, de Jürgen Habermas, d'Adorno, il est notamment l'auteur de *Traduire : théorèmes pour la traduction* (Gallimard, coll. Tel), et d'un très grand nombre d'articles de référence qui font de lui l'un des fondateurs de la traductologie

Aimée Lahaussois

Researcher in the History of Linguistic Theories Laboratory at the Université Paris Diderot. She works on three Tibeto-Burman languages of Nepal and is interested in the methodology of description and documentation of endangered languages, notably the tools available for the collection and analysis of morphosyntactic data on oral languages (typological questionnaires, parallel and comparable corpora, transcription and translation practices).

Ingénieur de recherche au CNRS et membre du centre de recherche HTL, Université Paris Diderot. Parmi ses domaines de recherche on peut citer : trois langues tibéto-birmanes du Népal; les méthodes de documentation des langues en voie de disparition, particulièrement les outils de collecte et d'analyse de données morphosyntaxiques pour les langues orales (questionnaires typologiques, corpus parallèles/comparables, traditions de transcription et annotation).

Mairi McLaughlin

Associate Professor of French and an Affiliated Member of the Linguistics Department at the University of California, Berkeley. She specializes in French/Romance Linguistics and Translation Studies. She is currently working on a book that explores the origins and evolution of the language of the French press (1631–1789) and is also producing a digital and critical edition of Urbain Domergue's *Journal de la langue françoise* (1784–1795) to be published by Garnier.

Enseignant-chercheur au Département de Linguistique à l'University of California à Berkeley. Ses recherches portent sur la linguistique française/romane et la traduction. Elle travaille actuellement sur un ouvrage qui étudie l'origine et l'évolution de la langue journalistique française entre 1631 et 1789, et prépare une édition numérique annotée du *Journal de la langue françoise* (1784–1795) de François-Urbain Domergue.

Patricia Minacori

Former technical and scientific translator who is now a professor and Director of the Program in Research and Professionalization in the Department of Applied Languages at the Universite Paris Diderot. She has published extensively in peer-reviewed journals in both English and French. Her research interests include technical and scientific translation with a specific focus on the elements that constitute the comprehension phase as well as translation assessment. She also works on technical communication and its relationship to translation within the framework of complexity as defined by Edgar Morin.

Ancienne traductrice technique et scientifique. Elle est actuellement enseignant-chercheur et Directrice du Programme de Recherche et Professionalisation au Département de Langues Appliquées à l'Université Paris Diderot. Ses recherches concernent la traduction technique et scientifique et notamment les éléments constitutifs de la phase de compréhension, ainsi que l'évaluation de la traduction. Elle travaille aussi sur la communication technique (technical communication), ses liens avec la traduction, dans un contexte de complexité, selon Edgar Morin.

Scott L Montgomery
(Keynote Speaker / Conférence plénière)

University of Washington, Seattle. His current research interests include: history of science; translation and science; language studies; intellectual history of Europe, China, and Islam. Recent books include: *A World History of Scientific Cultures* (2015); *Shape of the New: Four Big Ideas that Built the Modern World* (2015); *Does Science Need a Global Language? English and the Future of Research* (2013); *Science in Translation: Movements of Knowledge in Culture and Time* (2001).

Enseignant-chercheur à l'University of Washington à Seattle aux USA. Ses recherches actuelles portent sur : l'histoire de la science, la traduction et la science, étude du langage, l'histoire intellectuelle de l'Europe, de la Chine et de l'Islam. Dernières publications : *A World History of Scientific Cultures* (2015); *Shape of the New: Four Big Ideas that Built the Modern World* (2015); *Does Science Need a Global Language? English and the Future of Research* (2013); *Science in Translation: Movements of Knowledge in Culture and Time* (2001).

Elisabeth Navarro

Associate Professor in the Department of EILA (Intercultural and Applied Language Studies) at Université Paris Diderot. She is a member of the Research group CLILLAC and works in the field of "languages and identities."

Enseignant-chercheur à l'UFR EILA (Etudes interculturelles et langues appliquées), Université Paris Diderot, et member du centre de recherche CLILLAC. Elle travaille sur la question de « langues et identités ».

Sündüz Öztürk Kasar

Professor and Head of the Department of Western Languages and Literatures of Yıldız Technical University (Istanbul). Her research focuses on topics in linguistics, semiotics and translation studies; she s works in the field of semiotics of translation.

Professeur et Chef du Département des Langues et Littératures Occidentales de l'Université Technique de Yıldız (Istanbul). Ses recherches portent sur des sujets en linguistique, en sémiotique et en traductologie; elle travaille particulièrement dans le domaine de la sémiotique de la traduction.

Sandrine Peraldi

Director of research at ISIT (Institute of interpreters and tranlators), and a member of the research group CRATIL. Her research areas: onto-terminology, discourse analysis, corpus linguistics, machine translation.

Directrice de la Recherche à l'ISIT (Institut supérieur d'interprètes et de traducteurs), et membre du centre de recherche CRATIL (ISIT). Ses recherches sont axées sur : onto-terminologie, analyse discursive, linguistique de corpus, traduction automatique

Elise Pestre

Associate Professor in the Department of Psychoanalytical studies at the Université Paris Diderot and is a member of the Centre de Recherches Psychanalyse Médecine et Société (CRPMS). Her research focuses on globalization and subjectivity, specifically on the effects on subjectivity of displacement in refugee populations. She is also interested in contemporary phenomena of segregation, the issue of collective violence and trauma as well as the notion of psychic translation.

Enseignant-chercheur à l'UFR Etudes Psychanalytiques, Université Paris Diderot, et membre du Centre de Recherches Psychanalyse Médecine et Société (CRPMS). Ses recherches sont axées sur : globalisation et subjectivités, incidences subjectives du déplacement chez les populations réfugiées. Elle s'intéresse également aux phénomènes ségrégatifs contemporains, à la question des violences collectives et au trauma ainsi qu'à la notion de traduction psychique.

Rémy Potier

Associate Professor in the Department of Psychoanalytical studies at the Université Paris Diderot and is a member of the Centre de Recherches Psychanalyse Médecine et Société (CRPMS). His research focuses on the psychological issues with new medical technologies, interdisciplinary and methodological issues between psychoanalysis and epigenetics, and clinical listening devices in hospital settings.

Enseignant-chercheur à l'UFR Etudes Psychanalytiques, Université Paris Diderot, et membre du Centre de Recherches Psychanalyse Médecine et Société (CRPMS). Ses recherches sont axées sur : enjeux psychiques des nouvelles technologies médicales, enjeux interdisciplinaires et méthodologiques entre psychanalyse et épigénétique, dispositif d'écoute clinique en milieu hospitalier.

Philippe Provençal

Researcher at the Natural History Museum of Denmark. He obtained his Ph. D. degree for his thesis *A Lexicographic Survey of Arabic Animal Names* from the University of Copenhagen, Denmark. He specializes in the history of biology (i.e., zoology and botany) in the Arab world as well as the history of Arabic vocabulary that relates to it.

Chercheur au Muséum de l'histoire naturelle de Danemark. Ayant obtenu le doctorat pour sa thèse *Enquête Lexicographique sur les Noms d'Animaux en arabe* à l'Université de Copenhague, Danemark, il s'est spécialisé dans l'histoire de la biologie (zoologie, botanique) dans la civilisation arabe ainsi que du vocabulaire arabe leur appartenant.

Olivier Putois

Associate professor in the department of Psychology at Strasbourg University, and member of the Lab "Subjectivity, Social Link and Modernity"(SuLiSoM). He teaches clinical analytical psychology and psychopathology. After a PhD focused on perception and subjectivization drawing on philosophy and psychoanalysis, he works in psychoanalysis-oriented clinical psychology on the relationship between identity, identification and transmission, especially in the fields 1° of early interactions and intergenerational transmission, and 2° the psychical impact of genetic diseases.

Enseignant-chercheur en psychologie et psychopathologie cliniques analytiques à la Faculté de Psychologie de l'Université de Strasbourg et membre du laboratoire Subjectivité, Lien Social et Modernité (SuLiSoM). Après une thèse sur la subjectivation et la perception à la croisée de la philosophie et de la psychanalyse, il travaille aujourd'hui principalement en psychologie clinique d'orientation analytique sur le rapport entre identité, identification et transmission, notamment 1° dans le champ des interactions précoces et de l'intergénérationnel, et de 2° des incidences psychiques des maladies génétiques

Ward Van de Velde

Researcher in the Centre de recherche en linguistique appliquée TERMISTI, Bruxelles, Belgique) at the FreeUniversity of Brussels (Belgium). He is interested in communication in hospital settings, corpus linguistics, medical and administrative terminology, CAT tools and text readability.

Chercheur au Centre de recherche en linguistique appliquée TERMISTI, Bruxelles, Belgique) à l'Université libre de Bruxelles (Belgique). Il s'intéresse à la communication hospitalière, à la linguistique de corpus, aux terminologies médicale et administrative, aux outils de TAO et à la lisibilité des textes.

Florence Xiangyun Zhang

Associate Professor in the Chinese Studies Department at Université Paris Diderot (France). She is a member of the East Asian Civilizations Research Center (CRCAO). Her main research areas include translation theory, literary translation in China, theatrical language translation, translation of spoken style language in literature

Enseignant-chercheur à l'UFR Langues et Civilisations de l'Asie orientale, à l'Université Paris Diderot, et membre du Centre de recherche sur les civilisations de l'Asie orientale (CRCAO). Ses recherches actuelles sont axées sur : théories de la traduction, pensées chinoises sur la traduction, traduction du langage dramatique, traduction du style oral dans la littérature.

Table des matières